Praise for *The W*

'[Keir Starmer] could do worse than read this b

'Thoroughly researched... *The Wild Men* bring
should not have forgotten.'

Simon Heffer, *Daily Telegraph*

'A highly readable, enjoyable and informative book.'

John McTernan, *Financial Times*

'A meticulously researched collective biography.'

Andrew Marr, *New Statesman*

'Excellent.'

Daily Express

'Superb.'

Robert Hardman, *Spectator*

'An engrossing account of the perilous course charted by Ramsay MacDonald... David Torrance illuminates all of this brilliantly.'

Alan Johnson, *Guardian*

'Torrance tells an absorbing, meticulous and balanced story.'

Chris Mullin, *Spectator*

'Torrance tells the story of each of this engrossing era's main principals in a series of crisp, meticulously researched chapters. It was a fascinating period, and this is a timely, even racy account.'

Roger Alton, *Mail on Sunday*

'David Torrance's lucid account, *The Wild Men*, tells a lot of the story through a series of well-crafted and elegantly written mini-biographies of the leading players, a good device for navigating a turbulent period of complex events and issues.'

Andrew Rawnsley, *Observer*

'In *The Wild Men* David Torrance, a biographer and clerk at the House of Commons, tells the story of MacDonald's rise and the first Labour government, its people, policies and purpose, with sympathy and fastidious attention to detail. His reading and research are exemplary.... [A] fascinating portrait.'

Jason Cowley, *The Sunday Times*

'An accessible, entertaining and well-researched history... It is a welcome study of a period that should be better known. A collection of rich portraits of the leading figures of the government ... Torrance has skilfully brought the history of the first Labour government alive.'

Literary Review

'Admirable, thoroughly researched and very readable account... Torrance offers rich character sketches and takes us through the often difficult history of the government with exemplary skill.'

Allan Massie, *Scotsman*

'Tightly focused... even-handed... [an] in-depth study.'

'Lively, interesting [and] based on an impressive amount of archival research. A highly readable guide to a landmark historical episode.'

Richard Toye, author of *Age of Hope: Labour, 1945, and the Birth of Modern Britain*

'With meticulous reconstruction and careful judgement, this is a fascinating piece of work with some intriguing parallels for our own times.'

Peter Hennessy

'Torrance's book is (and I don't think I have ever described a political history book in these words) riveting. It is a joy to read; it is highly illuminating; it is – to me – a revelation.'

NetGalley review

'Deeply researched.'

Socialist Worker

'Of all the books and treatises issuing from the centenary of the first Labour Government, few will match David Torrance's splendid new work, *The Wild Men*.'

Herald

'An insightful, analytical study... Torrance has conducted some superb and dogged research into previously overlooked archives.'

Ian Cawood, *Times Literary Supplement*

'Authoritative...A compelling account of the first Labour administration.'

Jim Wilson, *Sunday Post*

'Rooted in robust research, the author casts a fresh eye on Labour's rise to power.'

Baroness O'Grady, Labour peer, *House Magazine*

'A fine historical prompt...There is much that [Keir Starmer] – and we – can learn from [the first Labour government].'

Prospect

'Much to inform and delight...the book is framed as a series of portraits of the main players and reflects much detailed new research. It is well written, easy to read and will prove an important historical resource.'

Julie Langdon, *The Tablet*

'The great strength of the work lies in the biographical studies of "The Wild Men" themselves, especially the chapters devoted to the Prime Minister.'

The Critic

THE WILD MEN

The Remarkable Story of Britain's First Labour Government

DAVID TORRANCE

BLOOMSBURY CONTINUUM
LONDON · OXFORD · NEW YORK · NEW DELHI · SYDNEY

BLOOMSBURY CONTINUUM
Bloomsbury Publishing Plc
50 Bedford Square, London, WC1B 3DP, UK
29 Earlsfort Terrace, Dublin 2, Ireland

BLOOMSBURY, BLOOMSBURY CONTINUUM and the Diana logo are trademarks
of Bloomsbury Publishing Plc

First published in Great Britain 2024
Paperback 2025

ISBN: PB: 978-1-3994-1147-9; eBook: 978-1-3994-1144-8; ePDF: 978-1-3994-1145-5

2 4 6 8 10 9 7 5 3 1

Typeset by Deanta Global Publishing Services, Chennai, India
Printed and bound in Great Britain by CPI Group (UK) Ltd, Croydon CR0 4YY

To find out more about our authors and books visit www.bloomsbury.com
and sign up for our newsletters

CONTENTS

PREFACE

What was it Marx said about history? The hardback edition of *The Wild Men* opened with the line 'All anyone could think of was clothes' and, more than a century later, that again was true during the current Labour government's turbulent first hundred days. First as tragedy, second as farce.

It began when the *Sunday Times* revealed that the Labour peer Lord Alli had been given a Downing Street pass after donating £32,200 of 'work clothing' and 'multiple pairs of glasses' worth £2,485 to party leader Sir Keir Starmer. This had been declared, but not properly. Next came news of £6,134 in designer clothes from the same donor for the Prime Minister's wife, Victoria, which was not declared. Lady Starmer was subsequently pictured attending London Fashion Week in an outfit 'rented' from designer Edeline Lee. 'Freebiegate' then spread to Angela Rayner, the Deputy Prime Minister (£3,550 worth of clothes from Alli), and Rachel Reeves, the Chancellor (£7,500 worth from another donor, Juliet Rosenfeld).[1] The Conservatives, still licking their wounds from a brutal election defeat, couldn't believe their luck and made hay.

In 1924, the sartorial commentary had a snobbish quality, a disapproving sneer at the inability of working-class ministers to dress appropriately; in 2024 it was the reverse, surprise at (mostly) working class ministers wearing designer labels having spent years in opposition promising to 'reset' politics after myriad Tory scandals. It didn't help that some posited defences were less helpful than others. Foreign Secretary David Lammy protested that 'unless you're a billionaire' some politicians had to 'rely on political donations' to 'look their best'. Reeves said she could understand that 'to a lot of people it looks a bit odd',[2] while Culture Secretary Lisa Nandy added that although voters wanted a 'well turned out' government its ministers could not give the impression of 'living very different lives from them'.[3]

A (partial) climb down inevitably followed. On the eve of a remarkably gloomy party conference in Liverpool, Number 10 announced that the Prime Minister, his deputy and Chancellor would no longer accept clothing donations. More than a week later, Sir Keir also repaid £6,000 worth of hospitality and gifts received since entering No 10 but held on to his suits, dresses for his wife and football tickets.[4] Pat McFadden, the Chancellor of the Duchy of Lancaster, said a revised Ministerial Code would clarify declaration rules, and Tom Baldwin, the Prime Minister's biographer, urged critics to stand back and 'recognise the idea that Keir Starmer is in politics for a few suits and a couple of Taylor Swift concerts is ludicrous'.[5]

It took the commentator David Osland to make the connection with the first Labour government a century earlier. Sir Keir's 'resort', he wrote, 'to exactly the same "I did nothing wrong/it was within the rules" excuses MacDonald advanced for hobnobbing with a biscuit baron really does take the biscuit'.[6] But as with the supposed award of a baronetcy in return for shares and a Daimler – a story broken by the *Daily Mail* towards the end of MacDonald's first premiership – nuance was the first casualty of a prolonged media storm. As one Cabinet minister told the *Guardian*: 'Waheed [Alli] is a millionaire and he already has a peerage. What more can he possibly want?'[7]

Presciently, in its review of the hardback edition of *The Wild Men*, *The Economist* concluded that Sir Keir Starmer 'could do worse than read this book to ponder what history can teach'.[8] At that point – February 2024 – the consensus was that a general election would take place in the autumn. Instead, on 22 May Rishi Sunak took almost everyone by surprise when he asked the King to dissolve Parliament. Polling was to take place on 4 July – US Independence Day.

Of Sir Keir's reading habits I have no inside knowledge. As one academic study noted, his leadership had shown 'relatively little' interest in Labour's past.[9] During the election campaign, however, there was a belated sign that the Labour Party had become a little more relaxed about the (for many) uncomfortable events of 1924. On 4 June, its Twitter/X account posted a video entitled 'This is the power of a Labour government' featuring grainy footage of Keir Hardie, Ramsay MacDonald *et al.* An unnamed narrator stated that:

> 100 years ago, 24 years after its founding, the Labour Party formed its first government. While it only lasted a matter of months, in that short time it passed legislation to build more affordable housing, improve protection for tenants, extend educational opportunities and increase welfare spending.[10]

The video then moved on to the more familiar, and generally less contested, territory of 1945 and all that. But for a party which had long ago excised 1924 from its official narrative, this was a significant change of tone. As the historian Malcolm Petrie observed in another review, both Starmer and his predecessor Jeremy Corbyn had 'endorsed a reading of Labour history in which the vital electoral triumphs are those of 1945, 1964 and 1997'; neither had 'found any inspiration in 1924 or 1929'.[11]

Petrie added that it was difficult to read accounts of the 1924 government without seeing 'contemporary parallels', but when it came to the election result there was no comparison: instead of winning 191 seats (as in December 1923), Labour secured 411 MPs, although its 33.7% share of the vote was not far in advance of that achieved (33.3%) at the October 1924 election which marked the end of that first administration. Such are the vagaries of first past the post. The Liberal Democrats, meanwhile, garnered the most MPs for a third party (72) since H. H. Asquith's tally of 158 in late 1923.

There were also echoes of the past in the Labour government formed by Sir Keir Starmer following his landslide victory. It was, as many observers noted, the most working-class in decades, perhaps since 1924 when the sight of trade unionists occupying the corridors of power had been genuinely shocking. The gender balance, however, could not have been more different: almost half Starmer's Cabinet were women, an incredible advance on the solitary junior minister appointed in January 1924.

Among the junior ministers was Lord Ponsonby of Shulbrede, great-grandson of Arthur Ponsonby, who had deputized for Ramsay MacDonald at the Foreign Office in 1924. And in an echo of MacDonald's troubles with his Scottish law officers, for some undisclosed reason it took until 29 August to appoint an Advocate General for Scotland (Cat Smith KC, daughter of former Labour leader John).

At his first press conference on Saturday 6 July, Sir Keir told reporters that some ministers had been to the Privy Council that morning 'to receive their seals' which, he added, 'was a moment in history'.[12] At that meeting, the new Prime Minister made affirmation as First Lord of the Treasury, after which he 'kissed' the hand of King Charles III, great-grandson of George V – the monarch who had initially feared but then revelled in the appointment of his first Labour ministers.

Only a few Cabinet ministers were required to be sworn as Privy Counsellors, as most (including the Prime Minister) were already the Right Honourable. This was not, as in 1924, an almost wholly inexperienced government. Thereafter, several ministers swore or affirmed their Oath of Office and received their seals. Angela Rayner had to do so twice, first as Secretary of State for Levelling Up, Housing and Communities, and second as Secretary of State for Housing, Communities and Local Government following a departmental name change. 'I had to go back to the king again to do it all over again,' she later told an audience in her Ashton-under-Lyne constituency. 'The king said "hmm, back again so soon".'[13]

Following that second Privy Council meeting on 10 July, Wes Streeting (Secretary of State for Health and Social Care) and Peter Kyle (Secretary of State for Science, Innovation and Technology) shared pictures of their seals on Twitter/X, obviously as proud to have received royal approval as had been Arthur Henderson *et al* on a gloomy January morning in 1924. This time there was no commentary on what ministers wore as they arrived at Buckingham Palace, although *The Times*' sketch-writer Tom Peck noted that when the House of Commons met for the first time on 9 July, Labour MPs 'wore red; a bubbling ocean of red dresses, red ties'.[14] Catherine Bennett in the *Observer*, meanwhile, took aim at some other media outlets for 'reducing Labour women to the sum of their outfits'.[15]

Ramsay MacDonald's first government did not last long enough to experience its own State Opening, but on 17 July the Sovereign delivered the first Labour King's Speech since that of George VI in 1950. It promised 'mission led' government based on economic growth, John Wheatley-style house building, greater devolution (in England), House of Lords reform and a new 'Council of the Nations and Regions' to foster collaboration between the Prime Minister, devolved First Ministers and mayors of combined authorities.[16] Following her dramatic resignation as the Prime Minister's chief of staff, Sue Gray was later appointed 'envoy' to the nations and regions.

Sir Keir underlined the importance of intergovernmental relations by embarking on a three-nations tour of the UK immediately after the election, parlaying with a new SNP First Minister in Edinburgh, a troubled Labour First Minister in Wales (Vaughan Gething later resigned) and the recently nominated Michelle O'Neill (Sinn Féin) and Emma Little-Pengelly (DUP) in Belfast. Later, the Prime Minister drank Guinness with the new Irish Taoiseach Simon Harris at Chequers. The 21st-century iteration of the 'Irish Question' looked likely to preoccupy Labour's seventh premier just as it had its first a century before, not to mention the legacy of Empire which had caused Ramsay MacDonald relatively little trouble: Foreign Secretary David Lammy provoked a Tory storm when he announced the UK would cede sovereignty over the British Indian Ocean Territory after almost two centuries under the Crown.

The historian Jonathan Davis observed that when Labour formed its first government in 1924:

> dealing with Russia (in its Soviet guise) was high on the agenda, forging a new relationship with Europe after the First World War was an urgent necessity, and issues in the Middle East after the end of the Ottoman Empire needed careful consideration. One hundred years on...the government led by Keir Starmer will find that it again needs a coherent foreign policy to deal with Russia, Europe, and the Middle East.[17]

There is nothing new under the sun. When it came to public spending, *The Economist* observed that Chancellor Rachel Reeves looked set to demonstrate the sort of 'fiscal austerity' exhibited by Philip Snowden a century earlier, with another Labour government keen to demonstrate that it was not, contrary to its opponents' charge, 'addicted to taxing and spending'.[18] In her first speech as Chancellor, Reeves spoke of inheriting 'the worst set of circumstances since the Second World War' but warned that 'a large majority in Parliament' did not mean she had 'the licence to row back on the principles of sound money and economic responsibility'.[19]

What of the Prime Minister? Initially, the consensus appeared to be that Sir Keir's first weeks in office demonstrated authority and seriousness, something underlined by his response to riots in England and Northern Ireland in early August. Yet as he neared the end of his first hundred days, there was widespread talk of drift, a sense his government lacked a clear sense of what it was actually for. Even before all this, several reviewers of *The Wild Men* had taken care to highlight what one called Labour's 'tradition of treating its leaders as betrayers of the party's fundamental beliefs'. In 1924 Ramsay MacDonald had been criticized by left-wingers for being insufficiently committed to socialism, as were Harold Wilson in the 1960s and Tony Blair in the 2000s. Asked in May

2024 if he would use a certain adjective to describe himself, Sir Keir replied:

> Yes, I would describe myself as a socialist. I describe myself as a progressive. I'd describe myself as somebody who always puts the country first and party second.[20]

During the general election of 2024, however, there was little talk of 'wild men' (or women), although the Conservative MP Sir Geoffrey Cox warned of the UK 'sleepwalking into a one-party socialist state' possessed of 'untrammelled power'.[21] As I noted in the original edition of this book, history might not repeat, but it sure does rhyme.

Dr David Torrance
Peckham, October 2024

INTRODUCTION

All anyone could think of was clothes. As members of the first Labour Cabinet prepared to collect their seals of office at a meeting of the King's Most Honourable Privy Council, the enormity of the occasion was almost lost amid sartorial considerations. As all but a few of the new Ministers of the Crown had no previous ministerial experience, most lacked the requisite dress. Conscious of this, the King had set aside the usual requirements; the result was an extraordinary array of different outfits at Buckingham Palace.

As Philip Snowden, the new Chancellor of the Exchequer, later recalled, several of his colleagues 'managed to drag from some obscurity a frock-coat and silk hat which might have been fashionable a generation before',[1] while others were at a loss. Viscount Haldane, a veteran Liberal minister and one of the few to be properly attired, tried one of his old coats on the Secretary of State for War, Stephen Walsh, although his diminutive stature meant it reached near his boots. It had more satisfactory results on William Adamson, the Scottish Secretary.[2]

The newspapers were equally preoccupied with dress as ministers arrived amid the 'deep gloom' that 'enshrouded' the Palace. J. R. Clynes (the Lord Privy Seal) wore 'a black soft hat and a muffler of indeterminate hue beneath his dark tweed overcoat', Tom Shaw (the Minister of Labour) 'boldly' donned a green-grey overcoat and a soft hat, while 'Willie' Adamson 'carried an unfurled umbrella'. It was curious, added one correspondent, to see the Lords Haldane and Parmoor, 'who have all the appearance of distinguished members of the older parties, walking slowly together amongst the trades union Ministers'. Most arrived on foot, but Jimmy Thomas, the Colonial Secretary, turned up in a plum-coloured limousine.[3]

Clothing would come to symbolize the tension at the heart of the first Labour government. Some of its members wanted to prove, contrary to an infamous assertion by Winston Churchill, that they *were* 'fit to govern',[4] and that meant conforming to the sartorial standards of previous Liberal and Conservative administrations; others were impatient to demonstrate that a socialist government was more interested in delivering radical policies than dressing up. Ramsay MacDonald, the illegitimate son of a farmhand who had the previous day kissed hands as Prime Minister, belonged in the former camp, as did Arthur Henderson, a Scots-born iron moulder, 'Jimmy' Thomas, a Welsh railwayman, and Willie Adamson, a Fife coal miner. Never before had so many men from such humble backgrounds occupied the corridors of power.

John Wheatley, an Irish-born miner and publican and the incoming Minister for Health, belonged firmly in the latter camp, and defiantly wore a ten-year-old lounge suit to his first Privy Council meeting. Most, however, did their best to conform. A press photographer captured the 'arrival on foot of the tall lanky figure of Noel Buxton and the short Sidney Webb with his nanny-goat beard, both clad in knee breeches and evening dress, white shirt and tails'.[5] According to the future Labour Chancellor Hugh Dalton, Labour left-wingers were outraged, while he himself thought the duo looked 'ridiculous ... the dwarf and the stork, side by side in this get-up, crowned with opera hats'.[6] 'They are all engaged,' the former Liberal premier David Lloyd George told his daughter Megan, 'in looking as respectable as lather & blather will make them'.[7]

A total of 13 ministers were required to be sworn as Privy Counsellors before accepting their seals of office. As they stood waiting for the King 'amid the gold and crimson magnificence of the Palace', J. R. Clynes could 'not help marvelling at the strange turn of Fortune's wheel, which had brought [Ramsay] MacDonald the starveling clerk, [Jimmy] Thomas the engine-driver, [Arthur] Henderson the foundry labourer and Clynes the mill-hand, to this pinnacle beside the man whose forebears had been Kings for so many splendid generations. We were making history. We were, perhaps, somewhat embarrassed, but the little, quiet man whom we addressed as "Your Majesty" swiftly put us at our ease.'[8]

With the Prince of Wales (the future King Edward VIII) observing proceedings, Noel Buxton, the new Minister for Agriculture, watched as his colleagues knelt one by one in front of him to kiss the Sovereign's hand. Writing later in his unpublished memoirs, he observed contemptuously that Wheatley, 'who had always posed as a sort of republican, was apparently unable to get up again from the cushion, and looked as if he had been overcome by passionate loyalty to the Throne'.[9]

The King then declared Lord Parmoor Lord President of the Council, while afterwards Josiah Wedgwood (the great-great-grandson of the famous potter) had a separate audience in order to receive his seals as Chancellor of the Duchy of Lancaster. This he considered a 'ridiculous office',[10] an impression confirmed when the Tory grandee Austen Chamberlain teased him for having allowed himself to be fobbed off with a Duchy, 'where the worst he could do would be to pack a bench of magistrates instead of losing an Empire'.[11]

Others were equally underwhelmed. Charles Trevelyan, the new President of the Board of Education, complained that the King 'went through the ceremony like an automaton', while Sidney Webb, the President of the Board of Trade, likened the silence which followed the acceptance of his seals to 'a noise like a first-class railway carriage'.[12] When asked to reflect on the change of government, the King was said to have replied: 'My grandfather would have hated it; my father could hardly have tolerated it; but I march with the times.'[13]

Nearly all the new ministers walked back to Downing Street to attend their first Cabinet meeting, one or two carrying the little scarlet cases which contained their seals; Arthur Henderson was positively 'bursting with childish joy' over that which had just confirmed him as Home Secretary.[14] Now the attention moved to headwear. Another press photograph showed Jimmy Thomas sporting a bowler hat, MacDonald and Henderson toppers and Clynes a more plebeian homburg. Downing Street proved as atmospherically gloomy as the Palace. The Prime Minister walked across to Number 10 from the Foreign Office shortly before 4 p.m. as dozens of photographers asked him to pose in front of its famous black door. A watchful janitor opened it as he approached but MacDonald closed it so the interior light would not interfere with the flashlights.[15] The new premier's account of an historic day betrayed both his shock at what had just happened, as well as his apprehension at what was to come:

> Without fuss, the firing of guns, the flying of new flags, the Labour Gov[ernmen]t has come in. At noon there was a Privy Council at Buck[ingham] Pal[ace]; the seals were handed to us – and there we were Ministers of State … A wonderful country. Now for burdens & worries. Our greatest difficulties will be to get to work. Our purposes need preparation, & during preparation we shall appear to be doing nothing – and to our own people to be breaking our pledges.[16]

This was prescient, for over the next nine months the UK's first Labour Prime Minister would find himself battling on a number of fronts: for acceptance by voters, co-operation with not one but two opposition parties in Parliament (Liberals and Conservatives) and most of all for support from his own colleagues, many of whom were deeply uneasy that a party with only 191 MPs had taken office at all.

It is difficult from the perspective of 2024 to appreciate the alarm which greeted the prospect of a Labour government a century ago. The horrors of the Russian Revolution were still fresh in the minds of voters, especially that of the King (although he did not vote), who had lost his beloved cousin, the Tsar, and his family to Bolshevik bullets. More to the point, many craved stability following the devastation of the Great War and the turmoil of two general elections in as many years, not to mention several changes of Prime Minister: the Liberal Lloyd George had resigned in October 1922, the Conservative Andrew Bonar Law had quit on grounds of ill health in May 1923 and now, in January 1924, the Labour Leader of the Opposition had succeeded Stanley Baldwin as premier.

'What has been done will be done again,' runs Ecclesiastes 1:9, 'there is nothing new under the sun.' I had feared as I began to research this book that I would discover a faraway political country of which I knew little. On the contrary, I encountered much that was surprisingly familiar: a minority government grappling with financial instability, a housing crisis, industrial action and a troublesome left wing. Territorially, it also resonated, with complex negotiations over the Irish border and demands for Scottish Home Rule. Even its scandals felt contemporary: the premier's financial arrangements, allegations of cash for honours and the dramatic denouement concerning apparent Russian interference in domestic British affairs. History might not repeat, but it sure does rhyme.

The story has been told before. The American academic Richard Wall Lyman published his PhD as *The First Labour Government, 1924* in 1957.[17] It remains comprehensive and elegantly written although hampered by the unavailability at that time of archival material. Almost 40 years later John Shepherd and Keith Laybourn published *Britain's First Labour Government*,[18] a scholarly monograph which benefited from access to primary sources albeit more concerned with internal Labour politics than personalities. Beyond these two volumes and a handful of useful journal articles, the events of 1924 had become obscured, not only by subsequent mythologizing (and denigration) of Ramsay MacDonald, but by the relentless march of time. 'That,' a former Labour Cabinet minister confessed to the journalist Patrick Maguire, 'is the period of Labour history I know least about.'[19]

The Wild Men: The Remarkable Story of Britain's First Labour Government takes a different approach in several respects. First, it is biographical, the events of 1924 told via the men (and one woman) who together comprised that first, historic administration. Second, I have dug more deeply into primary and secondary sources, not only utilizing the rich collection of MacDonald's personal and public papers at Kew, but hitherto unstudied collections from his daughter Ishbel (at the British Library) and son Malcolm (Durham University), as well as the curiously underused memoranda and correspondence at the Royal Archives, for the use of which I must acknowledge the permission of His Majesty King Charles III. Third, given that this was the *United Kingdom*'s first Labour government, *The Wild Men* concerns not just England (with which previous authors have mostly been preoccupied) but also events in Scotland, Wales and particularly Northern Ireland. And fourth, I have wherever possible foregrounded female voices, not just that of Margaret Bondfield (the only non-male minister) but diarists such as Beatrice Webb and Dolly Ponsonby. British politics of the mid-1920s might have been dominated by men, but the same does not need to be true of its history.

Some context is necessary fully to appreciate the politics of this era. Only a year before MacDonald et al. took office, the United Kingdom of Great Britain and Ireland had shrunk by a fifth following the secession of the Irish Free State to form a newly self-governing Dominion within the British Empire. Certain executive and legislative powers had also been 'transferred' to the bicameral Parliament of Northern Ireland in May 1921, representing the UK's first experiment with what would later be called 'devolution'. Irish independence meant the House of Commons had gone from 707 to 615 Members. The United Kingdom was changing, and its governing traditions with it.

The Labour Party as represented in Parliament was equally as complex. David Marquand has called it 'a loose federation of local bodies and special interests rather than a unitary organisation with a single purpose', and its Members and MPs 'a haphazard collection of individualists rather than a disciplined political regiment'.[20] The first Labour government, argued the civil servant Percy Grigg, was no more 'homogenous or coherent' than the party. What he called the 'Trade Union element' supplied five-sixths of the party's funds and were more interested in moderate 'bread and butter' politics than the abstract economic and social doctrine favoured by the party's 'intellectuals', a second grouping which included both former Liberals and those who had emerged from the Independent Labour Party (ILP), a separate but affiliated party. Grigg called the ILPers 'Montagnards' (the most radical political group during the French Revolution) who followed 'the lead of the Clyde in Scotland and Mr. [George] Lansbury in England'. Inclined to be unhappy at the moderation displayed by the trade unionists and intellectuals, the Montagnards were impatient for the New Jerusalem. All sections of the party, whether moderate or extreme, had what Grigg considered a 'queer' regard for Soviet Russia, the latter on the basis it represented (or so they believed) Marxism in practice and the former because it had installed a government representative (as they also believed) of the working man.[21]

Political opponents and the press, meanwhile, lumped them all together as the 'wild men', and first we must examine how they came to form a government at all.

I

'A SERIOUS NATIONAL MISFORTUNE'

Stanley Baldwin was the antithesis of a wild man. Pipe-smoking, ostentatiously English and middle class, he had been Prime Minister since Andrew Bonar Law resigned due to ill health in May 1923. And having won a general election the previous year, the Unionist Party – as it was then known – had a comfortable majority of 74 in the House of Commons.

Yet it was an unsettled period in British politics: most of Ireland had recently seceded from the UK, the economic and social consequences of the Great War were still playing out, while on the Continent, the French had occupied the industrial heartland of defeated Germany as a *quid pro quo* for unpaid reparations. But what really concerned Baldwin was unemployment. He had gradually come to conclude that Imperial Preference – otherwise known as 'Protection' – was the only way to re-energize the economy, reduce the number of jobless and drive up wages. The trouble was that Bonar Law had pledged the previous year not to embark on such a drastic change in fiscal policy.

It seemed, however, that Baldwin had little to fear from Labour. James Ramsay MacDonald had only become Leader of the Opposition in 1922, when he returned to the House of Commons having lost his seat in 1918 due to his anti-war stance. MacDonald's colleague Philip Snowden had even warned against the temptation of a minority Labour government taking office, as he believed this would 'so discredit the party that the day when it would become the majority would be indefinitely postponed'.[1]

At Labour's annual conference in June 1923, party president Sidney Webb predicted that the party might win a majority in around 1927, transforming 'our present one-third of all the voters into two-thirds'. In his own address, MacDonald agreed that

> No sane person would undertake to form a Government with a majority of about half a dozen, or which did not exist at all. They had to get an absolute majority of the House of Commons before a Labour Government would stand a ghost of a chance of pleasing its people with its work, and a Government that did not please its Party with its work had better remain in Opposition.[2]

By October, Baldwin had made up his mind to call a general election and informed the Cabinet on the 23rd something that for many of them 'came as a bolt from the blue'.[3] The annual Unionist conference was due to take place in Plymouth at the end of October and in his keynote speech, Baldwin dramatically declared that: 'If we go pottering about as we are we shall have grave unemployment with us to the end of time. I have come to the conclusion myself that the only way of fighting this subject is by protecting the home market.'[4]

Those words set in motion a chain of events which, three months later, produced the first Labour government. 'Mr. Baldwin throws down a challenge,' declared Labour Party Secretary Arthur Henderson in Yeovil the following day. 'Of protection as against the Labour policy. That challenge we accept.'[5]

The judgement of Baldwin's Cabinet colleagues was markedly less enthusiastic. 'I believe a dissolution would be a profound mistake,' wrote Lord Salisbury, 'politically and tactically.'[6] According to Lord Beaverbrook, the Prime Minister 'appeared obsessed by the single desire to force that Election'.[7] It looked for a time as if there would be defections, while the senior Tory backbencher Sir Allan Smith said he could not support his party in any election campaign.

Having recently returned from a tour of Eastern Europe 'for reasons of health', Ramsay MacDonald told a luncheon party that Protection would not cure unemployment but, rather, hamper the UK's exports. The Labour leader instead proposed that the 'fight' ought to be Protection versus the Labour policy of a Capital Levy (a one-off wealth tax), which would take money 'from those who had gained most by the expenditure of the debt'.[8] Writing to Baldwin, the *Spectator* editor John Strachey reckoned MacDonald had done everyone a favour by framing the election as a choice between Protection or a Capital Levy. 'I do not want to vote for either,' he added, 'but ... if I was forced to a choice, I should certainly not vote for a Capital Levy.'[9]

Baldwin asked a reluctant King George V to authorize a dissolution, in response to which the fifty-eight-year-old Monarch presciently warned that 'his majority might be reduced, or that he might not get a majority at all'.[10] The Prime Minister again shocked his Cabinet colleagues by informing them on 13 November that a dissolution was imminent; some ministers thought he had gone mad and contemplated resignation. Sir Maurice Hankey, the Cabinet Secretary, remarked to his private secretary that Baldwin would 'be out of office in six weeks'.[11] Three days later the dissolution was formally approved by the King, who was afraid, according to the Earl of Crawford, 'of a Labour government, probably more so than circumstances justify'.[12]

Thus began what David Marquand has called 'one of the strangest election campaigns in British history'.[13] MacDonald kicked off Labour's campaign with a motor tour from London to South Wales. In Newport he joined the local candidate as they were carried shoulder-high and their car towed nearly a mile through the streets. MacDonald's son Malcolm, then a student at Oxford, was hastily adopted as the Labour candidate in Bassetlaw, Nottinghamshire.[14] In the Labour leader's own constituency of Aberavon, women pasted photographs of MacDonald on bed sheets and tied them in a line across their street.[15] Few appeared to notice the grammatical error in one of the party's election posters: 'Greet The Dawn,' it read. 'Give Labour It's Chance.'

The party's manifesto, *Labour's Appeal to the Nation*, claimed the government had admitted its 'inability' to tackle unemployment and attacked protective tariffs as fostering a spirit of 'profiteering, materialism and selfishness'. Instead it proposed 'national schemes of productive work' and a non-recurring graduated 'War Debt Redemption' (or capital) levy on all individual fortunes in excess of £5,000. It ended on an idealistic note, urging voters to eschew 'the squalid materialism that dominates the world today'.[16]

Throughout the campaign, Baldwin and his agents believed they were going to win. The only sour notes were the pronouncements of his estranged (and discreetly homosexual) son Oliver, who spent the campaign attacking his father's policies while campaigning for the Labour candidate in Islington.[17] On 4 December Conservative Central Office predicted a majority of 87 and when the Prime Minister left Downing Street for some final campaigning in Worcestershire, he joked: 'I don't want any bands here when I come back.'[18] On the eve of the poll, the Central Office forecast had risen to 95.[19]

In spite of this (misplaced) electoral confidence, Unionists warned of 'panic' if Labour was to win the election, predicting 'a run on the banks', drained gold reserves and even 'an enormous rise of food prices, followed by starvation'.[20] One unintended consequence of Baldwin's dissolution gamble, meanwhile, was a reunified Liberal Party. United in defence of Free Trade, the estranged former premiers Herbert Henry Asquith and David Lloyd George issued a joint manifesto on 19 November.

The first result on polling day – Thursday 6 December – rocked Unionist complacency. In the Exchange Division of Manchester, a Liberal defeated the Tory Free Trader Sir Edwin Stockton, whose seat had been assumed to be absolutely safe. Out of the 346 seats held by Unionists in the previous Parliament, the party lost 107 and gained only 18. Labour captured several seats from the Liberals and added a quarter of a million votes to its 1922 tally. In West Leicester, Labour's Fred Pethick-Lawrence beat Winston Churchill (then a Liberal) by more than 4,000 votes, while in West Newcastle Arthur Henderson was defeated. The opposition's main advance occurred in Greater London, where the number of Labour Members jumped from 16 to 37. A trio of female Labour MPs – Susan Lawrence (East Ham), Dorothy Jewson (Norwich) and Margaret Bondfield (Northampton) – were also returned for the first time. At Downing Street Tom Jones, the Deputy Cabinet Secretary, heard these results with 'undisguised joy' and amid cries of 'You Bolshevist!' from less radical colleagues.[21]

Remarkably, there was now an unprecedented three-way split in the House of Commons: the Unionists had 258 seats, Labour 191 and the reunited Liberals 158. Neither Labour nor the Liberals had won, but the Conservatives had certainly lost. Although the Unionists were by some margin the largest single party, Baldwin had asked the electorate for a mandate to introduce Protection, and on that issue his party was in a minority of 258 to 349. In the country at large, he had secured only 5,544,540 votes which could be said to favour his preferred policy, against a combined anti-Protectionist vote of 8,662,581.

Lord Curzon, the Foreign Secretary, was scathing. 'You have known for long how poor an opinion I had of Baldwin's fitness to be PM,' he told his wife, 'and now alas the world knows it too.'[22] Opponents were equally incredulous. Dolly Ponsonby, who was married to Sheffield Labour MP Arthur, wrote in her diary 'that Baldwin "the honest man" is a stupid man & cannot govern, even with the asset of the eternal pipe'.[23]

The Leader of the Opposition returned to London on Saturday 8 December to find the evening papers predicting that Baldwin would soon resign and advise the King to send for MacDonald. 'Election wonderful triumph,' he wrote in his diary while remembering those he had lost. 'M[argaret]! Were she here to help me. Why are they both dead – my mother & she.'[24] Writing in his own journal, the King was less elated: 'It is a very serious state of affairs & will give me great difficulties to get out of the impasse, as another election now is not out of the question.'[25] According to Sidney Webb, MacDonald later told him the idea of Labour taking office first occurred to him as he drove around Aberavon and realized the significance of the aggregate results.[26] On the train back to London, meanwhile, he had told Hugh Dalton, a defeated Labour candidate in Cardiff, that the Capital Levy had lost their party 50 seats.

Back at 10 Downing Street, Baldwin 'took a pull at his pipe and tried to put a cheerful face on the situation'.[27] 'You are placed in a great difficulty,' wrote Viscount Haldane with considerable understatement. 'The King's government has to be carried on.'[28] On being contacted by Lord Stamfordham, the King's private secretary, Baldwin spoke at length of the 'extraordinary and unexpected result ... which had upset every calculation made by the experts both on the Conservative and Liberal sides'.[29] He asked to delay his audience with the King so he might consult colleagues at Chequers.

Wild talk and even wilder schemes poured into Stamfordham's office. Some correspondents believed Baldwin should resign at once; peers suggested Viscount Ullswater (until recently Speaker of the Commons) step up; others pointed to Lord Grey (a former Foreign Secretary with fading eyesight); while the *Spectator* editor John Strachey pushed for a government of 'National Trustees' led by the former Liberal Chancellor and banker Reginald McKenna, who was not even an MP. Geoffrey Dawson, editor of *The Times*, thought Baldwin should meet the House first, following the precedent set by Lord Salisbury after similarly indecisive elections in 1885 and 1892. Indeed, by 9 December Stamfordham noted 'a remarkable change ... in favour of the Cabinet holding on until they met Parliament'.[30]

The King also suggested to Baldwin when they finally met on 10 December that he consider a 'working arrangement' with the Liberals, although the Prime Minister ruled this out on the basis that he had brought down Lloyd George's Liberal–Conservative coalition in October 1922 and simply could not facilitate another.[31] More to the point, instinct told Baldwin that a coalition with the sole aim of denying Labour office would be politically unwise. As party chairman J. C. C. Davidson observed a couple of days later, any 'dishonest' attempt to 'deprive Labour of their constitutional rights' would be the 'first step down the road to revolution'.[32]

Other Unionists speculated as to Labour tactics. Lord Birkenhead thought MacDonald might – if invited to form a government – delay meeting Parliament until March 1924, leaving

> only time to bring in a Budget, which might include a Levy on Capital, increase of Death Duties and Super-tax. This would, naturally, be defeated in Parliament and then Mr. Ramsay MacDonald would go to the country with what would be regarded by the mass of the electorate as the most popular Budget that had ever been produced. The Labour Party would sweep the country and be in office for the next 5 years.[33]

While such a scenario also appealed to some on the Labour left, by this point MacDonald had announced his intention to instigate a vote of no confidence in Baldwin's government as soon as the Commons met. The prospect of this succeeding provoked hysterical predictions that the 'forces of order' would be paralysed, public finances shattered and Britain reduced to 'an outlaw state'. There would be no protection, ran another alarmist headline, 'for anyone who wears a clean collar'.[34]

The instincts of some in the Labour Party had been to reject office. On Sunday 9 December, MacDonald consulted two Liberal converts to socialism, Sydney Arnold and Hastings Lees-Smith, both of whom 'strongly advised' him 'not to try Cabinet' on the basis it would lack party support, 'fail' and then 'be overwhelmed at election'. The economist John Hobson, however, took the opposite view. As MacDonald wrote in his diary, he was inclined

> to risk it, make national appeal on policy & European settlement, improve unemployed schemes, housing, coordinate pensions & committees on agriculture, National Debt – all

a preparation for an election & selecting if possible time & issues, trying to increase country's confidence in meantime.[35]

The following day, MacDonald was relieved to find *The Times* opposed to Baldwin's immediate resignation, which gave him time to dictate a memorandum on a possible 'programme' for office. Later, Arthur Henderson, Philip Snowden, Jimmy Thomas and J. R. Clynes joined MacDonald at the Pimlico home of Sidney Webb, where all 'agreed that we shd. take office'. 'Unanimous that moderation & honesty were our safety,' noted the Labour leader in his diary. 'Agreed to stand together.'[36] In Snowden's account, MacDonald told them he 'was appalled at the poorness of the material', the Parliamentary Labour Party (PLP) comprising 'new and undisciplined members who would expect the Labour Government to do all sorts of impossible things'. The Capital Levy, meanwhile, was ditched as an 'electoral millstone'. Snowden also recalled Henderson expressing 'some misgiving about leaving the appointment of Ministers wholly to MacDonald'.[37]

Despite this apparent unanimity, Arthur Ponsonby, who had been comfortably re-elected in Sheffield, was 'very much afraid' of his party being 'taken in by the allurements of possible office'. His preferred policy was to 'force' the other two parties into a coalition and then 'hit hard at them both', although he was later 'converted' to assuming office 'provided it was not accompanied by any agreement with other parties'. But Ponsonby's doubts returned when, at a luncheon on 11 December, MacDonald told him that the charismatic trade unionist Jimmy Thomas would be his choice as Foreign Secretary. 'This quite took my breath away,' Ponsonby later wrote. 'I cannot imagine anyone less suited for the job.'[38] Whatever these doubts, Ponsonby – who coveted only a junior ministerial post – was clearly exhilarated: 'I feel as if I were in a dream … A Labour Government about to be formed!'[39]

On 12 and 13 December the situation was considered by the National Executive of the Labour Party, then by a joint meeting of it and the General Council of the Trades Union Congress, and finally by the executive of the Parliamentary Labour Party. At each of these gatherings MacDonald pointed out that

> if the Labour Party were to refuse office after defeating the Government with the aid of the Liberals, and if Asquith were then to form a Government instead, the Liberals would sit on the Government benches. The Opposition front bench, and most of the other Opposition benches as well, would be occupied by the Conservatives. The Labour Party would be relegated to the position of a group, and would probably sit below the gangway on the Liberal side of the House.[40]

In other words, the party would look irrelevant, its aspirations to govern evidently lacking in seriousness. On this basis, the National Executive resolved that 'the Parliamentary Party should at once accept full responsibility for the government of the country without compromising itself with any form of coalition', a sentiment shared by the TUC and the ILP.[41] On 13 December the PLP met at Eccleston Square and joined the growing consensus. Later, a myth formed that, to quote Manny Shinwell, MacDonald 'unexpectedly accepted office without consulting the Party Members', but that simply was not true.[42]

MacDonald also had no intention of forming a coalition with anyone, telling the *Manchester Guardian* editor C. P. Scott that the effect of the election had 'been to dig both deeply and broadly a ditch between Liberalism and Labour', not least because all over the country the Liberal fight had been 'dirtier than the Tory'.[43] 'The responsibility of so sudden and unexpected an assumption of office,' reflected Sidney Webb, 'gave the Party a shock which sobered even the wildest of the shouters.'[44]

Although Lord Haldane still believed the Conservatives would come to some sort of arrangement with the Liberals, he relished having 'come into sudden prominence'. The Lord Chancellor (Lord Cave) told him it was his 'duty to save the state by taking office', while MacDonald telephoned to ask for a meeting. On 10 December he offered Haldane 'anything' if he agreed to help

Labour form a government.[45] As Haldane told his sister Elizabeth: 'They lay great stress on my joining otherwise, they think, chaos.'[46] If that was a reference to inexperience, he had a point. Only Arthur Henderson and J. R. Clynes had Cabinet experience from the wartime coalitions, as did Stephen Walsh as a junior minister.

By Friday 14 December it had become clear, at least at Court, that the King ought to send for Ramsay MacDonald once Baldwin had faced the Commons, 'interpreting the general feeling of the people of the country that, true to British ideas, the Government, whoever they may be, should have a fair chance',[47] although Stamfordham, whose words these were, also fretted that the Monarch might make an inappropriate remark, lacking 'the calmness which such a situation demands'.[48]

The following day, Ramsay MacDonald arrived in his native town of Lossiemouth. Usually, he reached the Moray coast unnoticed; on this occasion he was greeted by enthusiastic crowds in both the market town of Elgin and 'Lossie', which were connected by a railway line. At his final stop, local fishermen and their wives 'cheered themselves hoarse', railway engines whistled and in the harbour sirens 'raised a great din'. Later that day, MacDonald and one of his sons visited the golf links at Stotfield before walking to Covesea Lighthouse three miles along the coast.[49]

With Baldwin having resolved to meet the Commons and MacDonald intent on defeating him once he did, it remained for the Liberals to articulate their position. Addressing newly elected Liberal MPs at the National Liberal Club on 18 December, Asquith denied any negotiations between himself and other party leaders, 'directly or indirectly, officially or unofficially, above ground or subterranean, aerial or by wireless'. He argued that as Free Trade had not been 'decisively rejected' by the electorate, his party 'controlled the situation' and would 'not move a finger to continue or connive at the prolongation' of the 'disastrous stewardship' of Baldwin et al. Asquith then got to the point:

> The days of the present Government are numbered. It seems to be generally assumed that, as the second largest party in

the House of Commons, though they number less than one third of its members, [Labour] will be ready to assume the responsibilities of Government. This may reassure some trembling minds outside – if a Labour Government is ever to be tried in this country, as it will be, sooner or later, it could hardly be tried under safer conditions.

David Lloyd George then rose to move a vote of thanks for Asquith's 'wise' speech, adding that the 'united' Liberals valued his guidance 'under the most difficult conditions with which the party has ever been confronted'.[50]

Asquith's pronouncement, Lord Haldane told his mother, 'makes it evident that the Liberals, or the bulk of them, will join with Labour in defeating the Government on the Address, and Ramsay MacDonald will be sent for'. He added that

The City is in a panic at the thought of a Labour Government and is cursing Baldwin for bringing on this election. All the old ladies are writing to their brokers beseeching them to save their capital from confiscation ... I have had a message from Baldwin begging me to join the Labour Government and help them out. I will come in on my own terms and have not yet told MacDonald what these are.[51]

The Labour leader made his response to Asquith a few days later in Elgin. After expressing fears there would be an attempt 'to wangle the Constitution' to exclude Labour from office, MacDonald likened the Unionist government to 'a corpse waiting for a coffin to be brought in and for the undertaker to screw it up':

This corpse lay in various departments, conducting foreign affairs, labour affairs, watching over delicate and complicated developments in our industries that might at any moment lead to open dispute; and all for what reason? Because everybody knew that the most likely alternative was a Labour Government.

MacDonald ended with an appeal, in the 'spirit of the Constitution', for 'fair play and for plain dealing', warning that the price of continuing 'tranquillity', maintained by his party in the face of all sorts of 'demagogic and revolutionary temptations', was 'gentlemanly and honest politics'.[52]

Some in the Labour movement remained uneasy. 'His striking appearance & very remarkable abilities carry him a long way,' conceded Dolly Ponsonby in her diary. But 'will not his excessive caution & his odd devious ways of getting at things, let us down'? Elsewhere, visions of the Red Flag fluttering over Westminster continued to reduce prominent figures to hysteria. Philip Snowden found himself having to reassure a countess that Labour's first act in office would not be to 'cut the throats of every aristocrat and steal all their property',[53] while Winston Churchill thundered that it would

> be a serious national misfortune such as has usually befallen great states only on the morrow of defeat in war. It will delay the return of prosperity, it will open a period of increasing political confusion and disturbance, it will place both the Liberal and Labour parties in a thoroughly false position … Strife and tumults, deepening and darkening, will be the only consequence of minority Socialist rule.[54]

2

'THE MOST HORRIBLE JOB IN MY LIFE'

By the time of the Liberal leader's clarifying remarks, Ramsay MacDonald had retreated to Lossiemouth, far away from the gossip and intrigue of Westminster. This was characteristic, though it did little to dispel charges of aloofness. His only party companion was the recent Labour convert General C. B. Thomson, although this was more for golfing companionship than political advice. Over Christmas, MacDonald faced an unenviable task: not only did he have to find enough men (and all but one was a man) to complete an administration, but he had to square various factions of his party. 'It is very sad,' he wrote to the journalist Sir Alexander Mackintosh, 'that several of the old cronies have their eyes shut but, perhaps, they are mercifully spared – no one need envy me my job.'[1]

As MacDonald brooded on the Morayshire coast, newsreels profiled 'The Man Who Would Lead Labour', complete with images of the 'little Scotch fishing village where he was born' and commentary on the 'modest home of the knickerbockered man, whose advent to Power would mark a change in our history as revolutionary as Magna Charta'. His children Ishbel and Malcolm were introduced to cinemagoers, as was the cigarette preferred by the putative premier to the pipe 'so cherished by Mr Bonar Law and Mr Baldwin'.[2]

One of the first appointments intimated by MacDonald had been that of the trade unionist James (or Jimmy) Thomas as Foreign Secretary, something which had come as a 'great shock' to Arthur Ponsonby. He told the Labour leader that Thomas would 'be a most unpopular appointment in the party ... I admire his eloquence but he is not trustworthy and he is far keener on getting credit for settling rather than on the thing being settled.'[3]

Not intending to take any chances, Ponsonby leaked the possible appointment to the *New Leader* and *Manchester Guardian*, the latter being particularly hostile to Thomas. He also wrote to colleagues such as Charles Trevelyan, who agreed with Ponsonby that the only tolerable appointment would be MacDonald himself. This lobbying worked, for on 18 December – the same day Asquith addressed Liberal MPs at the National Liberal Club – Ponsonby heard from the journalist Henry Massingham that MacDonald intended to take the Foreign Office in addition to the premiership. 'But,' he reflected in his diary, 'with the daily difficulties in the H[ouse] of Commons, the question is, can he?'[4]

It is possible Ponsonby had overinterpreted a casual remark, for there is little evidence that Thomas coveted such a prestigious post, and MacDonald was 'much puzzled' by the *Manchester Guardian* story. 'I have you still down for Home [Office],' MacDonald told Thomas, 'but the Colonies, with Ireland in, remember, is a big and difficult job and I have put in two or three [names] and then removed them.' 'The jig-saw is an intricate problem,' he added. 'Henderson tells me that the T[rade] U[nion] side is disturbed lest it does not get enough!'[5]

During a conference at Thomas's Dulwich home before MacDonald headed north to Lossiemouth, Jimmy's seventeen-year-old son Leslie had been despatched to find a copy of *Whitaker's Almanack* 'so that we might see exactly what constituted a full government'.[6] Already certain Labour MPs were being ruled out. Frank Hodges, 'they both agreed, had the brain but not the standing, and [George] Lansbury the standing but not the brain'.[7] At this stage, Philip Snowden as Chancellor was the only firm appointment in MacDonald's mind.

In another letter to Thomas, MacDonald said he had come to realize that the details of an administration were

twice as difficult as we thought that night. The mass of appointments for which we have absolutely no one qualified, is perfectly appalling ... It would take me six months to straighten it all out and would entail hundreds of interviews, but the worst of all is that I must speak to people who, if they care to give me away, could pull me down before anything had been solidified.[8]

Eventually, Thomas settled for the Colonial Office. 'He is quite pleased with himself,' reported Arthur Henderson to Sidney and Beatrice Webb.[9] Writing in the *Sunday Times* on 23 December, the Colonial Secretary-to-be said a Labour government would

not set out immediately to destroy the Empire, to disregard the rights of property, or to start for a system of equality. That is only the idea of foolish and misguided people. They will endeavour to show that in the affairs of the State they can bring experience and a single-minded effort to make the test of government not the advantage or monopoly of a few, but the right of the many.[10]

'Uncle Arthur', as Henderson was known within the Labour Party, presented another problem, for he had lost his Newcastle constituency at the general election. He appeared open to the idea of going to the Lords from which, by convention, at least two Secretaries of State were drawn. This was a little embarrassing, for Labour had a minimal presence in the Upper House and MacDonald had proposed its abolition in the 1890s. Now he found himself in the awkward position of creating new peers.

On 20 December, Henderson wrote to MacDonald seeking his approval not to stand again in Newcastle as well as clarity on the 'line to be followed' in the wake of Asquith's speech.[11] The Labour leader told him he had drafted two preliminary lists of ministers: in one he had left Henderson out altogether on the basis that he devote himself to organizing the party at large; in the other he had put him down as Chairman of Ways and Means (Deputy Speaker), which was not even a ministerial position. Philip Snowden considered this 'offensive' (indeed it apparently 'outraged' Henderson), perfectly illustrating 'what tactless things

McDonald could do'.[12] Unperturbed, Henderson wrote with alternative suggestions for the Chairman of Ways and Means, signing off with the hope that his leader was 'enjoying what free time you can snatch from your work'.[13]

Nor was MacDonald particularly close to John Wheatley, one of the leaders of the Clydeside group of left-wing Labour MPs. But when the Labour leader wrote on 14 December asking if he 'would be disposed to consider coming into the team',[14] Wheatley's response was almost deferential. 'It was noble of you to think favourably of me after all the trouble I gave you last session,' he wrote, but after 'careful consideration' he had 'decided to place my services at your disposal'.[15]

The 'trouble' to which Wheatley referred had been a debate on the Scottish health estimates in June 1923. James Maxton, another Clydeside MP, had likened proposed cuts to the 'murder' of children and accused a Conservative MP present of being 'the worst murderer of all'. When Maxton refused to withdraw his remarks, he, Wheatley and two others were all suspended from the House. This put the radical Clydesiders at odds with MacDonald and hinted at a 'dichotomy between gradualism and the rapid introduction of socialism' which was also to become a feature of the first Labour government.[16]

The media predicted a Clyde breakaway within a month of Labour ministers accepting office, a prospect MacDonald had cleverly averted by offering Wheatley and his associates James Stewart and John Muir ministerial posts. 'Wheatley finally fixed,' the Labour leader noted with satisfaction in his diary.[17] But the exclusion of even more Clydeside representatives, for example James Maxton and Tom Johnston, created a degree of resentment, particularly when briefing suggested it was because they had not 'got the brains'. The Independent Labour Party (ILP) organizer Patrick Dollan even accused MacDonald of being oversensitive to 'the fear of the Anglo-Saxons against too many Scots in the Cabinet'.[18] The charismatic Dumbarton MP David Kirkwood was more pragmatic, suggesting they should 'gie [give] the man [MacDonald] a chance'.[19]

Lunching with the Webbs on 31 December, Arthur Ponsonby reflected that the Labour leadership was 'always inclined to be a little anti-I.L.P. and pro-trade unionist and ... have far too good an opinion of Haldane'.[20] Indeed, since the election MacDonald had come to realize that with the former Liberal Lord Chancellor in his Cabinet, he would simultaneously gain a knowledgeable heavyweight while disarming potential critics of the first Labour government. The two men had communicated briefly earlier in December, but from Lossiemouth MacDonald got down to business, asking if Haldane might consider taking education ('I want there a good man, earnest, efficient'), the Lord Chancellorship, Admiralty or the India Office. 'I have,' added MacDonald, 'several awkward corners to get around.'[21]

To this, Haldane replied at once. Sympathizing with the Labour leader's 'inherently difficult task' he observed that

> If the Labour proposals to the country are so well thought out and so reasonable that sufficient fair-minded people are likely to be of opinion that Labour ought to have its chance, all may shape itself well ... But if the new Government does not commend itself, Labour will be out for a long time.[22]

Haldane ended his rather verbose letter with an invitation for MacDonald to come to Cloan, his country home, which he did on 4 January 1924. There it was agreed that Haldane would once again become Lord Chancellor, albeit shorn of day-to-day legal business in the Lords and at the Privy Council, which was to remain the preserve of Lord Cave, the outgoing Tory incumbent. In the time saved, Haldane was to reorganize both the Committee of Imperial Defence and the Lord Chancellor's Office. Afterwards, Haldane told the poet Sir Edmund Gosse that the Labour leader was

> quick at the uptake and I get on with him excellently. But he is terribly new to affairs, and the colleagues are much worse. Still, if it comes off, I do not despair of being able to interpret to the

country a new order of things which is bound to come anyhow, and which will not be so very different from the old.[23]

By the Christmas of 1923, the idea of a Labour government had gradually become more acceptable, and the political hysteria of early December subsided. Stanley Baldwin even considered it his duty to see MacDonald installed as his successor and Labour moderates strengthened at the expense of extremists. Wiser Unionist heads also realized that the 'howl of rage' directed at the Liberals for facilitating a Labour administration gave the prospects of 'good hunting' in future elections.[24]

Asquith was also clear that a Labour government must be given 'a reasonable chance',[25] telling Lord Stamfordham he would only support Labour measures with which his party agreed, although he conceded this might not satisfy the 'extreme wing' of the Labour Party: 'the young lions will be hungry and want to be fed, if they are not, they will roar and then will bite and this will bring disaster.'[26]

Writing to Baldwin, Leo Amery, the First Lord of the Admiralty, reckoned the Liberal strategy was to push out the Unionists and Labour in succession, thus gradually establishing for themselves the position of the only 'effective alternative to Labour'. But, he added, Labour shared the Unionists' desire to break up the Liberal Party and would thus 'be drawn into a friendlier attitude towards ourselves'. He continued:

I am sure that the real healthy and natural division of parties in this country is between constructive Conservatism on the one side, with a policy of Empire Development and national economic organisation, and on the other hand Labour Socialism with its ideas of levelling up by taxation, nationalisation etc … Meanwhile it is to the interest of both of us to clear the ground of the Liberal Party, which stands to-day for nothing more than an organised hypocrisy and not for any real political faith. We may each hope to get the larger share of the carcass but meanwhile the great thing is to get the beast killed and on that we can be agreed.[27]

In an interview with the American publication *Collier's Weekly*, MacDonald appeared to agree, predicting a time in which

> there will be only two [parties] – the Conservatives, who represent capital, and the combined forces who favour a government by the people. I believe that they will see the wisdom of combining under the banner of the Labour Party rather than the half-hearted principles of the Liberals.[28]

Not all Conservatives shared Amery's long view. In a letter to *The Times*, the former Tory MP George Terrell railed against the 'Communists, the wild men, the work-shy, the ignorant and the illiterate' upon whom Labour relied for support in Parliament,[29] while the City of London Conservative and Unionist Associations urged Baldwin to support a Liberal government in order to exclude those 'wild men' from office. The Prime Minister simply replied that such co-operation was impossible in light of Asquith's remarks at the National Liberal Club.

There were also ongoing jitters at Sandringham, where the King and Queen were spending Christmas. The Sovereign had been disturbed by the speeches of some Clydeside MPs, particularly a prediction from Campbell Stephen that the monarchy would 'end' were MacDonald to be refused a dissolution shortly after taking office. The King telephoned his private secretary, who was at Windsor, and instructed him to make discreet inquiries as to the lay of the land. As it happened, the Labour candidate Hugh Dalton (recently defeated in Cardiff) was visiting his father John, a former chaplain to Queen Victorian, tutor to George V and now a Canon of Windsor. As he later recounted, Hugh told Lord Stamfordham that he

> looked forward to the extinction of the Liberals and a return to the two-party system. He said he hoped it wouldn't be rich against poor. He dreaded that. He said that 'a Liberal financier' had told the King that 'the day Ramsay MacDonald kisses hands three hundred million pounds will leave this country' ...

I said such talk was all nonsense anyhow, and very unpatriotic as well.

Stamfordham passed all this on to the King, who read it aloud to the Queen, leaving them both 'slightly reassured'.[30] The Duke of Windsor, then the popular Prince of Wales, later recalled his father being 'in considerable doubt' as to how Labour leaders would 'conduct themselves towards him' were they to become Ministers of the Crown.[31]

MacDonald, too, had succumbed to anxiousness regarding possible financial panic and asked Jimmy Thomas if anything could be done 'to stop this sort of thing'. The *Financial Times* duly obliged early in the new year, Thomas having told the newspaper there was no cause for alarm: 'I cannot conceive of a Labour Government taking office [and] doing anything that should shake confidence not only in the stability, but in the future of this old country.'[32]

MacDonald had also instructed Thomas to convey to the King that he was 'anxious in every possible way to save him trouble and worry', a message he believed 'might smooth matters and also strengthen our hands'.[33] The King was acutely conscious that with a three-way split in the Commons he 'may have to come to grave and momentous decisions'.[34] On 28 December Thomas telephoned Stamfordham to say that

> If the King asks Mr. Ramsay Macdonald to form a Government he will undertake to do so. In spite of all the evil prognostications of the Press, no extreme legislation will be introduced or violent administrative changes carried out: 'no playing up to the Clyde Division'! But an endeavour to carry on the Government on sound lines.

Doubtless relieved, Stamfordham asked Thomas to tell MacDonald that there was no uneasiness on the King's part because 'he never doubted their loyalty or patriotism and felt sure the best interests of the Country would be the primary aim of their policy'.[35] There had, of course, been minority governments in the past, but never the situation produced by the recent election. It was not altogether clear a government with only 191 MPs would possess the same prerogatives and rights of that in a stronger position.

It seems Thomas was unconvinced by Stamfordham's reassurances. On New Year's Day he visited the King's private secretary at Windsor and asked, 'point blank' if the King was 'alarmed at the prospect of a Labour Government'. A startled Stamfordham obviously said 'no' and countered by asking if MacDonald would have the 'backing of his party' were he to accept office. Thomas said yes, 'with the exception of a few', a minority the party hoped to 'shed ... by degrees'. Thomas predicted a Labour government would 'live with the guillotine hanging over us: our enemies waiting & watching for the slightest chance of tripping us up'. Passing all this on to the King, Stamfordham observed that Thomas clearly believed 1924 was 'to be the beginning of a new era'.[36]

Lunching with his brother Sir Frederick (who was Keeper of the Privy Purse) on 3 January, Arthur Ponsonby was assured that the King was not being 'influenced by all the anti-Labour talk', although 'Fritz' urged them to 'keep on good terms with the King'. 'The Anti-Labour propaganda is fierce and furious,' observed Arthur Ponsonby in his diary. 'We are regarded as a band of inexperienced and ignorant navvies.'[37]

MacDonald's diary entry for 10 January reflected gloom amid the exhilaration:

Times of sad reflections and gloomy thoughts. The people of my heart are dead; their faces on my walls, they do not share with me. Had much difficulty in returning [to London]. How vain is honour now ... But I have to work out my destiny. So I returned to the world of politics & premierships, & a press that wonders why I take so little delight in publicity.[38]

During the Lloyd George coalition, Stamfordham had lobbied in vain for the office of Lord Chamberlain (which, among other duties, censored West End plays) to become permanent and non-political. With Labour on the cusp of office, he felt this reform had become inescapable, not least because Labour 'simply could not produce the men of aristocratic lineage and private means who traditionally occupied these great offices of State'.[39]

MacDonald had already intimated via Jimmy Thomas that the King should 'retain all the present officials if so desired on the understanding that they do not politically antagonise the Government'.[40] The King therefore decreed that the Earl of Cromer, Lord Chamberlain since 1922, would be made permanent, while Lord Shaftesbury would be reappointed Lord Steward, and that once Lord Bath retired as Master of the Horse, Lord Granard would become his permanent successor. Three lords-in-waiting ('a superior brand of equerry') were also to be appointed by the King (rather than the government) and relieved of their political responsibilities in the House of Lords. The Prime Minister, however, would continue to nominate three lesser Household officials to act as whips in the Commons.[41]

These reforms, however, caused much unhappiness, with Sir Frederick Ponsonby warning that by making the three 'White Wands' (the lords-in-waiting) non-political, the King would 'be cutting himself off from the Labour Party'.[42] Lord Stamfordham countered that:

The King will make the changes at <u>Ramsay MacDonald's request</u>. His Majesty has <u>not</u> refused to have anything to do with the Labour Party – on the contrary he will do everything to help Ramsay MacDonald in an exceptionally difficult position, and the latter has already expressed his gratitude for the helpful communications received from His Majesty with regard to the future.[43]

That the three Commons whips would still need to be suitably attired caused further anxiety. 'I feel afraid that they will clamour for plain clothes,' Stamfordham had told the King on 2 January.[44]

Contrary to subsequent accounts, the King made a real effort to 'understand the special difficulties and embarrassments of his new Labour Ministers', and they in turn were quite willing to dress appropriately, although drawing the line at knee breeches (through fear of ridicule) and full dress (on grounds of cost). The King minuted:

> This question of uniform is becoming very intricate & confused. Whatever decision the Cabinet Ministers come to, I will agree to, but they must all do the same. It would look very odd if some were in uniform and some in evening clothes at a Levée ... In no case do I expect anyone to get more than the Levée coat; full dress is not necessary on account of the expense.

Lord Stamfordham even ascertained that Moss Bros had some Levee Dress 'from £30 complete', information he passed on to Ben Spoor, Labour's Chief Whip.[45]

On Sunday 6 January, C. P. Scott of the *Manchester Guardian* found MacDonald at work in his study looking 'fagged and anxious' and surrounded 'with a vast litter of papers'. The Labour leader told him a 'deluge' of post had prevented him having any sort of rest in Lossiemouth and that he was about to engage a fourth secretary to ease the burden. When Scott urged greater communication with the Liberals, MacDonald showed a 'curious sensitiveness', saying 'there must be an end to the flaunting of Labour's dependence [on the Liberals]. It might be tolerated once, it might be tolerated twice, but after that, if repeated, he should speak out strongly.'[46]

No sooner had MacDonald returned to London than he was lobbied by colleagues regarding another appointment. The Newcastle MP Charles Trevelyan alluded to their 'rather difficult friend' in a letter dated 6 January, observing that 'the very qualities which may make him difficult as a colleague will make him a worse trouble if he is outside ... an injured hero to thousands of our supporters and the best Liberals'. He meant the French-born journalist and scourge of the Belgian Congo E. D. Morel, whom Trevelyan unconvincingly depicted as 'deeply loyal' to MacDonald. 'Nothing could shake our feeling which grew during the war years,' he added, 'that there is no one except you who is big enough to give Europe the necessary lead.'[47]

According to the Scottish communist Willie Gallacher, MacDonald privately assured Morel he would be appointed Foreign Secretary.[48] This seems unlikely, for the archival evidence suggests MacDonald simply did not want Morel anywhere near his government. In a terse note, the Labour leader told Morel he had 'tried hard' to secure him a junior ministerial post but had 'completely failed', offering the rather lame excuse that he was 'not in complete control'.[49] Arthur Ponsonby, like Trevelyan a supporter of Morel, believed that 'there was only one post available for him, under-secretary at the Colonial Office, and [Jimmy] Thomas flatly refused to have him'.[50]

On the evening of 8 January, the Foreign Office official (and future Conservative MP) Duff Cooper went to the Royal Albert Hall to witness what had been billed as a 'Labour Victory demonstration'. 'It was a very tame show,' recorded Cooper in his diary. 'It struck no note of revolution but rather one of respectable middle-class nonconformity. They sang hymns between the speeches which were all about God.'[51] It was indeed a surprisingly sober affair, an 'almost solemn act of dedication', as the journalist Henry Massingham put it, 'rather than the flaming signal of Party triumph'.[52] This was clearly deliberate, with MacDonald observing that the year 1924 was

> not the last in God's programme of creation. The shield of love and the spear of justice will still be in the hands of good and upright men and women, and the ideal of a great future will still be in front of our people.[53]

MacDonald also took care to rebut ongoing speculation regarding an immediate dissolution. 'We are not going to undertake office in order to prepare for a General Election,' he made clear, 'we are going to take office in order to do work.'[54]

Slightly alarmed by a succession of speakers 'so formal and uninspired as to suggest that the official policy was doomed to failure', the new Northampton MP Margaret Bondfield made a point of raising the 'pitch', pointing 'out that office was not merely or only a responsibility – it was also an opportunity'.[55] 'We want to make Westminster the workshop of the nation,' she declared, an 'enthusiastic determination' which spread, 'like electricity, through the meeting'.[56] This closed with renditions of 'The March of the Workers' and 'The Red Flag'.

The House of Commons had met for the first time earlier that day while on 9 January an expanded Parliamentary Labour Party gathered at the House of Commons. On 10 January, MacDonald saw Stanley Baldwin while Jimmy Thomas reassured Lord Stamfordham that Labour's 'programme would be of so moderate a character that he was afraid it would disappoint the Tories'.[57] Stamfordham also informed the King that no prospective Labour ministers had been the subject of police reports regarding subversive activities. Indeed, Sir John Anderson, permanent secretary at the Home Office, expected a Labour government would 'be as anxious as their predecessors' to be kept informed of 'what the Communists and extreme Members of their Party are doing and saying'.[58]

Further proof of the inevitability of office came when Sir Maurice Hankey, the Cabinet Secretary, paid a covert visit to MacDonald at his Belsize Park home on Saturday 12 January:

> I was taken up to a small room at the very top of the house – almost an attic or garret, with books all round, books and papers all over the tables, and Ramsay in the middle of them looking gaunt and thin and wearing a very ancient and threadbare 'sporty' coat. I took to him at once, and vice versa I think.

Once Sir Maurice had ascertained the Labour leader's support for the fledgling Cabinet Secretariat and Committee of Imperial Defence, he once again ran 'the gauntlet of the Press' and returned to Downing Street.[59] A few days later, Lord Stamfordham, clearly mollified by his communications with Jimmy Thomas, concluded that 'the sooner the Labour Party comes into power the better'. 'Personally I am not alarmed,' he wrote to a friend, 'and, unless they are upset by their own extremists, it would not surprise me were they to remain in office for some time, during which they may do considerable good.'[60]

On the eve of the State Opening of Parliament, MacDonald asked Lord Haldane if he would host a dinner for senior colleagues at his Queen Anne's Gate home. To this Haldane readily agreed, and his sister Bay acted as hostess. 'The King's Speech dinner went off remarkably well,' he later wrote to his mother. 'At Bay's suggestion I provided both lemonade and orangeade. The unofficial cabinet meeting which followed was a remarkable display of competence and also of conservatism.'[61]

The King's Speech on 15 January betrayed no sign of an expiring Cabinet, while the Monarch noticed that the Royal Gallery was 'full of friends of Labour members who had asked for tickets'.[62] The following day Susan Lawrence became the first female Labour MP to make a maiden speech, while a boisterous Jimmy Thomas mocked Winston Churchill and the Duke of Northumberland for their apparent belief that 'the baskets [were] ready for their heads'. Finally, on 17 January the Manchester MP and former Labour leader J. R. Clynes moved an amendment to the Loyal Address, respectfully submitting to the King that 'your Majesty's present advisers have not the confidence of this House'.

This was the test Baldwin had been expecting since mid-December, and in response he frankly admitted to having no expectation of remaining in office. But while Labour and the Unionists were keen to move to an immediate division, the Liberals insisted on a three-day debate. 'I propose,' declared Asquith, 'to vote, and to advise all my friends to vote for the amendment.' Arthur Ponsonby thought Asquith 'more brilliant' than he had ever heard, keeping the House 'in fits of laughter'. The following day, Ponsonby noticed that both the Prince of Wales (the future Edward VIII) and Duke of York (the future George VI) were in the Commons gallery, doubtless 'longing' for David Kirkwood, the Clydeside MP, 'to perform'.[63]

The delay meant MacDonald had some breathing space in which to put the finishing touches to his first administration, the composition of which had now been in gestation for five weeks. On 18 January he saw Lord Chelmsford, Lord Haldane having already established that the former Viceroy of India was 'well disposed' to becoming First Lord of the Admiralty despite having 'been a Conservative all his life'.[64] Chelmsford later told the courtier Alan Lascelles he had agreed on the basis that 'he should never be asked in Cabinet to give an opinion on any party question'.[65] Clement Attlee thought he had been appointed as he 'would be able to deal with admirals'.[66]

The law officers proved troublesome. Henry Slesser, the Labour Party's legal adviser, was MacDonald's preferred candidate for Attorney General, but he had been defeated at the election so was instead to be nominated as Solicitor General without a seat in the House. In his place, the forty-three-year-old MP for Wallsend, Patrick Hastings, was offered the office of Attorney General and the requisite knighthood. 'My inclination was to decline,' he later wrote, 'and if I had known what the next year was to bring forward I should most certainly have done so.'[67] By this point, the Liberal lawyer (and former Conservative MP) Lord Parmoor was also on board as Lord President of the Council.[68]

On 18 January, MacDonald heard back from George Lansbury, who had presumptuously told Arthur Henderson it would be 'a great honour and privilege to serve in the first British Labour Cabinet'. The Labour leader, however, offered him only the non-Cabinet transport ministry, which the Poplar MP rejected on the basis it would 'involve no participation in the formation of general policy'.[69] Lansbury had recently suggested at a public meeting that the King was being pressured into denying Labour the fruits of victory, adding that one previous monarch had 'lost his head' for standing 'up against the common people' and 'George V would be well advised to keep his finger out of the pie now.'[70] Given that the King was especially sensitive to such comments, MacDonald most likely did not want to antagonize the Monarch by including Lansbury, who was 'always speaking so wildly and indiscreetly at meetings', in his Cabinet.[71]

There was no such problem when it came to the Edinburgh MP and accountant William Graham, who on 19 January gobbled up the offer of Financial Secretary to the Treasury, telling MacDonald he 'could not have proposed anything more to my liking, by training and experience'.[72] Graham had been tipped for the Scottish Office, although he was clear 'no man would willingly go there, as the Office is one of the most thankless in the Government'. Instead, he was to support his friend Philip Snowden, long ago earmarked for the Treasury. Snowden later recalled that MacDonald

> threw across the table to me a pencilled note written on an envelope which said: 'I want formally to ask you to accept the office of Chancellor to the Exchequer.' I nodded my acceptance. I should think there would be no precedent for such an informal offer and acceptance of a Cabinet post.[73]

Sidney Webb, meanwhile, was confirmed as President of the Board of Trade (which included responsibility for unemployment), colleagues – though not Webb himself – having convinced MacDonald that the Fabian intellectual deserved something more substantial than the 'Cinderella' post of Minister of Labour.[74]

Webb urged MacDonald to make Margaret Bondfield the first woman Cabinet minister (she would instead become a non-Cabinet Parliamentary Secretary), while he later complained that 'nationalist feeling' meant South Wales had to be represented by Vernon Hartshorn (as Postmaster-General) and Scotland by William Adamson (with Cabinet rank as Secretary for Scotland), meaning the first Labour Cabinet numbered 20 rather than 14, several others having demanded senior positions.[75] Charles Trevelyan, meanwhile, was delighted to be offered 'the place he wanted above all others', the Board of Education. 'I no longer have only six children,' he told his wife Molly, 'I have six million.'[76] 'By

Thursday I may be Lord Chancellor again,' Haldane informed his mother. 'How odd! I do not deserve it, but it is a duty.'[77]

Having failed to locate John Wheatley, meanwhile, MacDonald despatched a note to the Cosmo Hotel (where Wheatley was staying) asking him to become under-secretary at the Ministry of Health with responsibility for housing. It seems Wheatley, bolstered by colleagues, declined, which forced MacDonald to offer him a Cabinet position. Arthur Ponsonby was also offered (and accepted) the post of under-secretary at the Foreign Office. MacDonald's approach, noted Dolly Ponsonby in her diary, was 'to put into central offices men very able in certain directions but knowing nothing of the job they are given. Thomas knows nothing of the Colonies. Wheatley only in Parliament a year and made a Cabinet minister.'[78]

Although his task was virtually complete, MacDonald clearly found it gruelling. 'Cabinet making worse than I thought,' he wrote in his diary on 19 January:

> All but two or three disappointed ... One after another behave as though I misled them in offering anything but a Cabinet place. To-day a wild letter has come from the wife of one who refused subordinate office which will give a sleepless night. I feel like an executioner, I knock so many ambitious heads into my basket. After this, every man will be my enemy.[79]

The fact the Labour leader was not a Privy Counsellor necessitated a degree of choreography, for Lord Cave (the Lord Chancellor) was quite clear that 'no person should be allowed to kiss hands as Prime Minister or First Lord of the Treasury without first being sworn as a member of the Privy Council'.[80] This meant two meetings of the Privy Council, one before MacDonald kissed hands, and another at which he and other senior ministers would receive their seals of office.

While Sir Maurice Hankey sorted out all that, the debate on the Address reached its conclusion on Monday 21 January, during which Margaret Bondfield delivered her maiden address on women's unemployment, patronizingly described by one correspondent as 'the first intellectual speech by a woman the House had ever heard'.[81] In his own contribution, MacDonald asked for 'fair play' once he formed a government. Baldwin promised it, while Neville Chamberlain churlishly blamed the Liberals for having brought about a socialist administration. 'It was they [the Unionists], not we, who invited the judgment of the electorate,' countered Asquith. 'They have got it.' Austen Chamberlain said the former premier had just 'sung the swan song of the Liberal party'.[82]

It was the 'fullest house' Arthur Ponsonby had ever seen and 'in a scene of great excitement' Labour's amendment was carried with a majority of 72, larger than many had expected.[83] Some ten Liberals voted with the Unionist government and half a dozen more abstained. Several Members then tried to continue the debate with another amendment condemning socialism, but the Speaker gave that short shrift and the amended Address was carried by 328 to 251. 'A revolution in English [*sic*] politics as profound as that associated with the Reform Act of 1832,' observed the *Annual Register*, 'had been carried through with a smoothness and rapidity that two months earlier would have been thought impossible.'[84] 'So I am be P.M.,' MacDonald wrote in his diary. 'The load will be heavy & I am so much alone.'[85]

The Labour leader's pocket diary blandly set out his appointments for 22 January:

10.30	Party
12	Buckingham Palace Privy Council
2.45	Commons
4.20	Buckingham Palace
5	Ministers
8	Dine Sir Maurice Hankey[86]

While MacDonald faced the PLP, Baldwin's Cabinet convened for the last time. The original plan had been for the Labour leader to be sworn of the Privy Council at noon, after which he would immediately be invited to kiss hands and form a government, but given that the motion for adjournment still stood in Baldwin's name, this would have created a constitutionally (not to mention socially) awkward situation in which the new premier (MacDonald) would find himself sitting on the government front bench as an ex-premier (Baldwin) moved it.

Instead, it was agreed the King would ask MacDonald to form a government on him being sworn a Privy Counsellor but that he would not kiss hands until *after* the adjournment. At the last minute, the Palace 'turned sticky' and wanted to postpone everything until the Commons next met on 12 February, but Sir Maurice Hankey put his foot down and eventually 'won all parties round' to the original plan.[87] At noon, therefore, the Labour Leader of the Opposition was sworn a member of His Majesty's Most Honourable Privy Council. 'He talked so steadily that I could hardly thank him,' recalled MacDonald of his first meeting with the King. 'Most friendly.'[88] 'He impressed me very much,' the King wrote in his diary, 'he wishes to do right thing. Today 23 years ago dear Grandmama died, I wonder what she would have thought of a Labour Govt.'[89]

Lord Stamfordham provided a fuller account of the King's first audience with MacDonald:

> He assured the King that, though he and his friends were inexperienced in governing and fully realised the great responsibilities which they would now assume, nevertheless they were honest and sincere and his earnest desire was to serve his King and Country. They may fail in their endeavours: but it will not be for want of trying to do their best.

The King specifically raised George Lansbury having gone 'out of his way to express a threat and a reminder of the fate which had befallen King Charles I', pointing out to MacDonald that he had little expected 'to occupy his present position'. He had, added the Monarch, 'served in the Navy for 14 years – and thus had opportunities of seeing more of the world and mixing with his fellow creatures than would otherwise have been the case'. Having established his everyman credentials, the King also wondered if MacDonald had 'fully considered the heavy responsibilities and duties incurred by undertaking the office of Secretary of State for Foreign Affairs in addition to that of Prime Minister'. He mentioned that Lord Salisbury had also done so and, as a consequence, neglected his work as premier. MacDonald replied 'that for the moment he had no one to appoint to the Foreign Office, but perhaps later on he might be able to hand it over to someone else'.[90]

Then, at 2.45 p.m., the outgoing Prime Minister (Baldwin) moved that the House of Commons adjourn until 12 February. When he announced that the King had been 'graciously pleased' to accept his government's resignation, one Labour MP cried: 'Thank God for that!'[91] 'One or two ineffective speeches,' judged the Prime Minister-designate, 'I took no part & declined to be drawn.'[92] By 4.30 p.m., MacDonald was back at the Palace, where the King formally appointed him Prime Minister and First Lord of the Treasury.

There followed another long talk, during which the King expressed his concern at the prospect of the Soviet Union being officially recognized. The new Prime Minister argued that other European countries were preparing to do so and that, if UK did not, it would miss out on economic opportunities:

> The King said he was sure that Mr. Macdonald would understand how abhorrent it would be to His Majesty to receive any representative of Russia who, directly or indirectly, had been connected with the abominable murder of the Emperor, Empress and their family, the King's own 1st cousin, and H.M. hoped that the representative might be a minister and not an ambassador.

Finally, the King referred to what he called an 'unfortunate incident' at Labour's Victory rally at the Albert Hall, by which he meant the singing of 'The Red Flag'. In response, MacDonald

> spoke very openly and said he was sure the King would be generous to him and understand the very difficult position he

was in vis a vis to his own extremists: and he could assure His Majesty that, had he attempted to prevent the 'Red Flag' being sung on that occasion, a riot would inevitably have ensued.

The Prime Minister added that it had required all his 'influence' to stop it being sung again in the Commons the previous evening. His party 'had got into the way of singing this song', he lamented, 'and it will only be by degrees that he hopes to break down this habit'.[93] 'King plays the game straight,' observed MacDonald in his diary later that day, 'though I feel he is apprehensive. It wd. be a miracle were he not.'[94]

MacDonald then returned to his room at the Commons, to which, fresh from his own audience with the King, Sir Maurice Hankey was summoned to 'drill' the new ministers on the formalities for another meeting of the Privy Council. Lord Haldane needed no such tuition and instead practically 'carried off' the diminutive Stephen Walsh, who was to be Secretary of State for War, 'to dine with him in order to instruct him how to behave with his Generals'.[95] When General – now Lord – Thomson, the new Secretary of State for Air, whispered to Hankey that the Prime Minister was 'at a loose end as regards dinner', the Cabinet Secretary invited MacDonald to have dinner and champagne at the United Services Club. As Sir Maurice recalled, the

only vacant table was in the far corner of the big dining room. We had to walk past a number of tables occupied by retired Colonels and Admirals of highly correct Tory politics. Many of them looked at us open mouthed, pausing twixt cup and lip as I filed down the room followed by the tall, frock-coated figure of the new and sinister Labour Prime Minister. That he should dine in their club on his first night in office![96]

'On my way home,' wrote Hankey's deputy Tom Jones in his diary, 'saw the evening placards, Lenin dead (official) Ramsay MacDonald Premier.'[97]

Sidney Webb later judged it was 'impossible not to admire the skill with which Macdonald had surmounted his difficulties', his government having been greeted with a 'universal chorus of approval' and not a little surprise that Labour could have produced 'so reputable a list'.[98] Inside the Cabinet room on 23 January, Lord Chelmsford met most of his colleagues for the first time, with the exceptions of Haldane (who had brokered his appointment), Sidney Webb and possibly Lord Parmoor. And while the Labour Party 'growled a little' at the inclusion of Conservatives, it was 'so pleased at all difficulties being surmounted that it did not kick'. More to the point, no one could pretend that a Cabinet containing Haldane, Parmoor and Chelmsford 'was either contemptible, or likely to ruin the Empire'. 'The stupidest old Tory,' wrote Charles Trevelyan, 'somehow felt that the Navy was safe for a year or two.'[99] John Shepherd and Keith Laybourn calculated that eight of the Cabinet's 20 members were drawn from the middle classes, one-fifth from the upper-middle-class, but the rest from the manual working classes, including three miners.[100]

With Cabinet ministers having taken their statutory oaths of office on 23 January, ministers were now able to appoint their deputies and under-secretaries. Jack Lawson, Financial Secretary to the War Office, later recalled the satisfaction of hearing his mother telling journalists (in her Northern accent) that she had 'sometimes walloped thoo … and that thoo sometimes needed it',[101] while Margaret Bondfield was chairing a TUC General Council meeting when she received a note from Tom Shaw asking her to become his Parliamentary Secretary at the Ministry of Labour. A 'revolution' had been accomplished, wrote the journalist Mary Agnes Hamilton: a 'woman was a member of a British Government'.[102]

John Scanlon, an Independent Labour Party activist, was baffled by the allocation of some minor offices, for example Manny Shinwell, 'who knew nothing whatever about mines but a little about ships, was made Minister of Mines, whilst Mr. Frank Hodges, who knew a lot about mines and nothing about ships, was sent to the Admiralty'.[103]

In the House of Lords, meanwhile, 'the young De La Warr and the aged Muir MacKenzie' became Lords-in-Waiting, albeit 'with no more than [Lords] Russell and Kimberley to whip'.[104] The daily papers were more interested in the less aristocratic ministers, the *Liverpool Daily Courier* noting that with 'a few exceptions' members of the government had 'come from the cabin and the mean streets'.[105] Asquith thought them 'for the most part a beggarly array',[106] while his wife Violet presciently predicted the new government would 'suffer for the timidity & inefficiency of its members' rather than for its 'violence'.[107]

Lord Stamfordham, on the other hand, could not help 'feeling optimistic', believing it 'just possible' that in the country's 'somewhat parlous condition they may prove to be the needful remedy'.[108] Writing in his diary, meanwhile, Henry 'Chips' Channon wondered at a Labour government being 'in power in England' (*sic*), asking: 'Is this the beginning of the end?? ... Will our heads fall off?'[109] How, asked Jack Lawson rhetorically,

> could the men of the mines and factories, the multitudes from the long lines of brick streets, hope to stand beside the makers of a science, a literature, and a mechanical world which was the wonder of all men? Their Press answered, Impossible. And lo while they were proving its impossibility the thing was done, and strange things were afoot in Government Departments.

It was, he added, worth living to have been 'one of the first of the new tribe to walk into those great buildings in Whitehall'.[110]

3

Ramsay MacDonald as Prime Minister: 'A mass of contradictions'

The new Prime Minister was an enigma. 'This or that man claimed to know him,' observed the journalist Sir Alexander Mackintosh. 'They came in contact with him as a lover of books or an enthusiast for art, or a perfervid Scot, but there was a realm to which he invited no man's company. He retired to thoughts among which he dwelt alone. The result was that he seemed a mass of contradictions.'[1]

Those contradictions were emphasized by media profiles. 'A Scotsman representing a Welsh constituency in a predominantly English Assembly,' observed *The Times*, 'a Liberal in early manhood destined to become the hero of the Socialist movement in Great Britain, an "intellectual" whom the manual workers of the Labour Party acclaim as their chosen leader.'[2] To the Liberal journalist Henry Massingham he was 'not eloquent, but a statesman. A man of principle, but not a fanatic.'[3]

But most of all they emphasized the new premier's humble origins, the facts of which lay in striking contrast to his professional or upper-class predecessors. 'No other holder of the highest office under the Crown has risen from such lowly circumstances as James Ramsay MacDonald,' gushed one early hagiography. 'No other … has had more sensational experience of the ups and downs of political fortune.' Those, it added, who had pictured him as a 'wild man' were 'astonished when they see and hear him'.[4]

The life of James Ramsay MacDonald was indeed the stuff of a romantic novel. Born illegitimately to a ploughman called John MacDonald and raised by his mother (Annie Ramsay, a servant) and grandmother, what his biographer David Marquand called the 'insecurities of a fatherless boy' never quite faded. MacDonald left Lossiemouth as a young man to help set up a boys' club at a Bristol church and, when that failed, embarked upon a scientific career in London. When that was scuppered by a breakdown, he became private secretary to Thomas Lough, a radical (Irish) Home Ruler. MacDonald was also active in the Fabian Society, Scottish Home Rule Association and Keir Hardie's Independent Labour Party, which he joined in 1894.

A quixotic bid to represent Southampton in Parliament brought MacDonald together with Margaret Gladstone,[5] whose private income enabled them to travel widely. Together they had six children: Alister (born in 1898), Malcolm (1901), Ishbel (1903), David (1904), Joan (1908) and Sheila (1910). In 1900, MacDonald became secretary to the Labour Representation Committee, in 1906 the MP for Leicester and in February 1911 chairman of the Parliamentary Labour Party. The rest of that year, however, was blighted by tragedy: diphtheria took MacDonald's son David, eight days later his mother passed away in Lossiemouth, and in July Margaret developed blood poisoning and died a few months later.

A devastated MacDonald sought solace in his work, but at the outbreak of the Great War he found himself at odds with the pro-war majority of his own party. He resigned as chairman and helped set up the Union of Democratic Control (UDC) to campaign for parliamentary control of foreign policy alongside Arthur Ponsonby, Charles Trevelyan and E. D. Morel, all former Liberals. This made MacDonald incredibly unpopular. In 1915 the tabloid newspaper *John Bull* revealed his illegitimacy, his Lossiemouth golf club expelled him as a member and, finally, at the 'khaki' election of 1918 he lost his Commons seat.

But in a remarkable comeback, by 1922 MacDonald was again in Parliament and became Leader of the Opposition after beating

J. R. Clynes by 61 votes to 56, his stand against the war having 'endeared him to the Left' and his steady support for 'gradualist' methods having 'made him acceptable to the Right'.[6] Strategically, MacDonald had a clear aim: to complete the political realignment which had begun during the war, 'elbow the Liberals aside and make Labour the permanent alternative to the Conservatives in a new two-party system'.[7]

Although a Labour government had been in prospect since the general election in December 1923, its advent still felt unreal. 'It was almost unbelievably pleasing to wake up one morning and find that the sun had risen not simply on the natural world around me,' wrote Malcolm MacDonald, then an Oxford undergraduate, 'but also – after a long, long seemingly endless night – on the MacDonalds' fortunes.'[8]

With Malcolm at university and his mother having died more than a decade earlier, the key figure in MacDonald's domestic and social world became his twenty-year-old daughter Ishbel, then in a midst of a three-year diploma in domestic science at King's College for Women. Her studies were swiftly abandoned when Bay Haldane (the Lord Chancellor's sister) helped her take over the premier's 'awkward rambling house' in Downing Street. 'You must be very careful, Miss, not to speak to reporters,' the office keeper (Mr Berry) told Ishbel, 'or you might say something your papa would not like you to say.'[9] The *Evening News* called her the 'College Girl Hostess of No. 10'.[10]

It fell to Ishbel to manage much of the daily business at Number 10 alongside Rose Rosenberg, MacDonald's personal secretary since 1923, and Miss Byvoets, a formidable Dutch housekeeper usually based in Lossiemouth. Incoming premiers were expected to furnish the residence themselves, so Miss Byvoets, Bay Haldane and Ishbel's aunt Florence (Gladstone), visited auctions to buy linen, china and silver. Food was bought from and delivered by the local Co-op, while the family occupied only state rooms which were heated at government expenses as they 'had to pay for [their] own coal and light'.[11] As Prime Minister and Foreign Secretary, Ramsay MacDonald earned £5,000 a year, taking only one salary rather than two, although this was reduced to £3,500 after tax. There was no entertainment allowance.

In late January, Alexander Grant, the managing director of McVitie's and inventor of its famous digestive biscuit, made MacDonald an offer. The two men had known each other since their respective childhoods in Forres and Lossiemouth, Grant's father and MacDonald's uncle having worked together as guards on the Highland Railway. Although Grant was a Unionist, he took great delight in his friend's political success. He was also a generous philanthropist and had recently endowed the Advocates' Library in Edinburgh so it could become a National Library of Scotland. Grant's offer was a loan of £40,000 so that, as MacDonald explained to his solicitor, he would not have 'to worry about income' while 'absorbed in public duties'.[12] This was to be divided into £30,000 of Preference Shares in McVitie & Price, from which the Prime Minister would receive a dividend twice a year, and £10,000 to be invested in Trust Securities. Grant also offered a Daimler, which would be maintained (together with a chauffeur) from the share income.[13] The money was paid into MacDonald's bank account, after which he purchased the shares as if he were a private investor, something contrived as Grant did not 'want any of the people' at his Manchester office 'to know anything about our transactions'.[14] A share certificate was sent to Downing Street in the middle of March but the arrangement was not made public.

Meanwhile there was also Chequers, recently gifted to the nation by Lord Lee of Fareham, and which the MacDonalds visited for the first time on 2 February 1924. Press photographs showed MacDonald and his daughter Joan standing at the entrance to its garden, above which was the legend: 'All care abandon, ye who enter here.' The Prime Minister took that seriously. At Chequers he refused to wear evening dress, instead 'putting on tweeds first thing in the morning and taking them off last thing at night'. Malcolm was also within motoring range of Oxford and would invite friends to spend a day in its spacious grounds. 'In those days its endowment ran to every luxury,' reflected Ishbel in an unpublished memoir. 'None of it was out of public funds.'[15] During his first weekend there, the Prime Minister ruminated on the domination of ministers by officials. 'Details are overwhelming & Ministers have no time to work out policy with officials as servants,' he wrote in his diary, 'they are immersed in pressing business with officials as masters. I must take care.'[16]

Ishbel distanced herself from Beatrice Webb's Half-Circle Club, which aimed to teach Labour women how to behave at official functions. The Prime Minister's daughter thought it so 'awful' she would have 'nothing to do with it',[17] although she did agree to a meeting of ministers' wives at Downing Street pending the establishment of a permanent Labour Club. On Ishbel's own initiative, she also instituted a weekly 'At Home' at which the spouses of Labour MPs could enjoy a 'homely cup of tea'. Although Webb found Ishbel an 'attractive creature ... simple and direct in speech and manner', she fretted about the impact of 'this vortex of luxurious living and silly chatter', having long suspected that her father preferred 'the company of Tory aristocrats and Liberal capitalists to that of the trade union officials and the I.L.P. agitators'.[18]

MacDonald had no such qualms. 'My dear Ishbel is splendid,' he told his diary. 'The little maid is sedate as a judge and reminds me every day of her mother.'[19] The Prime Minister insisted on breakfast at 8 a.m. as it was the only meal he and his children could have together. Initially, Ishbel hated Downing Street for what she called its 'moods ... stark unhomeliness and impromptu furniture', although this later gave way to affection. When her post became overwhelming – 'begging letters, invites to open bazaars, to be on committees, to be a patron ... letters from mad people' – Ishbel considered having a secretary of her own but 'was too scared'. Only decades later did she admit to being 'miserable ... always struggling to keep in my depth but determined never to show it'.[20]

As had been clear shortly after the election result, MacDonald missed acutely the presence of his late wife Margaret. Randall Davidson, the Archbishop of Canterbury, made a point of reading the Prime Minister's published tribute to Margaret,[21] which he considered 'a really fine picture of a remarkable woman'. He even wrote to MacDonald, noting the

> difference between what the taking of this great trust means to you now and what it would have meant had she been here to share it with you. That such a trust is shared, and such a burden half borne, by a true wife is a fact which no living man can realise better than I, with my experience of 45 years of what it means.[22]

In a separate letter to the Bishop of Winchester (Edward Talbot), Davidson judged MacDonald's new government to have 'a popular reception ... fifty times more favourable than any one we had dreamed of'. He added:

> Somehow or other there seems to be a general belief that they are going to do their jobs very well, and I find some people thinking that they may have a long spell of office. Some men of experience think just the opposite. I had a walk with [the Unionist politician] Hugh Cecil yesterday, and he said he expected them to be out by Easter.[23]

Visiting Number 10 for the first time under the 'new regime', Tom Jones, the Deputy Cabinet Secretary, was asked by the Prime Minister for his opinion of the political situation. He agreed with the Archbishop of Canterbury that Labour's position in the country 'was distinctly high'.[24]

The new government's first act was the *de jure* recognition of the Union of Soviet Socialist Republics,[25] the Labour manifesto having promised 'the resumption of free economic and diplomatic relations with Russia'. There was a rumour at the time that MacDonald, influenced by his officials, contemplated a U-turn, something which led the journalist J. L. Garvin to warn Jimmy Thomas that any delay would be 'morally disastrous ... dissensions on your own side, jeering on the other, a golden moment lost'.[26] That, however, was not the Palace's concern. Lord Stamfordham had written to Lord Haldane on 25 January to warn against the Soviet Union sending an ambassador, with whom the King would have to shake hands. In the event, Moscow sent a chargé d'affaires and the Monarch was spared any physical contact.[27] Arthur Ponsonby, MacDonald's under-secretary at the Foreign Office, found it almost 'incredible' to have assisted in the recognition of a country 'about which I have spoken and written so much'.[28]

That same day (1 February) the Prime Minister attended a Pilgrims' Dinner to welcome the new US Ambassador to the Court of St James's, Frank B. Kellogg. Randall Davidson wrote of the 'enthusiasm' which greeted MacDonald's first public speech from a largely Tory audience, observing that he did not think it

> wholly satisfactory that a man who is personally committed in the larger sense to a Socialist programme should be welcome in that kind of way by a great body of Anti-Socialists; for it seems to me to weaken the gravity of the great political, if not to some degree, even moral issues, which are at stake.[29]

'I went round and sat with [MacDonald] at night at 10 Downing Street and went through despatches,' recorded Arthur Ponsonby on 17 February. 'He is wonderfully quick and shrewd [but] a little inclined to observe unnecessary conventions and to be pulled towards the right.'[30] Others had been swift to comment on MacDonald's workload, or, rather, his long-standing propensity to work too much. Constitutionally incapable of delegation, his son Malcolm could remember him 'looking up a train in the railway timetable for one of his junior ministers',[31] while on several occasions, Sir Ronald Waterhouse, a private secretary inherited from Stanley Baldwin, found the Prime Minister still working at between two and four in the morning. Initially, MacDonald stipulated that all correspondence marked 'private' or 'personal' ought to reach him unopened but given that his postbag contained hundreds of letters a day (with many of them so marked), Waterhouse soon protested.[32] 'The silliest little letter had to be acknowledged,' remembered Ishbel. 'Many that could have been dealt with by secretaries received personally dictated replies, and old friends had their letters answered in Daddie's own hand.'[33] 'My working day stretches from 7 am to 1 am, with occasional extras,' wrote MacDonald on 10 April, 'but I enjoy it.'[34]

Despite allegations of aloofness, the new Prime Minister tried to be more open and accessible than his Unionist predecessors. A barrier erected across Downing Street on Bonar Law's instructions (to keep out the unemployed) was removed while MacDonald made a point of walking the short distance between Downing Street and the House of Commons. Ishbel could remember him bursting out of his study, his secretary trailing behind, answering questions as he put on his coat and then pacing 'down Downing Street with people running along with him trying to shake his hand and saying "Good old Ramsay!"' In Ishbel's account, her father disliked the 'commotion' but liked the exercise and ability to escape the feeling of 'superiority' conveyed by being driven such a short distance.[35] Others, not least party colleagues, had already begun to draw a different conclusion.

What most raised suspicions were MacDonald's relations with the King. Despite Christmas jitters, relations between George V and his new Prime Minister soon became those of 'unhesitating mutual confidence'. The Monarch, judged his official biographer Harold Nicolson, was attracted by MacDonald's 'quiet moderation, by his unfailing considerateness, by the deliberate blend in his manner and voice of silk and tweed, of cosmopolitan distinction and Scottish sense'.[36] Jane Ridley was blunter in judging that the King needed MacDonald in order to contain the 'deferential, respectable working class within a moderate Labour Party and split them off from the Bolsheviks and Red Clydesiders'.[37] This fitted in nicely with the Prime Minister's general political strategy, though at the same time he seemed to be genuinely impressed by the King's 'evident eagerness to do everything within his power to help the new Government'.[38] In the Sovereign, judged Sir Samuel

Hoare, MacDonald found an adviser 'ready to give him a definite and straightforward answer to the questions that were worrying his over-sensitive mind'.[39]

'I have,' the King wrote to his mother, Queen Alexandra, on 17 February, 'been making the acquaintance of all the Ministers in turn & I must say they all seem to be very intelligent & they take things very seriously. They have different ideas to ours as they are all socialists, but they ought to be given a chance & ought to be treated fairly.'[40] Lord Stamfordham, meanwhile, worried that figures like Beatrice Webb would look 'for relaxation in certain forms of Court etiquette, even to the extent of their curtsies',[41] while Lord Cromer, the newly permanent Lord Chamberlain, suggested that Bay Haldane and Margaret Bondfield (the only female minister) be consulted as to the 'individual wishes of the ladies of the Labour Government and the wives of Members of Parliament' when it came to sort of social occasions they would like to attend.[42] The King and Queen Mary eventually held an afternoon tea party at Buckingham Palace at which they 'took great pains to make things easy for everyone'. On 19 February Ishbel met the King and Queen for the first time, finding Mary 'very stiff & inanimate',[43] but the Prince of Wales friendlier when he came for lunch at Downing Street the same month. She speculated that the King 'hoped Daddie might help him to keep the headstrong Prince in order'.[44] Indeed, when the heir to the throne suffered a concussion while horse racing, the Prime Minister wrote him a rather obsequious letter begging that he 'refrain from taking chances that no doubt offer you an exhilarating temptation' but risked 'a serious mishap'.[45]

Chips Channon, meanwhile, found London 'restless', with lots of people gathered in front of Buckingham Palace, 'friendly, protecting crowds who vaguely thought the King in danger'.[46] Realizing that many of his subjects still regarded the new government with what Malcolm MacDonald called 'horrified prejudice', the King took the unprecedented step of holding a State banquet in honour of the Prime Minister and his 'ex-railwaymen, ex-coalminers, and ex-other manual workers Cabinet colleagues'.

Sitting to the Queen's right, MacDonald found himself distracted by a finely dressed man whose face looked familiar. When this figure later congratulated the Prime Minister on 'a grand day of peaceful revolution', he diplomatically asked when they had last met. Smiling, the man asked if MacDonald remembered

> a night about 30 years ago when three poverty-stricken young men who had come to London to seek their fortunes went together to hear a lecture by Lord Kelvin at the Royal Institution; and when the lecture was over, and they left the hall and put their hands in their pockets they found they hadn't enough money between them to pay their bus fares home! So they walked miles through the night back to their digs.

Finally recognizing himself as one of those poverty-stricken young men, MacDonald asked if the man was Dr Dawson. Not exactly, he replied, 'I'm Lord Dawson of Penn.' 'In the long years since the poverty-stricken youths had met,' recounted Malcolm MacDonald, 'one of them had become the King's Physician, and the other was now his Prime Minister.'[47] The King's banquet was also notable in that it served as an introduction between the Marchioness of Londonderry and MacDonald, who bonded over a mutual love of the Scottish Highlands. A few weeks earlier, Josiah Wedgwood had remarked to Hugh Dalton that the fact MacDonald had 'no woman' made his predilection for society hostesses 'all the more dangerous'.[48]

The King liked to see his ministers at levees and Court functions in the traditional uniform: gold-embroidered coat, cocked hat and sword, with trousers by day and knee breeches in the evening. Yet as at the Privy Council meeting on 23 January, this meant sartorial matters continued to dog the new Labour government, upsetting left-wingers and provoking accusations of snobbery on the part of MacDonald et al.[49] The Lord Chamberlain suggested ministers might wear the 'dignified and unobtrusive plain black coat and knee-breeches of a parliamentary official', although knee breeches were considered a step too far by some (Jimmy Thomas delighted the King with his quip that 'of course poor Sidney Webb can't put 'em on. His wife wears 'em'). On 6 February the Cabinet agreed that three ministers drawn from a 'pool' of those who either owned or were prepared to obtain the necessary dress would attend the King at Court. Those who did not want to wear the requisite dress were to be exempted.[50] 'I held a levee at St. James,' the King wrote with satisfaction in March. 'The Prime Minister, Mr. Henderson and Mr. Thomas came in uniform, thereafter Ministers came in evening dress with tights, it lasted 1 hr & 5 mins, 92 people passed.'[51] The Commons Speaker, John Whitley (the last Liberal to hold the post), followed the same compromise for his own levees, which led to the amusing spectacle of War Secretary Stephen Walsh (in full dress) using the coal lift at the Strand Palace Hotel in order to avoid the public gaze.[52]

This option, however, did not apply to members of the Royal Household, which included the three 'White Wands' (or Commons whips) still appointed by the Prime Minister. Chief Whip Ben Spoor told Lord Stamfordham that while they did not mind wearing full dress they were all 'poor men' and did 'not want to spend more than they could help out of their £700 a year salary'.[53] They (Tom Griffiths, John E. Davison and John Parkinson) had only accepted office thinking the salary was £900 a year, and after some negotiation the Household arranged for the trio's salary to be restored to that level. The King also made them a gift of their Court uniforms. Stamfordham was embarrassed by the press coverage, particularly a 'tiresome' headline in the *Daily Express*: 'King's Democratic Revolution: Evening Dress and Knee Breeches. Debutantes' Feathers to be Abolished?'[54]

Even the Prime Minister's doting daughter admitted that he 'fancied' himself in Court dress, largely because he looked, according to Chips Channon, 'very distinguished'. 'He has a fine profile, like a Roman coin,' wrote Channon after one State ball.[55] Socially, observed David Marquand, MacDonald was 'exotic, in the way that a Canadian or an American might be'.[56] Even Arthur Ponsonby conceded he had 'never seen equalled' the 'tact and dignity' of MacDonald's greeting of diplomats on the King's birthday.[57] Lucy Baldwin (Stanley's wife) privately criticized MacDonald for the number of parties he attended, but not only did he enjoy them, he regarded such functions as part of his role as Foreign Secretary. In an interview with the *New Leader*, he also turned the argument against his critics:

> I have known people who showed vanity by the clumsiness of their clothes. A tattered hat and a red tie, a tone of voice and religious repetition of Marxian phrases, may be as indicative of a man who has sold himself to appearances as the possession of a ceremonial dress to enable him to attend ceremonies which are historical parts of his duties.[58]

As Ethel Snowden (the Chancellor's wife) observed in an article for *The Spectator*, had ministers attended Court functions 'in hobnailed boots, with unwashed faces and collarless shirts' while treating the King with 'a hectoring authority', such conduct would 'quickly have covered them with deserved contempt and ignominy'.[59] For the Prime Minister, it was reciprocal. 'If royalty had given the Labour Government the cold shoulder,' he wrote in his diary, 'we should have returned the call. It has not.'[60] Lord Birkenhead later told the King that the premier and his colleagues had been 'greatly impressed with the very fair treatment accorded to them by H[is] M[ajesty] ... The P.M. had become absolutely convinced that a Constitutional Monarchy was the only thing for this country.' When Birkenhead asked if he liked MacDonald, the King replied that he 'did and found that the P.M. had always considered H.M.'s interests and even kept H.M. better informed than other P.M.'s'.[61]

Stories of the new Labour ministers, 'about ninety per cent of them – apocryphal', became the talk of polite society. Lord Haldane heard that Jimmy Thomas had introduced himself at the Colonial Office by saying he was there to make sure there was 'no mucking about with the British Empire'; Stephen Walsh, the War Secretary, had made an 'excellent impression' on his generals by announcing he stood for 'loyalty to the King'; while the Foreign

Office was delighted to have received the 'courteous' MacDonald in exchange for the 'autocratic' Lord Curzon. 'Altogether,' added Haldane, 'the departments have given the new Government a very friendly, even cordial reception.'[62]

Others remained unreconstructed. Lady Cunard asked Sir Ronald Waterhouse if the Prime Minister had 'any table manners', an exchange he re-enacted for the amusement of MacDonald,[63] while Lady Carson thought all 'those Labour fellows' on the front bench were 'an awful looking lot'.[64] Some spread malicious gossip. Manny Shinwell recalled an allegation that the Prime Minister had been seen entering 'a discreet little flat' in the Adelphi,[65] while the novelist and Unionist MP John Buchan told Leo Amery that MacDonald was an illegitimate son of Lord Dalhousie and thus a half-uncle by marriage of Princess Patricia of Connaught and a kinsman of the King.[66]

The Parliament opening by the King on 15 January, meanwhile, did not reconvene until 12 February. The Prime Minister was cheered as he passed through the gates of the Palace of Westminster, large crowds still keen to witness the novelty of a 'socialist' premier. The House of Commons and its galleries were packed, and one journalist watched as MacDonald took his place on the Treasury Bench where once he had also seen Gladstone, Balfour and Asquith, 'acutely conscious of the political transformation which had occurred so suddenly'.[67]

'No Prime Minister has ever met the House of Commons in circumstances similar to those in which I meet it,' MacDonald told MPs in an atmosphere described as 'electric'. As for the government's sustainability, he said divisions on 'matters non-essential, matters of mere opinion, matters that do not strike at the root of the proposals that we make' would not be regarded as a vote of no confidence. MacDonald's remarkable speech then covered treaties (which he proposed ought to be routinely ratified by Parliament), foreign affairs (he had recognized Russia as a 'preliminary' to a broader settlement) and the League of Nations (which he hoped would be used 'more and more' for the settlement of disputes). Coalitions, added the Prime Minister, were 'detestable ... dishonest'; it was 'far better' for the political life of the country that Labour should express its views as 'an independent party', bring those views before the Commons and ask it to take 'the responsibility of amending, accepting, or rejecting them'.[68] In the first of his daily reports to the King, MacDonald said he had 'endeavoured to give the House a broad and comprehensive survey' of how his government proposed to act domestically and internationally.[69]

Responding the next day, the Conservative leader Stanley Baldwin again promised fair play before quoting the Russian revolutionary Grigory Zinoviev (often spelled 'Zinovieff' during this period) – 'the most powerful personality in the Government of Russia to-day' – as saying that Russia would 'support Mr. MacDonald as the rope supports the hanged man'. As Gill Bennett has observed, at this point Zinoviev and his associates 'were not sure whether they wanted to bring the Labour government down, or make use of it'.[70] Asquith, meanwhile, caused a stir when he left his seat below the gangway to stand at the despatch box on the opposition front bench, joking that it allowed him to see both his opponents as well as his friends.[71]

In Arthur Henderson's continuing absence, Labour's whipping arrangements left a lot to be desired. Ben Spoor, the Chief Whip, suffered bouts of recurring malaria and alcoholism, meaning he was often absent, leaving the Parliamentary Labour Party uncoordinated. Unhelpfully, two of Spoor's deputies, Tom Griffiths and Tom Kennedy, also suffered from poor health, meaning they either failed to attend to necessary business or fumbled it badly. Vivian Phillipps, the Liberal Chief Whip, complained that Labour failed to consult him about suspensions of the eleven o'clock rule, which left the government needlessly vulnerable in the division lobbies.[72] However much 'fair play' opponents professed to give Labour, the fact remained that the government lacked the 'two most powerful weapons' normally at its disposal: control of the parliamentary timetable and an automatic majority for government business.[73]

By early March, the Prime Minister wondered if he could 'stand it', fearing that 'practically continuous' sessions of Parliament would 'break down the machine'.[74] MacDonald was also concerned at the failure of his backbenchers to respond adequately to the 'new conditions', some of the 'disappointed ones' having become 'as hostile as though they were not of us'.[75] Beatrice Webb placed the blame on the Prime Minister himself, writing on 15 March:

> The relations between the leading Ministers on the Treasury Bench either do not exist or are far from cordial. The P.M. is unapproachable by [Arthur] Henderson, who is responsible for the Labour Party organization in the country; and apparently by [J. R.] Clynes, the Leader of the House. 'No. 10 and No. 11 see no more of each other,' said Henderson to me, 'than if they slept and ate a hundred miles apart'.[76]

E. D. Morel was one of the 'disappointed ones' and complained to Lord Parmoor of having been 'wiped out and forgotten'. In desperation, Morel suggested he become an under-secretary for the League of Nations, but representations from Parmoor and Arthur Ponsonby had no effect. All Morel got was a nomination for the Nobel Peace Prize on account of his long campaign against Belgian atrocities in the Congo, but while this was supported by MacDonald and most of the PLP, it generated press ridicule on account of Morel's recent exclusion from the ministerial ranks.[77]

Relations between MacDonald and the Clydesiders, or the Independent Labour Party, were initially cordial. James Maxton dismissed persistent talk of a split as 'misguided', although he warned that if the government turned 'back' then he hoped 'the men from the Clyde would rise up and protest'.[78] Maxton soon became restless, and on the unlikeliest of pretexts. By early February, the government still lacked a Lord Advocate, the Scottish law officer equivalent of the Attorney General for England and Wales.[79] The previous month MacDonald had offered this position to Rosslyn Mitchell, a solicitor who had narrowly failed to capture Glasgow

Central at the recent election, but on 25 January he had written to say he was 'no longer available' as he was unprepared 'to assume even the semblance of an office-seeker'.[80] On 30 January the Prime Minister headed north to Edinburgh, where he consulted with Lord Clyde, the Lord President of the Court of Session, and Condie Sandeman, Dean of the Faculty of Advocates.[81] Clyde gave MacDonald a memorandum which asserted that by 'long custom' both the Lord Advocate and the Solicitor General for Scotland were 'appointed from among the members of the Scottish Bar'.[82] This memo was published in *The Times* on 7 February, perhaps by way of explanation for what was to follow. On 11 February, the Prime Minister finally replied to Mitchell, saying he had been 'most disappointed' to discover that legislation would be necessary to qualify him for the appointment. 'In view of the present situation in Parliament,' he added, 'I had to abandon all thought of that.'[83]

Here MacDonald's judgement failed him. That Rosslyn Mitchell was not a King's Counsel, the basis of a 'technical' objection pushed by Lord Haldane and others, rested upon long-standing convention rather than statute (although a non-KC would also have no right of audience before the Scottish courts). The Scottish Council of the ILP had pointed this out to the Prime Minister, but when it also warned of 'grave dissension' should MacDonald leave 'the legal machinery in Scotland in control of our political opponents', the Prime Minister lost his cool, asking if their idea of a Labour premier was someone who thought themselves 'above all law and precedent'. After being bombarded with undignified begging letters from expatriate lawyers – including the Imperial constitutional expert Arthur Berriedale Keith ('My political views,' he pleaded, 'are in sympathy with Labour policy') – the Prime Minister admitted defeat and, with Cabinet approval, asked Hugh Macmillan, a leading member of the Scottish Bar and a Unionist candidate, to serve as his adviser on Scots law.[84]

After consulting Stanley Baldwin, Macmillan replied on 7 February saying he would accept 'on a basis entirely non-political'.[85] Haldane, naturally, wrote to congratulate him, while the press also hailed the Prime Minister for 'defying the intimidatory threats of the Clydeside brigade and appointing one of the best men available irrespective of political considerations',[86] which of course made matters worse. Maxton (for whom Rosslyn Mitchell had acted when he was prosecuted for sedition in 1916) was heard to swear that if he possessed the 'health and strength he would smash the Scottish Faculty'.[87] When the ILP assured MacDonald its criticism was not directed against him but the 'dictatorial' Faculty of Advocates for 'forcing Tory Lawyers into a Labour Government', MacDonald replied in a friendlier tone, saying that to 'apply the American doctrine of spoils is not only wrong, but would soon land us in trouble'.[88]

This incident clearly troubled MacDonald, for within a week he was urging Hugh Macmillan to find a Scots lawyer MP he could nominate as Solicitor General for Scotland:

I cannot conceal from you the fact that I am having terrible difficulties inside my Party in connection with these appointments ... If there were a Labour supporter with any decent qualifications for the post, it would smooth my difficulties very considerably. I shall not, however, sacrifice efficiency for that.

The Prime Minister opted for efficiency and agreed to the appointment of John Fenton, a forty-three-year-old recent KC and another Unionist.

The position of the Independent Labour Party (with which the Clydesiders were aligned) within the Labour movement undoubtedly deteriorated as a consequence of this and other perceived weaknesses. Although the ILP chairman Clifford Allen dined with the Prime Minister at Downing Street once a week, 'excitedly hopeful of influencing the Premier', as far as Fenner Brockway could make out it was Allen who ended up being influenced by MacDonald.[89] But as Richard Lyman has observed, not 'all Clydesiders were irresponsible, and not all in the Parliamentary Party were Clydesiders'.[90] George Lansbury's critique, like that of

E. D. Morel, was primarily motivated by bitterness at not being a member of the Cabinet. 'I am thoroughly distressed about the Party,' he wrote to Beatrice Webb on 14 March:

> Everybody seems so thoroughly cheerful, and thoroughly content with what we are doing, and yet we are doing nothing that is of any real worth. I certainly think the fact that we are so very satisfactory to our opponents ... and so very unsatisfactory to the poor devils on whose votes people like me got into Parliament, is a tragedy of the first water.[91]

Although Webb did not accuse MacDonald of treachery, 'for he was never a socialist', she saw him as 'a believer in individualist political democracy tempered in its expression by utopian socialism'. Where he had 'lacked integrity', she added, was

> in posing as a socialist, and occasionally using revolutionary jargon. If he succeeds in getting a majority of the electors into this revised version of reformist conservatism embodied in the Labour Party machine, things will move forward; the underlying assumptions will be changed by the rank-and-file workers, and the structure will necessarily adapt itself to the new outlook.

It seemed doubtful that the Prime Minister would have regarded this as a criticism, and within a few weeks Webb's opinion had hardened: 'There would be only one advantage in Labour remaining in,' she wrote on 14 April, 'and that would be the more complete disillusionment of the left wing about the sincerity of J.R.M.'s socialism and proletarian sympathies.'[92] Even those such as Arthur Ponsonby who sympathized with the likes of Morel found such criticism 'exceedingly trying'. 'I am here [the Foreign Office] from 10 am till 11 pm generally later every day & yet JRM & I are "betraying the cause",' he had written to Morel on 31 January. 'If that now – goodness me what shall we get later!'[93] The answer was much the same, and in March Ponsonby bemoaned 'the loquacity of our own members, many of whom think it much more important that they should deliver speeches than that the Government should get on with the business'.[94]

When the government pointed out that Liberal support was a necessary evil and not everything could be done in the first session, critics insisted 'that it would be better to go down with colours flying than to lower the flag in the hope of keeping the ship afloat'. The Labour MP Frederick Pethick-Lawrence occupied a 'middle position', sharing disappointment 'at the apparent inaction' but also believing 'the country would have been annoyed if the Prime Minister, having taken office, had almost immediately courted defeat'.[95] Addressing the ILP conference in York, MacDonald irritated some by rejecting the dictum that 'they were in office but that they had no power'. 'We are in office,' he declared. 'With power.'[96]

A reformulated PLP Executive and its chair Robert Smillie, a MacDonald loyalist, did its best to 'dissolve conflicts through benedictions of socialist rhetoric'. Broadly representative of backbench opinion, Lansbury served as vice-chairman of a group which included five members identified with the ILP, a few trade unionists, both female backbenchers and the simmering E. D. Morel. For the duration of the Labour administration, this acted as a liaison body between the government and the party, watching the progress of business in the House, advising MPs and nominating representatives for the various select committees.[97] Its ministerial members were J. R. Clynes, Ben Spoor and Arthur Henderson.

Taking Henderson's place as Acting Secretary of the Labour Party was the efficient and mild-mannered J. S. Middleton. During 1924 party literature acquired a new logo – a torch, shovel and quill symbol incorporating the word 'Liberty' – while officials fretted about what would later be called 'entryism'. Labour policy was that 'individual' members of the Communist Party of Great Britain (CPGB) could join if they accepted 'the Constitution and principles of the Party'.[98] During April, MacDonald inserted a small newspaper cutting into his pocket diary which alluded to communists being 'anxious to get inside the Labour Party in order to remove the Fabian element and establish a party on a definite class basis'.[99] This the Prime Minister was determined to avoid.

MacDonald's handling of his senior ministers was rather more successful. 'The Prime Minister's behaviour in Cabinet was perfect,' judged Sidney Webb. 'He was never discourteous, never overbearing, never unduly dogmatic, patient to everyone, watchful to give everyone a chance to speak; and ... quick to close the debate as soon as it was proper to do so.'[100] An alternative perspective was that of Josiah Wedgwood, still unhappy at his 'useless' appointment as Chancellor of the Duchy of Lancaster. He thought Cabinet from the inside 'not awe-inspiring':

> The three men of outstanding ability were Lord Haldane, Philip Snowden, and Charles Trevelyan whose post was almost as humble as my own. MacDonald made up his mind on nothing; Snowden on everything. Our constant preoccupation was how to keep the Party quiet and the permanent officials satisfied ... 'We must not annoy the Civil Service' was the slogan of the first Labour Government.[101]

This was churlish. Sir Maurice Hankey, the Cabinet Secretary, attended Cabinet meetings, and while Sidney Webb considered him prone to making 'extraordinarily inept' suggestions on policy, almost everybody else, the Prime Minister included, held him in high regard. This was reciprocated, for Hankey considered it a 'more business-like Cabinet' than any he had worked with:

> They read their papers and get up their subject, and, on the rare occasions where they do not complete their agenda, meet either the same afternoon or next day to finish up. There is never any accumulation of Cabinet business, and it is the first time I have ever known such a state of affairs in the seven years I have been at this work.

Hankey assigned the greatest credit to MacDonald, 'an admirable head of the Cabinet'.[102] Lord Haldane – who knew Hankey the best – agreed that MacDonald was 'a better chairman than Asquith ... He keeps us to the point and gets his decisions'.[103]

There were modest innovations. Instead of providing only a list of ministers present, a regular press communique was broadened to include a summary of Cabinet business.[104] This was intended to mitigate against inaccurate newspaper accounts of discussions, although MacDonald still grew concerned about 'speeches, interviews, and other communications to the public ... made by men in responsible positions dealing with Government policy'.[105] Another change concerned smoking. The old Cabinet convention had been no smoking before lunch, but when Jimmy Thomas arrived late to the new Cabinet's first meeting and, knowing nothing of the rule, continued to smoke, others lit their pipes and the convention went up in smoke. 'Only three of us don't smoke at all,' Charles Trevelyan told his father, a veteran of Liberal Cabinets. 'The only objection to it is that J. H. Thomas ... keeps his pipe always in the corner of his mouth while he talks.'[106] The puritanical Philip Snowden considered it 'an outrage', although even he conceded that it 'tended to the harmony of the proceedings'.[107]

At their first meeting on 23 January, Lord Haldane told his colleagues it was the practice to refer to each minister (other than the Prime Minister) not by his title but his surname, although this was not strictly followed. Still thrilled to be back in government, the Lord Chancellor acted as 'a sort of father to our whole team – the one man who knows the customs and etiquette of old Cabinets'. Indeed, the experience had given him a new lease of life, 'as if he were a boy of 25'. Haldane and his sister Bay talked of his return to office as 'the great Adventure'.[108]

One of the first decisions taken by the Cabinet was not to permit an official photograph. One newspaper had run a respectable artist's impression of ministers sitting around the Cabinet table,[109] while the *Daily Graphic* poked fun with a cartoon depicting the diminutive Stephen Walsh being ushered into the Cabinet room by a gigantic footman.[110] Writing to the Prime Minister on 6 February, J. S. Middleton, Acting Secretary of the Labour Party, urged a formal photograph in the Rose Garden 'simply as a historical record', although Rose Rosenberg cautioned that 'so long as we run the risk of this vulgar publication' MacDonald was 'not in favour'.[111] Finally, on 21 February the Cabinet agreed that an arrangement should be made with a 'first-class photographer' for a private photograph to be taken of the members of the Cabinet, whose copyright it would remain.[112] The photograph was not actually taken until 2 July. Once the head of Stephen Walsh had been crudely inserted, it was released to a hungry media.[113]

MacDonald's relations with the Fourth Estate ought to have been better than any of his predecessors given his own journalistic background, but he still resented the jingoistic *John Bull* having revealed his illegitimacy nearly a decade earlier.[114] In an attempt to repair relations, the journalist H. R. Stockman, who had long ago fallen out with his 'hero' Ramsay MacDonald, 'induced' the Press Club to give the Prime Minister a dinner on 15 March, the first time it had entertained such a distinguished guest.[115] Wisely, the Prime Minister charmed his 'fellow journalists' by dubbing them the 'makers and the unmakers of Governments'. Also present was Stephen Walsh, the Secretary of State for War, who said no press on earth wielded such power 'with the same sense of responsibility as did the British Press'.[116]

But as the Canadian press magnate Lord Beaverbrook observed, one novel feature of the first Labour government was that it lacked 'considerable newspaper backing'. Only the small-circulation *Daily Herald* supported the government, although as Beaverbrook noted it only really represented the 'extreme Left' of MacDonald's supporters.[117] Indeed, Sidney Webb believed the *Daily Herald* (which was edited by a left-wing Scot called Henry Hamilton Fyfe) did the party 'more harm than good', while the government also had to contend with the constant insinuation from the Unionist press that it was acting under pressure from its left wing, or indeed the 'terrifying bogey' of the Bolshevists.[118] Relations were especially bad with the *New Leader*, an ILP journal edited by Henry Brailsford and boycotted by MacDonald on account of what he saw as an attempt to dictate government policy.[119]

MacDonald, however, seemed on reasonably good terms with the Anglo-Scottish Mary Agnes Hamilton, an unsuccessful Labour candidate and *New Leader* reporter who usually wrote under the pseudonym 'Iconoclast'. The only journalist invited to Chequers during 1924, even she wrote of having met the Labour leader's

> unseeing eye; experienced the chill of going into his room ... and being looked at, if looked at at all, as though not there. Sitting at his desk he goes on writing or reading. When at last he lifts his eyes, they perhaps see but as often as not do not focus you. You feel like a blurred outline on a dissolving negative.[120]

Hamilton's initially anonymous biography of MacDonald (published as *The Man of To-morrow* in 1923 and revised in 1925 and 1929) became more critical with time, while David Marquand has speculated that Hamilton (a divorcee) hankered after a personal as well as professional relationship with the widowed Prime Minister.[121]

Another piece of prime ministerial patronage provided even the most critical newspapers with weeks of colourful copy. Having learned from his mistake over the Scottish law officers, MacDonald decided to throw caution to the Highland wind and break a long-standing precedent when it came to the Lord High Commissioner to the General Assembly of the Church of Scotland, the King's personal representative at the annual gathering of Scotland's 'national' church or 'Kirk'.

As with the Lord Advocate, this was subject to long-standing custom rather than hard law, the usual nominee being drawn from the peerage. On 13 March, however, *The Times* reported that the Labour government was clear there was 'no legal, constitutional, or statutory objection to the appointment of a commoner, and the choice has accordingly fallen upon Mr. James Brown'.[122] It was an inspired move, the inspiration for which came from the Scottish Secretary, William Adamson, who argued that after 300 years 'the appointment had to be looked at from a new angle'.[123]

Jimmy Brown was a miner MP in South Ayrshire, a Sunday School teacher and a Kirk elder. He and his wife Katie, who still occupied a miner's cottage in Annbank, awoke to find themselves famous, particularly in the United States. Even newspapers in England and Wales, usually unconcerned with Scottish ecclesiastical matters, treated it as a major news story. MacDonald was relieved that his 'somewhat risky decision' had come off,[124] although one member of the Court regarded the appointment as positively 'Gilbertian'. 'I suppose we have to face such things,' he added, 'and probably many others!'[125]

During the General Assembly in May, Brown was referred to as 'Your Grace' and accorded all the privileges usually granted to royalty, while his only innovation was the absence of alcoholic drinks at the usual functions. On entering the floor of the General Assembly, Brown was loudly cheered, and the *Scotsman* lavished praise on Mr and Mrs Brown for 'most worthily' carrying out their duties, fully justifying 'a choice that has proved as happy as it was bold and novel'.[126] Only the Stirling MP Tom Johnston dissented from this orgy of approval, lamenting that Brown had not used his appointment to do away with his 'knee breeches and silk stockings'. Brown's response, according to the journalist and future Labour MP Emrys Hughes, was to call Johnston 'a dirty beggar'.[127]

On 6 March the Prime Minister delivered an address to the Free Church in Brighton on the relationship between Christianity and socialism in which he refused to see any conflict between the two. 'The only security we can have is the security of cherishing the moral categories,' he preached, 'justice, fair play, honesty, and uprightness.' MacDonald's address made a favourable impression in religious circles, particularly his defence of what he called a 'Scotch Sunday' as affording much-needed space for earnest and detached thought.[128]

Of the Prime Minister's responsibility for English ecclesiastical appointments, MacDonald was less enamoured. Shortly after becoming premier, Lord Parmoor had arranged a dinner introduction between Randall Davidson, the Edinburgh-born Presbyterian who had become the Anglican Archbishop of

Canterbury, and MacDonald, who had been raised in the Free Church of Scotland. Usefully, the pair hit it off, avoiding politics but discussing forthcoming appointments – MacDonald had recently nominated George Bell as Dean of Canterbury – after which Davidson and his wife Edith drove the premier and his daughters back to Downing Street. They remained in close contact, particularly when the Prime Minister was required to fill an episcopal vacancy in Birmingham later that year, one candidate for which was F. L. Donaldson, who had played an active part in Labour politics. Here, too, MacDonald irritated some of his colleagues by passing over what seemed an obvious choice and instead opting for Ernest William Barnes, a distinguished mathematician and scientist who had also been prominent in the Union of Democratic Control.

Davidson had misgivings on account of Barnes' theological liberalism, while the *Church Times* attacked the Prime Minister for not being an Anglican and thus possessing only 'second-hand knowledge of the needs of the Church and of the wishes of priests and laity'.[129] When its editor, a left-winger called Sidney Dark, also protested by letter, MacDonald vigorously defended himself, warning that if there were objections to his appointments,

> the only way out of the difficulty is for the Church to cut itself off from the patronage of the State. It is really impossible for me to enter into matters for which I have no genius. I am a good Presbyterian and if any of my ancestors knew that I had fallen so far from grace as to take any part in the appointment of Bishops they would turn in their graves![130]

Whatever the controversies, Randall Davidson was 'immensely impressed' by the Prime Minister's 'thoughtfulness & care' when it came to such appointments.[131] Privately, however, MacDonald complained of letters arriving 'like snowdrifts'.[132]

By February 1924, meanwhile, threats to Stanley Baldwin's leadership had dissipated and he had resolved to use a (he hoped short) period in opposition to reunify and rejuvenate the Unionist

Party. He dropped his policy of Protection just as swiftly as Labour had the Capital Levy, encouraged the backbench 1922 Committee to expand and created a 'Consultative Committee', which later became known as the Shadow Cabinet. The party's name was also changed to 'Conservative and Unionist' in England and Wales, although north of the border it remained the 'Scottish Unionist Party'. The emphasis on 'Conservative' was supposed to foreground the party's message of 'safety first', particularly in the context of a Labour government.

In a significant speech, Baldwin said Labour's 'great source of strength' was that they had in their ranks 'a large number of men who believe in their policy'. He added that it was 'that feeling which sends so many of the workers of the party to canvass, to do propaganda, and to conduct the business of elections without payment or reward. It is a spirit which can only be beaten by a similar spirit in our Party.' Until Conservatives could emulate that spirit, added Baldwin, the party would be 'fighting with one hand tied behind our backs'.[133]

This led in June to the launch of *Looking Ahead: Unionist Principles and Aims*, which articulated the 'New Conservatism', an early example of the titular prefix later adopted by the Labour Party in the 1990s.[134] These New Conservatives, however, managed to have it both ways, arguing that Labour deserved a chance to govern while also denouncing its ministers as dangerous and irresponsible. Nevertheless, by Easter there was criticism that the 'wild men' were being given too easy a ride in the House of Commons, a charge taken sufficiently seriously for the Tory Chief Whip to issue a denial.[135]

The Liberals, meanwhile, were not making as much of their time in opposition as they might have hoped. Maurice Cowling had little doubt Asquith had allowed Ramsay MacDonald to form a government not just to make clear his party was not one of 'bourgeois reaction', but because he expected 'first to hold the balance in the House of Commons and then to turn out MacDonald and come into office himself whenever Labour incompetence made MacDonald's overthrow convenient'.[136]

But when Parliament rose for its Easter recess on 16 April, the Labour government remained, as far as anyone could judge, relatively popular. Sales of the *Daily Herald* had increased, as had those for weekly Hansard reports, while the House of Commons had become 'the most popular show in London'.[137] And if by-elections were any indication, then a Labour gain in West Toxteth and the Liberal collapse in Kelvingrove were straws in the electoral wind. David Lloyd George had been conscious from the start that if Labour succeeded in office, it would get all the credit, and if it failed the Liberals would get the blame for putting them in power in the first place.

By March, the man they called the 'Welsh Wizard' appeared to realize he had cast the wrong spell in having eased Labour's path to office 'without any understanding or conditions'.[138] He began to attack the government with renewed vehemence, accusing it of being unpatriotic, while twice during March and April the Liberals refused to support the government, first on the naval estimates and second on a clause in the Rent Restrictions Bill. Proportional Representation (PR) for elections to the House of Commons might have brought the two parties closer together, but although the Cabinet recommended support for the second reading of Liberal MP Athelstan Rendall's Bill following a request from Asquith, a 'stormy' meeting of the Parliamentary Labour Party – which resented what it perceived as a Liberal 'ultimatum' – instead backed a free vote, essentially killing it off. Believing its 'stock' to have risen, reported *The Times*, the PLP had 'no intention that anybody else shall steal their thunder'.[139]

Matters had already come to a head at a Liberal Party meeting held shortly before the recess, at which several MPs expressed resentment at the hostility shown towards them by Labour. During a public meeting at Llanfairfechan on 22 April, Lloyd George characterized this as 'a revolt against humiliating conditions' under which Liberals were expected to sustain a government which 'seemed to regard it as an offence which ought to be kicked out of the way'. Liberals, he added, were to be 'the oxen to drag the Labour wain over the rough roads of Parliament for two to three years, goaded along, and at the end of the journey, when there is no further use for them, they are to be slaughtered.'[140]

For his part, MacDonald had long despised Lloyd George, a feeling plain from his daily parliamentary reports to the King and in a letter to Baldwin which said Lloyd George's photograph at Chequers put 'the Devil into me and makes me feel anything but proud of my job'.[141] According to the Liberal journalist Harold Spender, the Prime Minister told him Lloyd George's 'only aim' was to 'destroy' him,[142] while MacDonald toyed with making a speech about how much honours had been 'degraded' by 'that cheap-jack'.[143] During a rant to C. P. Scott, the Prime Minister 'reverted again and again to this dislike and distrust of the Liberals. He could get on with the Tories. They differed at times openly then forgot all about it and shook hands. They were gentlemen, but the Liberals were cads.' In his final letter of the session to the King, MacDonald critiqued both his own side (the 'majority of the Ministers had had no experience in the art of government') but especially the Liberals, who 'would appear to be finding their position to be one of growing difficulty and embarrassment'.[144]

What of MacDonald's own standing? After four gruelling months he was undoubtedly worn out. Even in early February the Archbishop of Canterbury and Asquith had noticed that the Prime Minister was suffering from neuritis;[145] in March he was plagued by headaches and the after-effects of influenza, while by May Dolly Ponsonby thought he looked 'extraordinarily aged – his face grey & ravaged'.[146] Austen Chamberlain felt MacDonald's party was also exhausted, although he conceded that this was 'probably more felt in the House than in the country, where, I suspect that they have already gained many & are still gaining more Liberal votes'.[147] Sir Maurice Hankey agreed, telling Lord Smuts that Labour had 'so far received a great deal of good will from the British people' who, in Arthur Henderson's words, had shown a 'sporting feeling' that they 'should be given a chance'.[148]

While MacDonald remained 'an outstanding figure', there was no doubt in Arthur Ponsonby's mind that the Prime Minister felt 'safer and stronger in leaning to the right than the left and is almost impatient when reminded of his own and the party's past protestations'.[149] In the view of Beatrice Webb, MacDonald had enjoyed 'good luck, up to now; and persistent good luck usually means a strain of unusual talent, if not genius', although she remained uncertain as to whether he was 'a genius, a mere spinner of words, or a sufficiently able man to make a good job of the country's business'.[150]

There seems little doubt that MacDonald could be needlessly rude and aloof. Even his daughter Ishbel found it strange that he never

> realised how far a little word of encouragement would go with those around him. I don't suppose he needed encouragement. He could always see his goal & keep his eyes on it without looking to one side or the other. But I think it was his reserve which prevented him from giving words of encouragement, his fear of sounding gushing.[151]

In MacDonald's frequent absences, J. R. Clynes, the Deputy Leader of the House, became what he called the chief 'Aunt Sally' of the government.[152] It must have registered, meanwhile, that the Prime Minister appeared on better terms with non-Labour colleagues. Archbishop Davidson found him 'increasingly confidential' (though with 'a temper which might bias him at times'),[153] while the Conservative Lord Advocate Hugh Macmillan 'always found him most accessible', and indeed MacDonald reciprocated by speaking of the 'confidence' he had in Macmillan's judgement, both legal and political.[154] Lauchlan MacNeill Weir, the Prime Minister's Parliamentary Private Secretary, later put this down to snobbery, observing that while Henderson and Clynes were 'proud of their association with the working class, MacDonald was rather ashamed of it'.[155] It was doubtless true he possessed what Maurice Cowling called 'a Victorian pride in achievement and an obvious enjoyment of respectability and power achieved after years of struggle',[156] but even the impeccably well-connected

Lord Haldane thought the Prime Minister 'too fond of great dinner parties'.[157] MacDonald certainly derived enjoyment from such gatherings, particularly when 'ladies were surprised to find that the man they considered an ogre was a cultured man of charm'.[158]

As if to confirm such suspicions, he and Ishbel spent the end of April at Windsor. 'The King has been most friendly & appreciative,' MacDonald told his friend Alexander Grant. 'He tells me he reads my dispatches with the utmost approval.'[159] The Prime Minister had recently put Grant's name forward for a baronetcy in recognition of his 'public services'. Thanking MacDonald on 18 April, Grant said he hoped to be 'worthy' and would 'not be disappointed if you are unable to carry this through'.[160]

In timing which would later prove significant, MacDonald replied (from Windsor) regarding a 'difficulty' which troubled him 'just a little':

> If when I die it is announced that I leave behind me over £40,000, it will be a great shock to many of my folks in the country, but perhaps we can meet that differently later on when we have more time to put [our] private affairs in order. So long as I am in my present job all my private concerns have to go to the wall. If they had to be looked after they would come to wreck. Things are hard & but for the supporting good will of my friends I could not go on.[161]

The McVitie's shares and Daimler were clearly weighing on MacDonald's mind, not least their undisclosed nature. On 3 June, Grant's baronetcy appeared in the *London Gazette* as part of the King's birthday honours list. 'The Baronetage was a matter of raising revenue at its institution,' Lord Parmoor had written to Lord Southborough the previous month, 'and there has been no great improvement.'[162]

For Ishbel MacDonald, meanwhile, the 1924 London season was 'outstandingly busy'. There had been state visits from the

Queen of Romania and the King of Italy, and she was also to be presented at Court, something suggested by Mrs J. R. Clynes in a letter to the *Daily Herald*. At first, she protested ('to me it was the height of snobbery'), but when it was explained she could not attend banquets and other state functions as 'mistress of No. 10', there was a change of heart.[163] On 20 May, therefore, Miss Ishbel MacDonald was presented to the King and Queen by Lady Chelmsford.[164]

This, together with the government's continuing popularity, served as a rejoinder to Winston Churchill's claim three years earlier that Labour was 'not fit to govern'. 'He has been proved as wrong in prophecy as he has constantly been in policy,' judged the ILP MP Fenner Brockway: 'The question now is not whether Labour is fit to govern, but whether the older parties have ever been fit to govern. In two months the Labour Government has achieved for social betterment and peace more than any other Government has achieved in as many years.'[165]

4

Arthur Henderson: 'Uncle Arthur'

While the Home Secretary's nickname 'Uncle Arthur' appeared to suggest, as the political theorist Leonard Woolf observed, 'a rather stuffy, slow-going and slow-thinking professional politician', in reality Arthur Henderson was a figure of some political stature.[1] Many viewed him as a left-wing version of Stanley Baldwin: a decent, solid and respectable face of the Labour Party who, in spite of his thoroughly Celtic provenance, appeared to epitomize moderate Englishness.

If this sounded like a winning formula, it had not proved enough for Henderson to retain his Newcastle East constituency at the 1923 general election, the combined weight of Unionists and Liberals having 'proved too strong'.[2] But despite the loss of his seat and possible exclusion from the first Labour government, Beatrice Webb found him 'amazingly cheerful, good-tempered, and determined to do his level best in organizing for the next general election'.[3] On the contrary, MacDonald found Henderson 'evidently very sore at being out', adding in his diary that he spoke 'of what he wd sacrifice if he attended to the [party in the] country & was not in [the Commons], & asked for a safe seat'.[4]

Having rejected MacDonald's idea of him becoming Deputy Speaker and a subsequent offer of the War Office, Henderson held out for the Home Office and eventually the Labour leader agreed. On 23 January 1924, therefore, Henderson accepted his seals of office as Secretary of State for the Home Department, but while he was already a Privy Counsellor on account of his membership of Asquith's wartime coalition, he was still not a member of either House of Parliament. Then, two days later, Dan Hodges, the Labour MP for Burnley, died unexpectedly. Henderson had a route back to the green benches.

When the Liberals decided not to field a candidate, Henderson was left in a straight fight with H. E. J. Camps, a Unionist, who gratuitously linked the Home Secretary with the 'Red Peril' and what he called the 'Socialist Arbeiter Internationale'. The by-election campaign, however, proved uneventful until a week before polling, when Henderson made a speech saying that as 'regards both the territorial and economic aspects of the Treaty of Versailles, revision, in my opinion, is not only essential, but is very much overdue'.[5]

Although this pledge had formed part of Labour's manifesto, on Monday 25 February Ronald McNeill, the Ulster-born Unionist MP for Canterbury, asked in a Private Notice Question whether Henderson's statement represented government policy. The Prime Minister initially dodged this, saying he had only seen newspaper reports, but on being pressed insisted there had been no change. This was embarrassing for MacDonald, as he was compelled to choose between rebuking his Home Secretary or scuppering the prospect of an agreement with the French, and it probably did little to improve his perception of Henderson's judgement. The incident also revealed a deeper tension, between the Home Secretary's view that decisions of the Labour Party conference were binding and the Prime Minister's that they were little more than 'soundings of party sentiment' that could be ignored.[6]

On the eve of the by-election, McNeill revived his attack with a full debate in the House of Commons. He made a long and laborious speech to which the Prime Minister responded by sarcastically reminding McNeill that he, as a previous under-secretary for foreign affairs, had gone 'to his own constituency and, whilst his Government was quarrelling with France over its Ruhr policy, made a public speech hoping that France was going to be successful'. If McNeill intended to 'throw thorns' in the Prime Minister's path, he added, then he should prefer that 'the person chosen to do it should have a clean record himself'.[7]

On Thursday 28 February, Henderson won Burnley with 24,571 votes to Camps' 17,534, a majority of 7,037 on a 5.4 per cent swing to Labour.

There was great excitement in the Commons when news of the result came through, not least because many Unionists had expected Henderson to be defeated. At the beginning of the following week, Uncle Arthur was escorted to take the Parliamentary Oath by his two sons, Will, the MP for Enfield, and Arthur Jnr, the MP for Cardiff South, 'a novel spectacle', as the Prime Minister told the King, 'for which there can be few if any precedents'.[8] Watched from the Ladies' Gallery by his wife and daughter, the Home Secretary was 'a picture of parental radiance' as he 'calmly took the oath and subsided on the Treasury Bench as soon as he had shaken hands with the Speaker'.[9]

Like Ramsay MacDonald, Arthur Henderson was born illegitimately in Scotland, although in industrial Glasgow rather than rural Morayshire. His mother Agnes was a domestic servant, who in around 1872 moved with her sons to Newcastle upon Tyne, where she later married a policeman named Robert Heath. This made Henderson a Geordie by upbringing if not birth, and his Methodist faith forged what was known as a 'Lib–Lab' politician, admiring of Gladstone and a moderate member of the Iron Founders' Union.

In 1895 Henderson became agent to Sir Joseph Pease, the Liberal MP for Barnard Castle, who he succeeded in Parliament (on behalf of the Labour Representation Committee) when Pease died in June 1903. He served as chairman of the Labour Party between 1908 and 1910 and later encouraged Ramsay MacDonald to take on the same role. Thereafter the two men essentially built the party which took office in early 1924 – Henderson helped draft its constitution – although there was a parting of ways during the Great War. MacDonald opposed it while Henderson resumed the party leadership and accepted office as President of the Board of Education. He resigned in 1917 and, like MacDonald, lost his seat at the 1918 election. Thereafter they were reconciled, but never completely.[10]

Most of Henderson's biographers have agreed that he was not a good fit at the Home Office. His strengths, judged Mary Agnes Hamilton, lay in his 'bold grasp and tenacious drive in the application of large ideas', whereas being Home Secretary, which largely comprised myriad often difficult – not to forget politically unpopular – administrative responsibilities, provided limited scope for his considerable talents.[11] The department of the mid-1920s had seven divisions: Aliens Control, Children and Probation, Crime, Factories and Shops, the Channel Islands, Northern Ireland and Police. Henderson was therefore responsible for 'the King's peace' as maintained by the criminal justice system (in England and Wales), although in practice most Home Secretaries ranged much more widely. Through Henderson also flowed the prerogative of mercy. When the Joint Committee of Industrial Women's Organizations pressed for the abolition of capital punishment, he replied that he would be 'glad to be relieved of the responsibility', but added that abolition would require legislation, and on that front the government did not have the luxury of choice.[12]

David Howell also detected 'affinity' between Henderson's 'bureaucratic style and the conservatism of his senior officials'.[13] Sir John Anderson, a Scottish civil servant who would two decades later become Home Secretary himself, was efficient but conservative. Indeed, the first few months of Henderson's tenure were dominated by strike action, which reinforced 'his tendencies towards moderation and caution' and did not, as a consequence, enhance his reputation within the Labour movement.[14]

At the government's very first Cabinet meeting Henderson updated colleagues on the impact of an unofficial railway strike which affected food and fuel supplies. He and Jimmy Thomas, who had until recently been general secretary of the National Union of Railwaymen (NUR), had attempted to settle the strike before it began. Some in the NUR suspected Thomas wanted to lance a troublesome industrial boil in advance of receiving his seals of office, while MacDonald warned the NUR that a 'really serious strike' would be a 'very nasty blow to us and is to increase our worries so much as to spoil our prospects'.[15] In any event, this strike was over by the end of January, when the Trades Union Congress brokered a compromise agreement involving gradual changes to mileage payments.

On the very day the railway workers went back to work, however, dockers approved a national strike when their demand for a two-shilling-a-day wage increase was rejected by employers. The King feared this would be 'disastrous for the country'.[16] Inclined to agree, Henderson and his Cabinet colleagues dusted off the Baldwin government's contingency planning. This provided for two sets of institutions and procedures, one for normal times and another for emergencies. The former was a standing committee meeting periodically at the Home Office to co-ordinate government schemes; the latter comprising four specialized subcommittees co-ordinated by the Chief Civil Commissioner. Both systems were under the general supervision of the Cabinet-level Supply and Transport Organization (STO).

On 12 February, the Cabinet had resolved to establish an emergency committee to look at the STO plans chaired by Henderson and comprising Jimmy Thomas (on account of his experience with the railways), Stephen Walsh (the War Secretary) and Lord Chelmsford (First Lord of the Admiralty). Sir John Anderson was also present at the committee's first meeting the same day, at which he took the opportunity to recommend that the STO be reactivated. The Cabinet agreed and Josiah Wedgwood, eager to escape Duchy of Lancaster business, was made Chief Civil Commissioner, although he grumbled that it was 'bound to make him unpopular with both sides'. When J. C. C. Davidson, Wedgwood's Unionist predecessor, learned of the appointment, he told Wedgwood it was his duty to 'protect the constitution against a Bolshevik inspired General strike'.[17]

This perhaps represented the new Labour government's coming of age. Faced with a choice between giving the strikers what they wanted or reaching decisions in the public interest to prove it was 'fit to govern', Henderson et al. inevitably chose the latter path. As Ralph Miliband later put it, 'implicit' in this concern for the 'national well-being' was an acceptance that this 'was not compatible with the vigorous advancement of remedies for working-class ills and grievances'.[18] According to Hugh Dalton – whose account is supported by the journalist Norman Angell – the Prime Minister deplored 'all strikes'. Over lunch at the 1917 Club, he said

> This sort of thing will 'knock us out' if it goes on ... 'Some reductions' of wages may be justifiable. Strikes may prevent trade revival. The military may have to be used to run lorries. 'The complexities of the situation' may even become such as to compel us to have 'a national Government'.[19]

Although this account purposefully foreshadowed the 'betrayal' of 1931, it nevertheless captured a genuine tension between the government and the broader Labour movement. Angell, then acting editor of the *New Leader*, recalled MacDonald arguing that it was 'ridiculous' to pretend that 10 to 11 shillings a day, while certainly not 'enough', was a 'starvation' wage. The problem, the Prime Minister continued, was

> to show these people that if they did strike, they could not win in the present circumstances ... There was every sign that the trade of the country was looking up. At present the employers simply would not grant the extra 2s. Later on, when trade had revived and some small boom was on, they might.[20]

Perhaps conscious of these tensions, Josiah Wedgwood spoke of creating a strike-breaking plan 'more appropriate to a Labour Government'. He proposed ending the 'melodramatic air of secrecy about the whole business' and encouraged greater openness about government to dispel the quasi-fascist 'atmosphere' associated with previous efforts. Jimmy Thomas and Harry Gosling, the Minister for Transport, also managed to reach agreements with the major transport unions regarding the distribution of food. On 20 February Thomas reported to Cabinet that he preferred to 'feed people' with the assistance of the unions rather than in defiance of them.[21] Five days later, the strike was over, the government having pressured employers back to the negotiating table where they quickly conceded defeat. The STO, meanwhile, had got no further than Henderson authorizing the Admiralty to collect an emergency supply of yeast from Ireland.[22]

The successful dock strike, however, hardly discouraged future action, and within two weeks the Transport and General Workers' Union led by Ernest Bevin (a future Labour Foreign Secretary) had initiated yet another strike, this time one that threatened to paralyse London's public transport network. This was then under the control of three separate companies: trams, buses and trains. It began with tramway workers striking for increased wages and was followed by a sympathetic stoppage of bus drivers, both of which began at midnight on 21 March. The government's response was to appoint a court of inquiry, whose interim report three days later accepted the wage claim as justified but concluded that the only long-term solution was greater co-ordination of the capital's transport services.

On 26 March, however, Bevin announced that the railway unions were to close the London Underground two days later. Workers at the Lots Road power station in Chelsea – which supplied electricity to the Underground – also agreed to come out in sympathy. This raised the prospect of a general power stoppage in London, which prompted the Prime Minister to inform Bevin that if that happened the Cabinet could no longer 'stand aside'. The STO was reconvened and agreed that if the action went ahead then a state of emergency would be proclaimed. As Ralph Desmarais has observed, Bevin's 'belligerent disregard for the delicate position of the Labour government matched in reverse MacDonald's over eagerness to appear capable of ruling responsibly'.[23]

In the Commons, MacDonald told MPs the government would 'not act merely as a strike-breaking organisation' and that a Bill to tackle what he called the 'anarchy of individual competition' in London transport was imminent.[24] On Friday 28 March two ministers were hastily despatched to Knowsley (the Earl of Derby's country estate near Liverpool), where the King interrupted his horse racing to sign a proclamation activating the *Emergency Powers Act 1920* which, to quote Sidney Webb, 'made the Executive supreme'.[25] Later that afternoon, naval ratings were put on standby to help run transport services for civil servants, hospital patients and other essential workers. The government's promised London Transport Bill, however, proved enough for the employers and unions to compromise. An interim wage rise was offered, the Underground strike was called off and at midnight on 31 March the tram and bus workers also returned to work. On 1 April the emergency proclamation was revoked by the King.[26]

MacDonald and Henderson had deployed brinksmanship to bring the dispute to an end, and for the remaining seven months of the government's existence there were no further strikes or meetings of the STO. Labour's willingness, however, to use the strike-breaking apparatus of the previous Conservative government – measures once strongly criticized by Henderson – went down badly with some sections of the Labour movement. While the Home Secretary believed it was the consequence of a long period of trade depression, recent wage reduction and a reduced standard of living, he and his colleagues also resolved that contact should be made with the TUC General Council for an 'informal discussion' about the situation. Either during this meeting or shortly afterwards, Henderson apparently remarked that 'the epidemic of labour revolts' reminded him 'of what was happening in Russia in 1917 against the Kerensky government'.[27] This tactless observation also landed badly.

When the success of bus drivers encouraged builders working on the Empire Exhibition at Wembley to demand higher wages, Lord Stamfordham warned that the King 'could not perform' the opening ceremony scheduled for 23 April 'unless the Exhibition itself and the roads are in a satisfactory state of completion'. Sir Ronald Waterhouse, one of MacDonald's private secretaries, replied from Downing Street, emphasizing the Prime Minister's 'individual success' in bringing the transport strike to a conclusion, having chaired successive conferences of workmen and their employers which, together with a final exhausted statement to the House at 10 p.m.[28]

The second reading of the London Traffic Bill, meanwhile, drew fire from the Liberal and Labour benches but eventually passed with Unionist support. While Lord Haldane believed the government had 'gained a good deal of credit' by reaching settlements more quickly than a Conservative government would have managed (it was, he said, 'a great advantage to have influential trade-union leaders in the Government'), he also cautioned that there was 'a pretty strong tail which is trying to wag the dog, and the real problem of the Government is to educate a large section of its supporters in the problems of government'.[29]

Beyond the economic impact, the Cabinet was concerned about communist involvement in industrial action and on 15 April established another committee to investigate. This was chaired by J. R. Clynes and included Arthur Henderson, who was perhaps the most committed anti-communist among the Labour ministers. The Home Secretary later produced an extensive memorandum on the Communist Party of Great Britain (CPGB), in which he described its foundation and aims as well as financial aid received from the Soviet Union. Letters signed by Zinoviev came to Henderson's attention in May, urging the CPGB to enter 'direct touch' with the revolutionary movement in the UK. Questioned in the Commons about these communications, the Prime Minister merely said he presumed Russians innocent until proven guilty.[30]

The King shared his ministers' concerns and instructed Lord Stamfordham to seek assurances that the government had the communist movement 'well under control', as the Monarch had 'no doubt the Communists found that England was the most difficult country in which to exert their power and influence and, consequently, it was upon her that they were now concentrating their efforts'. Henderson told the King's private secretary that he regarded recent claims the recent railway strike had been initiated by the CPGB as 'froth' given British communists were so few in number and urged him to tell the King that while they had no doubt seized the 'opportunity of a strike ... to work their propaganda and to pose as the only friends of the strikers, there is no proof that they actually initiate the strikes'. However, he warned that the communists were

> out to damage the Labour Party, for they recognised that the policy of the latter is to ameliorate the many grievances, the airing of which affords the Communists their most effective ammunition. For this reason it would be playing into their hands were the Government to do anything which could be construed into persecution. At the same time the Government were ready, as they were in the tube strike, to act and act boldly if the law were broken.[31]

When it came to reinstating officers sacked following the police strikes of 1918–19, meanwhile, the Home Secretary showed himself to be inflexible and only superficially sympathetic. The strikes had arisen from grievances concerning pay and had culminated with the *Police Act 1919*, which established the Police Federation of England and Wales as the only officially recognized union for police officers. Several strikers were dismissed from their forces and lost their pension entitlements; a campaign for their reinstatement revived under the first Labour government, having already been adopted as both party and TUC policy.

On 7 April, however, there was apparently no dissent as the Cabinet agreed it 'could not assume the responsibility of approving the reinstatement of the dismissed strikers'.[32] While stating that his 'natural sympathies would be with the strikers', in a Cabinet paper Henderson said he could not even 'countenance' the reinstatement of the dismissed strikers 'without most seriously compromising' his position. The Home Secretary's stance, observed one of his biographers, was thus 'indistinguishable from that of right-wing Tories'.[33]

On 12 April Henderson wrote to John Hayes, secretary of the Police and Prison Officers' Union (PPOU) and the Labour MP for Liverpool Edge Hill, to explain that the 'legal and practical difficulties in the way of reinstatement' were very real but were not the 'sole consideration', although he did 'not think it would serve any useful purpose' for him to elaborate on those 'in any detail'. The Parliamentary Labour Party was unimpressed, criticizing the decision as 'directly contrary to party policy' and smarting at the lack of consultation.[34]

But while the PLP and PPOU both suspected Henderson of capitulating to his permanent officials, the King felt he had gone too far. Stamfordham was despatched to Chequers to communicate to the Prime Minister the 'astonishment, indeed almost alarm', with which the Monarch had read the Home Secretary's Cabinet paper. MacDonald made the obvious retort that the policemen concerned would 'not be reinstated', but Stamfordham shot back that His Majesty was nevertheless 'astounded at the regret openly expressed by the Home Secretary at the conclusions to which he was forced to come', particularly that his 'natural sympathies' would be with the strikers. The Prime Minister then added 'frankly' that

neither the King nor you can understand the psychology of a Trades Unionist Leader when he deals with such a question. He has been brought up to regard it as his duty to stand by his fellow members and should a strike be declared his natural impulse is to back them to the utmost of his powers. Now Mr. Henderson is faced with a case which he realises is a bad case – no case at all. He has to admit this but he cannot help feeling for and sympathising with the men who have suffered. It is in fact Henderson, Home Secretary, apologising to Henderson, Trade Unionist. I should not have written the Memorandum as Henderson wrote it: but I can realise what was in his mind.

The Prime Minister then suggested that the King see the Home Secretary personally, though he doubted whether Henderson had 'a sufficiently broad outlook to realise the King's feelings and attitude with regard to what he has expressed in writing'. Stamfordham said the Monarch would doubtless

> sympathise with Mr. Henderson's feelings qua a Trade Unionist: but on the other hand Mr. Henderson is now His Majesty's principal Secretary of State, who is responsible for all that affects law, order and justice in the country: and, obviously, His Majesty could not allow the above expression to pass by unnoticed.[35]

A couple of days later, Stamfordham also went to see Sir John Anderson, the permanent secretary at the Home Office and the principal author of the memorandum which had argued against reinstatement. He told the King's private secretary that he had been 'surprised' to secure the agreement of Henderson and the Cabinet so easily, not least because the commitment to reinstate the officers had been 'one of the most important questionnaires put to every Labour Candidate at the last General Election'. Given that context, Anderson did not place too much weight on the Home Secretary's expression of his 'natural sympathies', for he had said these 'would be' ('not are') with the strikers. Anderson urged Stamfordham (and therefore the King) to take a broader view, arguing that from the 'departmental point of view' the Home Office had 'achieved a victory – not only for today but in the future'. He continued:

> For imagine as a result of a General Election the Labour Party returned to power with a majority in the House of Commons and with a Prime Minister of more advanced views than those of Mr. Ramsay MacDonald – this question would probably again be raised and supported by the Government of the day, but what an unanswerable reply the Home Secretary would be able to produce in the unanimous decision of Mr. Ramsay MacDonald's Government.[36]

The King was appeased. At the next suitable opportunity, Stamfordham told the Prime Minister that the Monarch would 'express his satisfaction' that the strikers were not to be reinstated, adding that 'His Majesty thought that as Home Secretary [Henderson] had almost strained his sentiments of sympathy to a maximum.'[37]

An unhappy King, however, was the least of Henderson's concerns. On 11 May John Hayes read the Home Secretary's letter of 12 April (regarding 'the legal and practical difficulties in the way of reinstatement') to a rally of dismissed policemen, who then demanded action rather than excuses, a cry subsequently taken up by the PLP Executive. A few days later Lord Parmoor, the Lord President, brought the matter back to the Cabinet, which considered alternative courses of action: either arguing that a minority government could not command the necessary support for reinstatement or gradual 'absorption' of the men into other branches of government service. Ultimately, however, it concluded that anything short of reinstatement simply would not wash.[38]

A subsequent statement in the House of Commons made matters worse. Although Henderson offered a committee of inquiry, he also made clear his distaste for police strikes:

I have been a trade unionist for 41 years, but ... I draw a very wide distinction between an ordinary industrial dispute and a strike in what is a disciplinary service like the police force. Those of us who are prepared to bring about changes, either political or industrial, on constitutional lines, cannot make too clear the difference between the position of the military, the police force or ... the fire brigade, so far as taking a 'down tool' policy is concerned.[39]

Not only were these remarks seized upon by Clydeside MPs, but there followed a protracted dispute between the PLP and the Cabinet regarding the proposed inquiry's terms of reference. The Prime Minister rejected a compromise whereby the terms would have been limited to the question of *how* to secure reinstatement, but the committee (which had an anti-Labour majority, reflecting the composition of the Commons) outlived the government and, in December 1925, advised against reinstatement.[40]

During his interview with Lord Stamfordham, Sir John Anderson had alluded to two other 'difficult questions' which had faced Henderson upon his arrival at the Home Office: the case of ex-Inspector John Syme and 'alien immigration'. Many in the Labour movement believed Syme, who had suffered a mental breakdown after being demoted and eventually dismissed from the Metropolitan Police for alleged insubordination, had been a victim of harsh discipline, and Henderson broke with precedent in ordering that Syme be examined at Broadmoor by two independent practitioners.[41] On 30 April, Lord Haldane also appointed a judge-led inquiry, whose conclusions both the government and Syme gave an 'undertaking' to accept.[42] Mr Justice Talbot reported on 11 July,[43] stating while the handling of Syme's case had been far from ideal, there was nevertheless no basis for any compensation.[44] Syme subsequently approached the Home Secretary for redress, but received no reply.[45]

Henderson also came under pressure to make changes to the *Aliens Restriction (Amendment) Act 1919*, which had further restricted immigration to the UK. Section 1 of the Act gave the Home Secretary significant powers to alter existing controls via Order in Council, thus bypassing Parliament. The *Aliens Order 1920*, for example, compelled all migrants seeking temporary residence to obtain a work permit or demonstrate financial independence. Although some sections of the Labour movement feared being undercut by foreign labour, the TUC demanded that any self-supporting 'aliens' be given residence and that none should be deported on the basis of political offences committed in their own countries. Henderson, however, argued that deportation was rare and observed that anyone could declare themselves a political refugee in order to 'game' the system. The 1919 Act, therefore, remained the basis of UK immigration law for another half-century.[46]

Wales was another of the Home Secretary's eclectic responsibilities. One of his sons – Arthur Henderson Jnr – was the Member for Cardiff South, one of 21 Labour MPs returned at the 1923 general election.[47] Ramsay MacDonald also represented Aberavon and was regarded in industrial South Wales as something of a political messiah.[48] The Labour Party was conscious of rising nationalist sentiment. During 1924 two significant movements emerged: Saunders Lewis's Y Mudiad Cymreig (The Welsh Movement) and H. R. Jones' Byddin Ymreolwyr Cymru (The Army of the Welsh Home Rulers).[49] Jimmy Thomas, the Newport-raised Colonial Secretary, also saw himself as one of Wales's men in the Cabinet, and lobbied Henderson to designate Cardiff the 'capital' of Wales.

After much deliberation, Henderson wrote to Thomas on 6 March:

> The point seems to me to be this. As ordinarily understood a 'capital' is the place where the government of a country is centred and I do not see how there can be a capital of a country whose public services are not separately administered and where there is no separate judiciary.

The Home Secretary cited Belfast, the 'chief commercial city in Northern Ireland', which in 1921 had become the capital of that part of the United Kingdom 'not by any act of the Crown or any formal procedure but merely by evolution and the fact of the judiciary and public services administration being centred there'. Henderson continued:

> so far as I can gather any question of official recognition of Cardiff as the capital of Wales would be likely to create great controversy. I am told for example that Swansea might claim to be the Welsh capital and that there would be the most emphatic objection in the distinctively Welsh portions of Wales to the designation of Cardiff as the capital.

The matter, concluded Henderson, 'might well be allowed to rest',[50] as indeed it did until 1955 when Gwilym Lloyd-George (son of David), the then (Conservative) Minister for Welsh Affairs and Home Secretary, declared Cardiff the capital of Wales.[51]

Henderson was more proactive when it came to amending the existing Factory Acts. As a trade unionist and MP Henderson had long pressed for safer working conditions, and in promoting his planned Factory Bill he made a well-publicized tour of textile mills in Burnley (his new constituency) and other parts of Lancashire. In keeping with the government's general approach to industrial matters, he also organized a conference of employers and operatives in Manchester. Not only did the Home Secretary's Bill codify existing legislation, but it proposed additional safeguards for male, female and child workers, greater protection for workers against injury, an eight-hour day and 48-hour working week (as per the recent Washington Convention), rest intervals, improved lighting, heating, ventilation and sanitation, and finally a more extensive system of factory regulation by Home Office inspectors.

The Bill inevitably provoked opposition from employers' organizations ('perhaps the best possible testimony' noted the Labour historian Herbert Tracey, to its likely benefits) and when it came before the Cabinet, Henderson himself warned that a clause concerning paid holidays might jeopardize the whole measure. His colleagues agreed and approved the draft Bill minus that forward-looking proposal.[52] This ambitious piece of legislation, however, fell victim to a congested parliamentary timetable and the short lifespan of the government, although it stands as a tantalizing indication of what a lengthier spell in office might have produced.

5

JOHN WHEATLEY: 'A TRADITIONAL MR. PICKWICK'

On 22 February 1924, a month after the Labour government had taken office, the King received John Wheatley. 'He is an extreme socialist & comes from Glasgow,' he noted in his diary. 'I had a very interesting conversation with him.'[1] There are several accounts of the Monarch's first audience with his Minister of Health, most likely embellished in their retelling. In one version, the King asked searching questions about Wheatley's childhood, in response to which the minister painted a vivid picture of the grinding hardship endured by his parents and their eight children, who had inhabited a miner's cottage without drainage or running water. To this the King apparently listened in 'friendly sympathy' before asking rhetorically: 'Is it possible that my people live in such awful conditions?' Then, as the King bade the minister farewell, he reportedly added: 'I tell you, Mr. Wheatley, that, if I had to live in conditions like that, I would be a revolutionary myself.'[2] Another story had it that the Minister of Health simply told the King he 'would never lift a finger to change this country from a capitalist Monarchy into a capitalist Republic. Of course, when capitalism goes, the Monarchy will go too. But I hope there'll be no ill-feeling on either side.'[3]

John Wheatley was born on 19 May 1869 in Co. Waterford, Ireland, but grew up in Lanarkshire, his father Thomas, a labourer, having found work in the Scottish coalfields. The Wheatleys were raised as strict Catholics, and indeed that faith had a lasting impact on John's personal beliefs and political activism. After joining his father in the mines as a boy, Wheatley left aged twenty-four to work as a shop assistant and in a public house. In 1896 he married Mary Meechan, herself the daughter of an Irish migrant, and with his brother Patrick ran a grocery shop in Glasgow's East End. When that business closed in 1901, he sold advertising for the *Glasgow Observer*, a Catholic newspaper.[4]

In 1908, Wheatley set up his own publishing company, the proceeds from which allowed him to buy a substantial home and educate his children in fee-paying Catholic schools. Later, a newspaper owned by his company, the *Glasgow Eastern Standard*, provided usefully comprehensive coverage of Wheatley's political activities. Since 1910 these had centred around local government, where he specialized in and campaigned for housing at affordable rents. 'In appearance rather like the traditional Mr. Pickwick', Wheatley's was 'the iron hand in the velvet glove'.[5] In 1922, he led the 'Clyde group' of MPs to Westminster following their triumphant showing in the general election of that year.

The group's confrontational tactics brought Wheatley and his followers into conflict with MacDonald, who believed their intemperate rhetoric and parliamentary disruption would cost Labour support. Nevertheless, Wheatley joined the first Labour Cabinet. Speaking at a celebratory reception in Shettleston, the new Minister of Health said he represented the 'Clyde men in the Cabinet' and that his appointment recognized 'the magnificent lead in the direction of Socialism given by Glasgow to the whole country'.[6] But far from being a 'wild man' from the Clyde, the civil servant Tom Jones judged Wheatley to be 'Pale Pink' rather than 'Turkey Red'.[7]

Despite having surprised colleagues with his deference on becoming a Privy Counsellor, Wheatley generally eschewed Court functions. He especially liked telling the story of a letter his wife had received from a countess inviting her to attend a social event, to which Mrs Wheatley had replied 'regretting her inability to accept on the ground that she spent her time in Glasgow'.[8] 'To the Ministry of Health he brings the authority of an expert,' judged the journalist Mary Agnes Hamilton, 'he finds there an opportunity of immediate constructive work such as is open to none of his Cabinet colleagues.'[9]

But before Wheatley could get on with that constructive work, he was plunged into a major controversy concerning socialist rebels in London's East End. Social security, such as it was in 1924, rested upon Lloyd George's 1911 scheme of National Insurance, payments from which could be supplemented in certain circumstances by elected 'Boards of Guardians' operating under the *Poor Law Amendment Act 1834*. Several Boards had come under Labour control in 1919, including that in Poplar, where George Lansbury, the first Labour mayor, had also broken with tradition by assuming office 'without robes, mace or cocked hat'.[10] In 1921, the Poplar Guardians had voted to pay more than the nationally approved scales for claimants within its jurisdiction. The then Minister of Health, Sir Alfred Mond, issued an Order prohibiting these payments, but this was ignored by the Poplar Guardians, who then incurred short prison sentences for their defiance of the law. Faced with the prospect of a breakdown of local government – and possibly law and order – the government brokered a deal to get the councillors out of prison and introduce a measure of equalization.[11]

On 5 February 1924 – a week before Parliament reconvened – Wheatley received a deputation from the Poplar Board of Guardians, which included Edgar Lansbury, George's communist son.[12] They made several demands, chief among them that Mond's Order be rescinded. Wheatley replied that he had already decided to repeal it,[13] though he was careful to make clear he had 'not seen any evidence of a conspiracy on the part of the officials to act as the enemies of Poplar and Poplarism'.[14]

To Wheatley, his decision was uncontroversial given his Tory predecessors had ignored repeated breaches of Mond's Order, but the news – which broke on 7 February – provoked the first serious row of the new Labour government. *The Times* warned that other Boards of Guardians would take it as permission to be 'less careful with the ratepayers' money', while Sir William

Joynson-Hicks, Wheatley's immediate predecessor, gave notice that he intended to bring the matter before the House.[15] It was all, confessed Lord Haldane to his sister Bay, making him 'anxious about our position in Parl[iamen]t'.[16]

MacDonald was clearly furious and made a 'strong appeal' to his colleagues 'not to make public announcements or take administrative action on questions of great public interest ... without previous consultation with the Prime Minister'.[17] And when Parliament met on 12 February, he attempted to further limit the damage:

> Everybody knows perfectly well that the question of the cancellation of the Order had been again and again under consideration in the Department concerned. Everybody knows perfectly well that as a matter of fact the Order has never been effective. Everybody knows perfectly well that an Act of Parliament was passed in 1923 which changed the methods by which extravagance by boards of guardians was to be checked.

The Ministry of Health, added MacDonald, had taken it for granted that rescinding the Mond Order was 'a merely mechanical operation'.[18]

Asquith, the Liberal leader, begged to differ, warning the following day in 'the plainest and most unequivocal terms' that unless the government reconsidered its decision, he did 'not think there is the least chance of that administrative act receiving the countenance or approval of the House of Commons'.[19] By far 'the best policy both for us and the country,' added Asquith in his diary, 'is to give the Labour Government a free and full rope'.[20]

In a Cabinet memorandum, Wheatley argued that his action had been 'gravely misunderstood' and 'grossly misrepresented'. Nevertheless, he agreed to state publicly that repealing the Order did 'not involve or imply any general alteration in Poor Law Policy',[21] a riposte to a Liberal motion condemning Wheatley's action as 'calculated to encourage illegality and extravagance'.[22] On the afternoon of 26 February, the Minister of Health

defended his action at length in the House, concluding defiantly
that he had

> not surrendered to Poplar; I do not intend to surrender
> to Poplar. I have rescued my Department from a state of
> degradation. I have put my Department in a position in which
> it can and will enforce the law, and will do so fearlessly ...
> impartially and fairly. It is ridiculous to suggest that in so doing
> I have encouraged extravagance and illegality in any part of the
> country.[23]

Philip Snowden, the Chancellor of the Exchequer, considered his
colleague's performance a 'veritable triumph', while in the House
even Sir William Joynson-Hicks said he had 'seldom heard a
comparatively new Member make such an excellent speech'.[24] In
his daily report to the King, MacDonald also praised Wheatley's
oratory while taking a swipe at George Lansbury's 'vigorous and
emotional defence of what is known as "Poplarism"'.[25]

Although Beatrice Webb judged Wheatley to be 'a new star in
House of Commons dialectics, logical and humorous with first-rate
delivery',[26] the incident also revealed the Minister of Health's own
attitude to be deeply ambiguous, if not downright hypocritical.[27]
Iain McLean, for example, has contrasted Wheatley's private
remarks to Cabinet with his public utterances,[28] including one
in which he spoke of his 'great joy and pride in being associated
with Poplarism'.[29]

Wheatley also took up a Rent Restrictions Bill sponsored by
the Labour backbencher Ben Gardner which had been before the
House of Commons since 18 January. He was keen to respond to
a demand from Clydeside colleagues to remove the hard edges of
a previous Act introduced by Neville Chamberlain and ameliorate
conditions in the minister's native city of Glasgow, where evictions
had recently increased. What evolved into the Prevention of
Evictions Bill was introduced in early April and sought to prevent
courts issuing eviction notices for non-payment of rent in cases
of unemployment. In an impassioned speech which left a 'lump'

in Lloyd George's throat,[30] Wheatley painted a distressing picture of a sheriff officer informing a mother that if she and her children had not vacated their house by noon the following day then he would have no alternative but to put them and their furniture out onto the street. He recalled that on first joining the socialist movement he had been told it threatened the destruction of that sacred institution, the family. 'Here,' declared Wheatley, 'you have an order of things that not only threatens, but does it.'[31]

But the Bill had been rushed and was therefore flawed. Despite pressure from MacDonald, Wheatley had failed to produce draft government amendments until the night before the Cabinet was due to consider them. Nor had he run the unemployment clause past the law officers or factored in the likely objection of opposition parties. Even Beatrice Webb thought it was 'administrative folly to lay the obligation of relieving the unemployed on those who happened to be their landlords'.[32] In an attempt to rescue the Bill, J. R. Clynes, the Deputy Leader of the House, intervened to say – and apparently in contravention of MacDonald's instructions – that the government would substitute the unemployment clause with another enabling the unemployed to obtain rent assistance from public funds.

But when the Prime Minister himself introduced that new clause, it did no such thing, the Chancellor having flatly refused to provide yet another government subsidy. Pleading for the ailing Bill, Wheatley was reduced to selling it as 'an emergency measure', while James Maxton warned his own front bench 'that unless they secure the homes of the people of Glasgow I will show force in the streets of Glasgow defending them'.[33] Instead, the Bill was withdrawn, and another introduced by the Liberals which stiffened the existing law in favour of tenants but took no account of the unemployed. This passed with minimal opposition.

Wheatley's relations with the Prime Minister, already frayed by the Poplar incident, 'resolved themselves in cold formality',[34] and Iain McLean has been harsher than most historians in deeming the 'fiasco' almost entirely the Minister of Health's fault, Wheatley having ignored departmental advice that eviction due to unemployment was actually quite rare. Had he explored possible ways of minimizing evictions, 'without tying it to the question of unemployment, he could have yielded to the heavy pressure that Kirkwood, Maxton and Stephen were putting on him without checkmating the Government'.[35] Beatrice Webb simply described it as another 'example of Wheatley getting the Government into a deep hole, climbing out of it himself in a brilliantly successful speech, [and] leaving the Government still deeper down in the hole which he had made!'[36]

Wheatley also came under sustained attack because of his stance on birth control, which by 1924 was championed by the Birth Control Association (BCA) led by H. G. Wells and Dora Russell, wife of philosopher Bertrand. While they wanted to make basic contraceptive knowledge widely available, Ministry of Health guidance forbade doctors or health visitors from giving advice on contraception and reserved the right to withdraw funding from those who did. The BCA hoped Wheatley might change course, but when they lobbied him in early May it became clear the minister's adherence to contemporary Catholic thought would trump any political (or indeed public health) considerations.[37]

'Mr Wheatley had stirred a hornet's nest,' Dora Russell later wrote, and 'all through 1924 we buzzed and stung.'[38] The Minister of Health soon had to defend himself in Parliament and in late July he received another delegation, this time from the Standing Joint Committee of Industrial Women's Organisations. Standing firm, Wheatley drew a distinction between 'the question [of] whether or not birth control was desirable and whether or not it should be taught in a particular place and manner'. He told the Committee that the

> question was highly controversial and he doubted whether the working classes were really united on the subject. It seemed to him likely that if this subject were taught at maternity centres many women, not only on account of religious but on account of other objections too, would be deterred from attending the centres.

While diplomatically expressing 'no opinion' as to the case for teaching birth control, Wheatley said he was not prepared to sanction its introduction at maternity centres without 'the express authority of Parliament',[39] an obvious attempt to kick a difficult issue into the long grass. At the Labour Women's Conference held in mid-May, Marion Phillips (the party's women's officer) even attempted to prevent any discussion of the issue and pressured Dora Russell to withdraw her demand for a debate. 'Sex should not be dragged into politics,' declared Phillips, 'you will split the Party from top to bottom.'[40]

Wheatley's plans for housing, then in careful gestation, at least presented the prospect of redemption from all this perceived reaction and legislative ineptitude. Labour's manifesto had been ambitious, promising to 'abolish the slums' and 'promptly build an adequate supply of decent homes',[41] while in early February Wheatley had 'harangued' the relevant Cabinet committee with his vision for a ten-year programme 'of 200,000 houses per annum, each to cost exactly £500 and to be let at exactly 7s. per week'. Tom Jones, the Deputy Cabinet Secretary, was incredulous:

> How this stupendous sum is to be raised, and how prices and rents are to be kept static regardless of all market changes, he had no idea, and it had to be pointed out to him that his scheme implied the stabilisation of wages for ten years.[42]

In his epic speech to the Commons on 12 February, the Prime Minister had observed that previous governments had only 'touched the fringe of the problem' of providing homes for wage-earners which could be rented 'with some relation to their wage income'. By way of contrast, promised MacDonald, his administration wanted to 'get right into the heart of it'.[43] This might have proved difficult given that Labour had come to office without, as in so many other areas, a detailed plan beyond disliking bad housing conditions, but as Arthur Greenwood later observed, it became clear 'from the outset that nothing short of a great cooperative effort on the part of the state, the local authorities and the building industry would be insufficient to cope with the problem'.[44] The Minister of Health likened it to a 'treaty' between those three sectors.

At the end of January, Wheatley convened a joint meeting of building unions (which had 15 representatives) and employers (who had 19) and asked them to figure out what the industry required to meet the nation's housing needs. MacDonald seemed content to leave Wheatley to it, perhaps conscious that when it came to housing he possessed considerable expertise from his career in Scottish local government. Meeting with local authorities at the Ministry of Health on 15 April, Wheatley declared

> that we have here a unique opportunity. If the same spirit of goodwill, if the same spirit of making some little sacrifice, some little sectional sacrifice, whether it be political, or whether it be economic, be made by each section as has been done by the building industry, then, I think, we are on the way to creating an atmosphere of national unity that will go a long, long way towards getting us out of our present difficulties.[45]

By that point, Wheatley's National Housebuilding Committee had signed off its unanimous report. This recommended the government guarantee a 15-year housebuilding programme, overcome the haphazard and casual nature of construction and train workers to replenish wartime losses. As a *quid pro quo*, parties to the agreement were pledged to build 2.5 million houses by 1929, and for let rather than sale. A statutory committee was also to allocate work, and, in a separate memorandum from the Committee of Building Manufacturers and Suppliers, the manufacturer H. C. Johnstone promised a policy of non-exploitation.[46]

Between April and early June, Wheatley embarked on an energetic round of meetings intended to meet any outstanding objections. With considerable skill, he persuaded the Chancellor to accept the additional cost of a variable subsidy to local authorities. Snowden was assuaged by this being spread over several years and through his dealings formed 'a very high opinion' of his colleague's 'administrative ability'.[47] On 8 May, meanwhile, Wheatley made the striking observation that 'if a socialist may claim to be in any way a conservative' he was proceeding in a 'slow and conservative way' which, he believed, 'in the long run ... will be the quick way'.[48]

At the eleventh hour, Wheatley was faced with the bricklayers' union threatening to withdraw over concerns about pay and the admission of twenty-year-olds to apprenticeships. He immediately appealed to the Prime Minister, arguing that the

> matter is so important that I suggest you should intervene, see delegates from the bricklayers as quickly as possible, and put to them quite squarely whether they are prepared to risk wrecking the housing scheme of the Labour government by persisting in a course in regard to which they will have public opinion dead against them as well as the opinion of the operatives who were parties with them in the scheme of the National Housebuilding Committee.

Despite being consumed with his own crises, MacDonald instructed an official to inform the Minister of Health 'at once' that he would see the bricklayers with him the following Monday evening.[49] Through collective and decisive action, the crisis was averted.

Finally, on 3 June Wheatley made another 'brilliant speech' as he moved the resolution for his long-awaited Housing (Financial Provisions) Bill,[50] while three weeks later its nine clauses passed their second reading aided by another lucid speech. This stage was carried by 315 votes to 175, 128 of which were Conservative. It needed all Wheatley's remaining skill and energy to tackle no fewer than 76 amendments at the Bill's committee stage. At times, some feared for the corpulent Wheatley's personal health, but on 25 July he was again on the front bench to defend his Bill against criticism from his own side that it was too moderate:

> Why did I not introduce a Socialist Measure? I was not in a position to introduce a Socialist Measure. The country is not

ready for Socialism. I wish it were ready for it. I will devote my life to an honest effort to prepare it for Socialism. Meantime, I have to take the materials which are available and use them, however much I may disagree with them, in order to contribute, however slightly, to the betterment of my fellow men.[51]

Charles Masterman, the radical Liberal MP, told the House:

For over six months, with extraordinary patience and industry, and with a humour and a willingness to compromise, and with all the arts of one who might have been in this House for 20 years on the Front Bench, he has conducted a difficult Bill in such a manner as to disarm opposition, and he has always been ready to accept proposals which he knew would make the Bill better.[52]

On the day the Housing Bill was due to receive Royal Assent – 7 August 1924 – Wheatley had on a whim caught a train to Littlehampton (he liked the name), walked out of its station and into a field, where he lay down 'with his jacket under his head and his handkerchief over his face, and just slept'.[53]

Wheatley was rightly celebrated at the time for his 'single-mindedness, excellent negotiating skills and expert salesmanship',[54] as well as subsequently for the transformative impact his legislation had on public housing in Great Britain, even though in the first year of what became known as the 'Wheatley Act' only 2,486 houses were built. Despite belonging, as Iain McLean has observed, 'to a minority faction in a minority government', he had shown tactical shrewdness in producing a scheme which relied on 'known and trusted precedents'. Whosoever was the mother, Wheatley was undoubtedly the wet nurse. 'The solid brick terraces which march across the inner suburbs of every British city,' judged McLean, 'could not have been built without John Wheatley …They are the monument to the greatest of the Clydesiders.'[55]

Ministry of Health officials had already come to view Wheatley as 'an improvement' even upon Neville Chamberlain, hitherto their 'ideal' minister,[56] but during his parliamentary triumphs on the Housing Bill, the Labour Party had also been won over, attracting Beatrice Webb's attention as a 'possible successor' to Ramsay MacDonald given his 'unexpected and outstanding' success on the front bench.[57] The journalist John Scanlon later claimed Wheatley told him he would resign from the Cabinet once his Building Materials Bill – intended to give central government even greater control over house building – had become law. 'He had seen the futility,' observed Scanlon, 'of trying to do anything of permanent value to remedy the defects of Capitalism in a Government composed of men who did not believe in Socialism.'[58]

Although this was most likely untrue, Wheatley had certainly come to hold the Prime Minister in low regard, apparently remarking that if the Conservatives 'were an intelligent party' they would make MacDonald their leader. There was also tension within the once close-knit group of Clydesiders. While David Kirkwood acknowledged Wheatley's success as a minister, he wrote of a feeling 'he had left us'.[59] Writing to a friend, Lord Beaverbrook noted that the Prime Minister was being 'hard pressed inside his own party by Wheatley', who was

> certainly the coming figure, and some people profess to believe that he will overtake MacDonald in the race. But there is very little permanency about these revolutionary figures. He is only dangerous to MacDonald in so far as he is inexperienced and extreme. Let him cease to be so, and he becomes merely another clever subordinate with a good debating style. And it is difficult to remain violent in politics for office in England [sic], as you well know, is a great emollient and softener of rough edges.[60]

But as Richard Lyman has observed, even if Wheatley's Housing Bill 'was not exactly socialism, it was certainly statesmanship'.[61]

6

Philip Snowden: 'A free breakfast table'

If Arthur Henderson and Sir John Anderson had proved a good match at the Home Office, they had nothing on Philip Snowden and one of the most powerful departments in Whitehall. 'We must imagine with what joy Mr Snowden was welcomed to the Treasury by the permanent officials,' ran Winston Churchill's memorable account:

> [H]ere was the High Priest entering the sanctuary. The Treasury mind and the Snowden mind embraced each other with the fervour of two long-separated kindred lizards, and the reign of joy began.[1]

For the Chancellor it must indeed have been a satisfying moment. As one of his biographers, Colin Cross, has observed, the disabled young man who 30 years earlier

> had been ejected from the Treasury service with a £30 gratuity had now returned as head of the department. The minority politician who for eighteen years had been telling Chancellors of the Exchequer how to run their department had at last the opportunity to test his own capacity.[2]

Snowden was born in 1864 in a cottage near Cowling in the Yorkshire Pennines, the only son and third child of John and Martha, who were both weavers. Like Arthur Henderson he was raised a Methodist (Wesleyan), a faith which thereafter permeated his education and political outlook.

Snowden found work as a clerk at the Inland Revenue but at twenty-seven severely injured his back in a cycling accident and was paralysed from the waist down. Over the next two years he learned to walk again, while the political theory he imbibed during his convalescence converted him from Liberal to socialist politics. Although his Inland Revenue job was kept open, Snowden decided to resign from the Civil Service on account of his disability, thereafter enduring 'without complaint the pain and inconvenience of his partial paralysis',[3] walking with a limp and two sticks. With his gaunt face and sober dress, Snowden 'looked like a civil servant, not a propagandist, and spoke like a mixture of the two'.[4]

In 1894 Snowden was elected to Cowling's new parish council and in 1906 entered Parliament as the Labour MP for Blackburn, moving to the Colne Valley constituency at the 1922 election. Within the Labour movement, Snowden was an odd fit. Leonard Woolf believed he was about 'as progressive as a member of the Junior Carlton Club', his political faith limited to 'support of the Crown, the Church, and free trade'.[5] But while Snowden was a details man, Ramsay MacDonald was a visionary. 'This temperamental antagonism was emphasized by personal dislike,' observed the Clydeside MP David Kirkwood. 'They should have been divorced for incompatibility of temper. Instead, they continued their association for the sake of the family.'[6]

In the wake of the 1923 general election, it was obvious to everyone in the Labour Party that Snowden was destined for the Treasury, although not everyone was thrilled at this prospect. 'Snowden, who thinks he has a right to be Chancellor of the Exchequer,' wrote Beatrice Webb of the post-election gathering at her Pimlico home, 'is chicken-hearted and will try to cut down expenditure. He even demurred to a programme of public works for the unemployed. Where was the money to come from? he asked, with a Treasury clerk's intonation.'[7]

On 23 January Snowden was both sworn of the Privy Council and received his seals of office, an unusual but not unique experience for an incoming Treasury chief (Disraeli had been in the same position in 1852). 'I suppose that like every other Chancellor,' wrote Lord Beaverbrook, 'you will shortly be locked in a death grapple for moral mastery with the Bank of England.'[8]

Beaverbrook, however, proved wide of the mark. The Governor of the Bank of England was Montagu Norman, with whom – to quote Roy Jenkins – it was 'hardly an exaggeration to say that Snowden fell in love'.[9] In his memoirs, the Chancellor affected only to have had a 'vague idea of what a Governor of the Bank of England ought to look like' prior to their first encounter:

> He might have stepped out of the frame of a portrait of a handsome courtier of the Middle Ages. It took but a short acquaintance with Mr. Norman to know that his external appearance was the bodily expression of one of the kindliest natures and most sympathetic hearts it has been my privilege to know. I do not remember clearly what we talked about at that first interview. But the impression his character made upon me still vividly remains.[10]

If Snowden was in love with Montagu Norman, then William Graham, the Edinburgh MP who became Financial Secretary to the Treasury, was equally besotted with the Chancellor. Like Snowden, he had begun his career as a low-ranking civil servant, later funding a degree in economics at Edinburgh University through his journalistic income. And like the Chancellor, Graham was most definitely 'not one of the wild men' in the new government, although 'much more dangerous than his dapper appearance and his constant smile might suggest'.[11]

Graham was thrilled to have been appointed Snowden's second-in-command, further deepening their father–son relationship and what one observer called 'a natural affinity between the Yorkshireman and the Lowland Scot'.[12] MPs used to call them 'the happy twins', and as far as Snowden was concerned his deputy was the 'ablest and most competent holder of that office I have known'.[13] A veteran of the Royal Commission on the Income Tax, Graham had a photographic memory and could speak at length (if not with flair) without notes.[14]

Supporting Snowden and Graham at the Treasury was Sir Warren Fisher, the permanent secretary, and P. J. Grigg, the Chancellor's private secretary. Grigg was one of Churchill's kindred lizards, and later gushed over Snowden's popularity with the permanent officials. He was, he wrote, the

> ideal of what a Minister should be in that he gave a very clear lead on all questions of policy, interfered rarely, if at all, in matters of administration, gave decisions quickly and unequivocally, and then defended his decisions against all-comers with confidence and vigour – and nearly always with success.[15]

As a former permanent official himself, Snowden held the senior Civil Service in high regard. If he had one disappointment, it was the 'disreputable condition' of the Treasury buildings in Whitehall, which the Chancellor regarded as 'a disgrace to the State'.[16]

Like the Prime Minister, Snowden's salary as Chancellor was £3,500 after tax, although unlike MacDonald he did not have to maintain a residence at Downing Street. Presumably in an attempt to sweeten the deal for J. R. Clynes, who had been appointed Deputy Leader of the House, the Clynes rather than the Snowdens were to occupy Number 11, traditionally the Chancellor's official residence. Although Philip acquiesced with minimal fuss (his flat in St Ermine's Court was considerably cheaper to maintain), his wife Ethel was 'deeply offended' at being excluded from one of London's most desirable addresses. Beatrice Webb, who busied herself providing Mrs Clynes with a housekeeper, cook and butler, attempted to 'soothe' Mrs Snowden's feelings while privately lambasting her:

> She is a 'climber' of the worst description, refusing to associate with the rank-and-file and plebeian elements in the Labour

Party. Hence every class-conscious Labour man or woman listens for the echoes of Ethel climbing, climbing, climbing, night and day! Out of the Labour world into that of plutocrats and aristocrats.[17]

Webb's sneers were, for once, not misplaced. While Philip Snowden generally eschewed Court ceremonies, Ethel was later presented at Court, resplendent in ostrich feathers as she curtsied to the King and Queen.

The Snowdens were close to the former coalition premier David Lloyd George, who was a near neighbour in Surrey. When Asquith audaciously suggested the government jettison John Wheatley in return for Liberal support, Ethel told Lloyd George of her

> sympathy for the idea of a Union of all the Radical forces for common ends ... You cannot suspect me of sympathy with the wild men of the Party. You know I disapprove of the mischievous policy of Wheatley [but] under this influence [Asquith's attack] I have declined several invitations from Liberals and have warned my husband to behave with cautiousness.[18]

Lloyd George, meanwhile, later told Deputy Cabinet Secretary Tom Jones that Snowden's inaugural Budget would only succeed if it led 'to a first-class controversy'.[19] But this was not the Chancellor's style. Just over three months after taking office, he presented his first, and as it turned out only, Budget to the House of Commons on 29 April. This Snowden had prepared in harmonious consultation with the Treasury but in virtual isolation from his Cabinet colleagues, including the Prime Minister. Indeed, he had followed Asquith's advice not to give colleagues advance notice of his proposals on account of leaks, and so the first they learned of them was on the morning of the Budget. Only the King received advance sight, with Lord Stamfordham passing on the Monarch's congratulations and approval regarding a 'very substantial surplus'.[20]

The Chancellor regarded it as 'no part' of his job to formulate spending proposals, but rather to 'resist all demands for expenditure made by his colleagues and, when he can no longer resist, to limit the concession to the barest point of acceptance'.[21] He put it more bluntly at the Lord Mayor's Dinner, describing himself as a 'man with his back to the wall, fighting off a pack of ravenous wolves'.[22] Instead the Chancellor's goals were threefold: defending the principles of Free Trade, reducing the burden of indirect taxation (particularly if it impacted food prices) and lowering the National Debt, to which end Snowden had already announced a Treasury committee (which included Barbara Wootton, a Labour/TUC researcher not yet old enough to vote).[23] Beyond those three aims, he possessed no bold vision. While Roy Jenkins had little doubt that the 'milk of Gladstonian doctrine ran more purely through Snowden's veins than through those of any intervening Chancellor', he posited that the Grand Old Man himself, confronted with the challenging circumstances of 1924, might have been a 'little less rigid'.[24]

This was a fair assessment given that Snowden had inherited a relatively favourable budgetary situation, a surplus of just over £48 million, although this 'went automatically to the reduction of the National Debt'. With the Cabinet having signed off his proposals, Snowden left Downing Street with his Budget in 'Mr. Gladstone's battered despatch-box' and passed 'cheering crowds' all the way to the House of Commons, the usual novelty of Budget Day heightened by it being 'the first time that a Labour Budget was to be presented to Parliament'. He claimed there was no 'nervousness' at the ordeal before him, for he was not 'an emotional person',[25] which was remarkable given that no fewer than five former Chancellors awaited his speech inside the Chamber.

Snowden had refreshed his memory of Gladstone's Budget speeches and in his own jokingly apologized for his 'youth and inexperience' while pledging to be 'vindictive against no class and against no interests'. The Chancellor's main reductions targeted indirect food and non-alcoholic drink taxes. Duty on sweetened table waters was abolished completely but retained on unsweetened equivalents such as soda water, a clear nod to the drinking habits of the middle classes. Sugar duty, meanwhile, was cut at a cost of nearly £18 million, tea duty was halved (£5 million) while that on cocoa, coffee and chicory was also reduced. Dried fruits (mainly prunes) were also made cheaper, which allowed Snowden to wax lyrical about promoting the 'greatest step ever made towards the Radical idea of a free breakfast table'. In another class-conscious move, a cut in entertainments duty was concentrated on the 'cheap seats' in theatres and cinemas.

The Chancellor also targeted several wartime taxes. He scrapped Corporation Profits Duty (at a cost of £2 million), 'unloved by its [Free Trade] parents and reviled by its subsequent [Protectionist] guardians', while the coalition government's duties on imported manufactured articles such as cars, bicycles, musical instruments, clocks and cinema films – collectively known as the 'McKenna duties' after the Chancellor (Reginald) who introduced them – were also swept away, apparently without any discussion in Cabinet and on the basis that the country 'had given a most decisive verdict against such duties' at the election.[26] In order to avoid hardship on traders, however, Snowden announced the duties would expire on 1 August rather than immediately.[27]

Altogether, Snowden cut taxation to the tune of £38 million for the forthcoming fiscal year but left income tax, surtax and death duties completely untouched, something that came as a considerable relief to those who still, even in April, believed a Labour government intended to penalize the wealthy. Of the Capital Levy proposed by the Chancellor and his colleagues during the general election, there was no mention, it having been jettisoned on account of its electoral liability, uncertain yield and propensity to act as a magic money tree for Labour activists.[28] As Roy Jenkins has observed, the real skill of Snowden's statement, later published in pamphlet form as *The Housewife's Budget*, was that what it *did* benefited the 'have-nots', while what it *did not do* relieved the 'haves'.[29]

Budget speeches are well known for taking a toll on those who deliver them, and as the Prime Minister later told the King, this one 'proved too much' for Snowden's strength and he was 'unable to resume his seat without assistance'. Otherwise, MacDonald was full of praise for an old comrade with whom he had not always seen eye to eye:

> Crisp and clear in its delivery, lucid in the exposition of facts and figures, cogent and forceful in the presentation of argument, softened and enlivened by personal touches of wit and human sympathy which distinguished it from most of its predecessors the speech was regarded by all who heard it as being a masterclass.

The Prime Minister also expressed satisfaction at the 'moderation' of Snowden's proposals (rather revealing his lack of foreknowledge), which he said had brought 'delight' to the government's supporters, pleased the Liberals and 'surprised' the Conservatives.[30] As Roy Jenkins put it, if judged on the basis of whether Labour was 'fit to govern', then the Chancellor 'had been a brilliant success'.[31]

The reception inside the House, noted Colin Cross, was almost 'embarrassingly cordial'.[32] Asquith congratulated Snowden for 'proceeding upon a thoroughly sound financial basis', later telling Duff Cooper that William Graham and Snowden ('in that order') were 'by far' Labour's best men,[33] while Sir Robert Horne, the Conservative spokesman, said he had not 'ever heard a more clear or perspicuous statement with regard to our national finance'.[34] At the same time, however, the opposition required a clear line of attack, which manifested itself the following day when Horne (himself a former Chancellor) claimed Labour in government had devalued the pound vis-à-vis the dollar. 'We have paid millions,' he stormed, 'for the felicity of enjoying a Labour Government.'[35]

Not everyone on the left was impressed. When John Maynard Keynes suggested Snowden should have spent £100 million on construction engineering, Hugh Dalton remarked that it was 'a little humiliating to find ourselves less bold than this Liberal economist', but then the Chancellor did not approve of

Keynesianism.[36] The normally critical Beatrice Webb, however, admitted she and her husband Sidney (the Minister of Labour) had been 'wrong' about Snowden and that his Budget had been 'a great triumph', the 'Dark Horse' having 'turned out a winner'.[37] That old Liberal Lord Haldane concurred. 'I told you that Snowden would prove to be an orthodox financier,' he wrote to a friend. 'There is nothing socialistic about this budget.'[38] The Chancellor also promised the Parliamentary Labour Party that his Budget was 'the prelude to the next, it is a preparation for bigger things', which Richard Lyman took to mean his proposed tax on land values.[39]

For Snowden, the media response to his Budget was everything he 'could have desired', with even American journals giving it 'almost as much prominence [as] in the English newspapers'. He joked in his memoirs that if the chorus of praise was justified then he had 'achieved a remarkable, indeed a unique, success in presenting a Budget which had pleased everybody'. The Budget improved hitherto strained relations between the Labour and Liberal benches and even led to speculation that the government would call a 'snap' general election.[40] When a Conservative MP remarked that the Chancellor must have been born under a lucky star, Snowden responded: 'The virtue, oh Brutus, is not in our stars, but in ourselves.'[41]

Snowden's lighter side was not always obvious to colleagues. At times P. J. Grigg, his private secretary, thought the Chancellor 'misused his acidity of tongue and created unnecessary pain or resentment among his Cabinet colleagues', although when the battle at hand was over 'he allowed full rein to a private charm and humour which few could resist – not even those with whom he had been lately in conflict'.[42] Churchill agreed it would be wrong to think of Snowden as 'the spiteful, vindictive Death's-head of his caricatures'.[43]

Charm and humour was the norm for those in Yorkshire with whom Snowden remained close even as Chancellor. Indeed, the Chancellor considered the 'proudest day' of his life not his statement of 29 April but an event which took place three weeks later in Cowling.[44] Banners welcomed, in native dialect, 'Awr Philip', while the Snowdens took part in a 'wildly enthusiastic' meeting at the local Methodist Sunday School.[45] In the Chancellor's speech of thanks, he expressed a desire for his tombstone to read: 'He worked for the poor.'[46]

Visiting the Snowdens at their Tilford home a few months later, Arthur Ponsonby could not quite get over his 'wonder' at seeing his old friend established as Chancellor of the Exchequer. 'He is certainly,' wrote Ponsonby, 'the right man in the right place.'[47]

7

Charles Trevelyan: 'Secondary education for all'

The 1923 Labour manifesto had promised to 'give to every child equality of opportunity in Education', and although this sweeping pledge appeared vague, in this area (if not in others), the first Labour government possessed a firm idea of its intended action. R. H. Tawney's *Secondary Education for All: A Policy for Labour*, published by the party in 1922, was the canonical text, having proposed the expansion of secondary education, the abolition of fees and the raising of the school leaving age.[1]

While other European countries had placed education under the control of ministers, in England and Wales it was administered via the Board of Education, since 1899 a committee of the Privy Council. This Board had a 'president', which made its incumbent sound more powerful than he actually was. As Charles Trevelyan put it in his first major speech as Labour's first President of the Board of Education, he was 'no autocrat'; rather the education system was what he called a 'triple partnership' comprising the State, local education authorities and teachers. As Trevelyan explained:

> Even if I had an enthusiastic Parliament behind me ... even if Mr. Snowden were to offer me many extra millions for the development of Education, I could not, without the goodwill of the Local Education Authorities, make fundamental changes in our Education System ... I need the consent, co-operation

and the conviction of the people, expressed not only through Parliament but through the Corporations and County Councils.

The Board of Education, added Trevelyan, could 'point a direction', but not 'that the direction shall be followed'.[2]

It helped to some degree that Trevelyan was not new to his department, having served as parliamentary under-secretary between 1908 and 1914. Charles Philips Trevelyan was born in 1870 into an impeccably Liberal family. His father Sir George Otto Trevelyan had served as Secretary for Scotland in two Liberal governments, while his mother Caroline was the daughter of a former Liberal MP for Bury. Charles' younger brother was George Macaulay Trevelyan, who, like their maternal great-uncle Lord Macaulay, was an influential historian.

Family tradition had it that the eldest son (and heir to the family baronetcy) entered politics, so following his education at Harrow and Trinity College, Cambridge, Trevelyan acted as private secretary to the Earl of Crewe, the Viceroy of Ireland, before joining the London School Board. In the 1890s he toured North America and Australasia with Sidney and Beatrice Webb and in 1899 entered the Commons at a by-election in Elland. An earnest and rather sanctimonious young MP (H. G. Wells immortalized Charles and George as the Cramptons in his novel *The New Machiavelli*), in 1904 he married Mary (known as Molly) Katherine Bell, a younger half-sister of the archaeologist Gertrude Bell and daughter of the industrialist Sir Hugh. This happy partnership did much to soften Trevelyan's character, although his tactlessness delayed his political advancement until his appointment to the Board of Education in 1908. In government, he advocated taxation of land values, co-operation with Labour on social legislation and abolition of the House of Lords.

Liberal support for the Great War led to a break with the government if not his party, although Trevelyan's active opposition led to deselection and media vilification. But, as Beatrice Webb later reflected, he had clearly demonstrated 'modesty, tenacity and courage'.[3] Trevelyan and Ramsay MacDonald helped found the Union of Democratic Control, which campaigned for parliamentary control of British foreign policy, and Charles became its principal spokesman in the House of Commons. In February 1918, he declared that Labour rather than the Liberals was now best placed to combat social and economic privilege, although it took him until November to follow the logic of that assertion and actually join the Labour Party.[4]

Trevelyan's defection to the Labour Party further strained relations with his elderly father, and he was widely accused of betraying both his class and political heritage. In 1919 he was selected as the Labour candidate for Newcastle Central, a seat he won at the general election three years later. Back in Parliament, Trevelyan aligned himself with the Independent Labour Party and held his seat at the next election held in December 1923.

Trevelyan's appointment as President of the Board of Education was as inevitable as that of Snowden as Chancellor, while the announcement prompted a touching letter of paternal pride from Sir George, soon to celebrate his eightieth birthday:

It is a very great advantage indeed in any genuine and important office, to go to a department the working of which you familiarly know. It is a saving to time, and a source of confidence and comfort, which no one can imagine who has not experienced it, and likewise experienced its opposite.[5]

On 31 January Trevelyan, his wife Molly and 'some' of their six children (who all attended the Quakers' School at Sidcot) had lunch with Tom Jones, the Deputy Cabinet Secretary. Jones expressed his 'delight at finding a President of the Board of Education who had children of his own to educate' for he believed that 'childless' social reformers such as the Webbs 'laboured under serious disqualifications'. When Trevelyan asked what might be achieved in the present Parliament, Jones 'trotted' out the usual proposals:

> development of Secondary Education by taking off the embargo on free places; permission to local authorities to raise the school age to 15; removal of the embargo on adult education; re-organisation of the Board's finances; much closer contact with the local authorities and teachers' representatives.

'All through the meal,' recalled an impressed Jones, 'I had rather the feeling of being under inspection myself.'[6]

During February and March 1924, Trevelyan's plans gradually emerged in a series of press interviews. He told the *Evening News* of his intention to reduce class sizes (it was, he said, 'very uneconomic' to have classes of 50 or 60) and *Time & Tide* that children and young people should not suffer through an inability to pay fees.[7] In the *New Leader*, meanwhile, Trevelyan spoke of getting the country (by which he meant England and Wales) into a 'new frame of mind' when it came to education policy.[8]

The fullest outline of the direction Trevelyan intended to take was set out in a speech at Newcastle on 22 March, later published as *The Broad High Road in Education*. This began with a critique of recent coalition and Unionist education policy. 'A few thousands of pounds saved,' he sneered, 'were of more concern than a few thousands of children well started in life.' Classes, meanwhile, had grown larger, hundreds of highly trained teachers had become unemployed and waiting lists for places extended, all of which had failed to satisfy the 'aspiration for equality of opportunity' which had emerged from the trenches and munitions factories of the First World War.

Central to Trevelyan's vision was the teacher, whom he believed ought to be appreciated, adequately paid and not overworked. To that end he asked Lord Burnham to work out, in conjunction with teachers and local education authorities, 'a fair and adequate settlement of the great salary question'. Effective teachers, he argued, could not be expected to command 'a mob of children', and so instead of classes of 60 or 50, his goal was a 'maximum of 40'.

Trevelyan also took immediate steps to remove a restriction on local education authorities providing meals for 'necessitous' children and announced in Newcastle that he intended to press for an improvement in school accommodation, free up head teachers to promote extra-curricular activities and, ultimately, prepare for 'advanced Education' becoming 'a universal possibility and the common right of all children'. He had already provided (or rather restored) 200 scholarships for children from state schools who showed 'a promising capacity' for a university degree. Trevelyan deployed the analogy of a 'wide staircase' or what he called the 'broad high road':

> The sons of well-to-do parents go to Harrow, Eton, Winchester, Westminster schools, and then on to Oxford and Cambridge, irrespective of whether they are clever or only moderately intelligent. A boy has to be exceedingly dull not to have a full chance of education if his father has £400 a year to spend upon him.

The Labour Party, declared Trevelyan, would not be content until children of all citizens had 'the same chances as the children of rich citizens get to-day'.[9]

Trevelyan's evangelism was also in evidence when, the following month, he became the first President of the Board of Education to address the annual conference of the National Union of Teachers. He told them his main goal was 'to establish personal contact, understanding, and cooperation', and that he desired 'not only to create a new educational atmosphere, but to do things in that atmosphere'. As far as the State was concerned, declared Trevelyan, the era of 'stinginess and discouragement' was at an end:

> Don't look at your profession as a place for soft jobs, look upon it as a profession of noble adventure, and be ready to go and be missionaries of culture in sordid slums or dull villages. I

come here to let you know that I am a human being. (Cheers.)
The human contact is wanted in this work between you and
the Board of Education. Let us go forward together in this
great crusade in which after all I am only the standard bearer.
If the work is to be done, it is you who have got to do it.[10]

'They all stood up and clapped and cheered when I got up,' Trevelyan
later told his wife Molly. 'They cheered again when I sat down. It was
a remarkable ovation. They were entirely pleased with my speech.'[11]

A favourable reaction also greeted Trevelyan's address to the
Independent Labour Party conference in York, during which he
spoke of mobilizing the 'whole instrument' of central government
behind his vision:

If we have five years in power, we shall have twice as many
children getting an advanced education as are getting it now. If
we have ten years in power, we shall have all the children getting
an advanced education and all their teachers having a university
education. If we have ten years in power, there shall be no class
over 10 and most classes in the country shall not be over 30.[12]

While other ministers lived from day to day, fearful of the
government falling at any moment, Trevelyan was looking ahead
to five and even ten years in power.

There was a degree of consensus among Labour, the Liberals and
Conservatives when it came to at least one aspect of Trevelyan's
education programme: all three parties placed great emphasis
on what was then called the 'secondary' school, which actually
meant selective grammars ('elementary' schools were what
would later be termed 'comprehensives'). While Conservatives
regarded secondary schools as necessarily selective, even among
Labourites the mantra of 'secondary education for all' had never
been intended to mean any dilution of this tradition.

If there were differences, therefore, it was over the speed and
extent of reform, rather than its direction. A grievance expressed
within the Labour Party (but largely absent among Conservatives)

was that the existence of fees unfairly stacked the odds against the children of poorer parents. Trevelyan, therefore, supported increasing the number of free places at secondary schools, while Tories fretted that a greater number of scholarship girls and boys would compromise quality. R. H. Tawney urged Trevelyan immediately to increase the percentage of free places offered by secondary grammar schools from 25 to 40 per cent, while entirely abolishing fees within five years.[13]

This suited Trevelyan, not least because he was attuned to the hopes of Labour backbenchers who pressed for more aggressive and ambitious policies. He clearly enjoyed being President of the Board of Education, commanding his officials and feeling, as he told Beatrice Webb, 'his foot firmly on the ladder of political advancement'.[14] As a minister, however, Trevelyan 'monopolised' his departmental responsibilities, leaving his junior minister Morgan Jones (a former teacher) with nothing to do.[15] He was also something of a peacock. Before one Cabinet meeting Trevelyan caused 'a mild sensation' when he arrived wearing a brilliant green scarf. He was, judged the *Evening Standard*, 'one of the best-dressed men in the House of Commons'.[16]

That best-dressed man got his chance to shine at the despatch box on 22 July, when Trevelyan presented the education estimates to the House. Although these stood at the same level as the previous year (nearly £42 million), given the child population of England and Wales was in decline there could still be 'considerable expansion in educational activities', an effective increase of some £500,000–£700,000 which would 'allow for the beginnings of a new era of productive expenditure'. Class sizes were also falling.

Shrewdly, Trevelyan quoted from the Conservative Party's recently published statement of principles and aims, which included a promise that 'secondary and university courses should be brought within the reach of every child'. He therefore proposed a new 'national standard', suggesting that

whereas now there are less than ten per thousand of our population in secondary schools, we should set before ourselves the objective of doubling that number in the next decade, so that there may be 20 per thousand in the secondary schools. I should like to see throughout the country a standard of at least 40 per cent of free places instead of the present 25 per cent, and I should like to see large areas in the next few years experimenting with completely free secondary education.

As for raising the compulsory school age to fifteen, Trevelyan remained 'anxious' to encourage local education authorities to utilize section 4 of the *Education Act 1921*, a tacit admission that the response had so far been disappointing (only Bath and East Suffolk had prepared the necessary by-laws). Some education authorities feared that raising the leaving age might deprive children in their areas of work which would be taken by fourteen-year-olds from neighbouring, less progressive, districts.[17]

In an effort to encourage the 'poor' to keep their children in school beyond the age of fourteen, therefore, Philip Snowden had agreed to fund 50 per cent of maintenance grants for poorer children in elementary schools (up from 20 per cent), as well as 'a large part of the sum for the provision of free places in secondary [grammar] schools'. Trevelyan told MPs of other activities which would make, he believed, schools more 'human and civilising'. School trips to places of natural beauty or historic interest had increased, 'where in a few days they very often learn as much as in the duller round of school life they could learn in as many months'. And while some Members might 'delight to be troubled' by the crowds of children visiting the Empire Exhibition at Wembley, it had made him feel that in future 'we must manage to make it easier for troops of children to come to the Metropolis in years when there is no abnormal attraction'.

To those, concluded Trevelyan, likely to complain that there was 'nothing new' in these proposals or that he was 'not going fast enough', he alluded to his Newcastle speech in arguing that he could not 'build a single school or employ a single teacher myself' but merely 'promote progress by advocacy'. 'I have done already the biggest thing that I could do,' he said, 'which has been to create a new tone of activity and hope in the world of education. It now remains for my fellow-countrymen to co-operate in applying the new spirit to a new notable advance.'[18]

Trevelyan's performance attracted yet more paternal approval. To move the estimates, wrote his father Sir George, was 'the most complete and unmixed pleasure that a political career gives to a politician who is worth his salt ... I am very proud and pleased at your performance.'[19] Randall Davidson, the Archbishop of Canterbury, also 'cordially' welcomed the minister's 'encouraging words' about the 'non-provided' (or religious) schools and assured Trevelyan he was doing his 'very best' to bring about improvements. 'I had some good talk to Edward Wood [Trevelyan's Tory predecessor] about it all,' added Davidson, 'and I like to think of you and him working in harmony to the right end.'[20]

When it came to the grant for free school places, Trevelyan found it necessary to criticize the Exchequer's parsimony. In a remarkably courteous letter given the circumstances, Snowden reminded the President of the Board of Education that he had been unable to accept his original proposal for a grant of £3 for each free school place in excess of 25 per cent on the grounds 'that it was giving too much of the money away without achieving any result'. The Chancellor said that in

> such circumstances I rely on the watchfulness of my Department to safeguard me and my successors from future difficulties. In the present instance I understand that a further discussion has cleared up the difficulty and on the basis of a closer definition than we had hitherto understood of what constitutes a free place for the purposes of this grant we have been able to accept your £3 over 25%.[21]

In August, meanwhile, the Prime Minister asked Trevelyan to address Wales's National Eisteddfod in his place. Speaking, as he later told Molly, 'in an enormous shed with three roofs', he had 'captivated ten to twelve thousand Welshmen'.[22] Having praised

Glamorganshire for expanding its free grammar school places, Caernarfonshire for raising its school leaving age to fifteen, and Wales as a whole for having produced two Welsh premiers 'of humble origin',[23] Trevelyan said he looked to the Principality for 'leadership' in education:

> I want you to lead my land, not in jealous rivalry, or in contemptuous superiority, but in noble example. As your two great rivers the Severn and the Wye draw the inspiration of their streams ... and flow first through their native Wales then spread fertility and beauty down our English valleys ... So may the fertile sources of your national enthusiasm for democratic education first bless your own land with a frank and happy people – then influence and inspire England to like standards – until the fame and hope of your ideals becomes part of the common stock of the world.[24]

Trevelyan was essentially a romantic visionary, albeit one with a practical sense of what was realistically deliverable. As he later reflected, nine months of Labour rule had not been 'so important for what it accomplished as for what it presaged'. 'It enabled the people,' he said, 'to begin to picture to themselves what Labour would be able to do when it had a span of years to work instead of mere months.'[25]

8

'RABBITS OUT OF A HAT'

If taxes, housing and education were in safe (if not wild) hands, the same could not be said of the first Labour government's approach to unemployment. On this complex front, the 1923 manifesto had been ambitious, promising the 'immediate adoption' of national schemes of 'productive work' together with adequate maintenance for those who could not find jobs. These schemes were to include a 'National System of Electrical Power Supply', the development of transport by road, rail and canal, a 'living wage' for agricultural workers and, ultimately, public ownership of mines, railways and power stations. All these, claimed the manifesto, would not only provide a remedy for 'present distress' but constitute 'investments for the future'.[1]

When Ramsay MacDonald faced the House of Commons for the first time on 12 February, his ministers – for unemployment was not the preserve of a single department – had had three weeks in which to develop more detailed plans, but still the Prime Minister's speech included no definite proposals. Instead, there were more promises. Where previous governments had failed to bring employers and the employed together, Labour would ensure trade was 'reinvigorated', the dole 'gap' closed and 'co-operative enterprises' encouraged in agriculture.[2]

Within a week of that speech, however, J. R. Clynes, the Deputy Leader of the House, announced that a Cabinet committee had been established to consider public works schemes for the relief of unemployment, while the same day the Commons endorsed the government's first piece of legislation, the single-clause Unemployment Insurance Bill, which abolished the hated three-week 'gap' (which kicked in after 12 weeks' unemployment benefit). A second Act (with the same name) was the product of a Cabinet battle over the means testing of benefits. While some wanted to abolish this altogether, the Chancellor opposed it as being too expensive. The compromise was that those in receipt of the benefit ought to be 'genuinely seeking work', a test which was to be extended to all claimants. Payment of benefits, meanwhile, was extended from 26 weeks in a year to 41, while payments were raised from 12 shillings a week to 15 for women, and from 15 to 18 for men. The children's allowance was doubled to two shillings.[3]

Although important and useful measures, supporters of the government expected much more. The Prime Minister, according to Deputy Cabinet Secretary Tom Jones, realized the urgency of being able to make, preferably in July, a statement of his government's policy on unemployment 'which would meet the criticism that they had none'.[4]

The new Minister of Labour was Thomas Shaw, a Lancashire textile worker who had served as secretary of the International Federation of Textile Workers since 1911. Robust, blunt and popular, his grasp of industrial politics was not in doubt,[5] but Shaw's appointment put him under considerable pressure. His 'steady-going sagacity' was taken to be 'ineptitude' by proponents of radical measures, while his perceived weaknesses were eagerly exploited by political opponents.[6] Officials mainly remembered him for the pride he took in his private ministerial lavatory, which became known as 'Uncle Tom's cabin'.[7]

Shaw's Parliamentary Secretary was Margaret Bondfield, an altogether more capable figure. One of eleven children born to a lace-working family in Somerset, she was a shop assistant before helping establish (alongside Mary Macarthur) the National Federation of Women Workers. Bondfield achieved several significant firsts: she was the first woman elected to the Trades Union Congress executive (1918), its first female chair (1923), one of the first three women Labour MPs and now the first female minister in any UK government.[8] 'Small, dark-haired, bright-eyed, with an alert tilt of head [and] a humorous curl of lip', Bondfield had memorably declared at Labour's victory rally that the party wanted 'to make the House of Commons the workshop of the nation'.[9]

MacDonald tasked Bondfield with what he called the especially 'difficult question' of enabling women and juveniles to benefit from existing unemployment schemes. As she observed in her memoirs, the

> enormous mass of detail in the Department made it almost impossible to keep in touch with what was going on in connection with other Departments dealing with social services. We were a new team, most of us having to learn the rules of the House as well as master the details of Departmental business, with a gigantic mass of papers to be read, and – what I regard now as the great weakness, no real focusing point for action on any one thing because of the multitude of things to be attempted.[10]

As a consequence, the Ministry of Labour came under almost continuous fire from the opposition benches. Tom Jones recorded a 'deplorable speech' on unemployment during March,[11] in which Shaw asked if his critics thought the government could 'produce schemes like rabbits out of our hat'.[12] Bondfield's 'general forcefulness of character and deep sincerity', however, marked her out as a relative success.[13] MacDonald described Bondfield in glowing terms: her first ministerial statement had been 'performed in the most able manner', while he predicted that with a little more experience she 'should make a first-rate parliamentarian'.[14] 'Maggie Bondfield', declared the Conservative MP Lady Astor, was 'worth twice some of the men in the Cabinet'.[15]

When in early February Tom Jones discussed the unemployment problem with Sidney Webb, the President of the Board of Trade, he was disappointed to find a supposed expert on the subject 'reduced to prescribing a revival of trade as the one remedy left to us'.[16] Nevertheless, Webb – who alongside Arthur Henderson had authored the Labour Party's 1918 constitution – was made chairman of the Cabinet's Unemployment Committee and became the first of the new Labour ministers to speak in the House of Commons, taking questions on the Carriage of Goods by Sea Bill.[17] Derided as 'Nanny' by Conservatives,[18] others regarded Sidney and his wife Beatrice as 'cold, non-human, intellectual machines'.[19] Webb's committee attempted to understand why unemployment – which was concentrated in shipbuilding, engineering and cotton textiles – remained at 10 per cent. Sure enough, its first interim report stressed that the 'only real cure' was 'such a revival of normal trade activity as [would] automatically re-absorb unemployed workmen into their accustomed occupation'. But as Andrew Thorpe has noted, given trade had rallied quite strongly since the second half of 1923, 'this line did not seem wholly fanciful'.[20]

Sidney, recorded Beatrice Webb in her diary, was pleased to find his officials 'polished instruments, waiting on him hand and foot, seemingly acquiescent in any practicable policy'. Those 'instruments' were particularly impressed by Webb's handling of his first Board of Trade meeting. According to Beatrice, the permanent heads remarked to each other: 'These new men are very good – we have at last a business government – these men have trained minds.' The 'peculiar characteristic' of the new government, she added, was that 'every member, except perhaps [John] Wheatley, has been a public servant and not a profiteer'.[21]

As J. R. Clynes observed in his memoirs, it needed 'a workman to understand and settle justly the grievances of workmen'. He added that he

> could remember my own time in a cotton-mill, when I had to work in a sort of bathing-slip because of the intense heat, and when for months on end I never saw the sun at all except on Sundays. Other Labour Ministers had tried coal-mining, engine-driving and so on, and could speak with authority on needed reforms.[22]

Harry Gosling, the Minister of Transport, fitted Clynes' description perfectly. A veteran of London's wharves, he had risen to become the first president of the Transport and General Workers' Union, an office he held until his death. Gosling's task was to sort out transport in London, which by the mid-1920s was crammed full of buses that followed the most lucrative routes and neglected less profitable areas. A London Traffic Bill had been introduced in March and enabled Gosling to regulate services via a new London and Home Counties Traffic Advisory Committee.[23]

This meant, in Gosling's account, 'legislating in a triangle, with the Transport Workers' Union on one side, the omnibus and tramways undertakings on the other, and the political Labour movement forming a third party'.[24] But like Margaret Bondfield, Gosling felt hamstrung by constantly 'trying to reconcile almost impossible demands':

> All the time one was to provide a measure strong enough from the Labour point of view to carry that party, anti-Socialist enough to win the co-operation of the Liberals, and perhaps sufficiently retrograde to secure the necessary Tory support. Clause by clause such considerations had to be borne in mind as against what one felt was the real interest of the community.[25]

Despite these constraints, Gosling also oversaw the reconstruction of many of the country's main arterial highways; in September he cut the first sod on the Glasgow–Edinburgh road, an important stimulus for development in both cities. This was planned to accommodate the vastly increased motor traffic then envisaged, while J. R. Clynes wrote proudly of the trees planted and 'artistic' bridges built so that 'within fifty years, our road system would become one of the most beautiful and effective in the world'.[26]

While the manifesto commitment to bring the railways into public ownership was not pursued, Britain's mines were another matter. Upon his appointment as Secretary for Mines, the thirty-nine-year-old Manny Shinwell had protested that he was not a miner, to which MacDonald apparently responded that it 'would be wrong to put a man in the job who could not take an impartial view'. His clerks, recalled Shinwell, were also 'relieved' to see that a representative of the 'wild men of the Clyde' was, after all, 'a harmless-looking fellow'.[27]

In May Shinwell made parliamentary time for a Private Member's Bill to nationalize the industry. The rationale for this curious approach was that no mandate had been secured at the election for such a radical move, although the Secretary for Mines claimed the government 'whole-heartedly' accepted 'the vital principle embodied in the Measure'.[28] Predictably, the Nationalisation of Mines and Minerals Bill was roundly attacked, with David Lloyd George leading the charge. It was, he told MPs, 'the first concrete example of the new Socialism which is awaiting us'.[29] An alliance of Liberal and Conservative MPs rejected the Bill at its second reading by 264 votes to 168. Still, Shinwell had come to the attention of the Prime Minister, who shared his determination to pursue a moderate path. 'Everybody with whom I discuss the Government agrees that you have been splendid,' wrote the Prime Minister at the end of August, 'and if I could give you any opportunities of showing yourself to better advantage, you can depend upon my doing so.'[30]

On less friendly terms with the Prime Minister was Noel Buxton, the Minister of Agriculture and Fisheries. A recognized authority on agricultural (and indeed foreign) affairs, like Charles Trevelyan he was the privileged son of a baronet and a Liberal convert to socialism. Buxton looked, observed one early biographer, like a Van Dyke portrait, his neatly trimmed beard contrived to disguise injuries from an attempted wartime assassination in Romania.[31]

Having concentrated for so long on foreign affairs, Buxton admitted to feeling 'like a fish out of water' at the Ministry MacDonald asked him to lead in January 1924. He also grew frustrated that the minority Labour government had not forged better working relations with the Liberals, meaning it had

little more than an opportunity for propaganda. I might have used the unrivalled platform which we had, as the first Labour

Government, to make the country more acquainted with our policy for agriculture, through State control of the land, but the practical job was to get through my bill on wage regulation, and therefore to avoid antagonizing people as much as possible.[32]

With farm wages having fallen to pre-war levels, Buxton's Agricultural Wages Bill sought to restore the National Wages Board. When that provision was defeated by Liberals at its committee stage, Buxton was thrown into 'a novel alliance' with the Conservative Edward Wood, later Lord Halifax, who agreed to support separate wages boards in each county as long as the government did not insist on a minimum wage. Although this stipulation led trade unions to demand that the whole Bill be dropped, Buxton appealed over their heads for the Parliamentary Labour Party to support 'what would benefit the poorest class of workers'. It worked, and in the House of Lords Lord Salisbury (the Conservative leader) stuck with the Buxton–Wood compact to guide the compromise Bill to the statute book. 'I derive the greatest satisfaction from the knowledge,' wrote Buxton in his unpublished memoirs, 'that my departure from strict democracy inside the Labour Party was an example of sound principle.'[33]

The successful passage of the Act was not welcomed by the King, who though 'very friendly on the Norfolk neighbour line' (Buxton was the MP for North Norfolk) disapproved of legislation on farm wages.[34] Having recently endured a strike by workers on his Sandringham estate, the Monarch had managed to persuade Bonar Law's government not to go down this path but had no such luck with Labour's wild men. The *Agricultural Wages (Regulation) Act 1924* received Royal Assent on 7 August and immediately increased wages to a level long demanded by farm workers.

At around the same time Buxton's measure made its way through a Commons committee, William Graham, the Financial Secretary to the Treasury, attempted to get authorization for a modest increase in pre-war pensions in order to keep pace with a rising cost of living. Conservative MPs objected on the basis that the proposals did not go far enough, and Graham was forced to withdraw his resolution before reintroducing it on 5 June. When it then encountered more trouble, only a last-minute intervention from Stanley Baldwin – who argued that something was better than nothing – carried the day. Separately, the pensions of elderly parents and other dependants of men who had died on active service were increased, the seven years' limit for claims abolished and sickness benefits restored to widows and orphans.[35]

By May 1924, however, what Ethel Snowden described as 'a violent attack' had developed against the Labour government because of its 'caution and moderation' and failure to bring forward 'extreme Socialist schemes'.[36] As J. R. Clynes observed in his memoirs, Labour suffered because a number of its supporters 'expected us to do everything in a few weeks' – 'unemployment would immediately vanish, poverty would cease, opportunity and wealth would be suddenly equalised' – and, when it became clear they 'could not perform miracles', those supporters 'bitterly' abused the government.[37]

In his speech to the Labour Women's Conference in May, the Prime Minister said a Labour government attempting 'far-reaching social reconstruction work' might either indulge in stunts or 'get up in the morning in the spirit of a workman, and take one's coat off, and do the work quietly and steadily'.[38] The ILP's Unemployment Committee, meanwhile, suggested the government issue an 'ultimatum' to railway companies to proceed with a work plan or 'face the alternative of an immediate nationalization Bill'. The 'entire remainder of MacDonald's career,' observed Richard Lyman sardonically, 'only becomes comprehensible in the light of recommendations such as this'.[39]

Addressing the Commons on 20 May, Tom Shaw failed to produce another 'rabbit', frankly admitting that he had no hope of remedying unemployment during his term of office. With brutal effect, his Liberal predecessor Thomas Macnamara quoted something Ramsay MacDonald had written more than two years earlier regarding the 'risk' a future Labour Cabinet might run in offering 'doles instead of prosperity'. Macnamara suggested that when a suitable opportunity arose, the Prime Minister might state that:

> When we denounced doles and promised work we had no idea how difficult the task of making work would be. We have, therefore, sinned in error and when next we deal with the unemployment problem from the public platform we will add a word of praise instead of abuse for our predecessors because we must admit that, with the best intentions in the world, the most we can do is to follow in their footsteps, leaning far more heavily than they did on doles which we denounce but which in practice we have widely extended and developed.[40]

Two days later the former Conservative Minister of Health Sir William Joynson-Hicks joked about the many 'rabbits we have not yet seen' and moved to reduce the Minister of Labour's salary on the basis that the government had broken its election pledges. Once again, Shaw floundered, attempting to take credit for a 240,000 reduction in the jobless figures, before being reminded that this was 40,000 fewer than the previous year. And when the Minister of Labour spoke of having continued the previous government's unemployment schemes, Macnamara went into rabbit overdrive:

> The rabbit, which last year the Labour party said was the most puny, the most wretched, the most skinny creature that ever escaped a lethal chamber, is to-day lifted from the hat with ostentatious pride and self-satisfaction, and is smoothed down most affectionately by the right hon. Gentleman, and we are told that there never was a bigger or better developed animal.[41]

For once, Margaret Bondfield failed to rise to the occasion, 'courageously', as Philip Snowden sarcastically put it, pinning the blame for government inaction on the Liberals. If opposition MPs, she added, were going to discuss the 'parentage of the rabbit', then they ought to remember that a 'continuous succession' of governments with 'more or less solid and effective majorities' had also failed to tackle unemployment. She said it was

> perfectly clear that no one outside a lunatic asylum would have assumed that the Labour Government could, in a House in which we form a minority ... pass the legislation necessary to acquire the land of the country for the general purposes of the country; to acquire powers over the railway interests of the country, which would be of advantage to the whole community; to acquire control over those forms of property which stand in the way of development, the great roads and the waterways. These things cannot be done by administrative action. They can only be done by coming to a House of Commons with a majority sufficient to secure the necessary legislative powers.[42]

A few days after these exchanges, Beatrice Webb admitted in her diary that Labour had failed to put forward 'a practicable policy', for which its leadership was at fault ('and we among them') for having implied that the prevention of unemployment 'was an easy and rapid task instead of being a difficult and slow business involving many complicated transactions and far more control of capitalist enterprise than any one has yet worked out'.[43]

On 29 May, the Commons voted on the Conservative motion to reduce the Minister of Labour's salary, which, as it was taken to be a confidence issue, the Prime Minister told the King was 'the most critical day which the Government has had to face since it assumed office'. MacDonald himself had spoken for an hour, drawing attention to the 'magnitude and proportions' of the problem and 'the impossibility of working miracles within the short period of four months'.[44] Almost plaintively, he said:

> Until you have been in office, until you have seen those files warning Cabinet Ministers of the dangers of legislation, or that sort of thing, you have not had the experience of trying to carry out what seems to be a simple thing, but which becomes

a complex, an exceedingly difficult, and a laborious and almost heartbreaking thing.[45]

Defeat was only averted when Asquith appealed for 'fair play', and the government survived with a majority of 48.

Spooked by this close shave, the Prime Minister turned the problem of public works schemes over to a committee chaired by Philip Snowden, although the responsible minister (in his capacity as First Commissioner of Works) was actually Fred Jowett, a local government pioneer in his native Bradford. His contribution to the first Labour government, however, proved more picturesque.

The atmosphere at the Office of Works when Jowett first arrived, observed Fenner Brockway, 'suggested that the working-class had really taken command of Whitehall'.[46] He hosted a departmental reception to which he defied custom by inviting 'the most junior members of his staff, even the messenger boys' and paying as much attention to them as a senior permanent official.[47] As First Commissioner, Jowett was in effect a steward for all Crown property, not only government buildings but also Royal palaces and parks, the Houses of Parliament, ruins and even statues in central London.

Upon this modest canvass Jowett left some enduring impressions. He delighted the Cabmen's Union by allowing taxis to be driven through Hyde Park for the first time; suggested to the Postmaster-General that the Royal Fine Arts Commission have a hand in designing telephone boxes (it chose a design by Sir Giles Gilbert Scott); and authorized the Rima statue by Jacob Epstein as a memorial to W. H. Hudson, again in Hyde Park. Upon its unveiling in May 1925, MPs and art critics attacked it as pornographic. Perhaps Jowett's most enduring contribution, meanwhile, remains visible to anyone passing by the National Portrait Gallery just north of Trafalgar Square. At the foot of a statue commemorating Nurse Edith Cavell, he instructed the sculptor to cut 'deep' her memorable last words: 'Patriotism is not enough. I must have no hate or bitterness for anyone.'[48]

Shortly before the summer recess, Philip Snowden finally gave Parliament 'a long outline' of schemes intended to deal with the unemployment problem. 'We have a positive remedy for unemployment,' he declared confidently, 'but the positive remedy for a chronic disease does not effect a cure in a day and a night. The more positive the remedy the slower is its effect.'[49] True to form, Snowden rejected the idea of running or accelerating public works schemes simply for the purpose of providing jobs; the test, he believed, ought to be whether or not such a scheme was a sound investment in and of itself. Among his proposals was an acceleration of the road-building programme, a government subsidy for developing the sugar-beet industry and assistance for agricultural drainage schemes. The Chancellor also pointed to progress on a tunnel under the Thames, consideration of a road to the London docks and an engineering survey in connection with a bridge across the River Tay.[50]

By far the most significant proposal, however, was the planned development of electricity. By the mid-1920s there were no fewer than 532 generating stations in Great Britain, and the government – in line with its election promises – proposed that Electricity Commissioners be empowered to eliminate what Snowden called 'the great waste resulting from the deplorable dis-organisation of the industry'. This they were to do by promoting interchange between competing generating stations via a new 'National Grid'.[51]

This was exactly the sort of scheme in which the normally parsimonious Chancellor revelled. Not only would the (significant) cost be spread over three years but it would provide substantial work for the unemployed. The government intended to introduce the necessary legislation during the 1925 parliamentary session, but instead of standing as a major 'practical demonstration of what Labour in power could accomplish',[52] it fell to a Conservative government to facilitate what became the *Electricity Act 1926*. This measure was carried with the full support of the Labour Party.[53]

'No Government has ever done so much,' declared a pamphlet issued after the first Labour government's departure from office, 'to aid the unemployed as Mr. Ramsay McDonald's Ministry',[54] but of course that was hyperbole. In a valedictory speech to the 1924 Labour Party conference, the Prime Minister admitted that some of its legacy had been 'frankly patchwork':

> Problems like unemployment, an essential feature in the economic system and one that was aggravated by the political, financial and industrial disturbances of the war, and perhaps even more by the hot-headed follies of the peace, present an intricate system of adjustments that have to be dealt with in detail, involving labour, thought, experiment and change in supporting opinion.[55]

The first Labour government might have done its best, but that – even judged by its own standards – was not nearly good enough.

9

WILLIAM ADAMSON: 'FAR FROM REVOLUTIONARY'

When Hugh Macmillan, the Conservative Lord Advocate, first made the acquaintance of William Adamson, the first Labour Secretary for Scotland,[1] he was disarmed to hear him ask: 'You'll help us, won't you? You must remember I'm only a miner.' Then, recalled Macmillan, he 'added with a twinkle': 'You'll be surprised to find what a Tory I am.' Throughout their subsequent association, the Lord Advocate found Adamson to be 'far from revolutionary' but, rather, 'a real canny Scot and a very engaging personality, simple, straightforward, and friendly'.[2]

William Adamson, generally known as Willie, was born at Halbeath near Dunfermline on 2 April 1863, the son of a coalminer. Aged eleven, he began work in the same industry, remaining there for the next quarter of a century. Like many of his colleagues, Adamson's political career was a product of trade unionism. Initially active in the Fife and Kinross Miners' Association, by the time he became Scottish Secretary he was an influential figure in the Miners' Federation of Great Britain.[3]

The involvement of senior Labour figures in the wartime coalition led by David Lloyd George meant that in October 1917 Adamson succeeded Arthur Henderson as chairman of the Parliamentary Labour Party. It was not a happy experience. 'He has neither wit, fervour nor intellect,' judged Beatrice Webb, 'he is most decidedly not a leader, not even like Henderson, a manager of men.'[4] For several difficult years Adamson was the face of his party in the House of Commons. 'It was not a part for which he was well suited,' agreed Mary Agnes Hamilton. 'He is a worker, not a speaker.'[5]

Adamson therefore joined the government in 1924 largely on the basis of his long track record in the Labour movement. He certainly looked the part of a Scottish Secretary and, according to a contemporary biography, 'enjoyed letting his temporary subjects see him in his official capacity'.[6] 'The Government has a lot on hand,' Adamson told the Commons a few weeks after occupying Dover House, the Whitehall base of the Scottish Office:

> We wish to do everything possible to assist our people, either in the Highlands or the Lowlands, and any step that it is possible for us to take we will take gladly. We are here for one thing only, and that is to serve to the best of our ability the people whom we represent.

Although Adamson persuaded the government to take up his Private Member's Bill to enfranchise female voters at twenty-one,[7] otherwise the Scottish Secretary did not loom large during the nine months of the first Labour administration.

The fact that Labour (and Adamson) were theoretically committed to Home Rule (or devolution) for Scotland also created a paradox, for the Scottish Council of the Labour Party (SCLP) enjoyed no such autonomy. 'Had Scotland,' declared the chairman of the 1923 SCLP conference (J. R. Bell of the National Union of Railwaymen), 'been in the enjoyment of Home Rule it is certain that a Labour government would now be in power north of the Tweed.' At its March 1924 gathering, meanwhile, a majority of delegates demanded separate Scottish representation on Labour's National Executive.[8]

As a result, Adamson found himself an awkward conduit for a number of competing claims: was he Scotland's man in the Cabinet or the Cabinet's man in Scotland? Did he speak for the Scottish Council of the Labour Party or its NEC? Whatever the case, in April Ramsay MacDonald welcomed 'some distinguished and undistinguished Scots' to Downing Street for a performance by the Glasgow Orpheus Choir. A rendition of 'Scots Wha Hae' produced a 'severe crack' in the floor of Number 10 which, as Mary Agnes Hamilton observed, 'may or may not have had a symbolic meaning'.[9]

The Prime Minister's political hero had been James Keir Hardie – Labour's founder and first leader – and Hardie had unequivocally supported Scottish Home Rule. This pledge, first made in 1888, endured as the Labour Party grew in Scotland and across Great Britain. At the 1922 and 1923 general elections, almost every Scottish Labour candidate pledged support, while the national party endorsed what Liberals had once called 'Home Rule all round', a more holistic plan of constitutional reform (or decentralization) which also owed something to that other Liberal ideal of Imperial Federation. Home Rule was particularly strongly identified with the Clydesiders, who viewed themselves 'as advance agents of a hitherto unrepresented public, carrying with them some special authority of a new and final order'.[10] James Maxton even railed against a Scottish majority 'steadily voted down by the votes of the English members pledged to a policy of social stagnation',[11] an argument which would become a fixture of Scottish political discourse over the next century.

Two months before the election of December 1923, MacDonald had told the Educational Institute for Scotland there was 'nothing that gave him more backbone' as a Scottish Home Ruler 'than when he looked at the way in which Scottish education was being dominated by English prejudice':

In Scotland we had our separate law courts, our separate church establishment, our separate educational traditions, results, system, and psychology, better than in our sister country, as had been proved by history, and he said that if anything established the claim to Self-government and Self-determination, it was that difference, especially when the Scottish people in that respect were being crushed down, and their advantages taken away from them by hostile majorities from another nation that owed no allegiance to the Scottish people.[12]

But within weeks, MacDonald began to shed this nationalist fervour. On 3 January 1924, Roland Muirhead, a member of the Independent Labour Party active in the Scottish Home Rule Association (SHRA), wrote to the Labour leader urging action should he become premier. MacDonald's reply more than a week later signalled his retreat:

> I am afraid at the moment it is impossible for me with all the burdens of straightening out matters to go into the details about Scottish Home Rule. I am covered up under suggestions from my friends about everything that ranges from the most important matters in the world to the most insignificant. You will all have to keep me out for a little time until I make the general arrangements and then I will come in and tackle details. In any event the man who would have to handle the matter first of all at any rate would be the head of the responsible department.[13]

So, what changed? In his survey of Labour's constitutional policy, Peter Dorey identified three factors: ideological, economic and electoral. Ideologically, developments on the Continent had gradually convinced the party that nationalism was a destructive rather than a progressive force, while many Labour politicians had come to see it as potentially damaging to the unity and solidarity of the British working class, encouraging the idea that Scottish workers somehow had different interests to those in England and Wales.[14] Economically, meanwhile, recession had pointed the movement towards closer involvement with a unified 'British' economy.[15] As J. S. Middleton, the Labour Party's Acting Secretary, put it, he did 'not think [that] all the large measures in which the Scottish, English and Welsh peoples are interested necessarily depend upon self-government for their success'.[16] Finally, as the party became more electorally successful, the fear grew that a potentially secessionist movement might deprive it of a parliamentary majority. As a representative of the NEC remarked at the Scottish Council's 1923 conference, given 'England was always Conservative', it could be that 'the Celtic fringe' would 'save Saxon England from the folly of its own Conservatism'.[17]

Here MacDonald had something in common with his nemesis Lloyd George. In opposition he too had campaigned for Welsh Home Rule and presented himself as a nationalist, yet on becoming premier did little for his native Wales beyond some minor administrative reforms and symbolic gestures. The Clydesiders, meanwhile, decided to take the initiative. At a well-attended meeting organized by the SHRA on 27 April, the Glasgow Gorbals MP George Buchanan said his forthcoming Bill would leave only Customs and Excise, the Post Office and the Armed Services under the control of the Imperial Parliament.[18] And in his own notorious speech at that same meeting, James Maxton said he asked for 'no greater job in life than to make English-ridden, capitalist-ridden, landowner-ridden Scotland into the Scottish Socialist Commonwealth'.[19]

Even some of the Clydesiders felt ambivalent about such rhetoric, which leaned towards full independence from – rather than devolution within – the United Kingdom just a few years after the Irish Free State had followed precisely that path. Tom Johnston, who was to second Buchanan's Bill, hoped not for 'a narrow, sterile, wha's-like-us pride', but of a resurgence of 'that national feeling which seeks to cherish the distinctive quality and genius which is ours by birth, by tradition, by social custom, and which if cherished and strengthened may be to the glory and profit of all mankind'.[20] Again, this distinction between progressive patriotism and secessionist nationalism would become a familiar refrain.

George Buchanan moved the second reading of his Government of Scotland Bill on 9 May. This was the latest iteration of numerous attempts to legislate for a Scottish Parliament since the late nineteenth century, and he claimed its 'principle, if not every word of the Bill', was supported by 56 out of Scotland's 74

MPs. Buchanan, a Glasgow-born trade unionist, could not help but allude to recent events across the Irish Sea:

It may not be a characteristic of the Scottish race to make their demands in the same way as, say, the Irish people, but nevertheless, while their methods may differ and their steps may alter, the Scottish people are as sincere, and for the most part as anxious, for this Measure as even our friends in Ireland were for their own form of government.

But his (or rather 'our') proposals did not, added Buchanan, amount to 'a complete Scottish Free State' but were, rather, roughly equivalent to the devolved Parliament of Northern Ireland established in 1921. They may be debating, he observed, in an 'Imperial Parliament', yet at the same time MPs were required to vote on extremely local measures (he cited Harry Gosling's London Traffic Bill as an example). The SHRA and others, continued Buchanan, had 'tried constitutional methods':

We have sent a majority of advanced Members to this House. We have looked with hope and aspiration to have something done for our problems, and it has not been done. I do not blame Parliament, I blame its methods and make up ... In England you have the Home Secretary responsible for one part of the business; you have the Minister of Health responsible for housing; the Minister of Labour for his particular Department; but in Scotland it is a jumble up, and one man is supposed to be responsible for all.

That 'one man' spoke towards the end of the debate. But while Willie Adamson said the government gave the 'general principle' of the Bill its approval, at the same time it recognized that it raised

a large and vital issue which is of importance to this country as well as to Scotland, and what they suggest, [what] they are prepared to do is to appoint a Committee to examine this

whole question and report to the House. That Committee, they
suggest, should be arranged through the ordinary channels.[21]

As it was a Private Member's Bill, a 'closure motion' was
required to end debate on its second reading and put the
Government of Scotland Bill to a vote. But just as this was
supposed to take place, dozens of Conservative MPs rose to
continue the debate. This prompted George Buchanan to move
that the question 'be now put', but the Speaker declined, a
decision which led to a 'burst of outrage' as Ian Macpherson,
a former Liberal Chief Secretary for Ireland, James Maxton
and Neil Maclean all made their own attempts to move the
closure. Still the Speaker declined to put the question and
instead instructed the Commons Clerk to read the remaining
Orders of Business. This meant discussion had automatically
terminated and the Bill 'talked out'. 'There will be no Orders
read,' stormed David Kirkwood. 'You have no right, Mr.
Speaker, to refuse the Closure. I move the Closure now ... We
are going to have the Closure now ... We have not been treated
fairly. Where is the respect due to the House?'[22] Eventually
the Speaker, 'being of opinion that grave disorder has arisen',
adjourned the House.[23]

This was reminiscent of the rowdy scenes which had so
infuriated Ramsay MacDonald in the previous Parliament.
Strikingly, the Prime Minister reported these events to the King
with relish rather than anger. 'The debate came in like a lamb,'
he wrote in his regular parliamentary report, 'and went out like a
lion.' The failure to achieve a second reading 'proved altogether
too much' for the 'equilibrium' of the Clydesiders, 'which is
never capable of standing a very savage strain'. 'For the next ten
minutes pandemonium reigned,' the Prime Minister continued.
Kirkwood, Maclean and Maxton 'could be seen gesticulating
wildly and hurling abuse at the chair', but the Speaker, he said
approvingly, had remained calm. 'It was an unhappy incident,'
concluded MacDonald, 'only relieved by the conduct of the
Speaker who acted up to the best traditions of the Chair.'[24]

It was clear from this account that the Prime Minister believed the Clydeside MPs had become their own worst enemies, though with the happy consequence that he could more easily take no further action. His opportunity to make this clear came less than a week later, when Buchanan pleaded for extra parliamentary time. Coldly, MacDonald regretted that it was not possible 'in view of the state of public business', despite J. R. Clynes having indicated the previous day that, if possible, time *would* be made. Buchanan sarcastically asked if questions affecting Germany, the Ruhr 'and every other part of the world are to be given preference over questions affecting our own home conditions, and particularly Scotland?'. Neil Maclean then asked if the House was to understand that 'no further discussion' regarding the Government of Scotland Bill would take place that session, and that it would 'have to go through the same procedure' the following year should 'some Scottish Member be fortunate enough to get a place in the Ballot'. Even more coldly, the Prime Minister simply said: 'That is so.'[25] Reporting these exchanges to the King, as usual in the third person, MacDonald was even more self-satisfied:

> The Prime Minister's refusal to grant facilities [for further debate] appeared to create a little resentment amongst some of the Glasgow Members, but the Prime Minister by a short and somewhat unexpected answer knocked his critics off their balance and they had not recovered it in time to put another supplementary question before the next question was called.[26]

Thereafter the whole affair petered out, although even with government support it is not certain the Bill would have reached the statute book. On 15 July, David Kirkwood introduced another Private Member's Bill, this time to repatriate the Stone of Destiny from Westminster Abbey to Scotland, but this too failed to progress.[27]

The Cabinet, meanwhile, made desultory efforts to follow through with Adamson's promise of a committee 'to examine this whole question' by asking J. R. Clynes, the Lord Privy Seal, to prepare potential terms of reference. He quickly ruled out a Speaker's Conference such as that of 1919–20 ('not fruitful of useful results') and instead settled on a Royal Commission, which could be

> strictly limited in numbers, strong in its composition, and generally of a character to commend national approval. I feel convinced that only by such means could proposals involving such great constitutional changes be formulated with any chance of ultimately being passed into law.[28]

Cabinet, however, turned this down on the basis that constitutional matters ought to be investigated by MPs.[29] Adamson then suggested the following terms as the basis of discussion with opposition parties:

> To consider the formulation of a scheme of devolution whereby legislative and administrative matters relating solely to England, Scotland or Wales respectively might be dealt with by national legislatures, and constitution of such legislatures, their relation to the Imperial Parliament, their financial powers, and the scope of their jurisdictions and functions, and to report.[30]

Questioned in the Commons on 18 June, however, the Prime Minister said the government had been

> unable to secure the co-operation of all parties in setting up a Committee somewhat on the model of the late Speaker's Committee which inquired into this subject with some others. In view of the undertakings it has on hand already, the Government regret that it is impossible for them at the moment to pursue the matter further this Session.[31]

When he received the freedom of the City of Glasgow a few days later, MacDonald refused to meet local members of the SHRA,[32] which must have caused tension given the Prime Minister and his daughter Ishbel were being hosted by the pro-Home Rule Glasgow ILP Federation.[33]

On 21 July 1924, MacDonald received another delegation comprising Tom Johnston, Neil Maclean and Duncan Graham, for which he was briefed on attempts to legislate for Home Rule since 1908.[34] That trio of MPs left disappointed by the same excuses first articulated in May, as did a separate group of Liberal MPs. While Home Rule for Scotland ostensibly remained Labour policy, it was, judged Michael Keating and David Bleiman, simply 'too far down the list of national priorities for it to be worth putting the Government's survival at risk'.[35]

As a result, William Adamson cut a rather sorry and isolated figure. On 23 August he gamely attended the Scottish Home Rule Association's annual rally to mark the anniversary of the execution of patriot William Wallace. In his remarks, Adamson tried to keep the dream alive, saying he looked forward with 'confidence' to the time when Scottish legislation would be 'enacted by Scotsmen in a Scottish Assembly'.[36] Almost a year later, meanwhile, Roland Muirhead sent the Labour leader a letter full of resentment at his old comrade's failure to progress the cause:

Why the Government of which you were the head last year failed to support the Scottish Home Rule Bill, I cannot explain (a non-Socialist and non-party measure, just such a Bill as a minority Government might be expected to pass). I must candidly admit that [it] caused your stock as a Scotsman to fall heavily in my estimation.[37]

Ramsay MacDonald did not reply.

JIMMY THOMAS: 'NO MUCKING ABOUT WITH THE BRITISH EMPIRE'

For a few months after the fall of the first Labour government, James Henry Thomas liked to tell a story about his first day at the Colonial Office. On his arrival, a porter refused to believe he was the new Secretary of State. When Jimmy, as he was generally known, politely insisted, 'I *am* the Secretary of State', the porter turned to a fellow janitor and said, sotto voce: 'Poor fellow! Another shell-shock case!' 'It was certainly a shock,' Thomas would reflect, 'to be mistaken for a wandering lunatic.'[1]

The story captured something of Thomas's ebullience and self-deprecation mingled with a love of status. He was devoid of qualms about establishment plaudits and 'high' company, for as far as he was concerned that signalled the growing acceptability of the Labour movement. In what would become another familiar Thomas refrain, he believed it was 'a great and democratic Constitution' which 'enabled the engine-cleaner of yesterday to become a Secretary of State to-day'.[2]

Jimmy Thomas was born on 3 October 1874 at Newport, Monmouthshire, the illegitimate son of a domestic servant. Raised in poverty by his grandmother, a widowed washerwoman, he worked part-time as an errand boy from the age of nine, polished brasses in a chemist's shop and later joined the Great Western Railway as an engine cleaner, where he visualized the 'footplate of [a] G.W.R. locomotive as the height of human ambition'.[3] Active in the Amalgamated Society of Railway Servants, Thomas was elected the Labour MP for Derby in 1910, and three years later helped form the National Union of Railwaymen (NUR), of which he became general secretary in 1916.

The First World War made Thomas a major public figure, but while he personally supported the war effort, he also defended Ramsay MacDonald's right not to. Towards the end of the war, he called a halt to unofficial strikes in South Wales by threatening to resign from the NUR, while during another (this time official) strike in 1919 the Cabinet seriously discussed ordering his arrest. Thomas's 1920 publication *When Labour Rules*, meanwhile, sought to reassure the middle classes they had nothing to fear (and something to gain) from a Labour government committed to moderation and parliamentary government. By the end of 1923, he was a political and trade union 'fixer' of some stature.[4]

Following the indecisive election of December 1923, Thomas had become one of the few senior party figures to remain in close contact with the Labour leader while he was at Lossiemouth, although one commentator was puzzled by their apparent friendship:

> The Prime Minister is a man of affairs, Mr. Thomas is a man of the world. The Prime Minister is, so far as his duties permit, an assiduous reader. It is doubtful if Mr. Thomas ever reads anything but the cheaper newspapers. The Prime Minister is a serious-minded man. Mr. Thomas's mind is essentially frivolous.[5]

Thomas's private secretary believed the answer lay in his 'unfailing ... courage and spring', which made him 'a great source of strength to the Prime Minister, who had equal courage but much less resilience, and sometimes had to be fished-up out of the Slough of Despond'.[6] Thomas was delighted when MacDonald sent him to the Colonial Office, where he followed in the footsteps of Winston Churchill and the Duke of Devonshire.

Thomas made a point of retaining the services of the discreetly homosexual polymath Eddie Marsh, who had served both men as private secretary.[7]

Surprisingly, they hit it off, finding amusement in a caricature which showed them dressed as one another, the Colonial Secretary in evening dress, Marsh in corduroy trousers tied under his knees with string. It was, recalled Marsh,

> delightful to see him settling down in his startlingly novel position. He knew of course the tradition by which Civil Servants have no politics in their work … but one could feel that he wasn't quite sure whether this would hold good when the party was Labour, and that for a day or two he was slightly on the defensive. It wasn't long before this cat's-ice was broken, and entire confidence set in. He was a capital master and companion.[8]

Marsh told Hugh Dalton that while his 'old chief' had used a bell to get his attention, his 'new chief puts his head round the door of my room, and says: "Come 'ere, you b—!!"'[9] Thomas's first staff briefing ended with the declaration: 'Now, boys, let's have a beer all round.'[10] The Colonial Office was not used to such informality.

The timing of Thomas's appointment, however, was unfortunate, the Associated Society of Locomotive Engineers and Firemen (ASLEF) having declared a strike just as Stanley Baldwin's government left office. Given that Thomas was expecting a call any day from Downing Street, he engaged in a war of words with John Bromley, ASLEF's general secretary. 'The strike, as I anticipated, is a complete fiasco,' he told the press. 'The best evidence of that is the number of trains running this morning.' Undeterred, Bromley said he did not 'fear' continuing the action 'as long as is necessary', adding that Thomas's account of a meeting with railway colleagues was 'garbled and incorrect'.[11] When the King apparently asked about Bromley during a Privy Council meeting, Thomas said: 'You can take it from me, your Majesty, he's a bloody 'ound.'[12] A hostile article later accused

Thomas of 'shamefully abandoning' his trade union post 'in the face of the enemy' and 'beetling away to the Colonial Office'.[13]

Given that he guaranteed 'good copy', the press loved Jimmy Thomas. 'Less than forty years ago he was running to old women with headache powders,' gushed the *Daily Express*. 'Now he, more than any other man, is responsible for keeping unfrayed the cords of fellowship and understanding that bind the Empire together.'[14] The civil servant Tom Jones also considered him the 'ablest politician' in the new government, possessing a 'cold brain'.[15] 'He is sane, sagacious, balanced, patriotic,' judged the Earl of Birkenhead, 'in my opinion he is no more a socialist than, say, Lord Parmoor or Mr. Winston Churchill.'[16]

Thomas was contemptuous of 'narrow and little-minded' colleagues who made a fuss about who wore what to the Privy Council meeting on 23 January ('Our Constitution does not stand or fall,' he remarked, 'by the dress Ministers of the Crown wear on gala days').[17] He delighted in both formality *and* informality. When the Duke of Devonshire called on his successor, he was surprised to be grasped by the elbow as Thomas exclaimed: 'Why, it's Victor! How very nice of you to call.'[18] And when asked by 'a white-wanded equerry' if he would escort the Duchess of Atholl into a State ball, he replied, according to Henry 'Chips' Channon, 'in a very loud voice "Rather", and left his house-keepery little wife to fend for herself'.[19]

Inevitably, Beatrice Webb disapproved of Agnes Thomas, who she said was

> a retiring and discreet climber and has never pretended to be specifically Labour, and the daughters are so far removed from Labour circles that one of them, when asked by a partner at a Half-Circle Club dance whether she was a 'Fabian', retorted indignantly, 'No: I am a "Thomas"'![20]

Webb later repeated her snobbery about Thomas's 'deliberately persistent dropping of his h's' in a newspaper interview, calling it an 'artistic touch ... like the red rouge on a star actress's lips

... which adds style to his shrewd and witty speeches'.[21] Eddie Marsh thought his boss 'misplaced them with conscious art', while he left this vivid sketch of Thomas's typical approach to an after-dinner speech. He would begin by

> seizing on something that had fallen from a previous speaker, turn it to ridicule, and proceed to a series of outrageous insults which set everyone, including the victim, in a roar; and then, without any transition, to rise from this mood and say quite simply and seriously, often with moving eloquence, what he really felt and meant about the subject in hand.[22]

Thomas deployed that eloquence during his first public engagement as Colonial Secretary, an Australia Day luncheon at which he sat next to the Prince of Wales. Speaking of the UK having just passed through a 'momentous period; a sort of blood-less revolution', he added that neither the King nor his son had been at all 'apprehensive'. As we have seen, this was not entirely true, but Thomas was purposefully stressing the new administration's moderation. Loud cheers greeted Thomas's conclusion, that the same constitution ('so broad, so wide, so democratic') which had transported him from Unity House to the Colonial Office, 'must be preserved, and the Empire which provides it must be maintained'.[23]

No part of the Empire continued to cause greater concern than that closest to Great Britain. Although the fledgling Irish Free State was a Dominion rather than a colony, relations between Dublin and London were Thomas's responsibility. The Free State, however, was wary, the new Colonial Secretary having 'never shown himself conspicuously friendly' to Ireland.[24] Tim Healy, the Governor-General of the Free State, identified a deeper problem, that the new Labour government was 'absolutely ignorant about Irish affairs'.[25] A Daily Herald correspondent also observed that 'Labour was weary of the Irish question and loth to provoke it to new life.'[26]

In opposition, Labour had supported all sorts of constitutional settlements before the Anglo-Irish Treaty had been signed in

December 1921, although in general terms it was pro-nationalist and anti-Ulster Unionist. Labour in government, therefore, 'had no Irish past to live down or to live up to'.[27] This, to a degree, was useful. As Tom Jones recorded of an early meeting, Thomas had

> no intention of being a passive instrument in the hands of the officials. Yesterday they had a Conference on the Irish Question ... [N. G.] Loughnane, our man in Dublin, put the case for the South with such conviction that Thomas rounded on him as an Irish Free Stater!

Under Article 12 of the Treaty – which had come into effect on 6 December 1922 – Northern Ireland had been faced with the choice of joining with the rest of the Free State or remaining a devolved part of the United Kingdom. As everyone expected, it chose the latter, but its 'opting out' had automatically triggered the formation of a Boundary Commission, which was to revise the border between the two parts of Ireland. The trouble was that Dublin and Belfast had wildly different interpretations of the Commission's remit. The former believed it would result in the transfer of Catholic-majority counties like Fermanagh and Tyrone to Free State jurisdiction, while the latter loudly declared it would surrender 'not an inch' of the territory assigned under the *Government of Ireland Act 1920*.

Although repeatedly delayed by the Irish Civil War and British political instability, Dublin had finally nominated its representative to the Boundary Commission in 1923, while Belfast continued to drag its feet in the hope that a more sympathetic and 'Unionist' government would eventually displace Labour from office. But until both representatives were in place, the Commission – as per the terms of the Treaty – could not be fully constituted, and the UK government was powerless to act. Much of Thomas's time, therefore, was spent attempting to break this apparently 'quite insoluble' impasse.[28]

Colonial Office officials feared that if London failed to 'honour' the Treaty then the Free State would abolish the post of Governor-General and the oath of allegiance to the King, thus 'virtually setting up a Republic'. Given that the whole object of the Treaty had been to keep the Free State under the Crown, this was considered an intolerable prospect. Tom Jones (an old Ireland hand regularly despatched to gather intelligence from what he disparagingly called 'the Irish bog') also worried that Dublin would 'take the matter' to the League of Nations, to which it had been admitted in September 1923; just the sort of 'spectacular play', he believed, 'which would appeal to them'.[29]

When an April 'conference' on the boundary problem broke up without agreement, officials were shocked to discover Thomas in his 'very Victorian' drawing room listening to reports of proceedings on a 'loudspeaker' and consuming an 'abundant supply of whiskey and soda'. As Tom Jones recalled, he was

> in no way dismayed at the result of the day's work, but when I suggested bringing the P.M. into the business he would not hear of it. He had full authority to act, the Cabinet would do what he advised, so would 'Mac' ... He is very proud of himself as a negotiator, but I fancy knowledge of his methods must be spreading. [When] Cope [another official] ventured to suggest that [Sir James] Craig might be placated with a peerage [to which] Thomas replied: 'He can have a b...y Dukedom if it will do the trick.'[30]

Sir James Craig was the ruddy-faced Prime Minister of Northern Ireland and leader of the Ulster Unionist Party which dominated the Parliament of Northern Ireland established in May 1921. An early test of the relationship between the two governments concerned Cahir Healy, who had been re-elected the Nationalist MP for the Westminster constituency of Fermanagh and Tyrone in December 1923. Following the assassination of a Unionist MP in May 1922, Healy and hundreds of others had been interned. While the Unionist government had released Healy as soon as Labour took office, he was still prevented from returning to his constituency. Ramsay MacDonald had made his feelings clear in a letter to Sir James Craig on 15 February, arguing that while the 'legal right' was not in question, it might 'raise an issue of constitutional privilege between the two Parliaments, and His Majesty's Government may be involved in a debate – in which the administration of your Government of the powers assigned to it may become a direct issue'.[31] Taking the hint, Craig quickly ensured Healy was able to resume his seat in the UK House of Commons.

London, however, proved unable to persuade Craig to compromise with W. T. Cosgrave, his Free State counterpart, over the boundary issue, its preferred alternative to the Commission required under the Treaty. MacDonald and Thomas tried to move things along by appointing Mr Justice Feetham, a Welsh-born South African judge, chairman, but still Belfast refused to appoint its representative. At the end of May the Prime Minister intervened and made one last effort to get Cosgrave and Sir James Craig to reach a compromise during a Chequers summit. As they waited for a delayed Cosgrave, MacDonald suggested to Craig that he preside over a conference at which maps and data pertaining to the border could be examined. Sir James politely suggested that he might have 'underestimated the complexity of the problem', illustrating his point 'by reference to the somewhat complicated pattern of the carpet'. When the Free State leader finally arrived, the discussion was polite but futile.[32] Cosgrave said the Irish people suspected London wanted 'to shelve the whole matter',[33] at which MacDonald resorted to eloquence, referring to the Treaty as 'but the dry bones of a settlement'. 'In the last two years you have clothed it with flesh,' he added, 'but we have yet to breathe into its frame the living spirit of reconciliation.'[34]

On 25 June several questions were formally referred to the Judicial Committee of the Privy Council, a sort of final court of appeal for the British Empire:

- Whether in the absence of a Commissioner appointed by the Government of Northern Ireland the Boundary Commission could be constituted;

- If the answer to this question was 'in the negative', whether the Governor of Northern Ireland could be instructed to make the appointment;
- Whether, if the question to this was also 'no', the UK government could make the appointment on Northern Ireland's behalf; and
- If the answer to this too was 'no', whether there was 'any constitutional method' of bringing the Boundary Commission into existence if the Northern Ireland Government maintained its refusal to co-operate.[35]

On 31 July the Judicial Committee answered all four questions in the negative, after which Thomas morosely informed the House of Commons that the government had no choice but 'to introduce legislation to give effect to what was the undoubted intention of the Treaty, and to press for the passage of that legislation through Parliament regardless of the consequences to themselves'.[36] That caveat was intended as a warning to Conservative 'die-hards' not to make trouble on something that had long been a non-partisan matter. But while Lloyd George immediately assured Thomas of Liberal support, Stanley Baldwin remained silent.

A minority Labour government had now come to appreciate Liberal and Conservative fears regarding the destructive effect of the Irish Question on the affairs of Great Britain. Quixotically, Thomas and his colleagues still hoped for a bilateral solution which might avoid the need for emergency legislation, and on 2 August Cosgrave and Lord Londonderry, the Acting Prime Minister of Northern Ireland (Sir James was ill) held lengthy talks with MacDonald and Thomas at Downing Street. The Prime Minister made 'a strong appeal upon the grounds of empire stability for the agreed boundary proposal' and hinted at the possibility of further 'constitutional changes' should the House of Lords try and block an amending Bill.[37] The King was also warned that if legislation – which was to give London the authority to appoint Northern Ireland's representative to the Boundary Commission – failed to clear either House of

Parliament he would be asked for a dissolution.[38] 'Did any P.M. have my burdens,' MacDonald asked his diary rhetorically. 'Conference with French & Germans, Anglo-Soviet negotiations, Ireland & now the murder of her wars.'[39]

Two days later Thomas and Arthur Henderson sailed to Dublin to persuade Cosgrave to give them more time before legislation was introduced at Westminster. To illustrate London's 'good faith', however, the government laid the proposed Bill before Parliament and promised to reconvene on 30 September rather than 28 October as previously planned. Reluctantly, Cosgrave agreed to yet another delay and on 4 August an Agreement – in effect a Treaty amendment – supplementing Article 12 of the 1921 accord was signed by MacDonald and his Free State counterpart.

Introducing the Irish Free State (Confirmation of Agreement) Bill on 6 August, Thomas appealed to the British people and press not to inflame old prejudices. The previous day Ramsay MacDonald had told Lady Londonderry, now a close friend, that while 'rigidly opposed to hasty legislation' his government also had to make clear it meant to 'keep faith' with its Treaty obligations. He also pleaded with her to get her friends 'to meet us reasonably within the period between now and the end of September' and not 'revive those evil passions of hate and strife'. If, added the Prime Minister, his government began to 'interpret' Article 12 for itself, it could only mean

> jumping out of the frying pan into the fire. You are all on the other side of the world of people and ideas from me and when I go from this I hope it will be never to emerge again from my own fireside; but whilst the sun is up and I doomed to bear these burdens and because I really did enjoy our talks, I beg you to help like a dear good woman to give us peace.[40]

A week later Lady Londonderry replied with a letter at once full of prejudice (the 'Southern Irish,' she wrote, 'are an inconsequential race ... very like children') and indignation at her friend's approach to Northern Ireland. If she and her friends were to help him, she argued, then he, too, 'must be reasonable too and keep the faith with Ulster':

> The truth is that in the past England has always ignored Ireland, when they had other things to think about. Then, either because they wanted the Irish vote to carry through some policy or other to clear the decks for other issues, their attention becomes riveted on this unhappy land and Great Britain proceeds to surrender everything, dignity and self respect not to mention loyal supporters.

Londonderry ended with an appeal to MacDonald's romanticism, noting that north-east Ulster had originally been 'won by a McDonald' who had cut off his left hand and thrown it from his boat 'on to the land which he claimed':

> Won't you another McDonald [*sic*], extend to us the other hand, the right hand of fellowship and maintenance and throw us the olive branch. This is my request to you. I am on the other side of the water, but not of the world, as you suggest … You may rely on my helping you all I can to keep the peace only you must help us too.[41]

The Irish Free State had declined to host a pavilion at the Empire Exhibition, which was opened by the King at Wembley on 23 April (St George's Day). Although long in gestation, Thomas realized this offered a perfect opportunity to showcase his party's fitness to govern both the UK and its sprawling Empire. Thomas stood proudly alongside the King-Emperor at the opening ceremony wearing full Court dress,[42] and in a later toast declared that the government 'intended above all else to hand to their successors one thing when they gave up the seals of office, and that was the general recognition of the fact that they were proud and jealous of, and were prepared to maintain, the Empire'.[43]

In his own speech, the King said the Exhibition represented the whole Empire 'in miniature'; Ramsay MacDonald, who first visited on 8 May, called it 'a doll's house representation of our great Commonwealth'. Costing £12 million and spread over 220 acres, it proved one very large and expensive doll's house, which included a replica of the Taj Mahal and a mountain of Australian butter. It also failed to break even, at least in part due to a run of phenomenally wet weather. Two weeks after the Exhibition opened, Thomas received the freedom of his native Newport. The Empire, he said in his acceptance speech, included the

> great Indian race of 300,000,000 people, brown but human. They were men and women with souls and aspirations, and then they had the black population – all part of the British Empire. Our job, our object, and our mission were to keep in mind that, however illiterate, however ignorant were these people, and however badly these people may have been treated in the past, here was a trust we had undertaken and which we should fulfil.[44]

These remarks revealed both contemporary racial prejudice and a rather clumsy attempt to distinguish Labour's Imperialism from that of the Conservatives.

What exactly this meant in practice was less clear. When the historian Sir Sidney Low rather patronizingly wrote that Thomas's appointment would help 'bring home to Labour' and 'to the English and Scotch working classes in general', a 'deeper and wider consciousness of the meaning and character of the world-realm for whose governance and guidance they are now, in large part, responsible', Thomas responded that one might 'infer' from his characterization that the Dominions and Colonies somehow 'belonged' to the UK. 'I want the working-classes of Great Britain,' he wrote, 'to think of these distant countries as belonging not to themselves but to the 70 million people who live in them.'[45] This, however, was difficult to square with using air attacks as a deterrent to tribal disturbances in Iraq, a policy William Leach, the under-secretary for Air, found himself defending in the Commons.[46]

Influential in guiding Labour's rather muddled approach to these questions was the Clydeside MP Tom Johnston. He had developed a 'positive' concept of Empire which was roundly attacked by those on the left, particularly communists, as little more than Imperialism-lite. To this, Johnston replied that socialism would not be advanced by the disintegration of the Empire, which would simply leave former British colonies, to quote Philip Snowden, at the mercy of 'the predatory designs of other powers'.[47] Pointing to the existence of other Labour governments in the Dominions, Johnston believed Imperialism 'might be made the greatest lever for human emancipation the world has ever known'.[48] A Commonwealth Labour Group even included John Wheatley and George Lansbury among its members.

To this Johnstonian vision, Thomas added a dollop of working-class sentimentalism. He argued that the Empire's foundations had been laid, 'not only by traders and explorers in search of wealth or fame', but also by 'humble men and women of British stock who left these islands for distant parts of the world, seeking only to secure a livelihood that was denied them at home'.[49] There were also lashings of paternalism. Thomas agreed with previous Tory governments that the UK's 'paramount duty' was to act as a 'trustee for the natives over whom she rules', then, 'gradually, by a process of educating and encouraging', he predicted, 'we can help these backward people to a greater sense of responsibility'.[50] In his Empire Day message of 24 May, Ramsay MacDonald waxed lyrical about 'exploring ships' which had carried 'our people, our institutions, our traditions, and our methods ... all over the earth'. He added:

> Our days of voyaging are not over. The world of mind and idea lies around us in unexplored tracts more vast by far than this earth was to our seamen, and the Commonwealth of Nations centring in this Motherland still hears the call to go out in an Elizabethan spirit of gallantry and doughtiness in search of liberty, justice, and peace.[51]

'Far from wanting to lose our Colonies,' declared J. R. Clynes, 'we are trying to keep them ... Labour prefers less imperialism and more common sense.'[52]

But if Labour preferred less Imperialism, appointing Lord Olivier, who had 20 years' experience managing British possessions in the Caribbean, Secretary of State for India seemed a curious move. Not only that, but the First Lord of the Admiralty was Lord Chelmsford, a former Viceroy of India who had publicly defended the 1919 Amritsar massacre and instigated repressive measures which provoked Gandhi's first civil disobedience campaign. Neither had dissented from the Prime Minister's message to the Gandhian Congress shortly after taking office, that 'no party in Britain' would be 'cowed by threats of force or policies designed to bring the Government to a stand-still'.[53] This was Imperial business as usual.

And if Olivier and Chelmsford were cautious pragmatists when it came to Indian nationalism, Josiah Wedgwood (who had hoped to get the India Office) and Charles Trevelyan were Radicals who believed a Labour government provided the perfect opportunity to accelerate the sort of Home Rule or Dominion status recently won by (most of) Ireland. MacDonald, however, sided with the pragmatists, and in February turned down Nehru's request for a round-table conference to prepare a new Indian constitution.[54] Two months later, the government even jettisoned the idea of direct talks with Indian leaders (Olivier thought them too 'upper-caste'), while in September MacDonald reluctantly agreed to more repressive legislation.[55] 'We have had beastly bad luck,' the Prime Minister later told John Wheatley, 'in the problems we had to face.'[56] The *Socialist Review* did not believe in luck, later judging India to be 'the one great failure of the Labour Government'.[57]

While Indian nationalists agitated for greater autonomy, the Union of South Africa (formed in 1910) was altogether more loyal to the Crown. Having clarified the timetable for the necessary Irish legislation, on 8 August Thomas set sail for Cape Town as head of the Empire Parliamentary Association's UK delegation accompanied by his wife Agnes and their two daughters. He was the first Colonial Secretary to visit since Joseph Chamberlain in the bitter aftermath of the Boer War.

General Hertzog, the South African Prime Minister and a Boer nationalist, greeted Thomas and the other delegates (which included the Conservative MP Sir Douglas Hogg, later Lord Hailsham) at Cape Town on 25 August. Soon Thomas's famed negotiating skills had won a notable concession, with Hertzog agreeing that South Africa would take part in the Imperial Conference planned for 1926.[58] Over the next ten days, the Colonial Secretary travelled to Durban, Bloemfontein, Johannesburg, Basutoland and Zululand, making a speech in every major city of the Union. Thomas said he was there neither 'to interfere nor to dictate', but provoked controversy when he pleaded for 'tolerance' on the 'Asiatic' question and, in an apparently humorous remark, said he did not want to treat South Africans 'as naughty children'.[59]

The Colonial Secretary, however, was compelled to cut short his trip on account of the Irish legislation due to be considered in late September. Upon his arrival at London's Waterloo Station his luggage caused something of a stir, comprising as it did 'a couple of parrots (in cages), poisoned spears (in my golf bag) given me by Zulu chiefs, and a bundle of rugs made of Kaross skins'.[60] Before leaving Cape Town a couple of weeks earlier, Thomas had linked the two Dominions in observing that just a few years earlier the Boers and British had been enemies. 'What a lesson for a stricken world!' he proclaimed, 'I hope that Ireland will follow your example.'[61] He and Sir Douglas Hogg, he quipped, could 'probably settle the Irish question on board ship'.[62]

II

VISCOUNT HALDANE: TIDYING UP THE CONSTITUTION

In his memoirs, Viscount Haldane left a detailed account of his typical working day during the life of the first Labour government. At just after ten o'clock each morning he would go to the House of Lords,[1] check that the day's judicial business was in progress and then spend an hour and a half tackling his duties as Lord Chancellor. Haldane and his permanent secretary, Sir Claud Schuster ('very quick and highly experienced'), would get that work 'launched' before noon, at which point he would walk over to Whitehall Gardens, where the staff of the Committee of Imperial Defence (CID) were already at work.

There, after settling the day's 'operations' with Sir Maurice Hankey, who was Secretary to the CID as well as the Cabinet, Haldane would preside over a small meeting of the Chiefs of Staff for the three branches of the Armed Services (Navy, Army and Air Force). After a 'brief interval for luncheon', he would return to the House of Lords to finish the day's business and correspondence. Finally, at 4.15 p.m. Haldane would change into his robes and take his place on the Woolsack. As Leader of the Lords, he would field questions of general policy from the government benches while Lord Parmoor, Lord President of the Council, dealt with foreign affairs and, in particular, the work of the League of Nations.[2]

Despite neither being a member of the Labour Party nor particularly well acquainted with Ramsay MacDonald before late 1923, Haldane had managed to place himself at the very heart of the first Labour government with command of a wide-ranging ministerial brief. Richard Lyman called him 'a valuable quarry', and it was one of which his ministerial colleagues would make good use.[3]

Richard Burdon Haldane was born at 17 Charlotte Square in the heart of Edinburgh's Georgian New Town on 30 July 1856, the second son of Robert Haldane, a lawyer, and his second wife Mary, who hailed from an eminent Northumberland family. The 'Haldanes of Cloan' straddled several generations and myriad professions. On his mother's side, Haldane was descended from Lord Eldon, a former Lord Chancellor, as well as Lord Stowell, a judge. Richard, who never married, wrote to his mother almost every day until her death aged 100 in 1925.

For six months Haldane studied German, philosophy and geology in Göttingen and then, more conventionally, law back in England. He was called to the English Bar in 1879, established chambers at Lincoln's Inn and took silk in 1890. Five years earlier he had also entered Parliament as the Liberal MP for East Lothian. Ideologically ecumenical, Haldane was friendly with both the Webbs (Beatrice considered him 'a successful lawyer, tinged with socialism')[4] and the Unionist statesman Arthur James Balfour, a fellow philosopher.

In 1902 Balfour (then premier) recommended Haldane become a Privy Counsellor, an unusual honour for someone who had never held public office, although three years later that changed when he became Secretary of State for War and subsequently Lord Chancellor in the Liberal governments of Sir Henry Campbell-Bannerman and H. H. Asquith. Viscount Haldane, as he became in 1911, modernized the Army via the Committee of Imperial Defence (established by Balfour in 1904), a valuable exercise given the outbreak of war in 1914. This was conveniently forgotten when the *Daily Express* led a jingoistic campaign against Haldane on the basis of his well-known regard for Germany. Although this was based on little more than xenophobia, Haldane twice offered to resign before being dropped from Asquith's coalition government in May 1915. A few years later David Lloyd George, now Prime Minister, asked Haldane to chair a committee on reforming the 'machinery of government', which reported in December 1918.[5]

By late 1923, most of those damaged politically by the First World War – not just Haldane but Ramsay MacDonald and Charles Trevelyan – were back in Parliament even if not completely rehabilitated in the eyes of the press and sections of the electorate. In retrospect, MacDonald's embrace of Haldane generated remarkably little controversy within the Labour Party beyond some low-level grumbling around Beatrice Webb's dinner table, although David Kirkwood probably spoke for the Clydeside MPs in observing that the former Lord Chancellor 'had rather too much say' in the formation of the first Labour government.[6] While he was an 'advanced' Liberal, Haldane was exotic rather than wild – the cartoonist Carruthers Gould depicted him as a talking penguin – and his status as a sort of 'father figure' to the new Cabinet was quickly accepted.

On the eve of taking office, Haldane wrote a touching letter to Asquith, whom he had served as a minister for seven years, almost apologizing for joining a government 'of which you are not the head'. 'Now it is a new period, and the adventure is both difficult and uncertain,' he added. 'It is not without misgiving that I face it. But I do not consider that I have the right to stand aside in this hour.' Asquith replied that Haldane was 'a far better judge than I can be of what, in these strange conditions, is your duty' and confessing 'to a profound distrust, not of the good intentions, but of the judgement of your new associates'.[7]

Towards the end of January 1924, another friend told Haldane his mind was 'full of hopes and fears' for the new government. 'If the wild men can be repressed, & the Govt. can settle the German question,' wrote the journalist Harold Begbie, 'then I believe Labour will have a remarkable victory at the polls.' He was also glad that Haldane's mother was 'alive to see this day'.[8] Just as Ramsay MacDonald's appointment as Prime Minister had salved old political wounds, Haldane's restoration to office given the manner of his exit was another satisfying vindication. 'He knew how much this meant to her [Haldane's mother],' judged Stephen Koss. 'And he had returned, however briefly, to the corridors of Whitehall, where he had always found the air more invigorating than that of the courtroom or library.'[9]

'I long to leave the constitution of Britain better than I found it,' proclaimed Haldane, 'and to perfect the machinery for the organization of defence, and I seem to have been given a chance!'[10] Today largely forgotten, the Committee of Imperial Defence had come to co-ordinate defence policy for the whole of the British Empire by the mid-1920s. While formal decision-making authority remained with the Cabinet and the Chiefs of Staff, the CID provided advice. And given its membership comprised Prime Ministers (UK and Dominion), senior Cabinet ministers, key civil servants and military leaders, this advice was usually followed.

Key to the growth of the CID's prestige had been Sir Maurice Hankey, who became its Secretary in 1912, four years before his appointment as the first Cabinet Secretary. As was clear from Hankey's covert meeting with Ramsay MacDonald in early January, initial fears that an incoming Labour government would abolish or neuter the CID proved unfounded. Presiding over its first meeting personally, the Prime Minister announced he had selected Haldane to act as chairman, although in reality Haldane had selected himself. The 'traditions' and functions of the Committee, declared MacDonald, 'should be continued on the same lines as in the past'.[11]

In this area at least, the Prime Minister was happy to delegate. For the next nine months Haldane ran the CID 'as a private empire in which neither MacDonald nor the Cabinet interfered'.[12] This effectively meant Haldane was Minister for Defence as well as Secretary of State for War, although the latter post was nominally held by Stephen Walsh, from whom little

Labour leader Ramsay MacDonald and the MPs Margaret Bondfield, Jimmy
Thomas and Robert Smillie at a 'victory' rally at the Royal Albert Hall on 8
January 1924. 'We are going to take office,' declared MacDonald, 'in order to
do work.'

Ramsay MacDonald, Jimmy Thomas, Arthur Henderson and J. R. Clynes
surrounded by well-wishers outside Buckingham Palace. They had just collected
their seals of office as, respectively, Foreign Secretary, Colonial Secretary, Home
Secretary and Lord Privy Seal. They look simultaneously shocked and delighted.

The 'biscuits' man Sir Alexander Grant playing golf with Ramsay MacDonald (watched by Ishbel MacDonald, middle left). Grant sought to resolve his childhood friend's financial concerns, but when he was awarded a baronetcy the press alleged 'cash for honours'.

Ramsay MacDonald sporting Court dress at a Royal levee in early 1924. The Prime Minister liked dressing up for State occasions, but some of his colleagues thought him rather too eager to please his society friends.

A miniature of Ishbel MacDonald by Winifred Cécile Dongworth. Her mother Margaret having died in 1911, Ishbel acted as her father's 'hostess' at Downing Street during the life of the first Labour government.

The first Labour Cabinet in the garden at 10 Downing Street. Initially reluctant to be photographed, ministers only agreed on the basis they would retain control of the image. An absent War Secretary, Stephen Walsh, has been 'inserted' second from the left in the middle row. Philip Snowden, the Chancellor of the Exchequer, is third left at the front.

John Wheatley (right) and Charles Trevelyan (left), respectively Minister for Health and President of the Board of Education, two of the first Labour government's more effective members.

William Adamson, who became the first Labour Secretary for Scotland, photographed in around 1920. 'You'll be surprised', he told the Unionist Lord Advocate Hugh Macmillan, 'to find what a Tory I am.'

The 1st Viscount Haldane, politician, lawyer and philosopher. His appointment as Lord Chancellor restored him to office nearly a decade after a jingoistic campaign had driven him from it. He wanted to 'tidy up' the ramshackle British constitution but could only achieve so much in the nine months Labour held power.

Fresh from his foreign policy triumph regarding German war reparations, Ramsay MacDonald featured on the cover of *TIME* magazine. He was generally considered a more effective Foreign Secretary than Prime Minister, although holding both offices proved exhausting.

Two years after the Irish Free State had seceded from the United Kingdom, the 'Irish Question' remained unresolved. MacDonald invited W. T. Cosgrave, President of the Executive Council of the Free State, and Sir James Craig, Prime Minister of Northern Ireland, to Chequers in an attempt to resolve the 'boundary' issue.

King George V as featured on 'Wembley' stamps commemorating the Empire Exhibition, which he opened in April 1924. Instinctively anti-Labour, he nevertheless went out of his way to demonstrate 'fair play' towards his socialist ministers. In return, the Labour Party came to perceive both constitutional monarchy and Imperialism in a more positive light.

Sir Patrick Hastings, the Attorney General for England and Wales. His botched prosecution of a communist journalist fuelled the so-called 'Campbell Case', which helped bring down the first Labour government.

Ramsay MacDonald addressing the October 1924 Labour Party conference. When this happened to coincide with the government's likely defeat on a censure motion, MacDonald declared: 'If there be an election the responsibility is not ours.'

Usefully for the Conservatives, the twin controversies of the Campbell Case and Russian Treaties dovetailed perfectly with its 'Red Bogey' campaign. This poster by Harry Woolley set the tone for the bitter general election of October 1924.

The Zinoviev affair as depicted in the *Illustrated London News*. A forged letter purporting to be from the President of the Third (Communist) International blew apart the 1924 general election campaign, the third in as many years. Also pictured are the Foreign Office official J. D Gregory, who many blamed for the controversy, and Christian Rakovsky, the Soviet chargé d'affaires.

was heard during the government's short life. Walsh's two under-secretaries were Clement Attlee, the future Prime Minister,[13] and Jack Lawson, who in a past life had worked as an orderly in Army barracks.[14]

The new Lord Chancellor used his long statement in the Upper House on 12 February (which echoed that delivered by the Prime Minister in the Commons) to emphasize business as usual when it came to defence policy, reassuring those who feared drastic cuts in armaments spending in favour of more progressive causes. This continuity also provided Haldane with political space to concentrate on administrative reforms: he established a permanent sub-committee of the CID comprising the three Chiefs of Staff and arranged for additional bodies to advise on wartime supply and the provision and distribution of manpower between the three Services, industry and agriculture. This was no easy task, owing to friction between the Army and Navy on one side and the relatively new Air Force on the other.[15]

The first battleground was Singapore. In May 1921 the Committee had recommended the construction of a British naval base on the strategically important island which then formed part of the Straits Settlements. Anticipating a future conflict in the Pacific, the CID believed a naval base would be vital to ensure the security of British interests – mainly Australia and New Zealand – in that part of the southern hemisphere. Separately, the Admiralty was also pushing for the construction of eight new naval cruisers.

On this, however, the new Labour government was determined to take a stand. On 21 February, the Prime Minister made clear that pressing ahead with the Singapore base would 'hamper' European confidence in his commitment to peace. Although he left open the possibility of a review should a base become a 'practical necessity', to all intents and purposes the scheme was dead. That same day Charles Ammon, the Parliamentary Secretary to the Admiralty, made the surprise announcement that 'in view of serious unemployment', the government had decided 'to proceed with the laying down of five cruisers – three of which will be built in the Royal Dockyards – and two destroyers'.[16] As Lord Chelmsford was in the Upper House, Ammon had to deal with hostile questioning in the Commons, including from the American-born Labour MP Ernest Thurtle, who asked contemptuously if the announcement was to be taken as a 'great moral gesture to the world'.[17] The Prime Minister argued that construction would keep 4,750 dockyard workers from losing their jobs. The route to disarmament, he told the Commons, was not to allow the Navy 'to disappear by wastage from the bottom', teasing a 'conception of pacifist principles' which was content for 'ships to fall to pieces'.[18]

Lord Beatty, the Admiral of the Fleet, was delighted that the Naval estimates (which included the cruisers) passed the House of Commons with a large majority, despite the public mood being strongly against armaments. As he wrote to his wife:

> Over 20 Liberal Members and the whole of the Labour Party and the whole of the Conservative Party supported the Admiralty, including extremists of every description, Pacifist, Communists, Socialists. It really is a very remarkable result and one which gives ample food for thought ... Who would have thought, a few years or even months ago, that we should see an overwhelming majority of the House support the proposition of a strong Navy?[19]

The cruiser announcement, however, also confirmed the need for economies in defence expenditure in order to reconcile the Labour left, something which would quickly sour Beatty's optimism. An attempt by the ILP MP Walter Ayles to reduce the size of the Army by 150,000 having been rejected by 347 votes to 13, in March the Cabinet approved MacDonald's decision not to ask Parliament to proceed with the Singapore base, 'since their policy was to support international co-operation through a strengthened and enlarged League of Nations',[20] not to mention honouring the spirit of the recent Washington Naval Conference, which had committed the UK, Japan and several other nations to disarmament. The Dominions had, of course, been consulted, but while Canada and the Irish Free State offered no view, Australia, New Zealand and Newfoundland all wanted to press ahead.

Australia and New Zealand were particularly furious, regarding the move as a betrayal by the Imperial government. Lord Beatty was also appalled, believing it would leave the Pacific at the mercy of the Japanese. Writing to his wife, Beatty believed Labour needed to be taught 'Imperialism'. 'It is quite extraordinary,' he observed angrily, 'the amount of real ignorance that exists in their minds on questions of the greatest importance.'[21] In concert with Sir Harry Batterbee, a veteran Colonial Office official, meanwhile, Sir Maurice Hankey attempted to change the Prime Minister's mind regarding the base. Batterbee had recently visited Singapore and suggested to MacDonald that he might regard construction of a base there as 'an expression of gratitude towards Australia and New Zealand for their help in the war'. This appeared to work, although a majority of the Cabinet (particularly Philip Snowden) remained opposed.[22] In Singapore, the colonial administration ignored Labour's instructions and continued with the necessary drainage work.

When it came to Singapore, Haldane believed that from a purely defensive point of view the base was desirable, although likely to cost considerably more than the £10 million anticipated by the CID, money he feared would be diverted from the Air Force, the expansion of which he considered more of a priority.[23] As Jake Vaughan has observed, Haldane basically 'steered a middle course between expansionism and unilateral disarmament'.[24] Confirming the Singapore decision in the House of Commons on 18 March, however, the Prime Minister further infuriated Hankey when he appeared to criticize the CID. Referencing Singapore, MacDonald said a Defence Committee with the premier as chairman was 'an excellent idea, and an excellent machine if it could work'. But, he added, 'it cannot work! It shows certain weaknesses wise or unwise.'[25] Although Sir Maurice did not doubt there were flaws in the current system of defence co-ordination, he suggested Singapore was not a good example, no other question having 'been more exhaustively studied in the last twenty years'.[26]

Another defence issue which pre-dated Labour's term of office was Egypt. Lord Curzon, the previous Foreign Secretary, had persuaded the War Office and Admiralty to relinquish the British Army's garrison in Cairo in advance of a likely electoral victory by the revolutionary nationalist Saad Zaghloul. As a *quid pro quo*, the UK was to maintain its exclusive right to 'protect' the Suez Canal, retain air bases at Heliopolis (near Cairo) and Aboukir, as well as station troops within striking distance of Cairo and Alexandria. Zaghloul did indeed win the election (with an overwhelming majority) and became Prime Minister of Egypt just four days after Ramsay MacDonald assumed the equivalent office in London.

Despite some grumbling from Lord Olivier, the Secretary of State for India, Stephen Walsh, the War Secretary, and Lord Thomson, the Secretary of State for Air, the Labour government supported Curzon's plan, although at the end of February the Prime Minister learned Zaghloul was demanding that the Suez Canal come under League of Nations control and for a complete end to the British military presence in Egypt.[27] The Committee of Imperial Defence consulted Field Marshal Viscount Allenby, the High Commissioner for Egypt, who said any restriction of the Suez Canal Zone would be strategically unwise.[28] In June, there was an additional crisis when Zaghloul also asserted Egypt's claims to Sudan. These were twice rejected by MacDonald, although the 'Anglo-Egyptian conversations', which continued between the two Prime Ministers until October, were incomplete by the time Labour left office in early November. In another neat piece of symmetry, Zaghloul's government itself fell a few weeks later.

Under Haldane's chairmanship, the Committee of Imperial Defence also finally killed off long-standing plans for a Channel Tunnel. First conceived in 1906, in June 1924 MacDonald had enthusiastically revived the proposal, which was supported by more than 400 MPs as well as prominent businessmen. The Prime Minister, however, made this subject to CID approval, specifically a sub-committee over which Haldane presided. The Lord Chancellor knew the scheme well, having played a part in the investigations which led the then Liberal government to veto it in 1907.

The issue turned on whether the commercial advantages of a tunnel would outweigh the security risks. Haldane's committee concluded that although passenger traffic might increase (albeit at the expense of steamship services), additional defence anxieties were unavoidable should the Continent become physically connected to Great Britain.[29] This was then referred to a full meeting of the CID, present at which were four living premiers – Balfour, Asquith, Lloyd George and Baldwin – and over which MacDonald presided. 'Amazed at [the] military mind,' he wrote in his diary, adding that it was 'in a rut where neither fresh air nor new ideas blow ... My burdens are so heavy & so many that I cannot take up the Tunnel at present, but it must be taken up. Meeting most unsatisfactory.'[30] A disappointed House of Commons was duly informed on 7 July.

Although most of Haldane's time was occupied with the Committee of Imperial Defence, he was also Leader of the Lords and Lord Chancellor, albeit shorn of the latter office's most high-profile judicial responsibilities – the Appellate Committee of the House of Lords and Judicial Committee of the Privy Council – which by prior arrangement were still in the hands of his Conservative predecessor, Lord Cave. To call the administration of the law in England and Wales complex would have been an understatement. While the appointment and discipline of court officials was the responsibility of the Lord Chancellor, their pay and expenses were a Treasury concern. A similar split applied to the County Courts, while the Home Office was also concerned with legal business for which the Lord Chancellor's Office was concurrently responsible. The Lord Chancellor himself was simultaneously a member of the Cabinet, president of the Supreme Court of Judicature and Speaker of the House of Lords.

All this, as one of his biographers has observed, brought 'pain and grief to Haldane's orderly mind'. His preferred solution, wrote Sir Frederick Maurice, was

> the creation of a Ministry of Justice, which should take over all the administrative functions exercised by the Lord Chancellor's department, the Home Office and the Treasury, and ... that the political head of this ministry should be a member of the House of Commons, and be responsible to that House for the patronage which he administered. In short he envisaged a separation of the judicial and administrative functions hitherto the responsibility of the Lord Chancellor.

This anticipated Blairite reforms of eight decades later, but the short life of the Labour government – not to mention vested interests – meant Haldane made little headway. Nor was he successful with his aspiration to transform the Judicial Committee of the Privy Council into a truly 'Imperial Court of Appeal'. As Lord Chancellor, meanwhile, Haldane nominated only one judge. Keen to avoid doing so 'in the last agony of the government's existence', Frank Douglas MacKinnon's appointment was rushed through on 5 October during the controversy surrounding the 'Campbell Case'.[31]

There were no grand plans for House of Lords reform. In 1924 it was an overwhelmingly hereditary body, with the exception of the Lords Spiritual (recently shorn of Welsh Bishops due to disestablishment in that part of the UK) and Lords of Appeal, then the only 'life' peers. The Cabinet did agree to support Viscount Astor's Parliament (Qualification of Peeresses) Bill,[32] which arose from the case of Viscountess Rhondda. She had succeeded to the title following the death of her father in 1918, but when she tried to take her seat in the Lords – arguing that the *Sex Disqualification (Removal) Act 1919* allowed women to exercise 'any public office' – Rhondda's claim was rejected. At the Bill's second reading on 17 July, Haldane did little beyond rebutting spurious objections that the admission of women would restrict the Royal Prerogative, although in any case it failed to progress.[33] The Lord Chancellor also ruled on another anomaly whereby 28 Irish representative peers – elected for life from among the entire Irish peerage under the 1801 Acts of Union – remained in the Upper House on the basis that the Anglo-Irish Treaty had made no explicit provision either for their retention or removal. Although he considered legislation, Haldane advised inaction, the consequence of which was that the last Irish representative peer did not 'die out' until 1961.[34]

When it came to the magistracy, however, the Lord Chancellor was considerably more proactive. The Labour Party had long complained of not being adequately represented among Justices of the Peace. Although these were not political offices, Lord Cave had already begun work on establishing Justices' Advisory Committees, which were intended to be cross-party and make recommendations to ensure a reasonable balance of political opinion was maintained among local magistrates.[35] On 31 July, Haldane received a delegation which included Labour MPs and the party's Acting Secretary, J. S. Middleton. They highlighted the 'grave disproportion' of Labour-supporting magistrates – only 719 (61 of them women) out of 9,621 – and asked that both the constitution of the Advisory Committees and ongoing appointments to the bench be speeded up.[36]

By the time Labour left office, Haldane had made a point not only of appointing Labour-supporting Justices but 'women members' too,[37] so that the proportion of new appointments was a more respectable 412 Conservatives, 237 Liberals and 280 Labour.[38] As Chancellor of the Duchy of Lancaster, Josiah Wedgwood was responsible for appointments in Lancashire, where he too pushed for working men and women to fill the local benches. Among his appointees was the radical feminist Selina Cooper.[39]

The Lord Chancellor also had the power to remove Justices of the Peace, something he exercised in August when he withdrew Albert Edward Dent from the Yorkshire bench on the basis that he was a passive resister against the local education rate. Haldane's view was that Dent's fellow magistrates would be put in an embarrassing position if presented with cases involving others who had refused to pay their rates.[40] The Cabinet's view, however, was that magistrates should not be removed on this basis,[41] and Haldane's intervention provoked a near split with Lord Parmoor, the Lord President and himself a magistrate. But 'for loyalty to the Prime Minister, and my colleagues', Parmoor told Sidney Webb, he had considered resigning from the bench in protest.[42] It fell to Sir Patrick Hastings, the Attorney General, to defend Haldane's decision in the Commons, but while he admired the Lord Chancellor as 'a great lawyer and a man of great intellect' he personally had 'always found him a nuisance'.[43]

The social if not intellectual highlight of Haldane's second tenure as Lord Chancellor came in July, when some 700 guests from the American and Canadian Bar Associations visited the UK. There were receptions at the Law Courts (at which Haldane accepted a statue of Sir William Blackstone), banquets at the Inns of Court and a side trip by some of the visitors to the Court of Session in Edinburgh. During a gathering in Westminster Hall at which the King and Queen were present, the North American guests were 'hushed with awe' as the Lord Chancellor's procession, all in full wig, entered the historic surroundings. There were comic scenes at a Buckingham Palace garden party. Someone had incorrectly told the guests they had to wear top hats (the King had, as usual, given Labour attendees the option of wearing lounge suits), a shortage of which led to one distinguished guest donning a collapsible opera hat, which 'shut up with a bang, to his great embarrassment, and the Queen's great amusement'.[44] Writing to his mother Mary when it was all over, Haldane said he had made 'innumerable speeches and shaken innumerable hands' and was in 'no doubt that the Americans and Canadians love a display of historic ceremony'.[45]

Sensing that Haldane was rather detached from the Labour movement, Sir Henry Slesser, the Solicitor General, asked if he would like to attend a meeting of the Parliamentary Labour Party. The Lord Chancellor accepted and was treated to an 'unusually obstreperous' session in which the 'Jacobins' shouted at MacDonald 'very rudely'. When Sir Henry asked if Haldane had enjoyed himself, he replied: 'Immensely, but like all happy experiences, I will not risk a repetition.'[46]

On 16 May, the Prime Minister opened a new Parliamentary Labour Club in Westminster[47] and paid Haldane what he considered a 'skimpy' tribute. 'However I have been seeing more of him,' noted the Lord Chancellor with satisfaction, 'and I think we are getting on as well as we ever shall.'[48] In his speech, MacDonald had alluded to Haldane spending a 'good deal of time' on the problem of how men, 'political leaders at one moment, business administrators at the next', could undertake the 'tremendous burdens' of government while remaining conscious of the bigger picture. This was a reference to what the Prime Minister envisaged as 'a Standing Committee, analogous to the Committee of Imperial Defence', whose function would be to provide the Cabinet with empirical data on the 'potential' as well as the immediate application of civil policy.[49]

Haldane called it a 'Committee of Civil Research' (CCR) and by August, following extensive consultation, he had a proposal for a CID-like body presided over by the Prime Minister but chaired by a nominated minister. Expert members appointed by the premier would then consider 'the development of economic, scientific, and statistical research in relation to civil policy and administration'. This clearly owed something to the similarly holistic Machinery of Government Committee chaired by Haldane towards the end of the First World War but, like that previous exercise, this too failed to attract the political backing necessary for its realization.

Preoccupied with foreign affairs and various political crises, much to Haldane's frustration MacDonald never signed off on the CCR. 'I begged him in vain for a few minutes to be diverted from his other and rather miscellaneous occupations,' he wrote in his memoirs. 'I could not get this, neither could I or the officials concerned procure his signature.'[50] Even in advance of this rebuff, Haldane had grown disillusioned with the man who had once offered him 'anything' in return for his support. Dining alone with Tom Jones, the Deputy Cabinet Secretary, on 7 July, the Lord Chancellor complained of MacDonald's aloofness from colleagues and needless blunders. 'He has courage but no passion,' he remarked wearily, 'no deep sympathy with the poor.'[51]

Sir Maurice Hankey nevertheless felt sure Haldane must 'feel glad' to have taken 'the plunge' and joined the Labour government in January:

> Had you not done so, I believe we would have had something like disaster on the defence side! You have given them a splendid start, and, provided you remain at the helm throughout the first term of office at the least, we shall have nothing to fear.[52]

'I am getting the Imperial defences into full order,' wrote Haldane on 13 September, 'but I want some months more before I can complete the work.'[53] The government, however, had weeks rather than months.

12

RAMSAY MACDONALD AS FOREIGN SECRETARY: CREATING A NEW ATMOSPHERE

Ramsay MacDonald had a complicated relationship with Lossiemouth. While he clearly adored the Morayshire town, it had not always loved one of its most famous sons as much in return. One point of tension was historic, the refusal of the town council to let a 'red bastard' build a home for his mother in the smartest, elevated part of Lossie, the other ongoing during his first term as Prime Minister, a wartime expulsion from the Stotfield Golf Club. The former was long forgotten, but the latter retained its ability to distress the unusually sensitive premier.

MacDonald's election in March to honorary membership of the Spey Bay Golf Club, 'for the great honours and distinction that you – a Moray man – have attained in becoming the head of His Majesty's Government',[1] had been welcome but did little to heal long-standing wounds. The following month, a Council member at the Moray Golf Club (which owned the Stotfield links) suggested MacDonald's membership be reinstated, but when this was put to a special meeting in Elgin in July, a majority vote in favour failed to meet the necessary two-thirds majority.[2]

In early August, Ishbel MacDonald, who remained a member of Stotfield, vowed not to play there that summer, as did her brother Malcolm, who agreed the behaviour of the Club had been 'disgraceful'. He wrote to Ishbel on 5 August to say he wished

those who are decent in the club would have some guts, and refuse to play until Foster and co [who were opposed to the readmission of MacDonald] had resigned, and then dictate an apology from the Club to be published in the press, saying amongst other things that the people who had wrangled the whole incident were a minority of drunkards whose actions were of no importance at all. Something drastic has got to be done before the club can clear itself of a bad disgrace.[3]

At the same time, Malcolm and Ishbel were keen to avoid taking any action which would 'annoy' their father, a sign of how close the trio remained during a challenging year.

The summer of 1924 had been particularly happy. MacDonald built a room for Ishbel in the garden at The Hillocks, where he would happily converse with sightseers over the fence. Ishbel believed they 'saved' her father from 'the danger of losing touch', while also cheering him up:

> From the time mummy died till he was prime minister he was a sorrowful man. People were afraid of him. He always seemed to be mourning. It was not often he was seen laughing. As prime minister the friendliness of the people, the exhilaration of victory, made him forget himself. He was a different man. He was on top of the world, full of fun and vigour. I like to think that my growing up and gradually becoming a companion was partly the cause of his new happiness.[4]

Even at The Hillocks, the Prime Minister was kept busy, working from breakfast until 8 p.m. and snatching only brief periods of relaxation. Hugh Macmillan, the Lord Advocate, once found him 'stretched on the grass reading one of Sir Walter Scott's novels'.[5] MacDonald told Lady Londonderry that Lossiemouth 'in any weather' brought him and his family 'health and happiness'.[6]

Although comfortable, The Hillocks was not exactly large, and must have felt overcrowded given the presence of a policeman for security, at least two offspring (usually Ishbel and Malcolm) and Miss Byvoets, the Dutch housekeeper with whom Ishbel was often at odds. Getting there also took time, involving at least three train journeys, although in February Lord Thomson, the Secretary of State for Air, offered to have MacDonald flown to Lossiemouth as long as his department had received 12 hours' notice.[7]

The main value of The Hillocks and Lossiemouth during 1924 was as a refuge from domestic and international affairs. Ramsay MacDonald's most distinctive move in January 1924 had been the decision to act as his own Foreign Secretary, a dual role last attempted by Lord Salisbury. Many at the time, including the King, doubted MacDonald's capacity to shoulder such a political and administrative burden. The courtier Lord Esher was virtually alone in thinking this 'twaddle'. 'There simply is no Foreign Secretary available except the P.M. himself,' he told Tom Jones. 'So it is futile to look for one.'[8]

Few, however, doubted the Foreign Secretary's grasp of the international scene. MacDonald had travelled widely with his late wife Margaret and, as Lord Haldane put it, 'interchanged views with a number of Continental statesmen', most recently as Leader of the Opposition. The result was something of the 'international mind which enabled him to understand and get the sympathy of foreign Ministers'.[9] Haldane, however, was disappointed not to be consulted more closely on foreign affairs, most likely on account of his association with the former Foreign Secretary Lord Grey, who was among those MacDonald blamed for the outbreak of the First World War. It was even suspected he hoped for that to become evident when he authorized the publication of pre-war archival material.[10]

MacDonald was aware, as David Marquand has written, that the 'sight of a Labour foreign secretary grappling successfully with problems which had baffled a Curzon or a Balfour' would do more to prove Labour's fitness to govern than any domestic achievement.[11] It helped that foreign affairs were largely conducted via the Royal Prerogative (i.e. on ministerial advice to the Crown), which offered MacDonald significant scope for executive action without recourse to Parliament, and therefore little need to worry about Labour's minority status. Indeed, Beatrice Webb was struck by what she called the 'unlimited autocracy' of the Prime

Minister, who 'alone determines what line he takes towards other countries'.[12] MacDonald neither referred foreign questions to the Cabinet nor even consulted his colleagues, which sat uneasily with his long-standing support – via the Union of Democratic Control – for 'democratic control' of foreign policy.

One plank of that policy was parliamentary approval for international treaties. These were traditionally handled under the prerogative, and Parliament had no say unless they required a change to domestic law. When MacDonald cooled on the idea of extending that say, Arthur Ponsonby, his under-secretary at the Foreign Office, saw it through, outlining what became known as the 'Ponsonby Rule' following a debate on the Treaty of Lausanne in April 1924.[13] Under this procedure, a treaty was to be laid in draft form before both Houses of Parliament for 21 days prior to ratification, during which MPs and peers could, if desired, discuss it. This did not satisfy E. D. Morel, who wanted legislation prohibiting 'secret' diplomacy rather than a mere convention.[14]

MacDonald's permanent secretary at the Foreign Office was Sir Eyre Crowe, who despite having a German mother and wife was decisively pro-French as well as vehemently anti-Soviet. He and other senior officials were apparently relieved by their new chief's personal charm (not to mention his intention to leave untouched the Secret Service) which was in sharp contrast to the stewardship of the more autocratic Lord Curzon. While Lord Parmoor (who was, in effect, minister for the League of Nations) found himself 'regarded as a cuckoo in the nest' and complained to MacDonald of civil service obstruction, the Foreign Secretary appeared content with the professionalism of his staff.[15] 'Nobody could have been more fluent in the radical rhetoric of the UDC,' observed Kevin Morgan of MacDonald. 'Few could have balanced this more delicately with the instinct of moderation.'[16]

When Labour formed its first government in January 1924, the Union of Soviet Socialist Republics (USSR) – a federation formed in 1922 – still had something of a pariah status. Vladimir Lenin, whose death coincided with the fall of Baldwin's government, had never held MacDonald in high regard, considering him a 'bourgeois pacifist and middle-class reformer', but the new Prime Minister and Foreign Secretary was nevertheless determined to end 'the pompous policy of standing aloof from Russia'.[17]

This meant ending the Soviet Union's seven-year isolation by granting *de jure* recognition of its government, which was given effect – again under the prerogative – on 1 February. As part of the recognition process, MacDonald invited Soviet representatives to London for a conference to discuss the treaties which were expected to flow from this restoration of diplomatic relations. Moscow despatched the Bulgarian-born revolutionary Christian Georgievich Rakovsky with the rank of chargé d'affaires, while the negotiations themselves were delegated by the Foreign Secretary to Arthur Ponsonby. On 14 April 'the Bolshevists', as *The Times* insisted on calling the Soviet delegates, met MacDonald in his room at the Foreign Office before being given lunch at Number 10. The premier asked them to meet him in the same friendly spirit in which he had invited them to London, and not to be influenced by attacks made on them while in the UK any more than he was by attacks made on him in Russia, most recently a particularly violent 'diatribe' from Zinoviev, the head of the Third International. 'We have taken the first step – and it was a pretty big one,' declared MacDonald. 'Let us together take the second step and justify the hopes of the many millions who look upon this meeting with so much expectation.'[18]

Europe at the beginning of 1924 was also badly in need of some Labour idealism. A year earlier, French and Belgian troops had occupied the Ruhr in response to a German default on deliveries of coal and timber required as reparations under the Treaty of Versailles. By the beginning of February, they controlled everything other than the British Zone. This weakened the Weimar Republic and prompted a German campaign of passive resistance in the heavily populated industrial region, while the invasion and subsequent hyperinflation pulverized its currency. In response, the Reparations Commission established under the Treaty established two expert committees to find a way of reconciling Germany's financial obligations with its diminished resources. The first of these – which was chaired by the American financier and former general Charles Dawes – started work shortly before Labour took office.

MacDonald and the Labour Party had long denounced what they considered the 'madness' of the 1919 Versailles settlement, which meant the onus was now on the Foreign Secretary to demonstrate he could 'create a healthier atmosphere'. Having recently met with five or six representatives of European nations on his travels in the Near East, MacDonald had detected what he described during the election as 'a sneaking feeling of shame on the part of those responsible for the evils in Europe'.[19] As he observed in his diary:

> France must have another chance. I offer cooperation but she must be reasonable & cease her policy of selfish vanity. That is my first job. Armaments & such problems that are really consequences must wait. The 'weather' must be improved. Already I see it is to take years of steady consistent work, & my official life may only be one of months.[20]

MacDonald made his first move just days after his appointment, persuaded by the Foreign Office to send a letter to the French premier Raymond Poincaré proposing 'strenuous action of goodwill'. Poincaré replied positively and at the end of February MacDonald sent a more detailed communication which acknowledged French claims while also warning of a growing feeling in the UK that France was determined to ruin Germany, thereby creating 'economic chaos' from which everyone would suffer. In March, meanwhile, the Foreign Secretary was delighted when US President Calvin Coolidge and his Secretary of State Charles Hughes took 'the fly' he had thrown to them in his first Commons speech on 12 February and declared their willingness to take part in disarmament talks. 'I shall not rush it, however, because the harvest is not quite ripe,' he told Lord Haldane. 'The corn is growing nicely and there is a tinge of yellow upon it – a little more genial weather will make it red.'[21]

Dawes published his report on 9 April. Long and technical, its central message was that Germany's annual reparations ought to be calculated on the basis of what it could afford to pay rather than what its creditors thought they ought to receive (i.e. the reparations should be significantly reduced). In addition, he proposed large international loans in order to stabilize the Weimar economy and a new currency called the 'Reichsmark'. Finally, Dawes insisted that French and Belgian troops must not 'impede' free economic activity in the Ruhr; in other words, they had to leave.

On 10 April, the UK government said it was prepared to accept the Dawes Report provided there was a general support for it among European nations, but the French gave it only grudging consent. MacDonald's willingness to embrace the scheme struck a chord with the public, and at the end of that month he was greeted by cheering crowds in his Aberavon constituency. At Briton Ferry he said the 'great contribution' a British Labour government could make to the peace and security of the world was 'to begin first of all not with grand programmes, but to establish a condition of friendly relations'.[22] Even Lord Beaverbrook formed 'great expectations' of MacDonald's European policy, believing it could 'bring France to the point of settlement with Germany'.[23]

On 9 May, the Foreign Secretary invited the French premier to Chequers, although this was delayed by Poincaré's resignation and replacement with the more left-wing Edouard Herriot, who finally crossed the English Channel on 20 June. By 22 June, the two premiers had agreed on an Allied Conference to which the French, Belgian, Italian and Japanese governments would be invited to send delegates, as well as two 'observers' from the United States. They were to negotiate a 'protocol' rather than a formal revision of the Versailles Treaty. Herriot and MacDonald also agreed to attend the opening of the Assembly of the League of Nations at the beginning of September.

Despite general public and press goodwill, sections of the Labour movement – particularly those associated with the Union of Democratic Control – viewed the Dawes Plan with profound apprehension given the party's long-standing opposition to reparations, however generously modified. E. D. Morel confronted MacDonald at a meeting of the PLP Executive, demanding to know what he would do if Germany did not accept any agreement. 'She must accept,' he replied, 'we shall make her accept', at which George Lansbury apparently remarked: 'That is what Lloyd George used to tell us in 1919.'[24] When UDC attacks continued, the government felt compelled to make clear it was a private body, prompting ministers such as Clement Attlee to sever ties.[25]

The Clydesiders were also unhappy, four of them (including John Wheatley) having visited the Ruhr in February 1923, after which they advocated some form of international control for the region. In his memoirs, Fenner Brockway recalled communicating one anti-reparations motion to a 'contemptuous' Prime Minister at Downing Street. 'What commands have you brought me today?' asked MacDonald sarcastically, in no mood to hear the Independent Labour Party 'damn' him over the Dawes Plan when everyone else recognized it 'as a great achievement of international reconciliation'.[26]

MacDonald also had to contend with an 'explosion' from the French when London failed to send Paris an official invitation to the London Conference (it deemed this unnecessary on account of the Chequers meeting). After ranting to the *Manchester Guardian*'s editor C. P. Scott about 'underhand, grasping, dishonourable' French politicians, the Foreign Secretary packed, in the acerbic words of Philip Snowden, 'his portmanteau for a week-end visit to M. Herriot in Paris'. There, as he also recounted to Scott, dinner took place at Versailles

in a room about three times as long as this the big dining-room at No. 10, about 50 feet long. There were present about 70 ex-premiers and would-be premiers – everybody, he added, in France wants to be a premier, if it is only for four days. I was seated in the middle of the long side of the table so had a good view of all the men opposite ... Mme Herriot, a very nice person, was seated next to me. I said to her 'can you tell me if there is an honest man here, besides your husband'. 'Yes', she replied, 'I think there are two'.

Despite MacDonald's prejudices, he and Herriot patched up their misunderstanding and the French premier even 'publicly expressed the opinion that the entente cordiale was now stronger than it had been since the Armistice'.[27] Frank B. Kellogg, the US Ambassador, thought the Foreign Secretary's speech at the opening of the London Conference on 16 July 'created the right atmosphere and struck exactly the right note'.[28]

Once the Allied delegates had reached an agreement they were joined by German representatives on 2 August, with regular daily meetings taking place in MacDonald's private room at the House of Commons. A crucial presence was the Foreign Office permanent secretary Sir Eyre Crowe, who bridged the gap between MacDonald's lack of German and the German delegates' rudimentary English.[29] Sir Maurice Hankey also found himself 'thrown together in great intimacy' with the Foreign Secretary during proceedings, and the pair were 'almost inseparable' in its last ten days.[30] It was a tremendously busy period. 'As soon as one thing is settled, another crops up,' MacDonald wrote to his aunt Bella. 'How it will end, or when, I know not. But for all one knows, it could end tomorrow with the most complete success.'[31]

It did not end that quickly, and the Foreign Secretary's diary entries demonstrate frustration with Germans as well as French. The latter were still 'chasing after will-o'-wisps in armed power, tricky diplomacy, stupid economics' while the former's 'long speeches and meticulous points' filled his heart with 'dread'. On 7 August MacDonald grappled with disagreement among the French delegates regarding the evacuation of French railwaymen from the Ruhr. At 11 p.m. he left to deal with his Foreign Office boxes, but when he returned his secretary rushed along the passage to meet him. 'Quiet,' he whispered, pointing to the Cabinet room and adding: 'They are in there still fighting & I have sent for refreshments.' The Foreign Secretary, meanwhile, 'slipped upstairs & went to bed'.[32]

MacDonald also had to mollify his anti-French and anti-reparations Chancellor, Philip Snowden. In an attempt to 'lubricate' proceedings, MacDonald proposed a small sacrifice of the UK's reparation claims (which were not, in any event, being paid) in favour of France, as well as supporting Dawes' proposal for a generous loan to Germany. Snowden, however, opposed lending any money unless the French evacuated the Ruhr immediately, rather than in a year as was being mooted. 'This is not merely a banker's demand,' he wrote to MacDonald. 'It is an investor's demand. No sane person would lend a penny to a country whose chief industrial area was occupied by foreign troops.'[33]

Although he had a point, what irritated the Foreign Secretary was the 'spiteful' way in which his Chancellor – who at one stage threatened resignation – expressed his opposition. 'Snowden absurdly mischievous,' MacDonald wrote in his diary. 'Raised every imaginable pettifogging point.'[34] When he and Hankey attempted a break to see George Bernard Shaw's play *Saint Joan* at the theatre, it was interrupted by telephone messages concerning 'a furious, wounded Herriot'. On returning to Number 10, the Foreign Secretary complained to Snowden that his

> remarks yesterday have played havoc & the whole French delegation has been mischief making the live-long day … what [Jimmy] Thomas would call 'the atmosphere' of this Conference has been destroyed. I cannot persuade Herriot that your remark about his position on arbitration was anything but a personal attack on his honour … [it has] made Herriot close up like an oyster and unless he is in a better frame of mind to-morrow, I fear this Conference may fail.[35]

'To-day has probably been the most critical day in the history of the Conference,' reported Patrick Gower (one of MacDonald's private secretaries) to Clive Wigram (the King's assistant private secretary). 'From morning until evening the game of chess has gone on continuously.'[36] The French had rallied the Italians,

Belgians and even the Americans to their claim to remain in the Ruhr for another year, and at one point further indelicate remarks from Snowden reduced Ambassador Kellogg to 'a trembling rage'.[37]

The London Conference brought MacDonald and Kellogg into unusually close contact. The Ambassador thought the Foreign Secretary 'at the height of his powers' during the conference, maintaining 'a remarkable poise ... and although I saw him frequently embarrassed, I rarely saw him give way to pessimism'. At the same time, Kellogg wondered 'whether his mind was sufficiently critical and incisive':

> He was not so good on detailed negotiation, lacking the patience necessary for that task. He could initiate negotiations and set them going splendidly, but he needed the help of others to carry them through, and he was not always sufficiently aware of that need, and did not have the gift of using others capable of helping him as fully as he might. He was therefore not skilled in conserving his own strength.[38]

Finally, on 16 August a protocol accepting the Dawes Plan and evacuation of the Ruhr was agreed, and with dramatic flair MacDonald staged a concluding handshake between Chancellor Marx of Germany and Prime Minister Herriot of France. In what Arthur Ponsonby considered an 'admirable'[39] closing speech, the Foreign Secretary thanked everyone 'from Premiers to typists', adding that the Conference had given Europe

> something better than an agreement drafted by lawyers and printed on paper – we all negotiated, discussed, put ourselves in each other's shoes. That is the greatest advance we have made. We are now offering the first really negotiated agreement since the war; every party here represented is morally bound to do its best to carry it out, because it is not the result of an ultimatum; we have tried to meet each other as far as the public opinion of the various countries would allow us.[40]

David Marquand considered this the 'high point' of MacDonald's first government, 'perhaps of his career'.[41] The King telegrammed MacDonald to 'heartily congratulate' him on 'bringing the conference to a successful conclusion',[42] while *Time* magazine put him on its cover. Patrick Gower told Clive Wigram the Foreign Secretary had been 'deeply touched' by the King's message, which had come into his hands just as the Conference closed, cheering 'him up tremendously' and sending 'him off to Scotland feeling very happy'.[43] 'I breathe like one with a load off his chest,' MacDonald told his diary.[44]

Although Lord Haldane worried that MacDonald would, as a result of his success, keep foreign affairs 'too much in his own hands', he conceded that 'Ramsay deserves all [the] credit' for his handling of the London Conference, believing that the UK's relations with France were now better than 'at any time since the war'.[45] Sir Maurice Hankey concurred, telling Wigram that the Foreign Secretary had

> displayed extraordinary resource, and great patience and courage. He really carried the whole Conference on his back, and overcame very great difficulties, both of a personal and political kind. It is a great comfort to know that we have a Prime Minister and Foreign Secretary who can handle a really difficult situation.[46]

Despite his earlier criticisms, even E. D. Morel gushed that MacDonald had 'achieved in six months what British statesmen have been trying vainly to accomplish for six years'.[47] In an article later quoted on Labour election posters, the Liberal journalist Harry Jones called the settlement with France 'a brilliant feather in his cap'. 'To have succeeded where Bonar Law, Baldwin, and Lloyd George failed,' he added, 'is a considerable achievement.'[48]

There were, however, notes of caution. While the *Daily Herald* acknowledged MacDonald's 'great success' as Foreign Secretary, it pointed to 'disadvantages in having no effective Prime Minister'.[49] The *Manchester Guardian* also carried an interview with Philip

Snowden in which he breached Cabinet collective responsibility by criticizing the reparations deal. It had, noted Mary Agnes Hamilton, been written up in a way that suggested 'first, personal conflict between the two men; and second, unflattering contrasts between the rigid straightforwardness of the one, and the supple sophistication of the other'.[50] For once, Arthur Ponsonby sided with the Foreign Secretary, criticizing the Chancellor's 'unaccommodating' stance.[51] 'The Snowdens lunched here the day after the interview,' recorded Beatrice Webb in her diary. 'It is clear that the Prime Minister has no friend in his Chancellor of the Exchequer.'[52]

Assessing the Labour government's prospects in May, Sir Maurice Hankey judged their 'best chance' to lie 'with a big success in Foreign Policy'.[53] The London Conference had certainly satisfied that, though the Anglo-Soviet Conference, which dragged on for four months and concluded shortly before the reparations protocol was agreed, did not fare as well. Part of the problem, judged Arthur Ponsonby, was that MacDonald was 'dreadfully bored at having to force his mind on to something else than that which is actually occupying him'.[54]

Ponsonby thus found himself directing negotiations but lacking authority, possessing the 'disadvantages without the advantages of a permanent official and the disadvantages without the advantages of a responsible minister'.[55] In general terms, the Soviet Union was prepared to pay compensation to British bond and property owners who had suffered losses as a result of the 1917 Russian Revolution but would only do so if the City of London raised money for a loan, something they insisted ought to be enshrined in one of two treaties between the UK and USSR. Ponsonby, however, insisted they negotiate directly with individual creditors, subject to a system of arbitration. During May, talks often looked likely to break down on this point.

During the Whitsun recess, MacDonald demanded that Ponsonby reach a settlement one way or the other by the end of June, perhaps with a view to freeing himself up for the London Conference due to begin the following month. 'It cannot continue,' he wrote impatiently. 'If any of our people stand in the way they should be told that they have to turn over a new leaf.'[56] It did not help that Soviet propagandists kept up a steady onslaught during the negotiations, including a 'blasphemous caricature' in *Pravda* which Lord Stamfordham trusted would 'be as repulsive and shocking to the Prime Minister as it is to the King'.[57] Zinoviev also slated 'MacDonald's infamy', something the Monarch flagged for the Foreign Secretary's attention, thinking it outrageous that such attacks continued as British delegates attempted to negotiate in good faith with their Russian counterparts.[58] MacDonald later complained to Rakovsky, arguing that Zinoviev's 'vituperation' had passed 'all bounds of decent political controversy'.[59]

Eventually, when Rakovsky made a minimal gesture towards meeting historic Russian obligations, the UK government agreed to guarantee a £40 million loan, despite MacDonald's assurances on 18 June that it had no intention of doing so.[60] At a decisive Cabinet meeting in late July, Snowden (supported by Jimmy Thomas, Lord Olivier and Josiah Wedgwood) attacked the proposed guarantee but with the 'very skilful assistance' of the Foreign Secretary and support from John Wheatley, Arthur Henderson and Sidney Webb, Arthur Ponsonby secured agreement. What dismayed him, however, was both the Foreign Secretary's lack of enthusiasm (MacDonald hoped the 'Bolshies would reject it')[61] and the Cabinet's almost entire ignorance of the negotiations. 'With few exceptions they did not seem to care very much,' he wrote miserably in his diary, 'all of them immersed in their own jobs.'[62]

Early on 5 August, however, the talks nearly broke down again regarding compensation for property owners. The Soviets wanted to pick and choose who got paid, an arbitrary approach the UK was understandably reluctant to sanction. On 31 July, Ponsonby had asked E. D. Morel and George Lansbury to bring pressure to bear on the Soviet delegates,[63] which Morel later spun as them having 'saved' the Anglo-Russian Conference, much to the irritation of MacDonald. Finally, a Board of

Trade official devised a formula Ponsonby believed would be acceptable to Rakovsky. He dashed over to Downing Street where, by a 'miracle', he

> met Snowden in the lobby, got him in a waiting room with a Treasury expert, a moment of hesitation but he accepted it, tore upstairs, found J.R.M. discussing holidays with Ishbel and knew him well enough to be sure that he must not be interrupted; mutton and apple tart almost stuck in my throat but I was rewarded for not bursting in. He turned to me, I explained the position, got his consent to the new formula and munching pie crust ran down to the House and made up my mind on the way to use the MPs and not the officials![64]

It was a shrewd move, for when the new formula was shown to Rakovsky by Morel, it was accepted. There had been no time to circulate printed copies of the revised agreement, and in giving a verbal summary to the Commons Ponsonby was not at his best. Sensing his weakness, Conservative and Liberal MPs 'combined to treat him atrociously' and accused the government of breaking its pledge not to guarantee a loan.[65] David Lloyd George called it a 'fake', a 'contract in which the space for every essential figure is left blank'.[66] The Conservative MP Cuthbert Headlam noted a 'general impression' that 'at the last moment' Labour's 'left wing took the bit between its teeth and practically forced' the government 'to come to some agreement'.[67]

Both treaties, however, were signed and sealed at just after 6 p.m. on 8 August. The first, a Commercial Treaty, provided that the UK should receive from the Soviet Union 'most favoured nation' treatment, in return for which Russia would receive benefits from the Exports Credit Scheme. Under the second agreement, the so-called General Treaty, Russia acknowledged the claims of British bond and property holders for compensation, but, under Article 6, there was merely a commitment to negotiate another Treaty regarding a government-backed loan, and only if the Soviet Union satisfied certain conditions. 'It was this doubly innocuous proposal,' observed Sir Henry Slesser, 'which was represented to the country as a surrender to Russia.'[68]

MacDonald even went out of his way to emphasize that the loan aspect of the General Treaty – if agreed – would be 'put before the House of Commons for rejection or acceptance'.[69] Together with the new Ponsonby Rule regarding parliamentary scrutiny, this meant the Russian Treaties could not possibly be ratified until after the summer recess. Aggrieved at not having received 'one word of relief pleasure commendation or sympathy' from the Foreign Secretary, Arthur Ponsonby was surprised to receive a letter urging him to keep his 'fighting spirit up' and not 'surrender'.[70] 'He is an extraordinary mixture,' he observed in his diary. 'He is inconsiderate and impersonal rather in the same way as [Campbell-Bannerman] was. I think it must be the Scottish temperament. I like his being sparing in praise. It makes a casual word of approval from him very valuable.'[71]

On 12 August the King saw MacDonald and they talked for nearly an hour, the Monarch having earlier expressed concern as to the 'Russian loan'. MacDonald told him he had signed the treaties as Foreign Secretary and not as Prime Minister, as if to imply a disagreement between the two. As Lord Stamfordham recounted:

> The Prime Minister said that the Russians had given us a 'most favoured nation' concession, such as had never before been given to any nation. They have promised again not to finance Communist Organisations in this country and spread propaganda. If they break this Clause it means no loan. I gather that the Prime Minister does not think that there is the slightest chance of a Loan being given, but was too tired to know much about the Treaty, which is entirely the doing of Arthur Ponsonby.[72]

Lord Haldane, who had been humiliated in the Upper House on learning of the treaties from Lord Curzon rather than his own colleagues, believed the 'awkward thing was the suddenness with which the new departure had been entered on, and the shock which this gave to public opinion'.[73] Writing in the *Daily Chronicle* under the headline 'Lulling the Middle Classes to Sleep', Lloyd George (who himself had negotiated an Anglo-Soviet trade agreement in 1921) claimed that, having spent the last seven months showing only its moderate face to the electorate, the Labour government had merely been waiting for the right moment. Then, he added dramatically,

> the mask of sweet reason and moderation will be torn off, and there will appear the stern face of the relentless enemy which has pursued private enterprise and individual property for fully a generation and at last tracked it down. Socialism is approaching skilfully under cover to the grand attack on the existing order of society.

As John Campbell has observed, the veteran Liberal statesman 'cannot himself have believed this blood-curdling nonsense', but it represented an escalation of Lloyd George's conclusion – first crystallized in April – that the 'patient oxen' ought to fight back and, in alliance with the Conservatives, bring its socialist masters to heel.[74] The tabloid press shared the Welsh Wizard's killer instinct, zealously taking up the anti-Bolshevist slogan: 'No Money for Murderers.' 'Things are moving ... and the worm is turning!' Stanley Baldwin told the *Spectator* editor John Strachey. 'The Liberals are in process of revolt against Labour. I don't know how far they will go but the movement has certainly begun.'[75]

MacDonald badly needed a holiday. 'I really cannot go on through the summer without a good break,' he had complained to Lord Parmoor while midway between the Anglo-Soviet and London conferences:

> If I get to Lossiemouth this week I shall only have a fortnight there now before starting for Geneva and the work that is ahead of me makes it pretty clear to me that that will be the end of my holiday. I really cannot go on with a holiday of a

short fortnight during which I shall have to deal with Foreign Office work every day.[76]

The Swiss city of Geneva was home to the Assembly of the League of Nations – the United Nations of its day – which MacDonald and Herriot had earlier agreed to visit during its September plenary session. Under discussion was the draft Treaty of Mutual Assistance proposed at the Assembly's fourth session in September 1923. This envisaged a system of collective assistance (including military) for any League member who was the target of aggression, which it was hoped would lead to a general reduction in armaments. On 30 May 1924, however, the Cabinet and Committee of Imperial Defence had expressed their opposition, with MacDonald calling the guarantee 'so precarious that no responsible Government will feel justified in consenting to any material reduction of its armaments in return'.[77] In its place, the League had prepared the Protocol for the Pacific Settlement of International Disputes (or the 'Geneva Protocol'), which placed more emphasis on the prevention of aggression via international arbitration. This, usefully, was supported by both the Labour government and most elements within the Labour movement.

Before travelling to the Continent, MacDonald managed to snatch a few days in Lossiemouth, his daughter Ishbel and Rose Rosenberg having headed north while the London Conference was still underway. He then spent a week at Balmoral with the Royal Family before heading back to London. 'This is a lovely place,' MacDonald told his aunt Bella. 'The Queen & I had a drive into the forest & then a long walk & back to tea. Tomorrow, if it keeps fine, the King & I are to go up the side of Lochnagar to some loch where there is a fine view.'[78]

MacDonald arrived in Geneva on 3 September and learned to his surprise that he was expected to make a speech. 'The Friends of the League,' he wrote in his diary, 'appealed to me to say something that would revive them, otherwise the League was dead.' He could hardly refuse and in his hotel room prepared a speech making four main points: the desirability of Germany joining the League, ratification of an optional clause in the Statute of the Permanent Court of International Justice, a wider system of arbitration and the calling of a 'General Disarmament Conference'. Detailed preparation for a speech was not his habit. 'The sentences simply come and go,' MacDonald later explained, 'I being a mere channel',[79] and as Kevin Morgan has observed, it is difficult to 'recapture the impression that his speeches appear to have made'.[80] Nevertheless his address, which spoke of 'blending the ideal with the real' and at one point compared arbitration to cloud-watching, was a resounding success with representatives of 54 nations. It was, declared the not uncritical *Manchester Guardian*, 'exactly the speech that the world has long needed from a British Prime Minister'.[81]

When the Prime Minister returned to London a few days later, it was left to Arthur Henderson and Lord Parmoor to pilot the Geneva Protocol through the League's Political Commission. Although France and nine other countries signed, the UK held off, pending consultation with the Cabinet and Committee of Imperial Defence, something Parmoor bitterly regretted. While Lord Haldane believed MacDonald had 'played the game splendidly' in Geneva, he also thought its implications had not been adequately considered.[82] The Admiralty objected to losing full control of its fleet, the Treasury and Board of Trade feared the impact of economic sanctions, while the Dominions (and the US) were also unhappy. Although the Cabinet accepted the draft Protocol on 29 September, the Foreign Secretary's eloquent speech looked unlikely to be matched by government action.

From Switzerland, MacDonald returned to London and then caught a train to Dundee, where he was due to receive the Freedom of the City on 9 September. Awkwardly, E. D. Morel was one of the city's MPs and led a delegation which greeted the Prime Minister on his arrival. Arthur Ponsonby had advised Morel in advance to talk of anything that was 'not remotely connected with politics',[83] so Morel welcomed him as 'the great peace minister'. MacDonald – who still bore a grudge against Morel – was graceless in response.[84]

On addressing the local Labour Party, the Prime Minister confessed to exhaustion, wondering if it would be possible in future 'with unscrupulous party fighting, with no mercy shown and no favour ever extended to one, for anybody ever to be Prime Minister of Great Britain for more than 12 months'. He also deployed his favoured agricultural metaphor for the conduct of foreign affairs:

> The man who knows how to do his work, who seeks legislation that is to be permanent, will work humbly, patiently, faithfully building up and up and up, dealing with the harvests as they ripen, never cutting green corn, but always watching and having somewhat of the powers of the Creator Himself, hastening the ripening of what is green, so that at the earliest possible moment it may be cut and gathered into our barns.[85]

This reference to the Almighty was typical of a 'hyperbolical strain' which had entered MacDonald's speeches,[86] but then he had always been something of a lay preacher. The following day, he was made a Burgess of Dundee before a crowd of 3,000, after which he and Ishbel, reported *The Times*, drove to Lossiemouth to 'complete his interrupted holiday'.[87]

But the weary Prime Minister had only a few days' respite. On 11 September, a new edition of his 1921 book, *Socialism, Critical and Constructive*, was published. In a new preface dated June 1924, MacDonald denounced Bolshevism as 'but an interlude in Tsarism' and warned that 'the revolutionary frame of mind created by the war had been a serious menace to the Socialist spirit of common service'. Coming amid his promotion of the Russian Treaties, this appeared hypocritical.[88] But this was a minor embarrassment compared with what followed. On Friday 12 September the *Daily Mail* reported – under a sensational double-column headline – that MacDonald had been deriving an income from 30,000 shares in the well-known biscuit firm of McVitie & Price. Not only that, but the newspaper had discovered via a diligent survey of the company's records at Somerset House that the shares had been transferred on 12 March by Sir Alexander Grant, the McVitie's chairman, controlling shareholder and a childhood friend of MacDonald. The fact that Grant had been granted a baronetcy a few weeks later was the final ingredient in a perfect tabloid tale. It looked like a straightforward case of cash for honours, although the reality was more nuanced.

While a 'thunderstruck' Sir Alexander was besieged by reporters at Manchester railway station, the Prime Minister tried to limit the damage. 'The capital is not mine, and I only technically own the shares,' he said in a short, and rather terse, statement to the Press Association. 'The matter has nothing to do with politics. Sir Alexander Grant got his baronetcy for public services, including the gift of the National Library to Scotland, of which most people know, and for which he has received the freedom of Edinburgh.'[89] By the following day, it had become clear that the purpose of the shares was to 'endow' a Daimler motor car for the Prime Minister's use. 'I am sick at heart to have to talk of this,' said MacDonald during another interview at The Hillocks, 'but I must protect my dear old friend in the enjoyment of the honour which the King so worthily bestowed upon him, and with which this act of personal kindness to myself had as much to do as the man in the moon.' He protested that he had not fancied himself

as the owner of a motorcar. It was against the simplicity of my habits. I took a long time to be persuaded, and letters are in existence which reveal the minds of us. In the end I agreed with this arrangement. A sum of money was to be invested in my name, and the income I am to enjoy during my lifetime so long as I keep a car, and at my death it is to revert to Sir Alexander Grant or his heirs. This is the full story of the incident.[90]

MacDonald repaid an old debt by granting this interview to the veteran journalist A. G. Wilken, one of the only reporters not to have abandoned him over his opposition to the war. With the world's press camped out in Lossiemouth, Wilken instead wired the story from his Central News agency in Elgin, making him 'a relatively rich man overnight'.[91]

Reading the newspapers in London, Beatrice Webb acknowledged 'extenuating circumstances':

> Grant ... may be said to have 'deserved a baronetcy'. MacDonald is taking an income, not from a stranger, but from a lifelong friend. Further, other statesmen have done exactly the same thing; but have hidden it up. MacDonald did it in a way which was bound to be discovered, and therefore it may be assumed he saw no objection to it. For all that, the bald facts look as if he had 'sold a baronetcy', not for party funds but for his own pecuniary benefit.

The 'blow', added Webb, was 'staggering: J.R.M. may not only have killed the Labour Prime Minister, he may have undermined, for a generation, the moral prestige of the Parliamentary Labour Party. Hitherto we have prided ourselves on being a party of incorruptibles. Shall we be so, even in our own sight, any longer?'[92]

As the row rumbled on, Sir Alexander added his own explanation late on Sunday evening:

> I felt that he was taking too much out of himself, and this was confirmed when I heard that he was travelling about by the Underground Railway. For instance, on the night when he delivered his fine speech at the Pilgrims' dinner [on 1 February] it had been arranged that after he left the hall he should take a train to Baker-street and travel thence by the Metropolitan Railway to a point near Chequers, where he was to go on by a Ford car.[93]

Lauchlan MacNeill Weir, MacDonald's PPS, was later scathing about this explanation, claiming the Prime Minister had never used the Underground while in office, 'for he had no need to do so' given he lived at Downing Street.[94] On 15 September, Grant wrote to the man he considered a 'brother', observing that what

MacDonald had long 'feared was to take place' had finally 'come like a flash of lightning':

> It seems to me to be a very poor world where one friend cannot be of assistance to the other ... but I do not think that any right-thinking people will allow themselves to be side-tracked by this ... it is only the opinion of good people that matters and that guides public opinion, however loud the others may be.[95]

Much rested on what 'good people' would make of Grant's baronetcy. According to Ishbel MacDonald, he had been offered this by the previous government but 'said he'd rather wait and get it from his friend JRM, who he was sure would be PM sooner or later'.[96] Even Philip Snowden, who was not by this stage inclined to be sympathetic, said it was 'within' his own knowledge 'that Mr. Grant's name had been on the waiting-list for a baronetcy before Mr. MacDonald became Prime Minister'.[97]

Although most 'right-thinking people' most likely concluded MacDonald had been naïve rather than corrupt, the 'biscuits' affair tarnished his reputation and amounted to a terrible psychological blow so soon after the 'highs' of the London Conference and his speech in Geneva. An indication of MacDonald's mood is to be found in a letter he wrote to Lady Londonderry on 13 September, when the row was at its peak. After alluding to 'wild propaganda', he lamented his imminent return to London:

> My moors and sky and sea were never more beautiful or more alluring, porridge and milk never tasted better. Nor a meal of pulse more pleasant and satisfying; and I have to bid them all farewell and return to decorum and high feasts and the great skies of a frowning world. Why not give you a General Election, when you can come armed with Bolshevist pamphlets...and send me about my business? Then I shall begin the Waverley Novels afresh and bless you to everlasting.[98]

On reaching London a few days later, the Prime Minister met a few Cabinet colleagues for an informal discussion about the forthcoming 'special session' of Parliament, the sole purpose of which was to pass legislation necessary to constitute the Irish Boundary Commission. Snowden saw at once that he was in 'a highly nervous condition', incapable of taking 'a calm and reasoned view on any subject'.[99] 'Poor Mac,' wrote Beatrice Webb, was suffering from 'mortified spiritual vanity'. He spoke

> gloomily about his 'being sick of it', the party had behaved so badly, the parliamentary executive regarding themselves as a court martial and the Daily Herald queering his pitch perpetually. 'Supposing we did come back in a majority, would you welcome it?' he asked. And when most of them replied 'Yes', he said that he thought it would be a grave misfortune, as the party (not the Cabinet!) was 'not fit to govern'.[100]

When Ben Spoor, the Chief Whip, told J. S. Middleton how 'depressed' and unwell the Prime Minister felt, the Labour Party's Acting Secretary despatched a sympathetic note:

> It is not surprising considering all the happenings of the last few weeks, and you certainly have not had the sort of break that would do you much good. When this was supplemented by the news, per wireless last night, that you had caught a chill on your way down, it made it all the easier to realise what a burden you are really bearing.[101]

Lord Haldane, meanwhile, believed that while the 'motor car incident' would not 'produce any explosion', it had rubbed 'the gilt off the gingerbread'. The result, he told Beatrice Webb, would 'be a tendency to disintegrate, which will be stimulated by other things. The Russian business is unfortunate. None but our own warm supporters will feel content with it. As to Ireland, we are in a better position, if we can take full advantage of it.'[102]

Haldane's assessment was shrewd. When on 21 September the Cabinet met for the first time since early August, the Irish problem had all but disappeared, with 'diehard' Conservative opposition having failed to materialize. Russia, however, had been simmering since early August and was about to come to the boil. The Conservatives and Liberals remained unhappy about the idea of the UK guaranteeing a loan to a country which daily advertised its intention to smash the 'capitalist' British Empire.

Asquith, the Liberal leader, made his views clear in a letter published on 22 September. Belatedly associating himself with the protests of Lloyd George, Lord Grey and several other prominent Liberals, he said Parliament should not 'countenance' – even provisionally – 'the guarantee by the taxpayers of Great Britain of a loan of undefined amount on unspecified conditions to the Soviet Government'. Rejecting the charge that this stance was informed by anti-Soviet prejudice, Asquith said his goal was something more business-like than 'crude experiments in nursery diplomacy'.[103] In a much-anticipated speech on 25 September, meanwhile, Winston Churchill said Conservatives and Liberals should combine to avoid 'subsidising tyranny', an intervention which marked the former Liberal's first intimation of public support for Stanley Baldwin.[104]

The Prime Minister responded on 27 September with a gibe at the 'nursery criticism' of his opponents, defending the Russian Treaties but meeting Asquith halfway in attaching certain conditions to the provision and guarantee of the loan.[105] Privately, however, MacDonald viewed the Liberals as a 'contemptible coterie with a lazy old man at their head'. 'The attack on the Russian Treaties looks less & less honest as one considers it,' he wrote in his diary. 'I am inclined to give the Liberals an election on it if they force it ... I do not relish the prospect of the state of things continuing.'[106]

Charles Ammon at the Admiralty felt MacDonald had taken his eye off the ball, apparently 'quite unaware of the growing antagonism to his Government's Russian policy'.[107] Writing in his diary on 24 September Arthur Ponsonby – the main architect of the Russian Treaties – agreed that he 'enters into the wood with no map decided on no particular path and he feels his way by instinct by quick momentary decisions in the light of the circumstances of the moment, manipulating as he goes'.[108] Addressing a meeting of the Parliamentary Labour Party a few days later, MacDonald's suggestion that a general election might be fought over the Russian Treaties was received with 'shouts of enthusiasm', although Ponsonby could not help noticing how 'tired and ill' the Prime Minister looked. He later told Ponsonby that if Labour continued in government he would no longer 'double' up as both premier and Foreign Secretary.[109] As Harold Nicolson noted in his authorized biography of George V, MacDonald had paid a 'formidable price' for having so rapidly 'altered the whole tone of international relations':

> The effort of those nine months was so gigantic that it damaged his health; his powers of assimilation, memory and concentration were seriously overstrained. The pressure of external affairs prevented him, moreover, from devoting to internal politics the close attention that they merited; mistakes were made. Above all, the cloud of overwork that hid the Prime Minister from his colleagues and supporters produced an impression of misty and even conceited aloofness – an impression which, as it hardened into a grievance, created an ever-widening rift between Mr MacDonald and the rank and file of his own party.[110]

When Parliament finally met on 30 September, it was clear to Philip Snowden and others that MacDonald had 'not recovered his nerve', and they 'feared what might happen when he had to face a merciless Tory Opposition and a Liberal Party by now no means friendly'.[111] Another storm was about to break, and the Prime Minister's response would determine the fate of the first Labour government.

13

SIR PATRICK HASTINGS: 'BY WHOSE REPRESENTATION?'

For most of his life, John Ross Campbell was known for being a 'case' rather than a human being. Born in Paisley to working-class parents in 1894, he started working as a grocer's assistant at fourteen. In 1912, 'Johnny' Campbell joined the British Socialist Party and at the outbreak of hostilities two years later was called up as a reservist, earning the Military Medal for conspicuous bravery during the Battle of the Somme. He joined the Communist Party of Great Britain (CPGB) upon its formation in 1920 and became a member of its central executive committee in 1923. Thin and quick-witted, Campbell was father to five stepchildren and two daughters with his wife Sarah, lived on a council estate and ate with printworkers at the *Daily Worker* canteen. A recognized authority on Robert Burns, he was as popular as a communist could be in the mid-1920s.[1]

Campbell was also a talented writer and propagandist and, on relocating to London in early 1924, became acting editor of the CPGB's *Workers' Weekly*. On 25 July, this carried an article specially addressed to 'the fighting forces', who were exhorted to form committees 'in every barracks, aerodrome, and ship' to lead 'a common attack upon the capitalists' and institute 'the reign of the whole working class'.[2] Although Campbell had edited the article, it was actually written by another British communist named Harry Pollitt. On 29 July, it was raised in the House of Commons,[3] with two more questions the following day. Rhys Davies, an under-secretary at the Home Office, simply said Arthur Henderson was 'considering whether any action is called for'.[4]

On 30 July, five days after the article appeared, the Director of Public Prosecutions, Sir Archibald Bodkin, met with the Attorney General, Sir Patrick Hastings, and sought his consent to institute criminal proceedings against the *Workers' Weekly* under the *Incitement to Mutiny Act 1797*. This was granted, though Sidney Webb later suggested Hastings believed he was 'merely being asked for a legal opinion' rather than the authority to prosecute the editor of a 'quite obscure organ of the British Communist Party'.[5] Given the Attorney General's legal experience, this scarcely seems credible.[6]

Sir Patrick, to be fair, was seriously overburdened, not least because he was the only one of the government's four law officers (two English and two Scottish) who actually had a seat in the House of Commons. As he complained in his memoirs:

The day was spent in one long rush between the Law Courts, Government departments, and the House of Commons. The night, or rather the early morning, was needed in order to get ready for the next day. Nothing that I began was I ever allowed to finish; and nothing was ever finished until something else was begun. Being an Attorney-General as it was in those days is my idea of hell.[7]

Born in London on St Patrick's Day 1880, Patrick Gardiner Hastings was named after the patron saint, both sides of his family having Irish provenance. Though outwardly respectable – his father Alfred had been a solicitor and his mother Kate a Pre-Raphaelite artist – the family oscillated between affluence and penury. Bankruptcy, wrote Hastings in his memoirs, 'was not a misfortune, it was a habit'.[8] After an unhappy schooling, he worked as a mining engineer in South Wales and served with the Suffolk Imperial Yeomanry during the South African War before being admitted to Middle Temple. With his parents unable to support him, Hastings saved enough to fund his call to the English Bar in 1904.

Two years later he married Mary Ellenore, whose father was a lieutenant-colonel, and together they produced two sons and three daughters as he became one of the busiest juniors at the common-law bar. Hastings took silk in 1919 and by the age of forty had 'all the cases that I wanted and perhaps more than I could do'.[9] Initially a Liberal, in 1921 he was adopted as the Labour candidate for Wallsend in Northumberland, defying expectations to win the largely industrial seat the following year. Beatrice Webb considered Hastings 'an unpleasant type of clever pleader and political arriviste',[10] and he did not take to the House of Commons, despising its tribalism as well as the often slow pace of parliamentary life. But as one of the only Labour MPs who was also a King's Counsel, in January 1924 Hastings reluctantly accepted office as Attorney General.[11]

By 2 August, a warrant had been issued for John Campbell's arrest and two days later Hastings was in his place on the front bench when the Home Secretary, Arthur Henderson, told him he had received a letter from some printers about the proposed prosecution of the *Workers' Weekly*. Sir Patrick asked for further information from the Assistant Director of Public Prosecutions, Sir Guy Stephenson, but by the time this reached him, the warrant had been executed, the offices of the newspaper raided by the police, and John Campbell placed in custody.[12]

On 6 August John Scurr, the Labour MP for Stepney Mile End, asked the Home Secretary 'under whose instructions' those proceedings had been instituted. Having been asked to respond on Henderson's behalf, Sir Patrick said that in his opinion the article 'constituted a breach of the law' for which the editor (Campbell) had accepted responsibility. During the angry exchanges that followed, James Maxton protested that the article 'mainly' contained 'a call to the troops not to allow themselves to be used in industrial disputes', a view he said (to a roar of approval) was 'shared by a large number of the Members sitting on these benches'. After the Speaker warned that further debate would be inappropriate given the matter was *sub judice*, Thomas Dickson, the Labour MP for Lanark, sarcastically asked the Attorney General if any Members expressing similar opinions to those in the article would also be subject to prosecution. As his colleagues shouted 'Yes!', Dickson added: 'If so, they will probably lose half their party.'[13] The Labour historian Francis Williams judged that such anger was directed not at the Attorney General but the Prime Minister, 'whom they suspected of not being so keen as some of his Cabinet colleagues on the Russian Treaty and of being glad of any chance to attack the Communists'.[14] Indeed, when John Scanlon, Sir Patrick Hastings' secretary, suggested the prosecution might be politically risky, Maxton 'sarcastically asked if wrecking the Government would be a tragedy ... that the sooner they were out the better, as every day they were in office led us further from Socialism'.[15]

But the behaviour of the Clydesiders, many of whom would have known Johnny Campbell personally, appears to have astonished Sir Patrick, who had somehow contrived not to pay any attention to internal Labour Party politics. On leaving the Chamber he asked to see Maxton and Sir Henry Slesser, the Solicitor General, as soon as possible. The former told him that Campbell was only acting editor of the *Workers' Weekly* and had a most distinguished war record as well as permanent injuries, although these were often exaggerated.[16] Asked for his opinion, Sir Henry appeared to concur with Maxton that the contents of the article did not fall under the 1797 Act, although he also agreed with Hastings that an unsuccessful prosecution would not be in the public interest.[17]

Sir Guy Stephenson, the Deputy Director of Public Prosecutions, later confirmed Maxton's account of Campbell's war record and added another key detail: the article had not in fact been written by the acting editor. At this point, the Attorney General decided the prosecution should not be allowed to proceed as it would most likely be unsuccessful and merely end up 'advertising Communism'. On meeting with Sir Patrick and Sir Guy, the Prime

Minister sought to blame the Director of Public Prosecutions (Sir Alexander Bodkin), in response to which the Attorney General said he accepted sole responsibility given he had authorized the proceedings.

In his subsequent account to the King of what he called a 'muddle', MacDonald said he had been 'furious' to learn of the prosecution, having known nothing of the case until he 'saw it in the newspapers':

> I sent for the Attorney General and the Public Prosecutor and gave them both a bit of my mind. They had acted without proper consultation and upon papers that gave them no sanction whatever for what they did. They replied that the whole matter should be dropped. I told them that as they had begun they had to go through with it.

Although this was not a wholly accurate account of what had transpired, the Prime Minister sought to excuse the incident as arising 'largely from the inexperience of some of my Ministers' as well as the 'slackness of business administration' in Whitehall.[18] He also conveyed the impression that any decision made by the Attorney General was subject to a prime ministerial veto.

Later, on 6 October, the matter came before the Cabinet, which in the absence of Sir Maurice Hankey was minuted by his deputy Tom Jones. Sir Patrick said he took 'full responsibility' but was prepared to terminate proceedings 'if the Cabinet so desired'. Arthur Henderson, the Home Secretary, said he had asked for a letter of apology from the printers, while Jimmy Thomas declared that 'nothing of this sort should happen without P.M. and Cabinet knowing of it'. MacDonald then said he would

> rather go through once started than show white feather. If you stop prosecution you will be asked all round what [you are] going to do. Editor is known – why not arrest him ... If [It had been] put to me I should not have sanctioned it. I know the men and the game. Now in [the] press and House of Commons.

Confusingly, such statements, that they should press on with the prosecution, were not matched by the Cabinet's conclusions, which were

  a. That no public prosecution of a political character should be undertaken without the prior sanction of the Cabinet being obtained.
  b. That in the particular case under review the course indicated by the Attorney-General should be adopted.[19]

As Sir Patrick later told the Commons, he 'left that Cabinet meeting with a decision at which I had arrived interfered with by nobody'.[20] In the words of the lawyer F. H. Newark, the Cabinet had 'asserted the right to interfere, and Hastings seems to have conceded that right. But in fact there was no political interference because the cabinet decided to adopt the course on which Hastings had already decided.'[21]

That decision was then put into effect. Shown the arguments for withdrawing the prosecution by Travers Humphreys, the senior Treasury counsel, Sir Patrick rejected them all except for Campbell's war record. On 13 August, therefore, a sceptical magistrate at Bow Street was informed that since

> process was issued in this case, *it has been represented* that the object and intention of the article in question was not to endeavour to seduce men in the fighting forces from their duty in the regiment or to induce them to disobey lawful orders, but that it was a comment upon armed military force being used by the State for the suppression of industrial disputes ... It has been possible for the Director of Public Prosecutions to accept that alleged intention of this article more easily because the defendant is a man of excellent character with an admirable military record.[22]

Humphreys' expression 'it has been represented', most likely inserted to flesh out what he considered an otherwise weak argument, provoked immediate controversy. While he later explained he was referring to 'the representations or statements made in the House of Commons and elsewhere at public meetings', John Campbell referred publicly to 'pressure of the rank and file' while the *Workers' Weekly* said withdrawal had come 'under severe pressure' from 'well-known' Labour MPs such as George Lansbury, James Maxton, John Scurr and 'many others'.[23] There was even speculation the CPGB would engage Sir John Simon (a Liberal) or Sir Douglas Hogg (a Tory) as counsel and call upon the Prime Minister to account for his 1912 defence of the trade unionist Tom Mann, who had been charged with an offence similar to that now withdrawn against Campbell.

Unhelpfully, this interpretation of 'representations' reinforced suspicions regarding the Russian loan, namely that the Prime Minister had caved under pressure from Clydesiders and communists. 'This then was the nub of the Campbell controversy,' observed the legal academic J. J. Edwards, for if 'substantiated ... such conduct on the part of the government was wholly unconstitutional'.[24] An editorial in *The Times* (under the heading 'By Whose Representation?') said it would

> constitute an interference by the Executive with the course of justice which should not be tolerated by the people of this country. To arrest a man on a grave charge and then to refuse, at the instance of someone, presumably in authority, to disclose the evidence when the accused professes to have a good defence, is not consistent with British ideas of justice. It undermines the confidence of the public in the procedure of our Courts of Law.[25]

Despite the furore, within a few days the 'Campbell Case' had receded from view. Even the King had been 'comforted' by his Prime Minister's account and was content to regard the affair, as MacDonald himself did, as a 'considerable muddle' rather than an ongoing concern.[26]

Within four weeks, however, it had returned like a bad penny. *The Times* reported on 20 September that Sir Kingsley Wood, a

Conservative MP who had a knack of getting under the Prime Minister's skin, intended to raise the Campbell Case once Parliament reconvened. Clearly panicked at this prospect, on 22 September MacDonald took the extraordinary step – during a gathering Hankey took to be a Cabinet meeting – of challenging the accuracy of the Cabinet minute dated 6 August, particularly conclusion (b) that the Attorney General's advice to withdraw the prosecution should be followed. As the Prime Minister later told C. P. Scott, Sir Maurice Hankey had

> been unable to attend and a substitute had been employed to take the minutes who took them all wrong. When Hankey brought them to MacDonald to be initialled he was in the midst of an important discussion ... on a proposed London Agreement. MacDonald scolded him for bringing them at such a time, contrary to his instructions, but Hankey persisted and said he thought he should look at item 5. MacDonald, still impatient, said, 'Well, is it all right?' and Hankey replied, 'Yes, I think so.' 'So I just initialled it,' said MacDonald and thought no more about it.[27]

As with MacDonald's earlier communication with the King, this was another partial account of events. What the Prime Minister did not realize was that Tom Jones had kept his raw notes from 6 August, which allowed the Cabinet Secretary and his Deputy to piece together an authoritative chronology of the minute and its subsequent approval by MacDonald.[28]

In a further indication of MacDonald's deteriorating judgement, he also told Hankey not to keep a record of the 22 September meeting, 'raising the possibility that the meeting became a non-event because MacDonald wanted no record of what had been talked about'. As Hankey's biographer John F. Naylor has concluded, the Prime Minister was 'prepared to discredit the Cabinet Secretariat for errors committed by the Executive'.[29]

This incident not only destroyed the hitherto close relationship between Hankey and MacDonald but also further diminished the Prime Minister's opinion of his Attorney General. 'Hastings is being overworked,' he complained to Hugh Macmillan, the Lord Advocate. 'The position is as you know that instead of having four lawyers on the front bench I have only one.'[30] Busy people make mistakes, and both MacDonald and Sir Patrick were exhausted. But whatever MacDonald's failures of judgement, he was not wrong to attribute some of the blame to his Attorney General, not least his failure to take into consideration the wider political, legal and disciplinary implications of his initial decision to prosecute. As F. H. Newark has observed, Hastings 'should have realised from the beginning' that the case 'could turn into political dynamite'.[31] In Ishbel MacDonald's account, her father had been 'let down by a clever lawyer who ... like so many other clever lawyers had not the instinct for parliamentary government'.[32]

To a degree, it was all humbug. Lord Haldane thought the idea that governments should never interfere with 'political' prosecutions absurd, while J. R. Clynes argued in his memoirs that the law officers regularly advised ministers whether or not certain proceedings ought to be initiated, for if 'this were not the case, what [was] the use of these officers?'[33] J. J. Edwards agreed, believing that some (if not all) of Hastings' predecessors as Attorneys General had often recognized the law officers' 'subservience to ... other members of the executive in the institution of criminal proceedings against particular individuals'.[34]

Humbug it may have been, but that humbug had exploded politically. On 25 September, Winston Churchill weaponized the Campbell Case during a rally organized by the Scottish Unionist Association in Edinburgh. Alleging that the 'Socialist Government' had 'perverted the administration of justice for political expedience', Churchill stated that

> Political pressure was brought to bear. A handful of obscure figures lurking in the background behind every Socialist administration made their power felt. The Government was terrified. The Attorney-General ordered the withdrawal of the

prosecution. An apologetic explanation was offered; the case fell to the ground, and the man walked off Scot free.

And if such things could be done by a minority Labour government, Churchill added gravely, 'we may judge for ourselves what may happen if a Socialist Government secures an actual majority of the House of Commons'.[35]

Parliament met on Tuesday 30 September, a month earlier than planned. Although this special sitting quickly became consumed by the Campbell Case, its primary purpose was tying up the loose ends of the Anglo-Irish Treaty. The Prime Minister himself moved the second reading of the Irish Free State (Confirmation of Agreement) Bill, telling the House that the 1921 agreement was 'a solemn contract' binding on both the 'Government then in power and on its successors'.[36] This much was uncontroversial, for there was no longer any Conservative appetite to defend belligerent Ulster Unionists. But, as MacDonald observed in his diary, the 'prosecution of a communist foolishly entered upon but much more foolishly, dropped, has enabled every hypocrite who does not agree with us to shout that we have been subverting the law & the constitution'.[37]

Earlier that day the Attorney General had responded to two Private Notice Questions regarding the abandoned prosecution of John Campbell. Sir Patrick equipped himself well, recounting the chronology of events since 25 July and coolly rebutting the idea that he had received any 'representation' from the defendant 'or from any person whatsoever'. Stanley Baldwin then asked whether the Prime Minister would allow time for further debate once the Irish Bill had been dealt with. 'We shall be guided by the course of the Debate to-night whether, in asking for that day,' added the Conservative leader, 'we couple it with a Vote of Censure.' An irritated MacDonald replied that he was 'not at all content to wait' and suggested that with at least two sitting days 'going blank' when the Irish Bill moved to 'another place' (the House of Lords) for consideration, one of them might be used for the purpose proposed by Baldwin. Asquith – who proposed his own critical resolution – concurred with the Prime Minister's 'reasonable' suggestion of an expedited discussion and the Conservative leader also consented.[38] Margaret Bondfield, then in Canada, believed this was the moment MacDonald's 'judgement deserted him'.[39]

Next, the Prime Minister responded to a Private Notice Question from Sir Kingsley Wood as to whether he had sanctioned the withdrawal of proceedings against John Campbell. He said:

> I was not consulted regarding either the institution or the subsequent withdrawal of these proceedings. The first notice of the prosecution which came to my knowledge was in the Press. I never advised its withdrawal, but left the whole matter to the discretion of the Law Officers, where that discretion properly rests. I never received any intimation, nor even a hint, that I should be asked to give evidence. That also came to my attention when the falsehood appeared in the Press.[40]

Sir Maurice Hankey called the first part of MacDonald's response 'a bloody lie', while Tom Jones, listening from the Commons gallery, said 'a shiver' went down his spine.[41] In his daily report to the King, the Prime Minister did not dwell on his misleading response but claimed 'misrepresentation' of the Campbell Case meant it had 'developed, at any rate for the time being, into an important political issue'.[42]

Events began to move quickly. The King and Queen were still at Balmoral when, on 2 October, Lord Stamfordham received a letter from the Prime Minister warning him that 'an end was approaching':

> The grace which was given to us for a month or two after we came in, has been steadily disappearing and the ordinary old-fashioned Parliamentary methods of attack ... have become more and more common ... Since I have been a Minister I have striven to give no advice to the Crown except what was impartial and issued from my sense of public duty ...

The decision of the Liberal Party yesterday, however, to move a resolution ... has made my course quite clear ... I see nothing for it but another appeal to the country as quickly as possible.[43]

That same day the Prime Minister was further tormented by a skilfully worded question from Sir Kingsley Wood asking if he would require the House to authorize an increase in his salary as First Lord of the Treasury. This clear reference to the Daimler affair of the previous month was compounded when Wood added that 'the present holder has found the emoluments of his office insufficient and has had to go to a private citizen', a remark greeted by noisy cries of 'Dirty!' from Labour MPs.[44] The Irish Bill, meanwhile, received its second reading after what MacDonald told the King was a 'masterpiece' of a winding up by Jimmy Thomas.[45] A last-ditch Ulster Unionist amendment moving for rejection of the Bill was defeated by 291 votes to 124.

A consensus regarding Ireland, however, did not mean the government was off the hook. 'As far as I am concerned,' declared Leo Amery in Birmingham, 'I do not care whether the Government is killed this week or at the beginning of next month, so long as it is killed.'[46] The Conservatives, the Prime Minister told the King, were 'clearly out for blood' while the Liberals remained 'enigmatic'; 'so these two Parties vie with each other in their struggles to usurp the position of Lord High Executioner'.[47] Eventually, it was agreed the censure debate would take place on Wednesday 8 October.

In yet another twist, a newspaper editor informed Sir Patrick Hastings that the Prime Minister, while at Lossiemouth the previous month, had told one of his reporters that he held the Attorney General entirely responsible for the 'muddle' of the Campbell Case and intended to ask for his resignation. Hastings called this a 'lie' and later challenged the premier in his room at the House of Commons:

MacDonald ... said that there had been some misunderstanding; he said that he had evolved in his mind an ingenious idea which might solve all his difficulties. He suggested that I should take all the responsibility upon myself, which I reminded him I had always done, and that I should then resign; that he would insist upon my immediately seeking re-election, and that all the members of the Cabinet should show their unbounded confidence in me by coming down to my constituency and speaking for me at the by-election.

With Hastings 'too much taken aback to think of a suitable reply', Jimmy Thomas filled the void by exclaiming, 'Mac, that's a damned dirty trick!' while adding, as Sir Patrick recalled, 'a few of those adjectives which anyone who knew Jimmy well would have expected'. When the Prime Minister attempted to excuse his proposal as 'merely a suggestion which had crossed his mind', the Attorney General said he would be unable to 'support' his statement of 30 September, which the Lord Advocate had already informed the premier was misleading. 'On that not very friendly note I left him,' wrote Hastings, 'and that was the last time I ever had a personal conversation with MacDonald.'[48]

The Cabinet met on 6 October to decide its response to the motions to be debated two days later, a vote of censure from the Conservatives and a Liberal amendment proposing a select committee inquiry. 'We are going to fight and refuse to accept the motions on Wednesday in any form,' recorded Haldane. 'If, as I expect, the Commons decide against us tomorrow we shall ask for a dissolution.'[49]

With fortuitous timing, the Labour Party conference opened at London's Queen's Hall on 7 October. 'If there be an election the responsibility is not ours,' declared MacDonald in his opening remarks, going on to contrast the Conservatives' 'straightforward motion of censure' with a Liberal amendment 'conceived in the spirit of medieval crookedness and torture'.[50] Charles Trevelyan thought it 'a magnificent as well as skilful speech', although he still believed 'defeat in some form' to be inevitable the following day.[51]

Lord Stamfordham was also proceeding on that basis. Since receiving the Prime Minister's gloomy letter on 2 October, he had sought 'soundings' from the other party leaders. While Baldwin was 'entirely in favour of a General Election and could not undertake to form Government', Asquith complicated matters by saying that while he thought it would be 'very difficult' for the King to refuse a dissolution, it was 'very unreasonable' for MacDonald to request one on the basis of the Campbell Case.[52] Seeking clarity, on 4 October Lord Stamfordham warned the Prime Minister that the King 'must be guided to a considerable degree by the nature of the issue upon which you would go to the country'.[53] Others advised, however, that to deny a dissolution would be 'tantamount to dismissal' of MacDonald.[54] This all proved academic. That evening, MacDonald dined with 'past and potential donors' to Labour's election fund at Downing Street, during which Lord Haldane pledged £1,000 from his own savings.[55] 'The question of election finance will have to be discussed by us this week-end,' Charles Trevelyan told his wife Molly. 'It is awful having three elections in three years. What must it be to those who have nothing in the offing.'[56]

As Sir Patrick Hastings walked to Parliament on 8 October, the streets were 'thronged' and he almost had to fight his way into the courtyard. 'In the House itself the galleries were packed,' he recalled, 'and even the lobbies were filled to overflowing.'[57] First, the Prime Minister asked the 'indulgence of the House' to correct his reply to Sir Kingsley Wood's question of 30 September. He explained that he had used

an expression which, when my attention was drawn to it two days afterwards, I had to admit went a little further than I ought to have gone ... [implying] that I had no cognisance of what was going on. I am very sorry. I did not mean to imply that. It was simply the concentration of my personal resentment at that gross imputation [that he had interfered] which made me for a moment forget that officially, and in conjunction with colleagues, the matter was talked about when no personal

considerations were in our minds at all. If I have misled any
hon. Members, I apologise for having done so.[58]

But instead of clearing the air, MacDonald's apology, to quote
Philip Snowden, 'made the position still worse, and actually
increased the impression of lack of frankness and candour'.
Colleagues on the front bench, added the Chancellor, hung 'their
heads in shame', while the Prime Minister dug himself deeper
under 'severe' cross-examination from Austen Chamberlain
(Conservative) and Sir John Simon (Liberal). John Wheatley
remarked to Philip Snowden that he had never known 'a man
who could succeed so well, even if he is telling the truth, in giving
the impression that he is not doing so'.[59] MacDonald's retraction,
recalled Sir Patrick Hastings, was 'heard in chilly silence'. It was,
he remarked, 'a most unfortunate atmosphere in which to start a
battle'.[60] The censure debate was to last seven hours.

Sir Robert Horne then moved 'that the conduct of His Majesty's
Government in relation to the institution and subsequent
withdrawal of criminal proceedings against the editor of the
Workers' Weekly is deserving of the censure of the House'. The
former Conservative Chancellor based his indictment mainly on
statements made by members of the CPGB (which he took at face
value) that the prosecution had been withdrawn under pressure
by certain Labour MPs. Sir Patrick Hastings, who felt 'disgust
at the whole proceeding and almost everyone connected with
them', followed with a further explanation of his actions which
impressed even his political opponents. 'It did not require the
roars from the Government supporters which arose when I sat
down,' he recalled, 'to make it plain that things were not going
quite as the Opposition had desired.'[61]

Next was Sir John Simon. Although he believed that Hastings
had satisfactorily explained his own conduct, he persisted in
moving the Liberal amendment seeking the appointment of
a ten-strong select committee to investigate and report on the
withdrawal of the prosecution. The Prime Minister then made a
further effort to recover the situation, denying the Cabinet had

mandated or instructed the Attorney General in any way, while repeating his opinion that a select committee inquiry could not possibly be impartial. He concluded with a warning that if the House passed either the main resolution or its amendment it would be the

> end of what hon. Members on all sides of the House will agree
> has been a high adventure – the end of a Government which,
> I think, has contributed much to the honour of the country,
> to our social stability, and which, when the country has an
> opportunity of passing a verdict upon it, will come again.[62]

The most memorable speech, which turned out to be his last in the House of Commons, was that of Asquith. He teased MacDonald for being oversensitive and recalled the precedents of the Jameson Raid and Marconi Affair to rebut the charge that a select committee would be biased.[63] Nevertheless, he offered that if one was appointed, Liberals would 'not ask for places upon it' to avoid any 'suggestion of a packed jury'.[64] The government offered no immediate response to Asquith's proposition, although the Cabinet had already decided to reject a judge-led inquiry, Royal Commission or reference to the Judicial Committee.[65]

At 8.45 p.m. the Cabinet met in 'conclave', during which Vivian Phillips, the Liberal Chief Whip, was asked by Jimmy Thomas if 'anything could be done to avoid a smash'. Phillips suggested a cooling-off period, that the government ask for an adjournment until the following day, something Thomas appeared to indicate 'would be accepted by the Government'.[66] The Prime Minister also received the 'additional offer' that if he accepted the Liberal amendment then Baldwin 'would withdraw his motion and the Government should remain in office'. Asked for his opinion, Sir Patrick Hastings said he would 'tell them to go to hell'.[67] The Cabinet, therefore, decided it would continue to oppose both motion and amendment, and that when Thomas wound up, he should 'be friendly, dignified, firm, fair, but that he should make it perfectly clear that, so long as the Vote of Censure and the

Liberal Amendment remained on the Order Paper, there could be no question of discussing any form of Inquiry'.[68]

Back in the House and after a few more speeches, Stanley Baldwin, hitherto silent but evidently in earnest consultation with his colleagues, made a dramatic intervention:

> We accept on this side the statements that have been made; we make no reflection on the honour of the Attorney-General and we consider that the right way of meeting this case, after having listened to the evidence which has been put forward, is to give the whole of our support to the Amendment which seeks for a committee of investigation.[69]

By this tactical stroke (for which myriad Conservatives claimed credit), the Leader of the Opposition secured the defeat of the first Labour government. Most Conservatives, as per Baldwin's instructions, voted with the Liberals *against* their own censure motion and *for* the Liberal amendment, which was carried by 364 votes to 198, a majority of 166. Two Conservatives, two Nationalists and 14 Liberals voted with the government.

As he left the Chamber, a 'genuinely distressed' Asquith told Philip Snowden 'that in all his Parliamentary experience he had never known a case where the Government had so wantonly and unnecessarily committed suicide'.[70] In what turned out to be his final parliamentary report to the King, the Prime Minister called it 'a strange crisis and a strange debate' permeated with an atmosphere of 'make-believe and humbug'. The Attorney General's speech had been 'a great personal triumph', Sir John Simon was 'a cold calculating lawyer with hardly a spark of humanity in his soul', while Jimmy Thomas had been in 'fighting form':

> The significant feature of the closing scenes was the tremendous enthusiasm and cheerful buoyancy of the defeated Party as compared with funereal gloom and depression which prevailed both in the Liberal and Conservative ranks. There were no

shouts of victory nor symbols of rejoicing, but almost an appearance of shame and self reproach over the fulfilment of an undignified and unworthy task.

The Prime Minister then ended this submission, as was customary, as 'Your Majesty's humble, obedient Servant'.[71] The Cabinet met briefly at 11.30 p.m. and resolved that MacDonald would see the King the following morning to ask for a dissolution. 'Cheering crowds waited outside but I escaped with a handful to Downing Street & am now going to bed,' wrote the Prime Minister in his diary. 'Alister & Ishbel came in with me to say goodnight. I am getting to like this room & leaving it touches me. This is the first time I have looked tenderly at it.'[72]

Why did MacDonald reject the Liberal amendment? Snowden, who would have given the opposition 'twenty committees if they had asked for them', rejected the post-hoc explanation that if the government had not surrendered over the Campbell Case, then it would certainly have been defeated, perhaps within a few days, on the Russian Treaties. 'There was no force in this reason,' protested the Chancellor in his memoirs, 'as the Prime Minister had already stated that on that question the Government would leave the House of Commons free to take what course it might decide.'[73] Margaret Bondfield, now making her way back to the UK from Canada, was even blunter: 'We did not fall on any ground of policy or principle. We fell just because Ramsay MacDonald lost his head.'[74]

Most likely MacDonald had simply had enough. Coming so soon after the biscuits and baronetcy affair, the Campbell Case meant he was 'exhausted in mind and body, carrying the burden both of a Prime Minister's day-to-day business and a succession of gruelling diplomatic negotiations with the great powers of Europe'.[75] Having travelled overnight from Balmoral, the King reached Buckingham Palace at 8.15 a.m. on 9 October, changed into a frock coat, had breakfast with the Queen at nine and saw his Prime Minister at ten. The King unhesitatingly granted MacDonald's request for a dissolution, 'as he had ascertained that no one would undertake to form a Government and ... even if such an arrangement were possible, a General Election was inevitable in the immediate future'. Although this aligned with the Prime Minister's own analysis, the King did not hold back, 'frankly' telling MacDonald that

> the Government had brought upon themselves the animosity of the Opposition by the Treaty made with the Soviet Government, which was unquestionably disliked in the country and by, to say the least of it, the unfortunate handling of the Campbell case by the Attorney General: and which, the King reminded the Prime Minister, he himself had admitted to His Majesty a few weeks ago at Balmoral, was one of the worse mistakes the Government had made.[76]

But while agreeing to a dissolution, 'the King deprecated the necessity for it, and expressed his regret that ... the appeal to the Electorate could not have been made upon a more vital issue than that of the abandonment of the prosecution of a Communist newspaper'.[77] The country, as the King wrote in his diary that evening, 'are tired of these constant elections'.[78] MacDonald, however, found the King 'most cordial' and the interview 'at times almost touching as we assured each other that we had done the best we could for each other'. After talking about 'revolutionary songs', historic riots and Ireland, the Monarch asked: 'You have found me an ordinary man, haven't you?'[79]

The Cabinet met at 11 a.m. and backed an immediate dissolution. As Parliament was customarily prorogued prior to a dissolution, this made necessary a short King's Speech. Following frantic deliberation with various permanent secretaries, Sidney Webb and Tom Jones had drafts ready for the Prime Minister and the King within a matter of hours.[80] Sir Maurice Hankey also arranged two meetings of the Privy Council, one at 3 p.m. to approve the Speech, and a second at 5 p.m. to agree the necessary Proclamations.

The Prime Minister then informed a surprised House of Commons that the King had consented to his request for a dissolution, the 'action taken' by the two opposition parties the previous evening having 'rendered an Election inevitable'. And to avoid a clash with forthcoming municipal elections, polling day was to be Wednesday 29 October, just 20 days' hence.[81] 'Blank dismay,' recalled MacDonald, 'settled upon the benches opposite and below the gangway.'[82] In the House of Lords, Lord Buckmaster asked why there was such 'extraordinary haste', to which Lord Haldane said ministers had been assured it was the 'desire' of the commercial and general communities 'to get rid of the Election, which is not of our creation, as soon as possible'.[83]

At 4 p.m., meanwhile, the Labour Party conference abandoned its agenda to hear a valedictory speech from its leader. MacDonald was on evangelical form:

> Back you go now from here, back to your constituencies, back to your parishes, back to your towns, back to your villages and start the fight, the greatest fight, the most memorable fight, involving the largest issues of any of the many fights that you and I have engaged in during the last thirty years.[84]

MacDonald also paid an affectionate tribute to the party's Acting Secretary, J. S. Middleton, who had first offered to become his assistant exactly 21 years earlier:

> I remember it well, when the Labour Party's head office was a back room, which was so dark and unsuitable for anything that we could not use it, at our little flat at 3, Lincoln's Inn Fields ... And Middleton, young and fresh, straight from his printer's case, ventured to suggest that if I wanted assistance, as I did, he would take his life in his hands and come up and do his best to help in building up the Party. There he is. (Loud cheers.) One of the most faithful, one of the quietest, one of the least self-seeking, and, above all, one of the most loyal of colleagues with whom it has ever been my good fortune to be associated.

Having urged delegates to campaign 'with that rugged force which drew people to them', the conference ended with delegates joining hands and singing 'Auld Lang Syne',[85] something MacDonald likened to 'a religious exercise'.

The House of Lords then considered the Irish Free State (Confirmation of Agreement) Bill, which by 6 p.m. was ready to receive Royal Assent. At this point, Lord Haldane was deep in philosophical discussion with the Solicitor General. As Sir Henry Slesser later recalled, the

> officials came to tell him that the [Royal] Commissioners were waiting for him to prorogue the Parliament. He ignored them and went on arguing about the definitions of Substance; and 'substantia' and their difference of meaning. It was nearly a quarter of an hour before he consented to be vested in his robes, wig and tricorn. Such an indifference about the fate of Government seemed to me to be truly philosophic.[86]

Having joined the Royal Commission, Haldane then delivered the King's gracious speech to peers sitting in the Chamber and MPs crammed behind its Bar. A Commission for Royal Assent and prorogation was then read, thereby ending the thirty-third Parliament of the United Kingdom of Great Britain and Ireland in the fifteenth year of the reign of His Majesty King George V. 'As Baldwin walked up to the Lords he too seemed depressed,' recalled MacDonald. '"You have done at least one big thing," he said – "The London Conference."'[87]

14

The 'Red Letter' Election

If the 1923 general election had been one of the strangest, that in 1924 was to be one of the most dramatic, the first, according to the journalist Mary Agnes Hamilton, in which 'the methods and discoveries of the new psychology were applied to an ignorant and highly suggestible mass mind'.[1] It opened with the Labour Party in surprisingly high spirits, the party conference having provided what Beatrice Webb called the 'most appropriate *mise en scene*' with its enthusiasm for Ramsay MacDonald:

> The Russian treaty and the withdrawal of the prosecution of Campbell have made the party solid and enthusiastic, all the querulous criticism or serious misgivings having vanished in a quite amazing way. Even the unsavoury Attorney-General stands out as a hero of social democracy; and as for the P.M., in spite of Court dress and the motor car, he has again become the idol of the left and the respected leader of the right of the labour movement respectively.

All the same, Webb wondered what was in the mind of 'the ordinary man who might, or might not, vote Labour, and on whom the result of the election depends'.[2]

Less sanguine was Arthur Henderson, who not only had to abandon his work on the Geneva Protocol but also plan an election campaign he predicted would be dominated by anti-communist propaganda.[3] In another swift piece of work, meanwhile, Sidney Webb prepared a manifesto, *Labour's Appeal to the People*, which was published the weekend after dissolution. What Ralph Miliband dismissed as 'a familiar mixture of cautious rhetoric, pious exhortation and piecemeal collectivism'[4] trumpeted achievements past and yet to come, while closing with the promise of 'a really Socialist Commonwealth'.[5]

Pledging a 'clean fight', the Prime Minister celebrated his fifty-eighth birthday on Sunday 12 October before boarding a train at Euston. 'They will hit you below the belt all the time,' he warned his supporters, 'but don't you do the same.' According to the Labour-supporting *Daily Herald*, 'people pressed around him, and women with babies in their arms rushed forward to shake him by the hand'.[6] As MacDonald's train headed north, it made brief stops at Rugby, Crewe, Carlisle and Motherwell. It was to be what his PPS Lauchlan MacNeill Weir called 'a triumphal tour on the modern American campaigning model'.[7]

In a keynote speech in Glasgow the following day, MacDonald attacked the Liberals and Conservatives for conspiring to turn Labour out of office on a trivial issue. 'It is our success that is our trouble,' he reflected. 'Had we made a mess of things, how happy they would have been. If I had made a mess of Europe, if my friend Wheatley had made a mess of it, we would not have been out. They would have given us a much longer tether.'[8] Ordinarily, political speeches were not broadcast during an election but given the short campaign, the British Broadcasting Company, then only two years old, agreed to transmit one from each party leader.

The Times estimated that between three and four million people were 'in a position to hear the Prime Minister if they so desired',[9] but if it had been MacDonald's intention to import his soaring platform oratory into the living rooms of wireless owners, it did not go to plan. Not being used to using microphones he often forgot to stand in front of it, and when 'a whispered intimation was made to him that it was going over badly', the Prime Minister sought to correct this by shouting. The result, recalled MacNeill Weir, 'was that he was either inarticulate or inaudible'.[10] Philip Snowden thought the broadcast 'almost unintelligible',[11] while Austen Chamberlain heard of people 'who had leanings towards him being quite put off after listening-in'.[12] In the hall itself, however, the speech was received with 'rapturous enthusiasm',[13] the Prime Minister hailing

> this extraordinary phenomenon of a Labour Government that has met kings and rulers of the earth, that has sat by them, that has conducted itself with distinction and with dignity (cheers); this Labour Government that has met ambassadors, that has faced the rulers of Europe on terms of equality; this Labour Government that has sent its representatives forth – and its representatives have been held as statesmen.

The local Glasgow politician Patrick Dollan even hailed MacDonald as 'the Gladstone of Labour'.[14]

Asquith opened the Liberal campaign at London's Queen's Hall on 14 October, describing MacDonald's oration as a piece of 'amazing rhodomontade' and complaining that his party's reward for trying to save the Labour government from itself had been jibes and ingratitude. Lloyd George then added dramatically that if it was left to Conservatives alone to fight 'the extremists of the Socialist Party, it will not be long before the existing order is overthrown'.[15]

At the same venue the following day, Baldwin launched the Conservative campaign, but it was his broadcast from the BBC's Savoy Hill studio on 16 October which made the biggest impact. Speaking intimately, he apologized for 'interfering' with the usual schedule, said what the country needed was a sane, common-sense government which did not get carried away with revolutionary theories or hare-brained schemes, and concluded with 'a gentle and courteous' thank you.[16] Mrs Baldwin even sat knitting in the studio to create the 'appropriate ambience'.[17] 'The result was a triumph,' observed Roy Jenkins. 'He had found a method of neutralising MacDonald's most effective political quality – his inspirational personal presence.'[18]

That personal presence was about to be stretched to breaking point. From Glasgow, the Prime Minister worked his way south in his now (in)famous Daimler, making speeches in practically every town through which he passed. While touring the industrial districts of north-east England he made an astonishing 27 speeches in a single day. Philip Snowden thought this 'a task beyond human endurance' and believed MacDonald's 'highly nervous condition' evident in Glasgow became more pronounced as his tour progressed.[19] It did not help that MacDonald was required to account for his inconsistency over the loan aspect of the Russian Treaties, which along with the Campbell Case dominated the campaign. 'If I said a thing in June which I found by August was wrong,' he protested unconvincingly, 'I certainly would change my mind. But that was not quite the situation.'[20]

In his Newcastle constituency, meanwhile, Charles Trevelyan had the benefit of enthusiastic workers and a well-oiled local electoral machine. Having once been cynical about the earnest young Liberal, H. G. Wells even offered to help, believing his work for education to have been of such 'outstanding value' that 'everyone who hopes for a happier, more civilized England should vote for you, irrespective of party associations'.[21] Molly Trevelyan threw herself into the campaign, though she was shocked by some 'terrible houses on the riverside, dark & stinky', confessing to her mother, Lady Bell, that she needed all her confidence before penetrating 'those noisome alleys' even though she found their inhabitants 'extraordinarily nice & friendly'.[22]

In North Camberwell, meanwhile, Charles Ammon boldly declared that in nine months Labour had done 'more for the peace of the world and for social legislation at home than the Coalition or Conservative Governments have done in eight years'.[23] Although MacDonald did not make it back to the capital, when he drove from Worksop to Sheffield Arthur Ponsonby thought it 'most touching to see men working in the fields or on the road drop their tools and come running with both their arms extended'. At the city's Hippodrome, Ponsonby and MacDonald addressed a crowd of 4,000 and 10,000 more outside.[24] Ponsonby predicted Labour would 'considerably increase its numbers but still be the second party'.[25]

In a typically fighting speech at Porthcawl, Jimmy Thomas sought to defuse the Campbell controversy by alleging that on four occasions Lloyd George's Cabinet had discussed controversial prosecutions,[26] while at another large meeting in Manchester the Prime Minister said the issue of the election was not whether his government had made mistakes: 'It has. I make a present of that to my opponents. What do I care? They can do what they like about it. We have made mistakes. That is not the issue. The issue is this: is the Labour Government going to have an opportunity of carrying on the work it has begun?'[27]

The Labour Woman, meanwhile, carried articles by Marion Phillips, the party's 'chief woman officer', urging 'the proudest housewives' to let their housework 'slide a little' for the campaign; MacDonald saying the majority necessary for Labour to do 'effective work' largely depended on the efforts of 'women in the Movement'; and J. R. Clynes claiming their opponents could not 'face the prospect of a second housewives' Budget'.[28] While such outlets were undeniably useful, of the main daily newspapers, only the *Daily Herald* (circulation: 300,000) supported Labour, meaning the sales ratio of anti- to pro-Labour publications was almost ten to one.[29]

By the deadline for nominations, Labour had increased its number of candidates from 420 to 500 and the Conservatives from 500 to 518, while the Liberals (not including ten ex-Liberals who stood as 'Constitutionalists') dropped from 443 to 333. The previous month MacDonald had tried to persuade his Conservative Lord Advocate to defect, pleading that he was in 'urgent need of a good Scottish lawyer in Parliament'.[30] Had Hugh Macmillan accepted, it would probably have riled the Clydesiders as badly as his appointment had earlier that year. Standing again in Glasgow Shettleston, John Wheatley had to endure sectarian attacks from his Conservative opponent, W. Reid Miller, a businessman with Orange Order connections,[31] while even more disturbing was J. R. Clynes' experience in Manchester, where one of his meetings was interrupted by a 'sinister procession' of figures 'clad in the dreaded robes and cowls of the Ku-Klux-Klan'.[32] Liberal and Conservative candidates also complained of often violent disturbances by Labour activists, prompting MacDonald to appeal to his followers to desist.[33]

But the disruption which most impacted meetings were chants of 'biscuits, biscuits, biscuits' in reference to the Sir Alexander Grant affair. Philip Snowden had no doubt this was used 'with damaging effect by canvassers who carried the slander from door to door'.[34] Particularly badly affected was Ishbel MacDonald, who campaigned on behalf of her brother Malcolm in Bassetlaw given his absence abroad on a debating tour. 'I hated that 1924 election,' she later observed, 'and have hated every election since.'[35] Only in Scotland, where Sir Alexander 'was held in the highest possible respect and esteem', did the affair apparently 'cut no ice at all'.[36]

Almost a week after the Prime Minister's tour had begun in the west of Scotland, he reached South Wales and his constituency of Aberavon to scenes of 'tremendous enthusiasm'.[37] Over the next ten days, MacDonald was required to make speeches which would be fully reported across the UK, which increased the likelihood of gaffes. In Barry, for example, he said that a party

> on the verge of being beaten and disgraced always tell lies, as they are doing now ... Why can't they make a decent intellectual fight of it, lay down their principles, put them against ours, and have an honourable set-to? Why do they slander us? Why, instead of having a great battle on a political principle, do they go about sniffing like mangy dogs on a garbage heap?

The press, noted Philip Snowden, 'pounced upon these words with avidity', something he believed had a 'great effect among a class of people' who had hitherto 'disregarded what his opponents said about him'.[38]

Writing to J. S. Middleton on 24 October, Rose Rosenberg reported that MacDonald was 'gradually getting over his tiredness'. 'He is really quite himself again,' she added, 'and you may tell any enquirers that there is nothing to fear concerning his health and the safety of his seat.'[39] But following the campaign from London was US Ambassador Frank Kellogg, who could not help feeling 'that the MacDonald of the election campaign ... was a different person from the MacDonald of the London Conference'. 'The strain of overwork had told upon him,' he wrote, 'and evidence that his nerves were taking their revenge was discernible in the hesitancies on some occasions and his precipitancy at others.'[40]

Writing to the Canadian politician Robert Borden, Lord Beaverbrook claimed MacDonald's central aim in instigating the general election had been to 'ruin the Liberal Party'. 'It is quite certain ... that he will attain his object,' he added. 'The Liberal Party is like the Spanish army in the Peninsula – quite good until brought into action.'[41] This was a brutal but accurate assessment, for even in Paisley Asquith struggled to connect with an electorate that had once eaten out of the Liberal leader's hand. Open dissent came from A. MacCallum Scott, a former Liberal whip, who denounced his party for appearing 'as a mere blank negative to Socialism'.[42] Winston Churchill, now contesting Epping as an 'Anti-Socialist Constitutionalist', echoed Lloyd Georgian hyperbole by telling his prospective constituents that 'spellbound by the lure of Moscow, wire-pulled through subterranean channels, Mr Ramsay McDonald [sic] and his associates have attempted to make the British nation accomplices in Bolshevist crimes'.[43]

Conservative Central Office had fashioned a 'Red Bogey' poster which depicted the Prime Minister turning his back on three downcast Dominion subjects offering 'Imperial Produce' in order to greet two grim-faced Cossacks. 'So this is Socialism!' it screamed. 'VOTE UNIONIST.' Usefully for the Tories, the twin controversies over the Campbell Case and Russian Treaties had combined to vindicate opposition cries of a Bolshevist Trojan Horse, which was ironic given this was precisely what MacDonald had worked so hard to combat since 1922. Sir Robert Horne spoke of 'Russian lice', Sir Thomas Moore said Soviet women had been 'nationalised', while even *The Times* observed that Labour's plans to build more power stations had also been a project 'dear to Lenin'.

Although Baldwin studiously avoided partisanship in his own campaign speeches, he was finally able to trade on the reputation he had carefully built up since his disastrous decision to call an election almost a year earlier. In Southend the Conservative leader said it made his 'blood boil' to read of the way in which 'Monsieur Zinoviev is speaking of the Prime Minister of Great Britain today'. At one time, he added, there had been a cry of 'Hands off Russia!' 'My word!' exclaimed Baldwin. 'I think it is time that someone said to Russia, "Hands off England!"'[44]

Grigory Yevseyevich Zinoviev was the archetypal Bolshevist of the British tabloid and Conservative imagination, and indeed references to him or his excitable pronouncements had punctuated the whole life of the first Labour government. Born in Ukraine to a Jewish family in 1883, during the 1920s Zinoviev was one of the most influential figures among the Soviet leadership as chairman of Communist International. And during Lenin's final illness in 1923-4, he had formed a triumvirate with Lev Kamenev and Joseph Stalin to deny Leon Trotsky his anticipated succession.

Even before the publication of a letter purporting to be written by Zinoviev blew apart Labour's election campaign, newspapers had carried similar smears. The *Daily Mail* claimed six members of MacDonald's Cabinet had been blackmailed into pressuring the Prime Minister to support the Russian Treaties against his will, while on 23 October the *Yorkshire Observer* revealed an exhortation for British democracy 'to follow Russia' in 1917 signed, among others, by MacDonald, Snowden, Charles Ammon and Fred Jowett, all now Ministers of the Crown. The following day, *The Times* even ran a story headlined: 'SOVIET SHIP AT

PORT TALBOT: Communists In Close Touch With Crew.' Port Talbot was close to McDonald's constituency.[45]

But it was again the *Daily Mail* whose seven-deck headline made the biggest splash on Saturday 25 October:

CIVIL WAR PLOT BY SOCIALISTS' MASTERS
Moscow Order To Our Reds
Great Plot Disclosed Yesterday
Paralyse the Army and Navy
And Mr MacDonald Would Lend Russia Our Money
Document Issued By Foreign Office
After *Daily Mail* Had Spread The News

The meat of the article alleged that the government had received the letter 'some weeks ago', which was not quite true but implied it had been suppressed. An accompanying editorial stormed that:

The country now knows that Moscow now issues orders to British Communists, and they are obeyed by the Communists here. The British Communists in turn give orders to the Socialist Government which it tamely and humbly obeys ... The whole history of the election is now explained. Here in this letter is the key. Behind the Bolshevik Treaty and behind the Campbell affair preparations are going forward for an 'armed insurrection' which shall repeat in Britain all the horrors from which Russia has suffered.[46]

That morning the Colonial Secretary Jimmy Thomas rose early at his hotel in Huddersfield and on buying a copy of the *Mail* rushed along the corridor to Philip Snowden's room, hammered on the door and shouted: 'Get up! We're bunkered!'[47]

The somewhat rambling letter purported to be from the Executive Committee of Communist International to the Central Committee of the Communist Party of Great Britain. Marked 'VERY SECRET' it was dated 15 September 1924 and predicted that the Labour government's attempts to normalize relations between the UK and the USSR would

> assist in the revolutionising of the international and British proletariat not less than a successful rising in any of the working districts of England, as the establishment of close contact between the British and Russian proletariat, the exchange of delegations and workers, etc., will make it possible for us to extend and develop the propaganda of ideas of Leninism in England and the Colonies.

Reading the *Mail* in Dundee, John Ross Campbell and Harry Pollitt, who together had produced a similarly controversial text in the *Workers' Weekly* that July, closely scrutinized the letter and immediately dismissed it as a forgery. So, too, did Zinoviev himself on 27 October, although his statement was not translated into English until the end of the year. Not only had he been on holiday on 15 September, but he would never have signed a letter 'Chairman of the Presidium of Executive Committee' or included 'Third' before Communist International. 'Everyone knows,' added Zinoviev, 'that the CP of Great Britain today has far more urgent business than the creation of a British Red Army.'[48] Such denials, however, carried little weight.

The Zinoviev Letter, or, rather, a copy of the letter, was telegrammed from the Riga station of the Secret Intelligence Service (SIS) to London on 9 October and reached the Foreign Office the day after Parliament was dissolved. This was assessed to be genuine by the SIS's Desmond Morton (although he later changed his mind), while separately other copies found their way – via the Conservative MP Guy Kindersley – to Conservative Central Office, where it was also believed to be genuine, and very probably from there to the *Daily Mail*.[49] The Conservative Party historian John Ramsden believed Baldwin's earlier reference to Zinoviev was 'too much to be explained away', suggesting he had been alerted to the document by his staff at Central Office.[50] On 22 October the London correspondent of the *Manchester*

Evening Chronicle had also predicted that before polling day 'a bombshell will burst and it will be connected with Zinoviev'.[51]

It took five days for that bombshell to make its way from the Foreign Office to the Prime Minister, who found it at around midnight – together with minutes from Sir Eyre Crowe (the Foreign Office's permanent secretary) and J. D. 'Don' Gregory (head of the Russian section at the Northern Department) – among files which had been sent to his Manchester hotel room. Crowe recommended that a formal protest be made to Rakovsky, the Soviet chargé d'affaires, and that the letter be publicized as the 'best and only defence against these treacherous proceedings'. Responding the following morning, the Prime Minister stressed the importance of ensuring the document was 'authentic' and that any protest must be 'so well-founded & important that it carries conviction & guilt'. If not, he added prophetically, 'it will do harm'.[52] When a draft Note of protest finally reached the Prime Minister on 23 October he amended – indeed strengthened – it in his own hand, though crucially he initialled only those amendments rather than the complete draft. His expectation was that he would see another draft as well as conclusive proof of the letter's authenticity.

Having received MacDonald's revision on the morning of 24 October, however, Sir Eyre Crowe decided to send this to Rakovsky immediately, while within a few hours he had also resolved to release both the Note of protest and the Zinoviev Letter to the press. Although J. D. Gregory and others doubted the wisdom of not checking with the Prime Minister, Sir Eyre had learned from the SIS that the letter was about to be published in the *Mail* and feared the government would be accused of withholding it. The Note of protest, signed with 'high consideration' by Gregory in the absence of the Foreign Secretary, stated that it was his 'duty to inform you that His Majesty's Government cannot allow this propaganda and must regard it as a direct interference from outside in British domestic affairs'.[53] It was delivered (together with the text of the Zinoviev Letter) to the Soviet Embassy at 4 p.m. and to the press two hours later. A surprised Rakovsky immediately drafted a reply stating categorically that it was 'a gross forgery'.[54]

Remarkably, news of publication first reached MacDonald not from the Foreign Office but from a *Daily News* journalist at one of his election meetings. As he recalled:

> I had two other meetings to take before returning to my hotel & it was late before I got back. I asked for information & was told that Sir E. Crowe assumed I wished for publication at once & referred to my initialled draft. But I had purposely refrained from initialling it so that I might see it again. Then a second telegram from Sir E. Crowe came correcting the statement that I had initialled it. I repeated my request for information & was told that it would be sent by a messenger. It came late that evening (Sat. 25th) & meanwhile I had to speak at Swansea and could say nothing.

Although MacDonald accepted that Crowe had 'no intention of being disloyal', he believed his 'anti-Russian mentality' had become 'uncontrolled', destroying 'his discretion' and blinding 'him to the obvious care he should have exercised'.[55]

The next morning, Sir Eyre told Lord Stamfordham it had 'never entered into the mind of anybody in this office' that MacDonald had not authorized publication. He also enclosed a copy of his explanatory letter to the Prime Minister which he suggested Stamfordham show to the King.[56] The Monarch responded to Crowe's 'extremely interesting' communication the following day, telling his private secretary that:

> Under the circumstances Crowe was quite right to publish the letter although it has certainly put the P.M. & his party in a hole & their opponents will make great capital out of it. But it would have been much worse if the *Daily Mail* had published it and the F.O. had remained silent. I suppose there is <u>no doubt</u> that Z's letter is <u>genuine</u>? I see the Communists say it is a forgery.[57]

The Monarch had a more open mind than most. Conservative Central Office, meanwhile, 'moved with devastating effectiveness' to orchestrate a press and speaker campaign capitalizing on the letter.[58]

In Huddersfield, meanwhile, Snowden and Thomas had telephoned MacDonald to ask what the hell was going on. 'He did not seem to be very much concerned about it,' recalled the Chancellor in his memoirs, 'and said that he did not know whether it was a fake or it was genuine. But he was making enquiries, and would refer to the matter in a speech.' But when the evening papers appeared without any response from the Prime Minister, Snowden grew frustrated, believing that every hour's delay 'strengthened the public belief that there was something in it which the Government were anxious to hide'. While some Labour candidates denounced the letter as a fraud, others took their cue from their leader and remained silent.[59] Speaking in Dundee on the Saturday evening, E. D. Morel threw caution to the wind and blamed J. D. Gregory, in whose name the Note of protest had been issued, for an 'act of treachery'.[60] 'I was in the storm of an election,' protested MacDonald, '& it never crossed my mind that this letter had any special part to play in the fight.'[61]

The following day, wrote Snowden, 'Labour supporters opened their Sunday papers greedily, hoping that the Prime Minister had made an explanation which would dispose of the bombshell', but again he had not.[62] J. R. Clynes was dumbfounded. 'A State matter of which the Government knew nothing was being discussed in every public-house in the country,' he wrote in his memoirs:

> As MacDonald had not instructed us in the matter, and still did not speak of it, we accepted the Soviet Minister's word, and disowned the forgery and everything connected with it. But our action alone, without that of our Prime Minister and Foreign Secretary, did not satisfy the country. People rightly asked why the one man in the Government who could speak with authority on foreign affairs remained mysteriously silent.[63]

On the afternoon of Monday 27 October, J. D. Gregory and his colleague William Strang arrived in Cardiff to 'explain the situation' but found themselves caught up in the carnival atmosphere of the election campaign. When the Prime Minister finally appeared, Gregory recalled that the 'poor man was exhausted out of all recognition'.[64] Furthermore, MacDonald had already made a speech in which he addressed the elephant in the room. After giving a lengthy chronology of events (which he had been sent in a memo), the Prime Minister promised to 'probe this thing right down to the roots'. But an unintended implication that he had been duped by his own civil servants ('I looked at the draft. I altered it, and sent it back in altered form, expecting it to come back to me with proofs of authenticity, but that night it was published') provoked cries of 'shame' from the audience. Although MacDonald had gone to great lengths to excuse them ('they honestly believed that the document was genuine, and on that belief they acted'), the damage had been done. A friend of Snowden's later told the Chancellor that the speech was 'so tragic' that others on the platform 'fervently prayed that it would open and swallow them up and put an end to the distressing spectacle'.[65]

It was not clear, however, what Snowden and others would have had the Prime Minister say. He could hardly have denounced the letter as a forgery for he did not know for a fact that it was, and if he had made such a claim, it ran the risk of causing further turmoil if it then turned out to be genuine. In a long speech at Sheffield the same day, Stanley Baldwin extracted maximum advantage from the 'Red Letter':

Did he [MacDonald] really mean that we should go through the election in ignorance of the letter? I do not think that can be the case, and yet his Party have been urging us to vote for them on the ground of the Russian Treaty, and on the ground that by their action the Labour Party have introduced a fresh era of brotherliness between the Soviet Government and ourselves. They could hardly have desired that the English public should come to a conclusion on this matter without seeing that correspondence.

This, as John Ramsden has observed, was 'masterly', creating the 'impression that MacDonald had lied without saying so'.[66]

On Tuesday 28 October, press coverage of MacDonald's Cardiff speech must have made depressing reading. *The Times* attacked the premier for exposing the Civil Service, 'which has no power publicly to defend itself, to attacks on policy for which the Minister alone is constitutionally responsible',[67] while the *Manchester Guardian* highlighted its major inconsistency: in making clear the Foreign Office had failed to provide proof of the letter's authenticity, the Prime Minister had simultaneously boasted that his government had acted with greater decisiveness than either the Conservatives or Liberals would have done in a similar situation. Asquith said he could not remember having read 'a more distracted, incoherent and unilluminating statement in the whole of his political experience'.[68]

Arthur Ponsonby, meanwhile, was furious that he – the minister most intimately acquainted with the Russian Treaties – had not been informed of the Zinoviev Letter. A Foreign Office official wrote to assure him he had not 'intentionally' been 'kept in the dark':

Gregory has just come back to say that he … was <u>very</u> sorry not to have marked the paper for you but at that time the paper had not assumed significance. He had written a brief minute against publication or any act. The whole incident is beyond words regrettable but I doubt it will influence the Election either way.[69]

And in a 'most secret note' from Neville Bland, Sir Eyre Crowe's private secretary, to Lord Stamfordham, the Foreign Office made further efforts to insulate itself:

The Zinovieff letter was obtained from an absolutely trustworthy agent in Russia and its receipt by the British

Communist Party was reported shortly afterwards from an entirely independent source in this country. It is unfortunately impossible to make this known, as the lives of our informants would clearly be seriously endangered.[70]

As with the Campbell Case, the blame for the Zinoviev affair cannot be exclusively pinned on an undoubtedly exhausted Prime Minister. Vernon Hartshorn, the Postmaster-General, later told the *Manchester Guardian* editor C. P. Scott that MacDonald's already 'broken' nerve had gone from 'bad to worse until his palpable and disastrous collapse at the close'. Similarly, Lloyd George claimed the premier's 'egotism' had 'become a disease' and affected 'his mental stability'.[71] Roy Jenkins was only slightly kinder in judging that 'once again MacDonald handled the matter with a mixture of ineptitude and shiftiness'.[72] Inexplicably relaxed in responding to communications from the Foreign Office, he had also failed to make his intentions regarding publication sufficiently clear, and was then damagingly tardy in responding once the story broke.

But the Foreign Office also did not cover itself in glory. In retrospect it seemed incredible that urgent business had been conducted by post rather than by telephone or telegram, while the Foreign Office's belief in the letter's authenticity appeared instinctive rather than robustly empirical. Sir Eyre Crowe's hasty decision to publish both the letter and the Note also failed to anticipate the likely impact on public opinion. Beatrice Webb blamed both ministry and minister, referring in her diary to 'the inept Foreign Office reply' as well as MacDonald's 'shifty and bungling management':

His task, be it said, has been intolerable, and made worse by wounded personal vanity over the motor-car episode and his prevarication about the Campbell prosecution. In this latest business of the Russian letter he has let his party, his Cabinet and the Foreign Office down – through carelessness or incapacity, [and] a total inability to take counsel.[73]

Similarly, Arthur Ponsonby believed that every person 'who touched the thing' – Gregory, Crowe and the Prime Minister – had 'made a hopeless hash of it'.[74] Making her way back from Canada, Margaret Bondfield reflected that even at that moment 'we could not draw the inevitable inference': 'We only felt discouraged; but if we had been wise we should have questioned far more seriously the qualifications of Ramsay McDonald for the Party leadership not because he was wicked, but because he was weak.'[75]

What of the impact of the Zinoviev Letter on the outcome of the election? To a degree it did little more than seal the deal on a Conservative victory which had already been secured, fitting beautifully, as the journalist Mary Agnes Hamilton put it, 'into the horrifying picture that had so assiduously been built up in the earlier weeks of the campaign'.[76] In that context, observed Philip Snowden, the letter's authenticity was 'immaterial', for had the Labour Party not already been associated in the electorate's mind with Bolshevism, then the Red Letter 'would have had no effect'.[77] This was surely true. As MacDonald himself later acknowledged, the 'important point was not the authenticity of the document but the use to which the document was put'.[78] A *Punch* cartoon, meanwhile, featured an unkempt ruffian in Whitehall carrying sandwich boards, one hand in his trouser pocket and the other holding a red flag. The board said simply: 'Vote for MacDonald and Me.'[79]

Susan Lawrence, one of Labour's three female MPs, believed that until what she called 'the fatal Friday' (when the letter and Note were published) she was 'doing very well' in East Ham, after which 'came the spectacular slide from Liberal to Conservative'.[80] This could also be discerned from Baldwin's closing tour of South-East Lancashire, a district which had been strongly Liberal in 1923 but now received the Conservative leader with surprising enthusiasm. Thus, the Red Letter helped scare middle-class Liberals into the Conservative fold, although in doing so it simply accelerated a pre-existing trend. 'The Zinoviev Letter no doubt increased the scale of victory,' judged John Ramsden, 'but it did not create it.'[81]

Polling took place on a Wednesday 29 October, less than two days after the Prime Minister's Cardiff speech. While the outcome of the election remained 'in the balance', Lucy Baldwin (the Conservative leader's wife) made a point of writing to Ishbel MacDonald to express her sympathy

> with your having to endure these attacks that have been heaped on your father by a certain portion of the press during the past few weeks. I suffered it myself through my husband after the last election ... this is the only day – polling day – that I could write to you without the possibility of my intentions being misunderstood.[82]

The Labour Party had not, observed Ralph Miliband, 'in any meaningful sense' won the election of December 1923 and 'nor did it, in any meaningful sense, lose that of October 1924'.[83] The party had gone into the election with 193 MPs, Oswald Mosley and G. M. L. Davies having accepted the Labour whip since January, but once all the results were declared, this had dropped to just 151. Paradoxically, however, the party's vote had actually increased by 1,139,241, which Sidney Webb called 'votes of confidence in Labour as a party of government'.[84] As Miliband also observed, while there was 'much that could be held against' the government on 'socialist grounds', most

> Labour supporters were not socialists, only anti-Conservatives. And, for those who did not want to vote Conservative, there was now no serious alternative to the Labour Party, just as there was no longer any serious alternative to the Conservative Party for those who would not vote Labour.[85]

In Northern Ireland, where neither Labour nor the Conservatives fielded candidates, the most significant result was in the two-member constituency of Fermanagh and Tyrone, where a huge swing to the Ulster Unionists displaced the two Nationalists elected in November 1923. 'Now no one will dare touch these counties,' exclaimed Lady Carson in her diary, a reference to Unionist fears regarding their possible transfer to the Irish Free State.[86]

Including those Ulster Unionists who took the Conservative whip at Westminster, the Conservatives had triumphed with 412 MPs, an increase of 154. 'The Conservatives have done very well in the election & have a clear majority in the H[ouse] of C[ommons] over the other parties of more than 200,' observed the King in his diary, 'so I hope at last we have got a stable Govt who will remain in for some years.'[87] The Sovereign's relief was nothing compared with that of Henry 'Chips' Channon, who praised 'England' for having 'returned to her senses':

> The era of privilege and *douceur de vivre* [sweetness of life] has come back to us and the good English people have recorded their faith in their leaders and aristocracy who after all have never let them down. The last election was apathy and annoyance … this time the country realised the dangers of socialism and would have none of them.[88]

Lord Rothermere told Lord Beaverbrook that the Zinoviev Letter – as publicized by his newspaper – 'had altered the situation to the extent of something like 100 seats',[89] while the Canadian politician Vincent Massey sent Baldwin a telegram. 'Thank God,' it declared, 'the Empire is safe.'[90]

The Liberal Party, meanwhile, had experienced an extraordinary collapse, a loss of 118 seats having reduced it to a rump of just 40. The most significant scalp was that of Asquith in Paisley, where Rosslyn Mitchell, the Glasgow solicitor whose appointment as Lord Advocate had been thwarted earlier that year, had beaten the Liberal leader with a majority of more than 2,000. The first Labour government and Asquith's elected parliamentary career, observed Roy Jenkins, 'perished together, the one after eight months, the other after 38 years'.[91] From this the Conservatives and Labour could derive mutual satisfaction, their desired two-party system having finally come to pass.

In Aberavon, meanwhile, Ramsay MacDonald's majority was reduced from 3,512 to 1,650, a Liberal candidate having done rather better than a Unionist the year before. In Bassetlaw, where his daughter campaigned on behalf of her brother Malcolm, Ishbel had cut the Conservative incumbent's majority to just 1,449. Writing to thank his sister, a 'surprised and delighted' Malcolm said he doubted his presence could have improved upon her result.[92] Unlike Malcolm, Margaret Bondfield had travelled 6,000 miles 'as fast as modern means of communication' would take her but had arrived too late to affect the result in her Northampton seat, where her victorious Tory opponents had made much of her 'gallivanting abroad'.[93] Although at this election Labour had fielded 22 women candidates, more than both the other parties combined, all those elected in 1923 were defeated, an outcome only partly mitigated by the victory of Ellen Wilkinson in Middlesbrough. In Newcastle, Molly Trevelyan told her mother that the local party now viewed her being 'as useful as a second candidate',[94] while Sir George Otto Trevelyan, a veteran Liberal MP and minister, wrote to congratulate his son Charles: 'Your return to Parliament was a strong personal pleasure to me, amidst much that I regretted, and much, all the country over, which I am beginning dimly to understand. But you are there, after such a storm.'[95]

As the storm settled, MacDonald made his way back to London and on his arrival at Paddington was almost carried by a 'cheering throng' from his railway carriage to a car containing two of his children. Seen off by a railwaymen's pipe band, the MacDonald trio then proceeded to Downing Street.[96] 'The experiences of this fight give one much sympathy with some of the assumptions of communism,' the Prime Minister reflected in his diary, that 'an appeal to the people can always be reduced to a dog fight which will be settled without reference to any serious issue.'[97]

The Cabinet met at 10.30 a.m. on Friday 31 October amid a general expectation that the Prime Minister would resign that day, even though the King was still at Sandringham. Everyone was present except Sidney Webb and John Wheatley, both detained in their constituencies, and Fred Jowett, who had been defeated in Bradford. A furious Philip Snowden (whose majority in Colne Valley had nearly doubled) later commiserated with the outgoing First Commissioner of Works on the 'great opportunities we have wantonly and recklessly thrown away by the most incompetent leadership' which ever brought a Government to ruin'.[98] This was echoed by the Chancellor's wife Ethel, who in Canada said Labour had 'been the victim of the worst leadership of modern times'. She later moderated this by acknowledging the 'ill-health and sheer nervous exhaustion' brought on by the Prime Minister's workload, but on returning home defended her original comments by saying: 'I said it because I believe it to be true.'[99]

When the Prime Minister entered the Cabinet room, observed Tom Jones, there

> was no demonstration of any kind. He was dressed in a dark suit, with a dark tie, looked pale and serious, and entered as if not certain what his reception was going to be. One gathered a general impression of everyone trying to maintain a cheerful countenance and determined to say nothing unpleasant about anybody or anything.

Following pleasantries, the Cabinet 'plunged' into an analysis of the election result. One minister had anticipated an increase of 20 Members, another had expected more, but all those present agreed that everything had been going well until the 'slump' caused by the *Daily Mail*'s story. 'The people lost confidence in us,' one minister observed, 'the women were frightened; speakers felt paralysed.'

Discussion then divided over the conduct of Foreign Office officials. Lord Haldane and Philip Snowden defended them throughout, but the Prime Minister said he considered 'the weakest part' of the Foreign Office case the fact that nobody there had 'phoned or wired, or in any way communicated the fact of publication to him'. This, agreed Jones, was certainly 'an amazing omission'. 'I felt,' observed MacDonald, 'like a man sewn in a sack and thrown into the sea.'

Another group led by Lord Parmoor and including Charles Trevelyan, Lord Thomson and Josiah Wedgwood was 'entirely out of sympathy' with Haldane and Snowden and demanded 'an enquiry which would table all the available evidence and expose our Secret Service'. It was plain to Jones that Trevelyan believed Crowe and Gregory had 'stooped to a mean political trick in order to damage the Labour Party', but the Prime Minister rebutted 'any such suggestion with energy'. Finally, it was agreed that a Cabinet committee comprising Haldane, Parmoor, Arthur Henderson and the Prime Minister should 'go into the question of the authenticity of the Zinoviev letter', although Jones was 'bidden to make no reference to the Civil Service aspect of the business' in his minutes.[100]

Addressing Oxford University's Irish Society that evening, the Irish Free State minister Kevin O'Higgins sardonically observed that since his appointment he had 'shaken hands with four English [sic] Prime Ministers and may be meeting my fifth any time now'. 'We are a little shocked in Ireland at the political instability of this country,' he added. 'We did hope that once Ireland as a bone of contention was withdrawn things would begin to settle down.'[101] Earlier that day, the formation of the Irish Boundary Commission had been announced after the UK government appointed the barrister and former *Northern Whig* editor J. R. Fisher to serve as Northern Ireland's representative. The Prime Minister wrote to thank George Glasgow for sending him a copy of his book, *MacDonald as Diplomatist*, joking that 'coming as it does now, it seems very much like an obituary notice'.[102]

On 1 November, MacDonald also wrote to Hugh Macmillan, the Conservative law officer whose appointment had caused him so much grief at the beginning of the year:

The short full day closes, & we shall soon be private persons again ... You have been a great comfort & support to me & I hope you have had some satisfaction in your work & that you will sometimes think of us not unkindly ... I am rather depressed for the time being, not at the results which have more hope than despair in them, but at the character of the attack. If this is how political contests are to be waged, our poor country has hard times in front of it.

MacDonald added that he had resolved to return to Sir Alexander Grant 'two luxuries with which he hoped to endow me', i.e. the McVitie's shares and Daimler. 'I must return to my drudgery again to make ends meet,' he told Macmillan, '& I shall give up all social engagements beyond a bare & necessary minimum.'[103] On Sunday 2 November, the Prime Minister visited Chequers for what he probably believed was the last time, a 'parting' he told his diary was 'most painful'.[104]

The Prime Minister also unburdened himself to Lord Stamfordham, saying that until 'an extraordinary change in the political atmosphere' he believed 'his party would have won, as up to that time wherever he went he heard praises of all that his Government had accomplished'. When Stamfordham (who, as usual, conveyed this conversation to the King) asked him if the Zinoviev Letter had affected the 'general mass' of electors, MacDonald

said No, but it had undoubtedly frightened the women and they as a rule had voted against the Government. He spoke with considerable bitterness of the calumny and abuse which had been heaped upon himself and his party – I did not allude to the strong abuse which he himself and some of his followers had heaped upon their opponents. He did, however, say that he had been unjustly reported, and that things which he had said in joke had been magnified into serious statements.[105]

The half-Scots Baldwin, amused to think that a MacDonald had been beaten by a Campbell (he meant John Ross), told Tom Jones he had not expected the Liberal rout to 'come so quickly'. 'The next step,' he added, 'must be the elimination of the Communists by Labour. Then we shall have two parties, the party of the Right, and the party of the Left.'[106] Speaking a few days later at the Reform Club, the now seatless Asquith said he had no regrets at having facilitated the 'experiment' of a Labour government. 'It has opened many eyes,' he argued, 'and it has been put an end to (as it was certain to be) the moment it threatened danger to our national interests and our national honour.'[107]

On the evening of 2 November MacDonald saw Rakovsky, who was angry that the Foreign Office would not accept his note branding the Zinoviev Letter a forgery, although the Prime Minister explained that this was because it alleged Foreign Office involvement. On 4 November the Prime Minister hosted a luncheon party at Downing Street at which Jimmy Thomas, Lord Arnold, Ben Spoor and Arthur Ponsonby were 'quite undismayed and quite sure that from the party point of view we have done the right thing'.[108] The Lord Advocate, however, found the premier 'in a strangely bemused state of mind over the change in his position' for which he 'could do little to console him'.[109] A final gloomy Cabinet followed at 3 p.m., during which the committee of inquiry delivered its anticlimactic findings:

> We do not hesitate to say that the evidence submitted to us gives no support to the allegation that leakage of information took place through some Department. By the nature of the case, some time must elapse before important pieces of evidence bearing upon the existence and the history of the document can be thoroughly examined and tested.[110]

It was then agreed the Prime Minister 'should forthwith place the resignation of the Government in the hands of His Majesty the King'.[111] 'As I looked round the table,' MacDonald later wrote, 'memory of all that had gone into life for me, & of those no longer with us, flooded my mind and almost my eyes.'[112]

At 5.30 p.m., MacDonald resigned during an audience with the King. 'I like him,' recorded the Monarch in his diary, '& have always found him quite straight.'[113] As ever, Stamfordham was on hand to flesh out his Sovereign's brief account:

> In taking leave of him His Majesty expressed regret at his resignation and also his complete satisfaction at the manner in which the Labour Government had carried out their work as regarded the King himself: the King said that he would always remember the consideration shown to him and to his wishes and added that he should always regard Mr. Ramsay MacDonald as a friend and that, whether in office or out of office, His Majesty trusted that he could always look to him to do the best for his country and for the Throne.

The King also deprecated references by some Labour MPs in the press to 'class war' which, in keeping with his earlier communication with Baldwin, he hoped MacDonald 'would do his best to assuage' (Jimmy Thomas had actually cautioned against 'damnable talk of class warfare'). The Labour leader complained about Winston Churchill referring to an 'ugly rush' to buy Court Dress earlier that year. His ministers had done so, protested MacDonald, to 'fall in with the King's wishes and to keep up the long-established Court traditions. These men were now angry and one had declared that he would never put on his Court uniform again.'[114] MacDonald later recorded that the King had been 'most friendly':

> Thanked me for what I had done ... Chaffed me about the Russian Treaty. Told him my successors would have to carry out the same policy. He hoped I was not to give up my car. Thought the attacks most unfair ... Hoped I would continue [to be] his friend as he would remain mine.[115]

Later, at 7 p.m., the King received 'Mr Baldwin & asked him to form a Govt which he agreed to do'.[116] He then gave the new premier a lecture about avoiding 'unruly disorder' in the House of Commons, leaving Viscount Esher with the strong impression that the King had been 'sorry to part with MacDonald'. 'Radicals and Socialists,' added Esher, 'are much nicer to Sovereigns than Tories.'[117]

It was certainly true that all those who left an account of Labour's first administration did so having radically altered their views of the King in particular and constitutional monarchy in general,[118] although as ministers prepared to relinquish their seals of office (which in those days was done in person) John Wheatley defied Lord Stamfordham's polite request that he wear a morning tailcoat and instead turned up in a short jacket.[119] 'We have lost office,' remarked the outgoing Minister of Health. 'We have gained the right to be ourselves.'[120] 'Tomorrow morning at 10.30 I deliver up the Great Seal to the King,' Haldane told his mother, adding that he would 'not be sad'.[121]

Jimmy Thomas made a point of accepting his departure from the Colonial Office with characteristic good humour, joking that the day after the election four 'magnificent' silver candlesticks had appeared on his office mantelpiece. 'What are they there for?' he asked an official, only to be told: 'Well, I don't know, sir ... but they had always been there till you came.' *The Times* praised his valedictory speech at Cutlers' Feast in Sheffield as 'a great ending to one of the few personal records in the late Administration which are not merely irreproachable but have a certain distinction'.[122] Returning to Unity House, Thomas joked that the parrot he had brought back from South Africa was 'no substitute for £5,000 a year, especially when the parrot dies so soon after knowing the result of my fate'.[123]

At the Board of Education, Charles Trevelyan held a most 'friendly & successful wake' as he bade farewell to 200 permanent officials,[124] while at the Foreign Office Arthur Ponsonby spent two days 'clearing up' and 'saying goodbye' but found to his frustration 'that blasted Zinovieff letter' still occupying everyone's attention:

How was it possible either to prove authenticity or forgery? Unless we could produce a man who saw Zinovieff draft it or produce a document which in itself could be proved beyond question to emanate from him it was useless trying to pretend an investigation was any good. J.R.M. will suffer in the party and to protect him his friends will attack the F.O ... Silence is my best course. But it will be difficult to allow people to say things which are manifestly unfair.[125]

Sir Eyre Crowe felt sure Haldane would be 'gratified' to learn that the Foreign Office now possessed proof Zinoviev had admitted to 'having sent the letter of Sept 15'. Sir Eyre also told Haldane, doubtless with considerable relief, that MacDonald had 'intimated to me that unless his political opponents persisted, he would do his best to let the matter peter out as quickly as possible'.[126]

The Prime Minister also spent 5 and 6 November distributing the spoils of office, telling the Irish Nationalist MP T. P. O'Connor that he never knew 'so many folks wanted honours'.[127] But fearing the omission of his Foreign Office private secretary (Walford Selby) would be 'misunderstood' in light of the Zinoviev affair, MacDonald was persuaded to abide with tradition and issue what *The Times* called a 'small' resignation honours list.[128] On 6 November, the Labour Party gave a dinner in MacDonald's honour at London's Great Central Hotel, which was also attended by Ishbel and her brother Alister, now a successful architect. They listened to what Arthur Ponsonby called 'forced hilarity' in response to a 'fairly good speech' from the ex-premier.[129] Finally, on 7 November, again observed by the Prince of Wales, the Foreign Secretary and his Cabinet colleagues 'gave up their Seals of Office & took leave'. They parted, added the King, 'the best of friends',[130] although Fritz Ponsonby later passed on to his brother Arthur the Sovereign's rather franker assessment of his first Labour ministers:

He liked MacDonald (though I think F[ritz] was restraining himself from quoting some critical remarks) he particularly liked Snowden and thought Henderson amiable. He did not care much for Wheatley and quite saw through Thomas – thought him a poseur and not genuine.[131]

On 11 November, Ishbel MacDonald was still at Number 10, a 'last survivor' awaiting a furniture van and looking forward to 'a quiet afternoon unmolested by the Tories that surround me'.[132] Her father, meanwhile, had taken to the hills of the West Country with his old comrade Lord Arnold. 'If friends fail,' he later wrote, 'the hill road never does.' MacDonald was amused to see Conservative election posters

> getting blurred and besmirched by the weather, staining the hoardings as they had stained the public mind, asking the electors to 'Vote for S[tanley] and Stability, Security, and Safety,' and, by way of variation, for 'Britons and no Bolshies,' [or] for 'the Union Jack and the British Empire.' Then came the woods and the hills and the sea, the Ship Inn with its noisy bar – and sleep.[133]

15

WHITHER THE WILD MEN?

On his way back to London following his tour of Devon and Cornwall, Ramsay MacDonald stopped at Shulbrede, the Surrey home of his former under-secretary at the Foreign Office, Arthur Ponsonby. 'He seemed to have recovered,' observed Dolly Ponsonby in her diary, 'said he had got his sleep back & told me what a nightmare the Election had been – towards the end he did not know what he was saying. This excessive over-tiredness no doubt explains a good deal & principally his bad judgement about the Zinovieff letter.'[1]

While Dolly felt a degree of sympathy for the now former Prime Minister, others viewed him in much the same way Conservatives had Stanley Baldwin a year earlier: as responsible for an unnecessary and damaging election and therefore in danger of losing the party leadership. Like his Tory counterpart, however, MacDonald pulled through. Urged to mount a challenge by Philip Snowden and John Wheatley, Arthur Henderson demurred, still of the view that the incumbent remained the best person for the job.[2] A Parliamentary Labour Party meeting in early December also found members in a restless mood. The left, wrote MacDonald in his diary, were

> out for my blood & had not the sense to restrain itself. Some members do no work but much talking & wish to turn floor of House [of Commons] into a sort of national street corner soap box. They are encouraged by our press which is in bad hands & we must fight them. The difficulties of the Party are

within more than without, & though I write 'the Left Wing': the inspiration really comes from those who were disappointed that I did not put them in the Ministry.[3]

Nevertheless, he was re-elected chairman of the PLP with only five dissentients (which included the Clydesiders James Maxton and George Buchanan) and perhaps as many as 30 abstentions.[4] E. D. Morel had died suddenly on 12 November, which had served to remove another likely source of internal discontent.

Despite what he had told Dolly Ponsonby at Shulbrede, however, MacDonald still struggled to get back to his 'old condition'. 'The strain of office was really frightful,' he told one correspondent in December, 'and probably no one will ever understand what it amounted to.'[5] Also suffering was Lauchlan MacNeill Weir, whom the Labour leader considered 'one of the most delightful men' he had ever worked with. Lord Dawson of Penn, the King's Physician and an old acquaintance of MacDonald's, had diagnosed MacNeill Weir with persistent ulceration and recommended surgery. The former premier also told Dawson of an imminent voyage to Jamaica and Panama. 'I am clean knocked out,' he admitted, 'and cannot get my head to work at all.'[6] A few weeks later MacDonald returned to England on the same ship as the new Scottish Conservative MP Robert Boothby, who detected in the Labour leader 'a sort of injured innocence'.[7]

In February 1925, Clifford Allen – who had spent 1924 trying to bridge the gap between MacDonald and the Independent Labour Party – told Arthur Ponsonby they

must allow Mac's holiday to end all reference to the personal failures of the past. We must assume that he really knows in his heart that he did badly in all the later stages and in much of the method of approach to policy in the first experiment of Labour Government ... Any further references to the past or to him will only revive his sensitiveness and put him on the defensive, when we ought to allow him to keep his own sense of 'sin' secret, and to benefit from it.[8]

By spring, unhappiness with the party leader had 'subsided but not entirely disappeared', although MacDonald's financial situation finally turned a corner. In December 1924 he had relinquished both his McVitie's shares (though he received dividends owing to the end of that month) and the Daimler,[9] but learned he had been bequeathed a life insurance policy by the Australian businessman Henry Markwald, an old ILP and Union of Democratic Control comrade.[10] This story had almost surfaced shortly after publication of the Zinoviev Letter,[11] but this time – and unlike the Grant loan – there was no controversy. Only in 1937 was the Prime Minister's salary increased to £10,000, while two years later a government driver was provided for the first time.

In June 1925, the Markwald legacy allowed MacDonald to move from Howitt Road to the Georgian Upper Frognal Lodge in Hampstead, which he filled with books.[12] To the Liberal journalist Harold Spender, experience of government had left the Labour leader 'much changed':

> He has joined the governing classes. He holds his Court. Like Cromwell, he has his own Peers the faithful Arnold, the romantic De la Warr, the tongue-tied Olivier, the martial Thomson. He has retired to the Highland fastness of London – Hampstead: and there he inhabits his castle.[13]

The novelist and Tory MP John Buchan, meanwhile, wrote to say he hoped Labour would 'come to its own as a true constitutional opposition, and the natural alternative Government'.[14]

The rest of the MacDonald story is well known. In June 1929 he returned to Downing Street as Prime Minister of another minority government, although this time Labour was the single largest party with 287 seats. The Cabinet looked in several respects like that of 1924, but within a few months the worst depression in a century was under way. In the midst of rocketing unemployment and a sterling crisis, the government agreed to resign in August 1931, but then George V persuaded MacDonald to head a 'National' government. Once British credit had been restored, ran the plan, an election would be fought along regular party lines.

Within weeks, however, the pound had been devalued and the Labour Party's National Executive voted to expel all those – MacDonald, Philip Snowden, Jimmy Thomas and Lord Sankey – who remained in office. In the election that followed, the National government was returned with a majority of nearly 500. 'In 1924 They Tricked You with a RED LETTER,' one campaign poster had warned. 'This Time It's GOING TO BE RED, WHITE & BLUE. DON'T BE HOODWINKED VOTE LABOUR.'[15] The 'official' Labour Party was reduced to just 52 MPs (led by Arthur Henderson) while 'National Labour' secured 13. Although Ramsay MacDonald remained Prime Minister, Stanley Baldwin, whose Conservatives had an astonishing 470 MPs, became de facto premier as Lord President of the Council. It became known within the Labour movement as the 'great betrayal'.

What of the other 'wild men'? Several returned to office with MacDonald in 1929, some to the same departments: Philip Snowden (Treasury), Charles – now Sir Charles – Trevelyan (Board of Education), Lord Parmoor (Lord President), Noel Buxton (Ministry of Agriculture) and William Adamson (Scottish Office). Others were promoted: J. R. Clynes became Home Secretary, Arthur Henderson Foreign Secretary, Sidney Webb (now Lord Passfield) Secretary of State for the Colonies and (separately) for Dominion Affairs, William Graham President of the Board of Trade and Thomas Shaw Secretary of State for War. Margaret Bondfield, meanwhile, became Minister of Labour, making her the first female Cabinet minister and subsequently also the first female Privy Counsellor. Although her memoirs echoed the general condemnation of MacDonald's actions in 1931, at the time she privately supported his decision.[16]

But while MacDonald found space, unlike in 1924, for the Poplar MP George Lansbury as First Commissioner of Works, the Clydesider John Wheatley, considered the main success of the first Labour government, was not invited to serve, in part because of his opposition to another minority administration. Although his landmark housing subsidies were ended in 1933, by that point around half a million houses had been built under the 'Wheatley Act'. Never in good health, Wheatley died shortly before his sixty-first birthday in May 1930 and left a sizeable sum in his will. A few months later Lord Thomson, who had once again become Secretary of State for Air, also died when the R101 airship crashed in France on its maiden voyage, killing 48 of its 54 passengers and crew. The tragedy was all the more poignant given that Thomson and MacDonald had initiated the Imperial airship development programme in 1924.

Although Philip – now Viscount – Snowden remained in the National government after the 1931 election as Lord Privy Seal, he resigned a year later and devoted his energies to increasingly bitter attacks on both it and MacDonald. At the 1935 election, he advised support for the Liberals, his first political love, and died of a heart attack two years later. William Graham, who had served as Snowden's Financial Secretary to the Treasury in 1924, had died in 1932 aged only forty-four, which some attributed to MacDonald's 'betrayal' but Snowden to the 'considerable strain' imposed by Graham's strenuous post-1924 activity.[17]

Sir Charles Trevelyan's second spell at the Board of Education, meanwhile, lacked the optimism of the first. When an Education Bill was delayed and then fatally amended, he grew bitter and resigned – unfairly blaming MacDonald – and lost his Newcastle seat in 1931. A decade later Trevelyan gave his family's Wallington estate to the National Trust but continued to live there until his death in 1958, which made him one of the first Labour government's longest survivors. Lord Passfield died in 1947, his wife Beatrice – the great chronicler of Labour politics – having predeceased him by four years.

Willie Adamson, meanwhile, was suspended from his Fife miners' union so established his own, although he managed to defeat his critics, rejoin his comrades, and retain his Dunfermline seat in 1929, returning to government as Secretary of State for Scotland, the Conservative government having elevated the 'dignity' of the office (and its salary) in 1926.[18] He lost his seat in 1931 and died shortly after failing to recapture it at the 1935 election.[19] Jimmy Thomas, who became Lord Privy Seal in 1929 and Secretary of State for Dominion Affairs in 1930, twice returned to the Colonial Office, although only for a few months in 1931 and 1935–6. Upon his expulsion from the Labour Party in 1931, Thomas was also ousted as general secretary of the National Union of Railwaymen, a position he had held since 1916. On being found to have leaked Budget proposals in 1936, he quit the National government and the House of Commons in quick succession, never returning to public life before his death in 1949.

On leaving the Woolsack in November 1924, Lord Haldane continued to lead Labour's small band of peers in the Upper House while remaining, at the suggestion of Stanley Baldwin, a member of the Committee for Imperial Defence. He also served as a Lord of Appeal, prepared his memoirs, and was elected Chancellor of St Andrews University just as his health declined in 1928.

In December 1924, Stanley Baldwin 'excised' an instruction in the Cabinet minute of 6 August 1924 – that no prosecution of a political character be undertaken without its prior sanction – as 'unconstitutional, subversive of the administration of justice and derogatory to the office of Attorney-General'.[20] Sir Patrick Hastings, who had been deeply and unhappily involved with the Campbell Case, returned to the Bar after leaving the Commons, wrote half a dozen plays and died at his London home in 1952. John Ross Campbell challenged Winston Churchill at the 1951 general election and lived until 1969, not long after the legal academic F. H. Newark had been surprised to find him running up the stairs at the Communist Party's London HQ, although this seems unlikely given he only had the back part of both feet due to treatment for trench foot.

If the Campbell Case lived on in law textbooks as a warning against mixing politics and prosecutions, the Zinoviev Letter became one of the Labour movement's enduring grievances. In December 1924, Lord Olivier wrote of a 'prevalent impression' that the first Labour government had been the victim 'of an election stunt got up by sensational journalism and Russian reactionaries, with the assistance of the secret service and certain elements in the Foreign Service',[21] while Ramsay MacDonald came to view J. D. Gregory as the main 'villain of the piece'.[22] When Gregory was suspended from the Foreign Office in 1928 for his role in a fraudulent currency operation, MacDonald sought to re-litigate the events of October 1924, but was humiliated by Baldwin in the House of Commons.[23] More than 70 years later Robin Cook, another Labour Foreign Secretary, commissioned a new investigation by historian Gill Bennett, who concluded the letter was almost certainly a forgery but that there was no evidence of an organized conspiracy against the Labour government by the intelligence services.[24] Cook said 'generations of Labour Party supporters and historians' had been vindicated and that the Labour government was 'confident' the letter had not been sent by Zinoviev.[25] After falling out with Joseph Stalin, Grigory Zinoviev had been arrested, put on 'trial' and executed in August 1936.

In June 1935, an exhausted Ramsay MacDonald finally relinquished office as Prime Minister and instead became Lord President of the Council, in effect a job swap with Stanley Baldwin. He remained in government even after losing his seat at an election that October, returning to Parliament at a Combined Scottish Universities by-election in February 1936. He remained in office for a further 17 months, an increasingly frail and forlorn figure, finally resigning in May 1937, shortly after the coronation of King George VI, who offered him a peerage. MacDonald declined, being less enamoured with such baubles than his critics had long alleged.

The seventy-one-year-old former premier and Labour leader spent a final summer at his beloved Lossiemouth and then sailed for South America with his daughter Sheila, dying of heart failure on board the liner *Reina del Pacifico* on 9 November. The nearest British territory was Bermuda, where thousands lined the streets of its capital Hamilton as MacDonald's coffin was pulled by gun carriage to the Cathedral of the Most Holy Trinity, where it lay in state. His body was returned to the UK aboard the light cruiser HMS *Apollo* and, after a public funeral at Westminster Abbey and private cremation at Golders Green, the former Prime Minister's ashes were taken to Lossiemouth by train. As a local newspaper reported:

> A hush seemed to fall on the town. Places of business were closed. Window blinds were drawn, flags flew at half-mast on the flagstaffs, and on the fishing vessels in the harbour, and small Scottish Standards and Union Jacks, which no doubt had their part in the Coronation celebrations in the summer, had been changed to simple symbols of mourning at some windows and doons.[26]

On 27 November 1937, the MacDonald clan and other mourners walked to Old Spynie churchyard overlooking the Moray Firth, where Margaret Ethel Gladstone had been buried 26 years earlier. Malcolm joined his parents in 1981 and Ishbel, who had acted as her father's hostess at Downing Street, the following year.

As David Marquand has observed, death often brings rehabilitation, but in the case of Ramsay MacDonald it 'brought more disdain'.[27] In 1938, Lauchlan MacNeill Weir, the PPS whose health had so concerned the Labour leader at the end of 1924, published a polemic entitled *The Tragedy of Ramsay MacDonald*, as full of mistakes as it was bitter invective. Nevertheless, it set the weather, and by the 1950s MacDonald's significant role in building support for the Labour Party and leading it into government for the first time had been removed from the public consciousness. 'On the left he was remembered only for his alleged perfidy in 1931,' judged David Marquand, who finally redressed the critical balance with a sympathetic biography in 1977. 'On the right he was barely remembered at all.'[28]

Only in 1957 did someone attach a commemorative plaque –
without consulting his family and curiously shorn of Northern
Ireland – outside MacDonald's birthplace in Lossiemouth:

1. GREGORY PLACE
BIRTHPLACE
Of
JAMES RAMSAY MACDONALD
1866 – 1937
FIRST LABOUR PRIME MINISTER
OF GREAT BRITAIN
1924

'I suppose really it has a certain brief charm,' Ishbel MacDonald
observed to her brother Malcolm, 'avoiding a list of
achievements.'[29]

16

REASSESSING BRITAIN'S FIRST LABOUR GOVERNMENT

> When you sit here 20 years from now, or in more extended premises, and survey the faults of your Labour Government, nine-tenths of your objections to us will consist of this: that, whilst we have had ideas that we wished to apply … the mere fact that we were in office or in power has not been tantamount to putting the authority into our hands to recreate the world.
>
> Ramsay MacDonald's speech on opening the
> Parliamentary Labour Club, 16 May 1924[1]

Judgements of the first Labour government have often verged on caricature. Josiah Wedgwood, for example, could 'recollect no meritorious step … save the recognition of Russia and the admission of taxis into Hyde Park',[2] while David Kirkwood believed it 'accomplished nothing and challenged nothing'.[3] Even academics have joined this reductive chorus. Kevin Morgan said it 'achieved little beyond the fact of its own existence',[4] while Gordon Brown, a future Labour Prime Minister, wrote that 'by anyone's standards … the Labour Government of 1924 was hardly a success'.[5]

There are many ways of assessing a government's record, and the 1923 manifesto, *Labour's Appeal to the Nation*, is not a bad place to start. Unemployment might not have been cured but progressive benefit reforms were implemented; agricultural salaries increased but there was no minimum wage; the Capital Levy was shelved but the National Debt reduced via Philip Snowden's

Budget, which also delivered on commitments to scrap food, entertainment and corporation taxes. Mines and railways were not nationalized, but roads were built, London transport reorganized and a 'National Grid' initiated. The slums were not eradicated, but the promise to 'build an adequate supply of decent homes' was set in motion.[6] Many governments with substantial majorities and fuller parliamentary terms have delivered less.

Ramsay MacDonald often likened the making of policy to growing corn and its delivery to harvesting, and it could be said his first government prepared the soil well. Every child did not get, as the manifesto promised, 'equality of opportunity', but Charles Trevelyan's spirited stewardship at the Board of Education improved relations with teachers and forged a cross-party consensus on selective 'secondary' education which endured until the 1970s. The ripest corn was housing, what MacDonald called 'the biggest piece of constructive industrial organization' ever attempted.[7] By 1927 even critics acknowledged the impressive pace of delivery with 273,000 homes completed and thousands of construction workers back in employment.[8]

In other respects – economic, Imperial and industrial – the first Labour government demonstrated a great deal of continuity with both its predecessors and successors. Clement Attlee attributed this to the party's lack of detailed policy planning, meaning there was 'no real decision as to what should be done first'. This stood in contrast with foreign affairs, which he judged the first Labour government's 'greatest success', not least because 'only in this sphere had policy been clearly worked out'.[9] The 1923 manifesto stated that Labour stood for

a policy of International Co-operation through a strengthened and enlarged League of Nations; the settlement of disputes by conciliation and judicial arbitration; the immediate calling by the British Government of an International Conference (including Germany on terms of equality) to deal with the Revision of the Versailles Treaty, especially Reparations and

Debts; and the resumption of free economic and diplomatic relations with Russia.[10]

That much of this had been delivered by the time Labour demitted office in November 1924 vindicates Attlee's assessment, while it is clear from contemporary accounts that MacDonald's handling of the London Conference and Geneva Protocol were regarded (even by critics) as genuine triumphs of patient diplomacy. That the latter remained unratified by the UK does not negate the point, for as Richard Lyman has acknowledged, the Locarno Pact of 1925 'owed much to MacDonald's back-breaking work in 1924'.[11] As Jake Vaughan has observed, the first Labour government 'marked a key stage in the evolution of Labour foreign policy from vague utopianism to a more practically-based approach'.[12]

If MacDonald and his party had a fault it was a certain naïveté regarding the Soviet Union, which led them to underestimate likely opposition to the Russian Treaties in Parliament, not to mention public (and royal) sentiment just a few years after a bloody revolution. Given its objectives, it is ironic that the first Labour government fell largely on the basis of alleged communist influence – the treaties, Campbell Case and the Zinoviev Letter – although the party's resulting determination to deny communists a place within the Labour movement helped it become 'the mass democratic organization which permanently replaced the Liberals in the two-party system'.[13]

The main charge against MacDonald has been that his absorption with foreign affairs – evident from his diary of the period – led him to neglect the home front. There is something in this, even if it is difficult to fault the decision taken in late 1923 to act as both Prime Minister and Foreign Secretary. The Earl of Birkenhead had once predicted that if he became premier MacDonald would be 'a kind of Labour Whig, seeking nothing but to curb the radical excesses of his more rabid followers'.[14] In this, he obviously succeeded, even if the behaviour of the Clydeside contingent often provided raw material for the charge – articulated most pungently by David Lloyd George and the

Daily Mail – that the government's moderation was a fig leaf for Bolshevist extremism.

In that context, it is also difficult to see how the first Labour government might have handled the Liberals differently. It has been argued that if the 1923–4 Parliament had 'set off with better intent' and more effective co-operation between Labour and Liberal whips, 'there might have been the foundation for a very different politics'.[15] But not only did the Liberals support most government legislation, the main reason for poor relations was the personality clash between MacDonald and the often-opportunistic Lloyd George. By spring 1924, the latter clearly realized his party had miscalculated and sought to bring down the government. Having concluded in 1922 that the House of Commons was not big enough for two progressive parties, MacDonald's policy of isolating the Liberals – and thereby forcing them to choose between Labour or the Conservatives – was fully vindicated by the 1924 election result.

At the same time, it is clear that MacDonald could be extraordinarily oversensitive, too easily wounded by criticism and self-pitying when confronted by the slings and arrows of political fortune. A propensity to drive himself too hard and neglect his health also created an environment in which damaging failures of judgement were more likely to occur. The Prime Minister's financial arrangement with a childhood friend was understandable but naïve, and had it been more diligently handled at the beginning of his premiership it might have caused much less embarrassment towards its close. The same was true of the Campbell Case. Although not entirely of MacDonald's making, he arguably made a bad situation worse with his predilection for dissembling over a handsome apology.

Stanley Baldwin called the Cabinet's handling of the Campbell Case 'unconstitutional', yet ironically one of the most significant achievements of Labour's first government was that the party was 'fixed permanently', as Sir Henry Slesser put it, on 'the habit of constitutionalism', continuing 'court, civil service and military and naval tradition unimpaired'.[16] This conservatism had moderately radical consequences. Not only did Court etiquette – socially and sartorially – begin to catch up with the twentieth century, but George V's friendly approach to the first Labour government was an important step on the monarchy's journey towards the studious neutrality which later characterized the reign of Queen Elizabeth II. The government and Royal Household were further separated (through the permanence of the Lord Chamberlain and other hitherto politically appointed officials) while the 1924 election helped put the 'final seal' on the convention that a dissolution request must be granted other than in certain specified circumstances.[17]

In other respects, however, it could not be argued that Labour government left much of a constitutional legacy, even if Lord Haldane's plans for a consolidated Ministry of Justice proved seven decades ahead of their time. There was only a single proactive change, the Ponsonby Rule on parliamentary consideration of treaties, which endured as an important constitutional convention until it took statutory form in 2005.

The territorial constitution, meanwhile, presents a mixed legacy, although one virtually ignored by often Anglocentric historians and academics. An exception is Ivan Gibbons, who has criticized what he called the government's 'legalistic, not to say conservative' approach to Northern Ireland during its term of office, more concerned with respectability than radical action.[18] It is difficult, however, to see what MacDonald and Jimmy Thomas, the Colonial Secretary, might have done differently, bound as they were by the Anglo-Irish Treaty, a fragile security situation and a mainland consensus that no more be heard of the Irish Question. From another perspective, MacDonald et al. handled political leaders in 'Ulster' and the Irish Free State with considerable tact, utilizing the Judicial Committee to provide the necessary clarity and, in the government's final act, constituting the Boundary Commission after a two-year delay.[19]

Labour's approach to Scotland, however, justifies the description 'conservative'. Despite a long-standing personal (not to forget party) commitment to delivering 'Home Rule', MacDonald's patriotic fervour cooled the moment it looked likely he would occupy Number 10. For once, the Clydesiders' irritation at their leader's haughty disregard was justified, with the Prime Minister almost relishing the opportunity to kill off George Buchanan's Bill in May 1924. Thereafter, MacDonald went through the motions of exploring potential reform but the party's commitment to devolution – as confirmed at its 1928 conference – became, much like Clause IV, 'largely symbolic', a principle to which the leadership paid lip service while no longer reflecting 'a serious heartfelt commitment'.[20]

This had consequences, for the failure of Buchanan's Bill pushed the Scottish Home Rule Association to pursue 'Dominion status' and the withdrawal of Scotland's MPs from Westminster, something which eventually fostered a more 'separatist' nationalism of which the Scottish National Party (formed in 1934) would become the most significant manifestation. MacDonald came to separate his personal patriotism from the 'rather tragic delusion of imagining that a Scotland made economically self-contained is going to make its tribute to the world'.[21] It would take the Labour Party another half-century to reconcile itself with legislative devolution, while in 2007 the SNP displaced Labour as Scotland's dominant political force. MacDonald would have recognized the irony of a minority government attempting to balance respectable moderation with the radicalism of its supporters.

To a degree, prolonged discussion of Labour's record in government obscures the fact that its most significant achievement was in taking office at all. From the perspective of 2024 the challenges of minority government are all too familiar, but it remains hard to fully appreciate the challenges created by the general election of December 1923: a three-way split in the House of Commons and an administration supported by fewer than 200 MPs. So, whatever its weaknesses, few Cabinets have ever 'governed Britain under more unprecedented and perplexing conditions'.[22]

Sir Patrick Hastings put it well when he described that first Labour government as 'a great adventure' consisting 'of an untried body of men, travelling in an unknown land, and surrounded by countless enemies'.[23] But despite their inexperience – only a handful of ministers had served in government before – many of the Cabinet discharged their duties well enough to earn the respect of their permanent officials and political opponents. And although Ramsay MacDonald disparaged coalitions, his first government was essentially that, not only an alliance comprising different factions of his own party – intellectuals, trade unionists and Clydesiders – but also former Liberals and even a few Conservatives. That he proved himself able to both assemble and sustain such an unlikely administration remains impressive a century later.

Furthermore, Labour's performance in government *must* be balanced against its minority status, something its critics at the time were noticeably reluctant to do. Faced with what Beatrice Webb called 'two oppositions' which could have combined to bring it down at any moment, it was obvious even to the critical eye that not much was likely to be accomplished under such conditions. Yet MacDonald and his colleagues packed a remarkable amount into nine months, experiencing all the triumphs, drama and mistakes normally associated with a full parliamentary term. Even Clement Attlee, surveying events from the perspective of 1937, did not doubt the 'utility' of his party's determination in 1924 to prove that Labour men and women could 'administer the country': 'The British elector is very sceptical of anything which he has not seen. The mere formation of a Labour Government and its existence for nine months registered a vital change in the political situation. Henceforth Labour was the alternative Government.'[24]

What else could Labour have done? Had MacDonald followed the left's strategy and demanded an immediate dissolution after Parliament's rejection of a radical socialist agenda, it seems highly unlikely Labour would have been returned with a larger number of MPs let alone the majority necessary to deliver the New Jerusalem. Instead, like the apostle Paul, the party put away childish things and chose the moderate, more constructive path. And although this made it, to quote Fenner Brockway, 'a Social Reform Government rather than a Socialist Government, a Liberal Government rather than a Labour Government',[25] the fact remained that it managed to be in office as well as in power, which was the only means by which it could deliver anything at all. If the lesson of 1924 was that only majority government stood any chance of delivery, then what better proof was there than occupying office as a minority in challenging times?

It took, as David Marquand has argued, some time for the Labour Party to get over its 'complex' about Ramsay MacDonald, something he attributed to 'an unwillingness to face painful truths about its own conduct and record'. Particularly after the 'great betrayal' of 1931, it became easier to blame one individual rather than acknowledge the more nuanced reality of 'a man of his own time facing the problems of his own time and applying or failing to apply the solutions of his own time'.[26] That judgement was formed more than half a century after the events of 1924, although at least one contemporary assessment was not far removed. When the journalist Mary Agnes Hamilton came to update her biography of the then former Prime Minister in early 1925, she observed that a 'stage on the road to to-morrow' had been accomplished, 'a light held up that, if temporarily obscured, glows behind the glass with the promise of fuller brightness'.[27]

For Labour the general election of 1923 had presented an opportunity, one the party grabbed with alacrity. Ramsay MacDonald and his colleagues had been dealt a very difficult hand which, for the most part, they played surprisingly well. This had not been guaranteed. The fledgling ministers might have been a disaster, spooking the City of London, offending the King and alienating moderate voters by attempting to pass 'extreme' measures. The Labour Party might have been rendered unelectable. But that did not happen, in part due to the skill of its leader and a few of his colleagues – most notably Snowden, Wheatley, Thomas and Trevelyan – but also on the basis of an occasionally compliant opposition, the fair-mindedness of voters and not a little political luck. As a result, the 'wild men' so feared in late 1923 had within the space of an eventful year shown they were competent men after all. Labour were fit to govern.

BIBLIOGRAPHY

PRIMARY SOURCES

Papers of Lord Charles George Ammon (PLCGA), Hull History Centre
Stanley Baldwin Papers (SBP), University of Cambridge
Lord Beaverbrook Papers (LBP), Parliamentary Archives
Noel Buxton Papers (NBP), McGill University Archives
Cabinet Papers and Conclusions (CPC), The National Archives
Cabinet Secretariat Records (CSR), Public Record Office of Northern
    Ireland
Lady Carson Papers (LCP), Public Record Office of Northern Ireland
Sir Winston Churchill Papers (SWCP), Churchill Archives Centre
Randall Davidson Papers (RDP), Lambeth Palace Library
Department of the Taoiseach Papers (DTP), National Archives of Ireland
Arthur Greenwood Papers (AGP), Weston Library
Lord Haldane Papers (LHP), National Library of Scotland
Iona Kielhorn Collection (IKC), The Hillocks, Lossiemouth
George Lansbury Papers (GLP), London School of Economics Library
Lloyd George Papers (LGP), Parliamentary Archives
Londonderry Papers (LP), Public Record Office of Northern Ireland
Lord Chancellor's Department Papers (LCDP), The National Archives
Ishbel MacDonald Archive (IMA), British Library
Malcolm MacDonald Papers (MMP), University of Durham
James Ramsay MacDonald Papers (JRMP), John Rylands Research
    Institute and Library
Ramsay MacDonald Papers (RMP), The National Archives
Papers of James Ramsay MacDonald (PJRM), National Library of
    Scotland
MacDonald/Grant Letters (MGL), National Library of Scotland
Alasdair Alpin MacGregor Papers (AAMP), National Library of Scotland
Hugh Macmillan Papers (HMP), National Library of Scotland
Eoin MacNeill Papers (EMP), University College Dublin Archives
J. S. Middleton Papers (JSMP), Labour History Archive and Study Centre
H. Montgomery Hyde Papers (HMHP), Public Record Office of Northern
    Ireland

E. D. Morel Papers (EDMP), London School of Economics Library
Ponsonby Archive (PA), Weston Library
Sydney Olivier Papers (SOP), Bodleian Library
Arthur Ponsonby Papers (APP), Shulbrede Priory
Dolly Ponsonby Papers (DPP), Shulbrede Priory
Royal Archives (RA), Windsor
Papers of the Scottish Secretariat and of Roland Eugene Muirhead (PSSREM), National Library of Scotland
Manny Shinwell Papers (MSP), London School of Economics Library
Archive of Lord Southborough (ALS), Weston Library
John Strachey Papers (JSP), Parliamentary Archives
James H. Thomas Papers (JHTP), Kent History and Library Centre
Treasury Papers (TP), The National Archives
Trevelyan Archive (TA), Newcastle University
Papers of Alice G. Vines (PAGV), National Library of Scotland
Papers of Beatrice and Sidney Webb (PBSW), London School of Economics Library

SECONDARY SOURCES

Adrian Addison (2017), *Mail Men: The Unauthorized Story of the Daily Mail*, London: Atlantic Books

Mosa Anderson (1952), *Noel Buxton: A Life*, London: George Allen & Unwin

Norman Angell (1951), *After All: The Autobiography of Norman Angell*, London: Hamish Hamilton

Anonymous (1924), *Ramsay MacDonald's Romantic Life Story By 'One who knows him': Britain's First Labour Premier*, London: Reynolds's News

Anonymous (1931), *The Scottish Socialists: A Gallery of Contemporary Portraits*, London: Faber and Faber

Clement Attlee (1937), *The Labour Party in Perspective*, London: Victor Gollancz

— (1954), *As It Happened*, London: Heinemann

Stuart Ball (ed.) (1992), *Parliament and Politics in the Age of Baldwin and MacDonald: The Headlam Diaries, 1923–1935*, London: The Historians Press

Rodney Barker (1972), *Education and Politics 1900–1951: A Study of the Labour Party*, Oxford: Clarendon Press

Lewis Baston (2000), 'Labour local government 1900–1999', in Brian Brivati and Richard Heffernan (eds), *The Labour Party: A Centenary History*, Basingstoke: Palgrave Macmillan

Francis Beckett (1998), *Enemy Within: The Rise and Fall of the British Communist Party*, London: John Murray

G. K. A. Bell (1935), *Randall Davidson: Archbishop of Canterbury*, Volume II, London: Oxford University Press

Gill Bennett (1999), *The Zinoviev Letter of 1924: 'A most extraordinary and mysterious business'*, History Notes 14, London: Foreign & Commonwealth Office.

— (2018), *The Zinoviev Letter: the conspiracy that never dies*, Oxford: Oxford University Press

John Bew (2016), *Citizen Clem: A Biography of Attlee*, London: Riverrun

Earl of Birkenhead (1924), *Contemporary Personalities*, London: Cassell

Gregory Blaxland (1964), *J. H. Thomas: A Life for Unity*, London: Frederick Muller

Margaret Bondfield (1948), *A Life's Work*, London: Hutchinson

Robert Boothby (1947), *I Fight to Live: Autobiography*, London: Victor Gollancz

D. G. Boyce (1988), *The Irish Question and British Politics 1868–1996*, Basingstoke: Palgrave Macmillan

Fenner Brockway (1942), *Inside the Left: Thirty Years of Platform, Press, Prison and Parliament*, London: George Allen & Unwin

— (1946), *Socialism Over Sixty Years: The Life of Jowett of Bradford (1864–1944)*, London: George Allen & Unwin

— (1977), *Towards Tomorrow: The Autobiography of Fenner Brockway*, London: Hart-Davis, MacGibbon

Gordon Brown (1986), *Maxton*, Edinburgh: Mainstream

David Bryn-Jones (1937), *Frank B. Kellogg: A Biography*, New York: G. P. Putnam's

John Callaghan (2007), *The Labour Party and Foreign Policy: A History*, London: Routledge

John Campbell (1977), *Lloyd George: The Goat in the Wilderness 1922–1931*, London: Jonathan Cape

John Campbell and Richard McLauchlan (2020), *Haldane: The Forgotten Statesman Who Shaped Modern Britain*, London: Hurst & Company

W. S. Chalmers (1951), *The Life and Letters of David Beatty: Admiral of the Fleet*, London: Hodder & Stoughton

Lewis Chester, Stephen Fay and Hugo Young (1968), *The Zinoviev Letter: A Political Intrigue*, London: Lippincott

Winston Churchill (1942), *Great Contemporaries*, London: Macmillan

J. R. Clynes (1937), *Memoirs 1924–1937*, London: Hutchinson

G. D. H. Cole (1948), *A History of the Labour Party From 1914*, London: Routledge & Kegan Paul

Margaret Cole (1955), *Beatrice and Sidney Webb*, London: Fabian Society

Maurice Cowling (1971), *The Impact of Labour 1920-1924: The Beginning of Modern British Politics*, Cambridge: Cambridge University Press

Colin Cross (1966), *Philip Snowden*, London: Barrie and Rockliff

Sibyl Crowe and Edward Corp (1996), *Our Ablest Public Servant: Sir Eyre Crowe 1864-1925*, Braunton: Merlin Books

Hugh Dalton (1953), *Call Back Yesterday: Memoirs 1887-1931*, London: Frederick Muller

John Davies (1994), *A History of Wales*, London: Penguin

Peter Dorey (2008), *The Labour Party and Constitutional Reform: A History of Constitutional Conservatism*, London: Palgrave Macmillan

Robert E. Dowse (1966), *Left in the Centre: The Independent Labour Party 1893-1940*, London: Longmans

J. J. Edwards (1964), *The Law Officers of the Crown*, London: Sweet & Maxwell

Mortimer Epstein (ed.) (1923), *The Annual Register 1923*, London: Longmans

— ed. (1924), *The Annual Register 1924*, London: Longmans

Richard J. Finlay (1994), *Independent and Free: Scottish Politics and the Origins of the Scottish National Party 1918-1945*, Edinburgh: John Donald

Russell Galbraith (2018), *Without Quarter: A Biography of Tom Johnston*, Edinburgh: Birlinn

William Gallacher (1947), *The Rolling of the Thunder*, London: Lawrence & Wishart

Alexander Gammie (1931), *From Pit to Palace: The Life Story of the Right Hon. James Brown, M.P. Lord High Commissioner to the General Assembly of the Church of Scotland*, London: James Clarke & Company

Martin Gilbert (1976), *Winston S. Churchill*, Volume V, *1922-1939*, London: Heinemann

Harry Gosling (1927), *Up and Down Stream*, London: Methuen

Thomas N. Graham (1948), *Willie Graham: The Life of The Rt. Hon. W. Graham*, London: Hutchinson

J. D. Gregory (1929), *On the Edge of Diplomacy: Rambles and Reflections 1902-1928*, London: Hutchinson

Percy J. Grigg (1948), *Prejudice and Judgment*, London: Jonathan Cape

Partha Sarathi Gupta (1975), *Imperialism and the British Labour Movement, 1914-1964*, New York: Holmes & Meïer

Richard Burdon Haldane (1929), *An Autobiography*, London: Hodder & Stoughton

Mary Agnes Hamilton (1924), *Margaret Bondfield*, London: Leonard Parsons

— (1924), *Fit to Govern!*, London: Leonard Parsons (published under the pseudonym 'Iconoclast')

— (1925), *J. Ramsay MacDonald (1923–1925)*, London: Leonard Parsons (as above)

— (1938), *Arthur Henderson: A Biography*, London: Heinemann

John Hannan (1988), *The Life of John Wheatley*, Nottingham: Spokesman

Sir Patrick Hastings (1948), *The Autobiography of Sir Patrick Hastings*, London: Heinemann

Simon Heffer (ed.) (2021), *Henry 'Chips' Channon: The Diaries: 1918–38*, London: Hutchinson

David Howell (1986), *A Lost Left: Three Studies in Socialism and Nationalism*, Manchester: Manchester University Press

— (2002), *McDonald's Party: Labour Identities and Crisis, 1922–1931*, Oxford: Oxford University Press

Keith Jeffery and Peter Hennessy (1983), *States of Emergency: British Governments and Strikebreaking since 1919*, London: Routledge & Kegan Paul

Edwin A. Jenkins (1933), *From Foundry to Foreign Office: The Romantic Life-Story of the Rt Hon Arthur Henderson, MP*, London: Grayson & Grayson

Roy Jenkins (1964), *Asquith*, London: Collins

— (1987), *Baldwin*, London: Papermac

— (1998), *The Chancellors*, London: Macmillan

Raymond A. Jones (1989), *Arthur Ponsonby: The Politics of Life*, London: Christopher Helm

Michael Keating and David Bleiman (1979), *Labour and Scottish Nationalism*, London: Macmillan

David Kirkwood (1935), *My Life of Revolt*, London: George G. Harrap

William Knox (1991), '"Ours is not an ordinary Parliamentary movement": 1922–1926' in Alan McKinlay and R. J. Morris (eds), *The ILP on Clydeside, 1893–1932: From Foundation to Disintegration*, Manchester: Manchester University Press

Stephen E. Koss (1969), *Lord Haldane: Scapegoat for Liberalism*, New York: Columbia University Press

Labour Party (1923), *Labour's Appeal to the Nation*, London: Labour Party

— (1923), *Report of the Twenty-Third Annual Conference of the Labour Party*, London: Labour Party

— (1924), *Can Labour Rule? No. 6, The Anglo-Soviet Treaties*, London: Labour Joint Publications Department

— (1924), *Labour's Appeal to the People*, London: Labour Party.

— (1924), *Labour's Great Record*, London: Labour Publications Department

— (1924), *Report of the Twenty-Fourth Annual Conference of the Labour Party*, London: Labour Party

— (1924), *Six Months of Labour Government*, London: Independent Labour Party Information Committee

Jack Lawson (1932), *A Man's Life*, London: Hodder & Stoughton

Keith Laybourn (2020), *The Independent Labour Party, 1914–1939: The Political and Cultural History of a Socialist Party*, Abingdon: Routledge

Fred M. Leventhal (1989), *Arthur Henderson*, Manchester: Manchester University Press

Rodney Lowe (1986), *Adjusting to Democracy: The Role of the Ministry of Labour in British Politics, 1916–1939*, Oxford: Clarendon Press

Richard W. Lyman (1957), *The First Labour Government, 1924*, London: Chapman & Hall

John McConachie (1988), *The Moray Golf Club at Lossiemouth 1889–1989*, Elgin: Moravian Press

J. Ramsay MacDonald (1924), *Margaret Ethel MacDonald*, London: George Allen & Unwin

— (1924), *Socialism: Critical and Constructive*, London: Cassell

Norman and Jeanne MacKenzie (eds) (1984), *The Diary of Beatrice Webb*, Volume One, *1873–1892: Glitter Around and Darkness Within*, London: Virago

— (eds) (1984), *The Diary of Beatrice Webb*, Volume Three, *1905–1924: The Power to Alter Things*, London: Virago

— (eds) (1985), *The Diary of Beatrice Webb*, Volume Four, *1924–1943: The Wheel of Life*, London: Virago

Ross McKibbin (1974), *The Evolution of the Labour Party 1910–1924*, Oxford: Clarendon Press

Sir Alexander Mackintosh (1945), *Echoes of Big Ben: A Journalist's Parliamentary Diary (1881–1940)*, London: Hutchinson

Richard McLauchlan (2023), *Serious Minds: The Extraordinary Haldanes of Cloan*, London: Hurst

Iain McLean (1999), *The Legend of Red Clydeside*, Edinburgh: John Donald

Lord Macmillan (1952), *A Man of Law's Tale: The Reminiscences of the Rt. Hon. Lord Macmillan P.C., G.C.V.O., LL.D., D.C.L.*, London: Macmillan

Lauchlan MacNeill Weir (1938), *The Tragedy of Ramsay MacDonald: A Political Biography*, London: Secker & Warburg

James Margach (1978), *The Abuse of Power: The War Between Downing Street and the Media from Lloyd George to Callaghan*, London: W. H. Allen

David Marquand (1977), *Ramsay MacDonald*, London: Jonathan Cape

— (1997), *Ramsay MacDonald*, London: Richard Cohen

Edward Marsh (1939), *A Number of People: A Book of Reminiscences*, London: Heinemann

Sir Frederick Maurice (1939), *Haldane 1915–1928: The Life of Viscount Haldane of Cloan*, London: Faber and Faber

Keith Middlemas (1965), *The Clydesiders: A Left Wing Struggle for Parliamentary Power*, London: Hutchinson

— (ed.) (1969), *Thomas Jones: Whitehall Diary*, Volume I, *1916–1925*, London: Oxford University Press

— (ed.) (1971), *Thomas Jones: Whitehall Diary*, Volume III, *Ireland 1918–1925*, London: Oxford University Press

Ralph Miliband (1961), *Parliamentary Socialism: A Study in the Politics of Labour*, London: George Allen & Unwin

Donald Mitchell (2014), *The Politics of Dissent: A Biography of E. D. Morel*, SilverWood

H. Montgomery Hyde (1960), *Sir Patrick Hastings: His Life and Cases*, London: Heinemann

— (1973), *Baldwin: The Unexpected Prime Minister*, London: Hart-Davis

Austen Morgan (1987), *Ramsay MacDonald*, Manchester: Manchester University Press

Kevin Morgan (2006), *Ramsay MacDonald*, London: Haus

A. J. A. Morris (1977), *C. P. Trevelyan 1870–1958: Portrait of a Radical*, Belfast: Blackstaff Press

Paul Mulvey (2010), *The Political Life of Josiah C. Wedgwood: Land, Liberty and Empire, 1872–1943*, London: Royal Historical Society

John F. Naylor (1984), *A Man and an Institution: Sir Maurice Hankey, the Cabinet Secretariat and the Custody of Cabinet Secrecy*, Cambridge: Cambridge University Press

Harold Nicolson (1952), *King George the Fifth: His Life and Reign*, London: Constable

John Julius Norwich (ed.) (2005), *The Duff Cooper Diaries*, London: Weidenfeld & Nicolson

Nicholas Owen, 'MacDonald's Parties: The Labour Party and the "Aristocratic Embrace", 1922–31', *Twentieth Century British History* 18:1, 2007

Earl of Oxford and Asquith (1928), *Memories and Reflections 1852–1927*, Volume 2, London: Cassell

Lord Parmoor (1936), *A Retrospect: Looking Back Over a Life of More Than Eighty Years*, London: Heinemann

F. W. Pethick-Lawrence (1943), *Fate Has Been Kind*, London: Hutchinson

Vivian Phillips (1943), *My Days and Ways*, Edinburgh: Pillans & Wilson (privately printed)

Martin Pugh (2010), *Speak for Britain!: A New History of the Labour Party*, London: Bodley Head

John Ramsden (1978), *The Age of Balfour and Baldwin 1902–1940*, London: Longman

— (1998), *An Appetite for Power: A History of the Conservative Party*

Report from the Select Committee on Ministers' Remuneration, Cmnd 170, 28 July 1930

Robert Rhodes James (1969), *Memoirs of a Conservative: J. C. C. Davidson's Memoirs and Papers, 1910–37*, London: Weidenfeld & Nicolson

— (1977), *The British Revolution, British Politics, 1880–1939*, Volume 2: *From Asquith to Chamberlain 1914–1939*, London: Hamish Hamilton

Jane Ridley (2021), *George V: Never a Dull Moment*, London: Chatto & Windus

Kenneth Rose (1983), *King George V*, London: Papermac

Stephen Roskill (1972), *Hankey: Man of Secrets*, Volume II, *1919–1931*, London: Collins

Clyde Sanger (1995), *Malcolm MacDonald: Bringing an End to Empire*, Liverpool: Liverpool University Press

John Scanlon (1932), *The Decline and Fall of the Labour Party*, London: Peter Davies

Robert C. Self (ed.) (1995), *The Austen Chamberlain Diary Letters: The Correspondence of Sir Austen Chamberlain with his Sisters Hilda and Ida, 1916–1937*, Cambridge: Cambridge University Press

John Shepherd (2002), *George Lansbury: At the Heart of Old Labour*, Oxford: Oxford University Press

John Shepherd and Keith Laybourn (2006), *Britain's First Labour Government*, Basingstoke: Palgrave Macmillan

Manny Shinwell (1955), *Conflict Without Malice*, London: Odhams Press

— (1981), *Lead With the Left: My First Ninety-six Years*, London: Cassell

Sir Henry Slesser (1941), *Judgment Reserved: The Reminiscences of the Right Honourable Sir Henry Slesser: Late Lord Justice of Appeal*, London: Hutchinson

Philip Snowden (1934), *An Autobiography*, Volume Two, *1919–1934*, London: Ivor Nicholson and Watson

Dudley Sommer (1960), *Haldane of Cloan: His Life and Times 1856–1928*, London: George Allen & Unwin

Harold Spender (1926), *The Fire of Life: A Book of Memories*, London: Hodder & Stoughton

Ernest Stanford, *James Ramsay MacDonald: A Memoir* (unpublished), Edinburgh: National Library of Scotland (unpublished manuscript)

A. J. P. Taylor (1972), *Beaverbrook*, London: Hamish Hamilton

Miles Taylor (2000), 'Labour and the constitution' in Duncan Tanner, Pat Thane and Nick Tiratsoo (eds), *Labour's First Century*, Cambridge: Cambridge University Press

J. H. Thomas (1937), *My Story*, London: Hutchinson

Hubert H. Tiltman (1929), *James Ramsay MacDonald: Labour's Man of Destiny*, London: Jarrolds

Herbert Tracey (ed.) (1925), *The Book of the Labour Party: Its History, Growth, Policy, and Leaders*, Volume I, London: Caxton

Charles Trevelyan (1924), *The Broad High Road in Education*, London: Labour Party

— (1927), *Education when Labour Rules Again*, London: Labour Party

Rhiannon Vickers (2004), *The Labour Party and the World*, Volume 1: *The Evolution of Labour's Foreign Policy, 1900–51*, Manchester: Manchester University Press

Alice G. Vines (1982), *The MacDonald Women: Margaret and Ishbel*, Edinburgh: National Library of Scotland (unpublished manuscript)

Graham Walker (1988), *Thomas Johnston*, Manchester: Manchester University Press

Nourah Waterhouse (1942), *Private and Official*, London: Jonathan Cape

Josiah C. Wedgwood (1940), *Memoirs of a Fighting Life*, London: Hutchinson

Duke of Windsor (1951), *A King's Story: The Memoirs of H.R.H. the Duke of Windsor*, London: Cassell.

Francis Williams (1950), *Fifty Years March: The Rise of the Labour Party*, London: Odhams Press

Philip Williamson (2007), *Stanley Baldwin: Conservative Leadership and National Values*, Cambridge: Cambridge University Press

Trevor Wilson (ed.) (1970), *The Political Diaries of C. P. Scott 1911–1928*, London: Collins

Ian S. Wood (1989), 'Hope Deferred: Labour in Scotland in the 1920s' in Ian Donnachie, Christopher Harvie and Ian S. Wood (eds), *Forward! Labour Politics in Scotland 1888–1988*, Edinburgh: Polygon

— (1990), *John Wheatley*, Manchester: Manchester University Press

Leonard Woolf (1967), *Downhill all the Way: An Autobiography of the Years 1919–1939*, London: Hogarth Press

Chris Wrigley (1990), *Arthur Henderson*, Cardiff: University of Wales Press

JOURNAL ARTICLES

Trevor Barnes (1979), 'Special Branch and the First Labour Government', *The Historical Journal* 32:4, pp. 944–7

J. P. Casey (1975), 'The First Labour Government and Office of Lord Advocate', *Northern Ireland Legal Quarterly* 26:1, pp. 18–29

Ralph H. Desmarais (1973), 'Strikebreaking and the Labour Government of 1924', *Journal of Contemporary History* 8:4, pp. 165–75

H. A. L. Fisher (1924), 'The Present Situation', *The Nineteenth Century and After* 95

Ivan Gibbons (2009), 'The First British Labour Government and The Irish Boundary Commission 1924', *Irish Studies: An Irish Quarterly Review* 98:391, pp. 321–33

Martin Johnes (2012), 'Cardiff: The Making and Development of the Capital City of Wales', *Contemporary British History* 26:4, pp. 509–28

Carolyn J. Kitching (2011), 'Prime minister and foreign secretary: the dual role of James Ramsay MacDonald in 1924', *Review of International Studies* 37:3, pp. 1403–22

Michael Meadowcroft (2018), 'The 1924 Labour Government and the Failure of the Whips', *Journal of Liberal History* 100, pp. 24–35

Stephen Clive Meredith (2012), 'A "Strange Death" Foretold (or the Not So "Strange Death" of Liberal Wales): Liberal Decline, the Labour Ascendancy and Electoral Politics in South Wales, 1922–1924', *North American Journal of Welsh Studies* 7, pp. 18–37

Kevin Morgan (2005), 'The problem of the epoch? Labour and housing 1918–1951', *Twentieth Century British History* 16:3, pp. 227–55

F. H. Newark (1969), 'The Campbell Case and the First Labour Government', *Northern Ireland Legal Quarterly* 20:1, pp. 19–42

Sheldon Spear (1978), 'Pacifist Radicalism in the Post-War British Labour Party: The Case of E. D. Morel, 1919–24', *International Review of Social History* 23:2, pp. 193–223

Andrew Thorpe (1996), 'The industrial meaning of "gradualism": the Labour party and industry, 1918–1931', *Journal of British Studies* 35:1, pp. 84–113

Graham Walker and James Greer (2019), 'Religion, Labour, and National Questions: The General Election of 1924 in Belfast and Lanarkshire', *Labour History Review* 84:3, pp. 217–39

UNPUBLISHED PHD THESIS

Jake Vaughan (2007), 'The first Labour Government and the civil service', PhD thesis, London: King's College

ACKNOWLEDGEMENTS

The late historian D. R. Thorpe, who was very encouraging to me as a young writer, once said that 'people, places and papers' were the essential components of political biography. All three have proved essential to the research and writing of *The Wild Men*.

First, people. For the first time in almost 20 years I worked with an agent, and Martin Redfern (formerly of Northbank) proved key in developing the pitch which was accepted by Tomasz Hoskins at Bloomsbury Continuum. I am very grateful to them both. Thanks also to Dr Conor McCormick of Queen's University Belfast for his hospitality in that fascinating city and for directing me towards several useful sources regarding the law officers. Both Jason Loch and my brother Michael read everything in draft and made helpful observations, while Mark Scott advised on the niceties of Court dress. I must also thank my House of Commons Library colleagues Greg Howard and Paul Little, who cheerfully tracked down obscure books, pamphlets and journal articles. John Curtis, another Library colleague, looked over the chapter on foreign affairs and pointed me towards a reference on prime ministerial cars.

Next, papers. The superb Parliamentary Archives threw up a number of useful sources, as did collections in England, Scotland and both parts of Ireland. Their respective archivists proved unfailingly helpful. Highlights were the often-overlooked papers at Windsor's Royal Archives, access to which was facilitated by Miss Allison Derrett, who also rectified my clumsily incomplete references. I am also indebted to two private archives, that preserved by Ian and Kate Russell at Shulbrede Priory (the Arthur and Dolly Ponsonby papers), and a modest but useful collection of correspondence in the possession of Jeni Freeman.

Finally, places. The highlight of my research trips were a few days at Lossiemouth on the beautiful Morayshire coast. There I met Iona Kielhorn, a doughty defender of her grandfather's legacy and an engaging host. Particularly memorable was being allowed to explore The Hillocks, where MacDonald planned his first government over the Christmas of 1923. Nothing could quite match enjoying lunch there after traipsing the sand dunes between Lossie and Covesea Lighthouse, just as Labour's first Prime Minister-to-be had done a century earlier.

Dr David Torrance
Peckham
September 2023

THE LABOUR GOVERNMENT
(22 JANUARY–4 NOVEMBER 1924)

Most appointments were announced on 22 January (exceptions are indicated below). Senior appointments were active from the acceptance of seals; junior positions from point at which the King was informed.

The Cabinet	
J. Ramsay MacDonald	Prime Minister, First Lord of the Treasury, Secretary of State for Foreign Affairs and Leader of the House of Commons
Viscount Haldane	Lord High Chancellor of Great Britain and Leader of the Lords
J. R. Clynes	Lord Privy Seal and Deputy Leader of the House of Commons
Lord Parmoor	Lord President of the Council
Philip Snowden	Chancellor of the Exchequer
Arthur Henderson	Secretary of State for the Home Department
James H. Thomas	Secretary of State for the Colonies
Stephen Walsh	Secretary of State for War
Lord Olivier	Secretary of State for India
Lord Thomson	Secretary of State for Air
William Adamson	Secretary for Scotland
Sidney Webb	President of the Board of Trade
Charles P. Trevelyan	President of the Board of Education
Lord Chelmsford	First Lord of the Admiralty
John Wheatley	Minister of Health
Noel Buxton	Minister of Agriculture and Fisheries
Thomas Shaw	Minister of Labour
Vernon Hartshorn	Postmaster-General

Fred W. Jowett	First Commissioner of Works
Josiah Wedgwood	Chancellor of the Duchy of Lancaster
Ministers not in the Cabinet	
Frank O. Roberts	Minister of Pensions (23 January)
Harry Gosling	Minister of Transport (24 January) and Paymaster-General (6 May)
Frank Hodges	Civil Lord of the Admiralty
Sir Patrick Hastings, KC	Attorney-General for England and Wales (23 January)
Sir Henry H. Slesser, KC	Solicitor General for England and Wales (23 January)
William Graham	Financial Secretary to the Treasury
Jack J. Lawson	Financial Secretary to the War Office
Ben Spoor	Chief Whip
Parliamentary under-secretaries (and respective departments)	
William Leach	Air
Lord Arnold	Colonies
Arthur Ponsonby	Foreign
Rhys Davies	Home
Robert Richards	India
Clement Attlee	War
James Stewart	Health for Scotland
Parliamentary Secretaries	
Charles Ammon	Admiralty
Walter B. Smith	Agriculture and Fisheries
Morgan Jones	Education
Arthur Greenwood	Health
Margaret Bondfield	Labour
J. W. Muir	Pensions
A. V. Alexander	Board of Trade
Manny Shinwell	Mines
William Lunn	Overseas Trade
Scottish law officers	
Hugh Macmillan, KC	Lord Advocate (as of 8 February)
John C. Fenton, KC	Solicitor General for Scotland (as of 18 February)

TIMELINE OF THE FIRST LABOUR GOVERNMENT

1923	
25 October	Stanley Baldwin's Plymouth speech precipitates a general election
12 November	Baldwin asks King George V to dissolve Parliament
6 December	General election
18 December	During a speech at the National Liberal Club, H. H. Asquith, the Liberal leader, makes it clear he will not prevent Labour from taking office
1924	
8 January	Ramsay MacDonald addresses a 'victory rally' at the Royal Albert Hall
15 January	State Opening of Parliament
21 January	Baldwin's government loses vote of no confidence
22 January	MacDonald is sworn of the Privy Council and 'kisses hands' as the first Labour Prime Minister
23 January	Senior ministers receive their seals of office from the King
21–29 January	Railway strike
1 February	UK grants *de jure* recognition of the Soviet Union
7 February	Press reports that John Wheatley has rescinded the Poplar Order
12 February	MacDonald addresses the House of Commons for the first time as Prime Minister
16–25 February	Dock strike
21 February	The Prime Minister cancels plans for a Singapore naval base
28 February	Arthur Henderson, the Home Secretary, wins the Burnley by-election

26 February	Liberal motion condemning repeal of the Poplar Order; government survives
22 March	Charles Trevelyan sets out his vision for education in a speech at Newcastle
22–31 March	London tram, bus and Underground strike
1 April	Arthur Ponsonby outlines what becomes known as the 'Ponsonby Rule' on parliamentary consideration of treaties
7 April	Cabinet agrees not to reinstate police strikers
9 April	Charles Dawes publishes his proposals for German reparations
14 April	Anglo-Soviet Conference begins in London
23 April	The King opens the Empire Exhibition at Wembley
29 April	Philip Snowden delivers his first Budget
9 May	George Buchanan's Government of Scotland Bill is debated in the House of Commons
29 May	A Conservative motion to reduce the salary of Minister of Labour is defeated
3 June	Sir Alexander Grant created a baronet
20–22 June	MacDonald holds talks with French premier Edouard Herriot at Chequers
7 July	Plans for a Channel Tunnel are shelved following opposition from the Committee of Imperial Defence
16 July	The London Conference on reparations begins
25 July	*Workers' Weekly* carries an article calling on the Armed Forces to lead 'a common attack upon the capitalists'
30 July	Sir Patrick Hastings, the Attorney General, authorizes criminal proceedings against *Workers' Weekly*
31 July	The Judicial Committee of the Privy Council rules that the Irish Boundary Commission can only be constituted if the Anglo-Irish Treaty is amended
2 August	German delegates join the London Conference
6 August	Cabinet discusses the 'Campbell Case'
7 August	Royal Assent is granted to the Housing (Financial Provisions) Act 1924
8 August	Commercial and General Treaties between the UK and Soviet Union are signed in London

13 August	The prosecution against John Campbell is withdrawn
16 August	The London Conference concludes with a protocol on the French occupation of the Ruhr and German reparations
3 September	MacDonald becomes the first UK Prime Minister to address the League of Nations
12 September	The *Daily Mail* reveals that the Prime Minister owns shares in McVitie's
22 September	Asquith publishes a letter attacking the Russian Treaties
30 September	Parliament meets to consider legislation amending the Anglo-Irish Treaty and the 'Campbell Case'
8 October	Government loses confidence vote in the Commons
9 October	Parliament is dissolved
10 October	A copy of the 'Zinoviev Letter' arrives at the Foreign Office
13 October	MacDonald's Glasgow speech is broadcast on the BBC
15–16 October	The Prime Minister sees the Zinoviev Letter for the first time
25 October	The *Daily Mail* publishes the Zinoviev Letter
27 October	MacDonald responds to the Zinoviev Letter during a speech in Cardiff
29 October	General election
31 October	Cabinet appoints a committee to investigate the Zinoviev Letter
4 November	MacDonald resigns as Prime Minister; Stanley Baldwin kisses hands
7 November	Labour ministers relinquish their seals of office

ENDNOTES

PREFACE

1 For a detailed summary of how the story unfolded, see Oliver Wright, 'How freebies furore went from bad to worse for Keir Starmer', *The Times*, 3 October 2024.

2 'Rachel Reeves defends £7,500 clothes funding with Labour under pressure over donations', *Standard*, 23 September 2024.

3 'Starmer will stop accepting clothes to show solidarity with public, says Nandy', *Guardian*, 21 September 2024.

4 'Keir Starmer pays back £6,000 for gifts received since becoming PM', *The Times*, 2 October 2024.

5 Steven Swinford and Oliver Wright, '"A lot of mistakes were made": concerns mount over Labour's messaging', *The Times*, 4 October 2024.

6 David Osland, 'When freebies for a Labour prime minister take the biscuit', Labour Hub website, 5 October 2024.

7 Kiran Stacey, '"He will hate this profile": how donor Waheed Alli became a Labour fixer', *Guardian*, 16 September 2024.

8 'Lessons for Keir Starmer from Britain's first Labour government', *The Economist*, 8 February 2024.

9 'Conclusions', *How Labour Governs* Report, Anglia Ruskin University website, July 2024.

10 The Labour Party on X, 'This is the power of a Labour government', 4 June 2024.

11 Malcolm Petrie, 'When Labour Was New: Labour's First Government', *London Review of Books*, 20 June 2024.

12 'Prime Minister's remarks at Downing Street: 6 July 2024', Number 10/ Prime Minister's Office website, 6 July 2024.

13 'Angela Rayner talks new Labour Government and meeting King Charles twice', manchesterworld website, 15 June 2024.

14 Tom Peck, 'Commons courtesies go right out of the window', *The Times*, 10 July 2024.

15 Catherine Bennett, 'Reducing Labour women to the sum of their outfits is suddenly all the rage', *Observer*, 14 July 2024.

16 'The King's Speech 2024', Number 10/Prime Minister's Office website, 17 July 2024.

17 Jonathan Davis, 'How Labour Governs: Labour and the wider-world', Anglia Ruskin University website, July 2024.

18 'Lessons for Keir Starmer from Britain's first Labour government', *The Economist*, 8 February 2024.

19 'Chancellor Rachel Reeves is taking immediate action to fix the foundations of our economy', HM Treasury website, 8 July 2024.

20 'Keir Starmer: I am a socialist who will put country before party', *Telegraph*, 27 May 2024.

21 'Sir Geoffrey Cox says Britain is "sleepwalking into a one party, socialist state"', GB News website, 12 June 2024.

INTRODUCTION

1 Philip Snowden (1934), *An Autobiography*, Volume Two, *1919–1934*, London: Ivor Nicholson and Watson, pp. 605–6.

2 Keith Middlemas (ed.) (1969), *Thomas Jones: Whitehall Diary*, Volume I, *1916–1925*, London: Oxford University Press, p. 267.

3 *Evening Standard*, 23 January 1924.

4 *The Advocate* (Tasmania), 7 January 1921.

5 Ernest Stanford, *James Ramsay MacDonald: A Memoir* (unpublished manuscript), Acc.6215/Box 4(c), Alasdair Alpin MacGregor Papers, Edinburgh: National Library of Scotland, p. 55.

6 Hugh Dalton (1953), *Call Back Yesterday: Memoirs 1887–1931*, London: Frederick Muller, p. 146.

7 John Campbell (1977), *Lloyd George: The Goat in the Wilderness 1922–1931*, London: Jonathan Cape, p. 84.

8 J. R. Clynes (1937), *Memoirs 1924–1937*, London: Hutchinson, p. 20.

9 Unpublished memoirs, CA RBD MS 951-2-012, Noel Buxton Papers, McGill University Archives.

10 Josiah C. Wedgwood (1940), *Memoirs of a Fighting Life*, London: Hutchinson, p. 186.

11 Paul Mulvey (2010), *The Political Life of Josiah C. Wedgwood: Land, Liberty and Empire, 1872–1943*, London: Royal Historical Society, p. 138. The Chancellor of the Duchy of Lancaster was responsible for appointing magistrates in Lancashire.

12 Kenneth Rose (1983), *King George V*, London: Papermac, p. 329.

13 J. R. Clynes, *Memoirs*, p. 20.

14 Norman and Jeanne MacKenzie (eds) (1985), *The Diary of Beatrice Webb*, Volume Four, *1924–1943 The Wheel of Life*, London: Virago, p. 11.

15 Unidentified newspaper cutting, 24 January 1924, Trevelyan Archive, Newcastle University.

16 Diary entry dated 22 January 1924, PRO 30/69/1753/1, Ramsay MacDonald Papers, Kew: The National Archives.

17 Richard W. Lyman (1957), *The First Labour Government, 1924*, London: Chapman & Hall.

18 John Shepherd and Keith Laybourn (2006), *Britain's First Labour Government*, Basingstoke: Palgrave Macmillan.

19 *The Times*, 26 December 2022.

20 David Marquand (1977), *Ramsay MacDonald*, London: Jonathan Cape, p. 285.

21 Percy J. Grigg (1948), *Prejudice and Judgment*, London: Jonathan Cape, p. 130.

1. 'A SERIOUS NATIONAL MISFORTUNE'

1 Colin Cross (1966), *Philip Snowden*, London: Barrie and Rockliff, 1966, pp. 192–3.

2 Labour Party (1923), *Report of the Twenty-Third Annual Conference of the Labour Party*, London: Labour Party, pp. 178–9, 204.

3 H. Montgomery Hyde (1973), *Baldwin: The Unexpected Prime Minister*, London: Hart-Davis, pp. 175–6.

4 *The Times*, 25 October 1923.

5 *The Times*, 27 October 1924.

6 Lord Salisbury and Viscount Novar to Stanley Baldwin, October 1923, D.4.1, Stanley Baldwin Papers, University of Cambridge.

7 'How the Socialist Government came into Power: A Three-Cornered Misunderstanding', Lord Beaverbrook Papers, BBK/G/12/6, Parliamentary Archives.

8 *The Times*, 2 November 1923.

9 John Strachey to Stanley Baldwin, 3 November 1923, D.4.1, SBP.

10 H. Montgomery Hyde, *Baldwin*, p. 184.

11 Stephen Roskill (1972), *Hankey: Man of Secrets*, Volume II, *1919–1931*, London: Collins, p. 352.

12 Jane Ridley (2021), *George V: Never a Dull Moment*, London: Chatto & Windus, p. 316.

13 David Marquand, *Ramsay MacDonald*, p. 295.

14 Clyde Sanger (1995), *Malcolm MacDonald: Bringing an End to Empire*, Liverpool: Liverpool University Press, pp. 40–41.

15 *The Labour Woman*, January 1924.

16 Labour Party (1923), *Labour's Appeal to the Nation*, London: Labour Party.

17 Oliver Baldwin was elected the Labour MP for Dudley in 1929.

18 Roy Jenkins (1987), *Baldwin*, London: Papermac, 1987.

19 *The Times* predicted a majority of between 27 and 59 seats.

20 Labour Party (1924), *Six Months of Labour Government*, London: Independent Labour Party Information Committee, p3.

21 Keith Middlemas, *Thomas Jones: Whitehall Diary*, Volume I, p. 258.

22 H. Montgomery Hyde, *Baldwin*, p. 95.

23 Diary entry dated 7 December 1923, Arthur Ponsonby Papers, Shulbrede Priory. Dolly (or Dorothea) was the daughter of composer Hubert Parry.

24 Diary entry dated 8 December 1923, PRO 30/69/1753/1, RMP.

25 Royal Archives (afterwards RA) GV/PRIV/GVD/1923: 8 December.

26 Mary Agnes Hamilton (1938), *Arthur Henderson: A Biography*, London: Heinemann, p. 232.

27 H. Montgomery Hyde, *Baldwin*, p. 196.

28 Lord Haldane to Stanley Baldwin, 8 December 1923, D.4.1, SBP.

29 Memo by Stamfordham, 8 December 1923, RA PS/PSO/GV/C/K/1918/14.

30 Memo by Stamfordham, 9 December 1923, RA PS/PSO/GV/C/K/1918/26.

31 Kenneth Rose, *King George V*, p. 324.

32 Robert Rhodes James (1969), *Memoirs of a Conservative: J. C. C. Davidson's Memoirs and Papers, 1910–37*, London: Weidenfeld & Nicolson, p. 189.

33 Memo by Stamfordham, 10 December 1923, RA PS/PSO/GV/C/K/1918/32.

34 Labour Party, *Six Months of Labour Government*, p. 3.

35 Diary entry dated 9 December 1923, PRO 30/69/1753/1, RMP.

36 Diary entry dated 10 December 1923, PRO 30/69/1753/1, RMP.

37 Philip Snowden, *An Autobiography*, Volume Two, pp. 594–7.

38 Diary entries dated 9 and 11 December 1923, APP.

39 Diary entry dated 13 December 1923, APP.

40 David Marquand, *Ramsay MacDonald*, p. 298.

41 Margaret Bondfield (1948), *A Life's Work*, London: Hutchinson, p. 253.

42 Manny Shinwell (1981), *Lead With the Left: My First Ninety-six Years*, London: Cassell, p. 81.

43 Trevor Wilson (ed.), *The Political Diaries of C. P. Scott 1911–1928*, London: Collins, 1970, p. 449.

44 Memorandum by Sidney Webb on the first Labour government, Passfield 4/18, Papers of Beatrice and Sidney Webb, London: London School of Economics Library.

45 Dudley Sommer (1960), *Haldane of Cloan: His Life and Times 1856–1928*, London: George Allen & Unwin, pp. 390–91.

46 Richard McLauchlan (2023), *Serious Minds: The Extraordinary Haldanes of Cloan*, London: Hurst, p. 203.

47 Stamfordham to John Strachey, 14 December 1924, STR/13/15, Strachey Papers, Parliamentary Archives.

48 Diary entry dated 14 December 1923, Davidson 14, Randall Davidson Papers, London: Lambeth Palace Library.

49 *The Times*, 17 December 1923.

50 *The Times*, 19 December 1923.

51 Sir Frederick Maurice (1939), *Haldane 1915–1928: The Life of Viscount Haldane of Cloan*, London: Faber and Faber, p. 143.

52 *The Times*, 23 December 1923. When a 'Tory paper' in Aberdeen said the Labour leader had described 'the Liberal Party as a corpse waiting for its coffin', MacDonald wrote to Jimmy Thomas to complain: 'I did nothing

of the kind ... This misreporting is getting terrible' (Ramsay MacDonald to Jimmy Thomas, 24 December 1923, U1625/C95, James H. Thomas Papers, Maidstone: Kent History and Library Centre).

53 Philip Snowden, *Autobiography*, pp. 607–8.

54 Robert Rhodes James (1977), *The British Revolution, British Politics, 1880–1939*, Volume 2, *From Asquith to Chamberlain 1914–1939*, London: Hamish Hamilton, p. 190.

2. 'THE MOST HORRIBLE JOB IN MY LIFE'

1 Sir Alexander Mackintosh (1945), *Echoes of Big Ben: A Journalist's Parliamentary Diary (1881–1940)*, London: Hutchinson, p. 98.

2 BFI Screenonline website: http://www.screenonline.org.uk/film/id/755970/synopsis.html

3 Arthur Ponsonby to MacDonald, 11 December 1923, PRO 30/69/1258, Ramsay MacDonald Papers, Kew: The National Archives.

4 Raymond A. Jones (1989), *Arthur Ponsonby: The Politics of Life*, London: Christopher Helm, p. 141.

5 MacDonald to Jimmy Thomas, December 1923, U1625/C94, James H. Thomas Papers, Maidstone: Kent History and Library Centre.

6 J. H. Thomas (1937), *My Story*, London: Hutchinson, p. 75. Leslie Thomas later became the Conservative MP for Canterbury between 1953 and 1966.

7 J. H. Thomas, *My Story*, pp. 165–6.

8 MacDonald to Jimmy Thomas, 19 December 1923, U1625/C93, JHTP.

9 J. H. Thomas, *My Story*, p. 167.

10 *Sunday Times*, 23 December 1923.

11 MacDonald to Arthur Henderson, 22 December 1923, PRO 30/69/1169, RMP.

12 Philip Snowden (1934), *An Autobiography*, Volume Two, *1919–1934*, London: Ivor Nicholson & Watson, p. 597.

13 Arthur Henderson to MacDonald, 18 December 1923, PRO 30/69/196, RMP.

14 Keith Middlemas (1965), *The Clydesiders: A Left Wing Struggle for Parliamentary Power*, London: Hutchinson, p. 135.

15 Gordon Brown (1986), *Maxton*, Edinburgh: Mainstream, pp. 151–2.

16 Keith Laybourn (2020), *The Independent Labour Party, 1914–1939: The Political and Cultural History of a Socialist Party*, Abingdon: Routledge.

17 Diary entry dated 21 January 1924, PRO 30/69/1753/1, RMP.

18 Gordon Brown, *Maxton*, p. 152.

19 William Knox (1991), '"Ours is not an ordinary Parliamentary movement": 1922–1926' in Alan McKinlay and R. J. Morris (eds), *The ILP on Clydeside, 1893–1932: from foundation to disintegration*, Manchester: Manchester University Press, p. 160.

20 Diary entry dated 31 December 1923, Arthur Ponsonby Papers, Shulbrede Priory.

21 MacDonald to Lord Haldane, 23 December 1923, MS 5916/67, Lord Haldane Papers, Edinburgh: National Library of Scotland.

22 Sir Frederick Maurice (1939), *Haldane 1915–1928: The Life of Viscount Haldane of Cloan*, London: Faber and Faber, pp. 144–6.

23 John Campbell and Richard McLauchlan (2020), *Haldane: The Forgotten Statesman Who Shaped Modern Britain*, London: Hurst & Company, p. 198.

24 John Ramsden (1978), *The Age of Balfour and Baldwin 1902–1940*, London: Longman, p. 183.

25 Roy Jenkins (1964), *Asquith*, London: Collins, pp. 500–1.

26 Memorandum by Lord Stamfordham, 19 December 1923, RA PS/PSO/GV/C/K/1918/67.

27 Leo Amery to Stanley Baldwin, 21 December 1923, D.4.2, Stanley Baldwin Papers, University of Cambridge.

28 *Liberal Magazine*, April 1924.

29 *The Times*, 9 January 1924.

30 Hugh Dalton, *Call Back Yesterday*, p. 146.

31 Duke of Windsor (1951), *A King's Story: The Memoirs of H.R.H. the Duke of Windsor*, London: Cassell, p. 187.

32 *Financial Times*, 5 January 1924.

33 MacDonald to Jimmy Thomas, 24 December 1923, U1625/C95, JHTP.

34 Stamfordham to Lord Cave, 27 December 1923, RA PS/PSO/GV/C/K/1918/78.

35 Stamfordham to the King, 28 December 1923, RA PS/PSO/GV/C/K/1918/85.

36 Stamfordham to the King, 1 January 1924, RA PS/PSO/GV/C/K/1918/97.

37 Diary entry dated 3 January 1924, APP.

38 Diary entry dated 10 January 1924, PRO 30/69/1753/1, RMP.

39 Kenneth Rose (1983), *King George V*, London: Papermac, p. 327.

40 Stamfordham to the King, 28 December 1923, RA PS/PSO/GV/C/K/1918/84.

41 Kenneth Rose, *King George V*, p. 327.

42 Sir Frederick Ponsonby to Stamfordham, 5 January 1924, RA PS/PSO/GV/C/K/1918/100. 'If the King is to abolish all political Officers permanently it will be a big jump,' Ponsonby argued in a later memo. 'If this is done temporarily only in the case of a Labour Administration, it may put the King in a position to be shot at by the scallywags of the Labour Party' (10 January 1924, RA PS/PSO/GV/C/K/1918/143).

43 Memorandum by Stamfordham to Sir Frederick Ponsonby, 21 January 1924, RA PS/PSO/GV/C/K/1918/160.

44 Stamfordham to the King, 2 January 1924, RA PS/PSO/GV/C/K/1918/98.

45 Harold Nicolson (1952), *King George the Fifth: His Life and Reign*, London: Constable, pp. 391–2.

46 Trevor Wilson (ed.) (1970), *The Political Diaries of C. P. Scott 1911–1928*, London: Collins, pp. 452–3.

47 Charles Trevelyan to MacDonald, 6 January 1924, GB 133 RMD/1/14/79, James Ramsay MacDonald Papers, Manchester: John Rylands Research Institute and Library.

48 William Gallacher (1947), *The Rolling of the Thunder*, London: Lawrence & Wishart, pp. 65–6.

49 MacDonald to E. D. Morel, January 1924, Morel/F2/1/12, E. D. Morel Papers, London: London School of Economics Library.

50 Raymond A. Jones, *Arthur Ponsonby*, p. 142.

51 John Julius Norwich (ed.) (2005), *The Duff Cooper Diaries*, London: Weidenfeld & Nicolson, p. 188.

52 Labour Party (1924), *Report of the Twenty-Fourth Annual Conference of the Labour Party*, London: Labour Party, p. 5.

53 *Scots Magazine*, November 1966.

54 *The Times*, 9 January 1924.

55 Margaret Bondfield (1948), *A Life's Work*, London: Hutchinson, p. 254.

56 Mary Agnes Hamilton (1924), *Margaret Bondfield*, London: Leonard Parsons, p. 160.

57 Stamfordham to the King, 10 January 1924, RA PS/PSO/GV/C/K/1918/138.

58 Stamfordham to the King, 10 January 1924, RA PS/PSO/GV/C/K/1918/137.

59 Stephen Roskill, *Hankey: Man of Secrets*, Volume II, pp. 353–4.

60 Stamfordham to Gladstone, 16 January 1924, RA PS/PSO/GV/C/K/1918/154.

61 Dudley Sommer (1960), *Haldane of Cloan: His Life and Times 1856–1928*, London: George Allen & Unwin, p. 396.

62 RA GV/PRIV/GVD/1924: 15 January.

63 Diary entries dated 18 and 19 January 1924, APP.

64 Haldane to MacDonald, 11 January 1924, PRO 30/69/1258, RMP.

65 Alan Lascelles to Sir Owen Morshead, 3 June 1952, RA PS/PSO/GV/C/K/1918/184A.

66 Clement Attlee (1954), *As It Happened*, London: Heinemann, p. 96.

67 H. Montgomery Hyde (1960), *Sir Patrick Hastings: His Life and Cases*, London: Heinemann, p. 131.

68 Parmoor was married to Theresa, a sister of Beatrice Webb, while his youngest son Stafford Cripps later became Chancellor of the Exchequer.

69 George Lansbury to Arthur Henderson, 15 January 1924, and Lansbury to MacDonald, 18 January 1924, Lansbury/28, George Lansbury Papers, London: London School of Economics Library.

70 John Shepherd (2002), *George Lansbury: At the Heart of Old Labour*, Oxford: Oxford University Press, p. 210.

71 Memorandum by Sidney Webb on the first Labour government, Passfield 4/18, PBSW.

72 William Graham to MacDonald, 19 January 1924, PRO 30/69/1258, RMP.

73 Philip Snowden, *An Autobiography Volume Two*, pp. 605 and 654.

74 Richard W. Lyman, *The First Labour Government*, p. 242.

75 Memorandum by Sidney Webb on the first Labour government, Passfield 4/18, PBSW.

76 A. J. A. Morris (1977), *C. P. Trevelyan 1870–1958: Portrait of a Radical*, Belfast: Blackstaff Press, p. 155.

77 Haldane to Mary Haldane, 20 January 1924, MS. 6007, LHP.

78 Diary entry dated 21 January 1924, Dolly Ponsonby Papers, Shulbrede Priory.

79 Diary entry dated 19 January 1924, PRO 30/69/1753/1, RMP.

80 Lord Cave to Sir Maurice Hankey, 9 January 1924, RA PS/PSO/GV/C/K/1918/133.

81 Mary Agnes Hamilton, *Margaret Bondfield*, p. 163.

82 HC Deb 21 January 1924 Vol 169 c601.

83 Diary entry dated 22 January 1924, APP.

84 Mortimer Epstein (ed.) (1923), *The Annual Register 1923*, London: Longmans, p. 9.

85 Diary entry dated 21 January 1924, PRO 30/69/1753/1, RMP.

86 Diary entry dated 22 January 1924, GB 133 RMD/2/22, JRMP.

87 Stephen Roskill, *Hankey: Man of Secrets*, Volume II, p. 355.

88 Diary entry dated 21 January 1924, PRO 30/69/1753/1, RMP.

89 RA GV/PRIV/GVD/1924: 22 January.

90 Memorandum by Stamfordham, 22 January 1924, RA PS/PSO/GV/C/K/1918/164.

91 HC Deb 22 January 1924 Vol 169 c696.

92 Diary entry dated 22 January 1924, PRO 30/69/1753/1, RMP.

93 Memorandum by Stamfordham, 22 January 1924, RA PS/PSO/GV/C/K/1918/164.

94 Diary entry dated 22 January 1924, PRO 30/69/1753/1, RMP.

95 Norman and Jeanne MacKenzie, *The Diary of Beatrice Webb*, Volume Four, p. 9.

96 John F. Naylor (1984), *A Man and an Institution: Sir Maurice Hankey, the Cabinet Secretariat and the custody of Cabinet secrecy*, Cambridge: Cambridge University Press, p. 135.

97 Keith Middlemas (ed.) (1969), *Thomas Jones: Whitehall Diary*, Volume I, 1916–1925, London: Oxford University Press, p. 264.

98 Memorandum by Sidney Webb on the first Labour government, Passfield 4/18, PBSW.

99 Charles Trevelyan to Gertrude Bell, 12 February 1924, CPT/1/2/20(212), TA.

100 John Shepherd and Keith Laybourn, *Britain's First Labour Government*, p. 67.

101 Jack Lawson (1932), *A Man's Life*, London: Hodder & Stoughton, p. 266.

102 Mary Agnes Hamilton, *Margaret Bondfield*, p. 163.

103 John Scanlon (1932), *Decline and Fall of the Labour Party*, London: Peter Davies, pp. 19–20.

104 Memorandum by Sidney Webb on the first Labour government, Passfield 4/18, PBSW. The twenty-three-year-old Earl De La Warr was the first hereditary peer to join the Labour Party; the seventy-eight-year-old Lord Muir Mackenzie was a Scottish KC.

105 *Liverpool Daily Courier*, 26 January 1924. The headline was 'CABINET MINISTERS FROM THE SLUMS'.

106 Roy Jenkins, *Asquith*, p. 501.

107 Violet Bonham Carter to Winston Churchill, 18 January 1924, GBR/0014/CHAR 2/137/1-4, Sir Winston Churchill Papers, Cambridge: Churchill Archives Centre.

108 Stamfordham to John Strachey, 23 January 1924, STR/13/15, John Strachey Papers, Parliamentary Archives.

109 Simon Heffer (ed.) (2021), *Henry 'Chips' Channon: The Diaries: 1918–38*, London: Hutchinson, p. 97.

110 Jack Lawson, *A Man's Life*, p. 267.

3. RAMSAY MACDONALD AS PRIME MINISTER: 'A MASS OF CONTRADICTIONS'

1 Sir Alexander Mackintosh, *Echoes of Big Ben*, p. 98.

2 *The Times*, 23 January 1924.

3 *Time* magazine, 4 February 1924.

4 Anonymous, *Ramsay MacDonald's Romantic Life Story By 'One who knows him': Britain's First Labour Premier*, Reynolds's News, 1924, pp. 1 and 28.

5 Margaret was no relation to the former Liberal Prime Minister.

6 Richard W. Lyman, *The First Labour Government*, p. 7.

7 David Marquand, 'Ramsay MacDonald', *Oxford Dictionary of National Biography* (hereafter *ODNB*).

8 Clyde Sanger, *Malcolm MacDonald*, p. 42.

9 Dudley Sommer, *Haldane of Cloan*, p. 399.

10 *Evening News*, 23 January 1924.

11 *Report from the Select Committee on Ministers' Remuneration*, Cmnd 170, 28 July 1930, p38.

12 MacDonald to Thompson, 4 February 1924, PRO 30/69/194, RMP.

13 Alexander Grant to MacDonald, 5 and 8 February 1924, PRO 30/69/194, RMP.

14 Alexander Grant to MacDonald, 14 February 1924, PRO 30/69/194, RMP.

15 Unpublished memoir by Ishbel MacDonald, Add MS. 89304/3/8, Ishbel MacDonald Archive, London: British Library.

16 Diary entry dated 3 February 1924, PRO 30/69/1753/1, RMP.

17 Letter from Ishbel MacDonald to Ben Pimlott, January 1980, Add MS. 89304/4/2, IMA.

18 Norman and Jeanne MacKenzie, *The Diary of Beatrice Webb*: Volume Four, pp. 12–17.

19 David Marquand, *Ramsay MacDonald*, p. 304.

20 Unpublished memoir by Ishbel MacDonald, Add MS 89304/3/8, IMA.

21 *Margaret Ethel Macdonald* was first published by the Women's Labour League in 1912 and was reprinted by George Allen & Unwin shortly after Ramsay MacDonald became Prime Minister.

22 G. K. A. Bell (1935), *Randall Davidson: Archbishop of Canterbury*, Volume II, London: Oxford University Press, pp. 1175–6.

23 Randall Davidson to Bishop Talbot, 27 January 1924, Davidson 14, RDP.

24 Keith Middlemas, *Thomas Jones: Whitehall Diary*, Volume I, pp. 270–1.

25 MacDonald did so without consulting the Cabinet.

26 J. L. Garvin to J. H. Thomas, 29 January 1924, U1625/C43, JHTP.

27 A chargé d'affaires was inferior in rank to an ambassador and did not need to be presented to a head of state.

28 Diary entry dated 10 February 1924, APP.

29 Diary entry dated 1 February 1924, RDP.

30 Diary entries dated 27 January and 17 February 1924, APP.

31 'The Living Past', 134/22/1-8, Malcolm MacDonald Papers, Durham: University of Durham.

32 Nourah Waterhouse (1942), *Private and Official*, London: Jonathan Cape, pp. 296–7.

33 Unpublished memoir by Ishbel MacDonald, Add MS 89304/3/8, IMA.

34 Diary entries dated 10 and 28 April 1924, PRO 30/69/1753/1, RMP.

35 Unpublished memoir by Ishbel MacDonald, Add MS 89304/3/8, IMA.

36 Harold Nicolson, *King George the Fifth*, p. 388.

37 Jane Ridley, *Never a Dull Moment*, p. 321.

38 Harold Nicolson, *King George the Fifth*, p. 388.

39 Ernest Stanford, *James Ramsay MacDonald*, p. 56.

40 Harold Nicolson, *King George the Fifth*, p. 389.

41 Memorandum by Stamfordham, 25 January 1924, RA PS/PSO/GV/C/K/1918/188.

42 Memorandum by the Earl of Cromer, 15 February 1924, RA PS/PSO/GV/C/K/1918/299.

43 Diary entry dated 19 February 1924, Add MS. 89304/3/8, IMA.

44 Unpublished memoir by Ishbel MacDonald, Add MS 89304/3/8, IMA.

45 Duke of Windsor, *A King's Story*, pp. 195–6.

46 Simon Heffer, *Henry 'Chips' Channon*, p. 97.

47 *Observer*, 2 October 1966.

48 Hugh Dalton, *Call Back Yesterday*, p. 144.

49 Nicholas Owen, 'MacDonald's Parties: The Labour Party and the "Aristocratic Embrace", 1922-31', *Twentieth Century British History* 18:1, 2007, pp. 1–53.

50 Cabinet Conclusions dated 6 February 1924, CAB/23/47/4, Kew: The National Archives.

51 RA GV/PRIV/GVD/1924: 11 March.

52 Philip Snowden, *An Autobiography*, Volume Two, p. 663.

53 Ben Spoor to Stamfordham, 29 January 1924, RA PS/PSO/GV/C/K/1918/205.

54 Stamfordham to MacDonald, 1 February 1924, RA PS/PSO/GV/C/K/1918/226.

55 Kenneth Rose, *King George V*, London: Papermac, 1983, p. 331.

56 David Marquand, *Ramsay MacDonald*, p. 404.

57 Diary entry dated 7 June 1924, APP.

58 *New Leader*, 18 April 1924.

59 *Spectator*, 31 May 1924.

60 Diary entry dated 12 May 1924, PRO 30/69/1753/1, RMP.

61 Memorandum by Clive Wigram dated 6 August 1924, RA PS/PSO/GV/C/K/1949/14.

62 Dudley Sommer, *Haldane of Cloan*, p. 400.

63 Nourah Waterhouse, *Private and Official*, p. 346.

64 Diary entry dated 12 May 1924, MIC665/18, Lady Carson Papers, Belfast: PRONI. Lady Carson was married to Sir Edward – by then Lord – Carson, a former Ulster Unionist leader.

65 Emanuel Shinwell (1955), *Conflict Without Malice*, London: Odhams Press, p. 94.

66 Kenneth Rose, *King George V*, pp. 331–2.

67 Sir Alexander Mackintosh, *Echoes of Big Ben*, p. 99.

68 HC Deb 12 February 1924 Vol 169 cc746-51.

69 MacDonald to the King, 13 February 1924, PRO 30/69/228, RMP.

70 Gill Bennett (2018), *The Zinoviev Letter: The Conspiracy That Never Dies*, Oxford: Oxford University Press, p. 33.

71 HC Deb 13 February 1924 Vol 169 cc852-57.

72 Vivian Phillips (1943), *My Days and Ways*, Edinburgh: Pillans & Wilson. This rule dictated that the Commons was automatically suspended at eleven o'clock each evening.

73 David Marquand, *Ramsay MacDonald*, p. 320.

74 Diary entry dated 2 March 1924, PRO 30/69/1753/1, RMP.

75 Diary entry dated 2 March 1924, PRO 30/69/1753/1, RMP.

76 Norman and Jeanne MacKenzie, *The Diary of Beatrice Webb*, Volume Four, pp. 17–18.

77 Donald Mitchell (2014), *The Politics of Dissent: A Biography of E. D. Morel*, SilverWood, pp. 194, 199–201.

78 Gordon Brown, *Maxton*, p. 157.
79 Two previous books on the first Labour government have erroneously referred to the 'Scottish Judge Advocate'.
80 Rosslyn Mitchell to MacDonald, 25 January 1924, PRO 30/69/686, RMP.
81 For the only comprehensive account of this episode, see J. P. Casey (1975), 'The First Labour Government and Office of Lord Advocate', *Northern Ireland Legal Quarterly* 26:1, pp. 18–29.
82 *The Times*, 7 February 1924.
83 MacDonald to Rosslyn Mitchell, 11 February 1924, PRO 30/69/686, RMP.
84 Arthur Berriedale Keith to MacDonald, PRO 30/69/686, RMP.
85 Hugh Macmillan to MacDonald, 7 February 1924, MS 25261, Hugh Macmillan Papers, Edinburgh: National Library of Scotland.
86 *Glasgow Herald*, 9 February 1924.
87 *The Times*, 11 February 1924.
88 File entitled 'Appointment of Scottish Law Officers', PRO 30/69/686, RMP.
89 Fenner Brockway (1942), *Inside the Left: Thirty Years of Platform, Press, Prison and Parliament*, London: George Allen & Unwin, p. 151.
90 Richard W. Lyman, *The First Labour Government*, p. 232.
91 George Lansbury to Beatrice Webb, 14 March 1924, Passfield 2/4/H, PBSW.
92 Norman and Jeanne MacKenzie, *The Diary of Beatrice Webb*, Volume Four, pp. 18–22.
93 Arthur Ponsonby to E. D. Morel, 31 January 1924, Morel F8/123, EDMP.
94 Arthur Ponsonby to E. D. Morel, 20 March 1924, Morel F8/123, EDMP.
95 F. W. Pethick-Lawrence (1943), *Fate Has Been Kind*, London: Hutchinson, p. 136.
96 *The Times*, 21 April 1924.
97 David Howell (2002), *MacDonald's Party: Labour Identities and Crisis, 1922–1931*, Oxford: Oxford University Press, p. 30.
98 *Report of the Twenty-Fourth Annual Conference of the Labour Party*, pp. 38–40.
99 Inserted between the pages dated 6–12 April 1924, GB 133 RMD/2/22, JRMP.
100 Memorandum by Sidney Webb on the first Labour government, Passfield 4/18, PBSW.
101 Josiah C. Wedgwood, *Memoirs of a Fighting Life*, p. 186.
102 John F. Naylor, *A Man and an Institution*, p. 139.
103 Dudley Sommer, *Haldane of Cloan*, p. 404.
104 *The Times*, 24 January 1924.
105 Sir Ronald Waterhouse to Arthur Greenwood, 6 February 1924, MS. Eng. c. 6227, Arthur Greenwood Papers, Oxford Weston Library.
106 Charles Trevelyan to Sir George Otto Trevelyan, 2 July 1924, CPT/1/7/67/49-51, TA.
107 Philip Snowden, *An Autobiography*, Volume Two, pp. 705–6.

108 Charles Trevelyan to Professor Basil Williams, 28 January 1924, CPT/1/2/20/172, TA.

109 *Christian Herald*, 7 February 1924.

110 *Daily Graphic*, 2 February 1924.

111 J. S. Middleton to MacDonald, 6 February 1924, PRO 30/69/175, RMP.

112 Cabinet Conclusions dated 21 February 1924, CAB 23/47/10, CPC.

113 Walsh was presumably unavailable when the photograph was taken.

114 James Margach (1978), *The Abuse of Power: The War between Downing Street and the Media from Lloyd George to Callaghan*, London: W. H. Allen, pp. 37–8.

115 H. R. Stockman to MacDonald, 16 February 1924, MID/18/62, J. S. Middleton Papers, Manchester: Labour History Archive and Study Centre.

116 *The Times*, 17 March 1924.

117 A. J. P. Taylor (1972), *Beaverbrook*, London: Hamish Hamilton, p. 220.

118 Memorandum by Sidney Webb on the first Labour government, Passfield 4/18, PBSW.

119 Trevor Wilson, *The Political Diaries of C. P. Scott*, p. 470.

120 Mary Agnes Hamilton, *J. Ramsay MacDonald*, pp. 174–5.

121 David Marquand, *Ramsay MacDonald*, p. 407.

122 *The Times*, 13 March 1924.

123 Alexander Gammie (1931), *From Pit to Palace: The Life Story of the Right Hon. James Brown*, London: James Clarke & Company, p. 88.

124 MacDonald to Hugh Macmillan, 7 April 1924, MS 25261, HMP.

125 General Sir William Birdwood to Clive, 20 March 1924, RA PS/PSO/GV/C/N/2556/28.

126 Alexander Gammie, *From Pit to Palace*, pp. 114–15, 124–5.

127 Russell Galbraith (2018), *Without Quarter: A Biography of Tom Johnston*, Edinburgh: Birlinn, p. 84.

128 Mortimer Epstein (ed.) (1923), *The Annual Register 1923*, London: Longmans, pp. 24–5.

129 *Church Times*, 8 August 1924.

130 Ramsay MacDonald to Sidney Dark, 13 August 1924, MS 3219 f179, RDP.

131 Diary entry dated, 4 February 1924, Davidson 14, RDP.

132 MacDonald to Lord Chelmsford, 16 August 1924, PRO 30/69/190, RMP.

133 John Ramsden, *The Age of Balfour and Baldwin*, p. 190.

134 John Ramsden (1998), *An Appetite for Power: A History of the Conservative Party Since 1830*, London: HarperCollins, p. 39.

135 John Ramsden, *The Age of Balfour and Baldwin*, p. 199.

136 Maurice Cowling (1971), *The Impact of Labour 1920–1924: The Beginning of Modern British Politics*, Cambridge: Cambridge University Press, p. 350.

137 Mary Agnes Hamilton, *J. Ramsay MacDonald*, p. 103.

138 John Shepherd and Keith Laybourn, *Britain's First Labour Government*, p. 109.

139 *The Times*, 2 May 1924.

140 John Campbell, *Lloyd George: The Goat in the Wilderness*, pp. 93–5.

141 MacDonald to Stanley Baldwin, 29 March 1924, Vol 159/230, SBP.

142 Harold Spender (1926), *The Fire of Life: A Book of Memories*, London: Hodder & Stoughton, pp. 274–5.

143 Diary entry dated 26 June 1924, PRO 30/69/1753/1, RMP.

144 MacDonald to the King, 17 April 1924, PRO 30/69/228, RMP.

145 Earl of Oxford and Asquith (1928), *Memories and Reflections 1852–1927*, Volume 2, London: Cassell, p. 210.

146 Diary entry dated 15 May 1924, DPP.

147 Robert C. Self (ed.) (1995), *The Austen Chamberlain Diary Letters: The Correspondence of Sir Austen Chamberlain with His Sisters Hilda and Ida, 1916–1937*, Cambridge: Cambridge University Press, p. 251.

148 Stephen Roskill, *Hankey: Man of Secrets*, Volume II, p. 366.

149 Diary entries dated 7 March and 17 April 1924, APP.

150 Norman and Jeanne MacKenzie, *The Diary of Beatrice Webb*, Volume Four, p. 27.

151 Unpublished memoir by Ishbel MacDonald, Add MS 89304/3/8, IMA.

152 J. R. Clynes, *Memoirs*, pp. 30–1.

153 Diary entry dated 20 May 1924, Davidson 14, RDP.

154 Lord Macmillan (1952), *A Man of Law's Tale*, London: Macmillan, p. 91.

155 Lauchlan MacNeill Weir, *The Tragedy of Ramsay MacDonald*, p. 137.

156 Maurice Cowling, *The Impact of Labour*, p. 366.

157 Lord Haldane to Bay Haldane, 7 April 1924, MS 6013, LHP.

158 Alice G. Vines (1982), *The MacDonald Women: Margaret and Ishbel*, Acc.13629/9, Papers of Alice G. Vines, Edinburgh: National Library of Scotland, p159.

159 MacDonald to Alexander Grant, 27 April 1924, MS. 25274/3, MacDonald/Grant Letters, Edinburgh: National Library of Scotland.

160 Alexander Grant to MacDonald, 18 April 1924, PRO 30/69/194, RMP.

161 MacDonald to Alexander Grant, 27 April 1924, MS. 25274/3, MGL.

162 Parmoor to Lord Southborough, 6 May 1924, MS. Eng. c. 7347, Archive of Lord Southborough, Oxford: Weston Library.

163 Unpublished memoir by Ishbel MacDonald, Add MS 89304/3/8, IMA.

164 *The Times*, 22 May 1924.

165 *The Times*, 10 March 1924.

4. ARTHUR HENDERSON: 'UNCLE ARTHUR'

1 Leonard Woolf (1967), *Downhill all the Way: An Autobiography of the Years 1919–1939*, London: Hogarth Press, p. 84.

2 Fred M. Leventhal (1989), *Arthur Henderson*, Manchester: Manchester University Press, p. 120.

3 Norman and Jeanne MacKenzie (eds) (1984), *The Diary of Beatrice Webb*, Volume Three, p. 432.

4 Diary entry dated 10 December 1923, PRO 30/69/1753/1, RMP.

5 Mary Agnes Hamilton, *Arthur Henderson*, p. 238.

6 Mary Agnes Hamilton, *Arthur Henderson*, p. 124.

7 HC Deb 27 February 1924 Vol 170 cc605-06.

8 MacDonald to the King, 4 March 1924, PRO 30/69/228, RMP.

9 Edwin A. Jenkins (1933), *From Foundry to Foreign Office: The Romantic Life-Story of the Rt Hon Arthur Henderson, MP*, London: Grayson & Grayson, p. 99.

10 Chris Wrigley, 'Arthur Henderson', *ODNB*.

11 Mary Agnes Hamilton, *Arthur Henderson*, p. 241.

12 Edwin A. Jenkins, *From Foundry to Foreign Office*, p. 107.

13 David Howell, *McDonald's Party*, p. 31.

14 Chris Wrigley, 'Arthur Henderson', *ODNB*.

15 Austen Morgan (1987), *Ramsay MacDonald*, Manchester: Manchester University Press, p. 105.

16 RA GV/PRIV/GVD/1924: 16 February.

17 Ralph H. Desmarais (1973), 'Strikebreaking and the Labour Government of 1924', *Journal of Contemporary History* 8:4, p. 168.

18 Ralph Miliband (1961), *Parliamentary Socialism: A Study in the Politics of Labour*, London: George Allen & Unwin, p. 105.

19 Hugh Dalton, *Call Back Yesterday*, p. 148.

20 Norman Angell (1951), *After All: The Autobiography of Norman Angell*, London: Hamish Hamilton, p. 244.

21 Ralph H. Desmarais, 'Strikebreaking and the Labour Government of 1924', p. 171.

22 Keith Jeffery and Peter Hennessy (1983), *States of Emergency: British Governments and Strikebreaking since 1919*, London: Routledge & Kegan Paul, p. 81.

23 Ralph H. Desmarais, 'Strikebreaking and the Labour Government of 1924', p. 172.

24 HC Deb 27 March 1924 Vol 171 cc1681-83.

25 Memorandum by Sidney Webb on the first Labour government, Passfield 4/18, PBSW.

26 Keith Jeffery and Peter Hennessy, *States of Emergency*, pp. 83–6.

27 Chris Wrigley (1990), *Arthur Henderson*, Cardiff: University of Wales Press, p. 149.

28 Stamfordham to MacDonald, 2 April 1924, PS/PSO/GV/C/K/1929/1, and Sir Ronald Waterhouse to Stamfordham, 4 April 1924, RA PS/PSO/GV/C/K/1929/3.

29 Sir Frederick Maurice, *Haldane 1915–1928*, p. 153.

30 Trevor Barnes (1979), 'Special Branch and the First Labour Government', *The Historical Journal* 32:4, pp. 944–7.

31 Memorandum by Stamfordham, 28 June 1924, RA PS/PSO/GV/C/K/1940/3.

32 Cabinet Conclusions dated 7 April 1924, CAB/23/47/19, CPC.

33 Chris Wrigley, *Arthur Henderson*, pp. 144–5.

34 David Howell, *McDonald's Party*, p. 31.

35 Memorandum by Stamfordham, 6 April 1924, RA PS/PSO/GV/C/K/1937/1.

36 Memorandum by Stamfordham, 8 April 1924, PS/PSO/GV/C/K/1937/5.

37 Stamfordham to MacDonald, 9 April 1924, RA PS/PSO/GV/C/K/1937/6.

38 Cabinet Conclusions dated 15 May 1924, CAB/23/48/7, CPC.

39 Chris Wrigley, *Arthur Henderson*, pp. 145–6.

40 David Howell, *McDonald's Party*, p. 32.

41 Mary Agnes Hamilton, *Arthur Henderson*, p. 242.

42 HC Deb 17 July 1924 Vol 176 cc565-66.

43 Cmnd 2193. See also RMD/1/8/7, JRMP.

44 *The Times*, 12 July 1924.

45 The second Labour government of 1929–31 would award Syme a modest 'medical' pension.

46 John Shepherd and Keith Laybourn, *Britain's First Labour Government*, pp. 95–6.

47 Stephen Clive Meredith (2012), 'A "Strange Death" Foretold (or the Not So "Strange Death" of Liberal Wales): Liberal Decline, the Labour Ascendancy and Electoral Politics in South Wales, 1922–1924', *North American Journal of Welsh Studies* 7, pp. 18–37.

48 *New Leader*, 30 November 1923.

49 John Davies (1994), *A History of Wales*, London: Penguin, p. 545.

50 Arthur Henderson to J. H. Thomas, 6 March 1924, U1625/C71, JHTP.

51 HC Deb 20 December 1955 Vol 547 cc310-1W.

52 Herbert Tracey (ed.) (1925), *The Book of the Labour Party: Its History, Growth, Policy, and Leaders*, Volume I, London: Caxton, pp. 258–9.

5. John Wheatley: 'A traditional Mr. Pickwick'

1 RA GV/PRIV/GVD/1924: 22 February.

2 Lauchlan MacNeill Weir, *The Tragedy of Ramsay MacDonald*, p. 139.

3 Hugh Dalton, *Call Back Yesterday*, p. 147.

4 Ian S. Wood, 'John Wheatley', *ODNB*.

5 Mary Agnes Hamilton (1924), *Fit to Govern!*, London: Leonard Parsons, p. 34.

6 John Hannan (1988), *The Life of John Wheatley*, Nottingham: Spokesman, p. 118.

7 Keith Middlemas, *Thomas Jones: Whitehall Diary*, Volume I, p. 270.

8 John Scanlon (1932), *Decline and Fall of the Labour Party*, London: Peter Davies, p. 67.

9 Mary Agnes Hamilton, *Fit to Govern!*, p. 34.

10 Richard W. Lyman, *The First Labour Government*, p. 13.

11 Lewis Baston (2000), 'Labour local government 1900–1999', in Brian Brivati and Richard Heffernan (eds), *The Labour Party: A Centenary History*, Basingstoke: Palgrave Macmillan, p. 453.

12 Edgar's daughter was actress Dame Angela Lansbury.

13 John Hannan, *The Life of John Wheatley*, p. 120.

14 Minute of deputation, 5 February 1924, MS. Eng. c. 6234, AGP.

15 *The Times*, 7 February 1924.

16 Lord Haldane to Bay Haldane, 7 February 1924, MS 6013, LHP.

17 Iain McLean (1999), *The Legend of Red Clydeside*, Edinburgh: John Donald, p. 213.

18 HC Deb 12 February 1924 Vol 169 cc751-53.

19 HC Deb 13 February 1924 Vol 169 c863.

20 Earl of Oxford and Asquith, *Memories and Reflections*, p. 210.

21 CAB 24/165/14, CPC.

22 HC Deb 26 February 1924 Vol 170 c319.

23 HC Deb 26 February 1924 Vol 170 cc350-51.

24 Keith Middlemas, *The Clydesiders*, p. 144.

25 MacDonald to the King, 27 February 1924, PRO 30/69/228, RMP.

26 Ian S. Wood (1990), *John Wheatley*, Manchester: Manchester University Press, p. 125.

27 David Howell (1986), *A Lost Left: Three Studies in Socialism and Nationalism*, Manchester: Manchester University Press, p. 26.

28 Iain McLean, *The Legend of Red Clydeside*, pp. 213–14.

29 Keith Middlemas, *The Clydesiders*, p.126.

30 Keith Middlemas, *Thomas Jones: Whitehall Diary*, Volume I, p. 277.

31 John Hannan, *The Life of John Wheatley*, p. 128.

32 Iain McLean, *The Legend of Red Clydeside*, p. 216.

33 Gordon Brown, *Maxton*, p. 158.

34 Keith Middlemas, *The Clydesiders*, p. 155.

35 Iain McLean, *The Legend of Red Clydeside*, p. 216.

36 Ian S. Wood, *John Wheatley*, p. 130.

37 John Hannan, *The Life of John Wheatley*, p. 130.

38 Ian S. Wood, *John Wheatley*, p. 146.

39 *The Labour Woman*, September 1924.

40 John Shepherd and Keith Laybourn, *Britain's First Labour Government*, p. 78.

41 Labour Party, *Labour's appeal to the nation*.

42 Keith Middlemas, *Thomas Jones: Whitehall Diary*, Volume I, p. 270.

43 HC Deb 12 February 1924 Vol 169 cc755-56.

44 *The Survey*, 15 November 1924, MS. Eng. c. 6234, AGP.

45 Notes of a deputation of local authorities, 15 April 1924, MS. Eng. c. 6232, AGP.

46 *Report of the Committee on the Building Industry*, Cmnd 2104.

47 Philip Snowden, *An Autobiography*, Volume Two, p. 700.
48 Notes of a deputation of local authorities, 8 May 1924, MS. Eng. c. 6232, AGP.
49 John Wheatley to MacDonald, 31 May 1924, PRO 30/69/211, RMP. Wheatley made his appeal on a Saturday.
50 MacDonald to the King, 4 June 1924, PRO 30/69/228, RMP.
51 HC Deb 25 July 1924 Vol 176 cc1725-26.
52 HC Deb 25 July 1924 Vol 176 c1703.
53 Ian S. Wood, *John Wheatley*, pp. 140–1.
54 John Hannan, *The Life of John Wheatley*, p. 134.
55 Iain McLean, *The Legend of Red Clydeside*, p. 218.
56 Keith Middlemas, *Thomas Jones: Whitehall Diary*, Volume I, p. 74.
57 Keith Middlemas, *The Clydesiders*, p. 172.
58 John Scanlon, *Decline and Fall of the Labour Party*, pp. 72–3. This Bill fell with the government in October 1924.
59 David Kirkwood, *My Life of Revolt*, p. 220.
60 A. J. P. Taylor, *Beaverbrook*, pp. 221–2.
61 Richard Lyman, *The First Labour Government*, p. 115.

6. PHILIP SNOWDEN: 'A FREE BREAKFAST TABLE'

1 Winston Churchill (1942), *Great Contemporaries*, London: Macmillan, p. 223. Less frequently quoted is Churchill's subsequent commentary that Snowden 'had to go on pretending he was a Socialist, the wordy champion of the class war and so on'.
2 Colin Cross, *Philip Snowden*, p. 197.
3 P. J. Grigg, *Prejudice and Judgment*, p. 135.
4 Duncan Tanner, 'Philip Snowden', *ODNB*.
5 Leonard Woolf, *Downhill all the Way*, pp. 84–5.
6 David Kirkwood (1935), *My Life of Revolt*, London: George G. Harrap, p. 222.
7 Norman and Jeanne MacKenzie, *The Diary of Beatrice Webb*, Volume Three, p. 431.
8 Lord Beaverbrook to Philip Snowden, 23 January 1924, and Snowden to Beaverbrook, 24 January 1924, BBK C/297, LBP.
9 Roy Jenkins (1998), *The Chancellors*, London: Macmillan, p. 277.
10 Philip Snowden, *An Autobiography*, Volume Two, pp. 613–14.
11 Mary Agnes Hamilton, *Fit to Govern!*, p. 77.
12 Anonymous (1931), *The Scottish Socialists: A Gallery of Contemporary Portraits*, London: Faber and Faber, p. 97.
13 Philip Snowden, *An Autobiography*, Volume Two, p. 655.
14 Thomas N. Graham (1948), *Willie Graham: The Life of The Rt. Hon. W. Graham*, London: Hutchinson, p. 144.

15 P. J. Grigg, *Prejudice and Judgment*, p. 136.
16 Philip Snowden, *An Autobiography*, Volume Two, p. 617.
17 Norman and Jeanne MacKenzie, *The Diary of Beatrice Webb*, Volume Four, p. 11.
18 Ethel Snowden to David Lloyd George, 19 February 1924, G18/8/12, Lloyd George Papers, London: Parliamentary Archives.
19 Keith Middlemas, *Thomas Jones: Whitehall Diary*, Volume I, p. 277.
20 Stamfordham to Philip Snowden, 26 April 1924, T/171/226, Treasury Papers, Kew: The National Archives.
21 Roy Jenkins, *The Chancellors*, p. 278.
22 Richard W. Lyman, *The First Labour Government*, p. 143.
23 *The Times*, 19 March 1924.
24 Roy Jenkins, *The Chancellors*, p. 278.
25 Philip Snowden, *An Autobiography*, Volume Two, pp. 638, 641–2.
26 HC Deb 29 April 1924 Vol 172 cc1587-610.
27 Lord Stamfordham told Snowden the King had expressed 'regret' regarding their abolition (Stamfordham to Philip Snowden, 26 April 1924, T/171/226, TP).
28 Andrew Thorpe (1996), 'The industrial meaning of "gradualism": the Labour party and industry, 1918–1931', *Journal of British Studies* 35:1, p. 92.
29 Roy Jenkins, *The Chancellors*, p. 280.
30 MacDonald to the King, 30 April 1924, PRO 30/69/228, RMP.
31 Roy Jenkins, *The Chancellors*, p. 282.
32 Colin Cross, *Philip Snowden*, p. 205.
33 John Julius Norwich, *The Duff Cooper Diaries*, p. 198.
34 HC Deb 29 April 1924 Vol 172 c1611.
35 HC Deb 30 April 1924 Vol 172 cc1681-1702. Sterling against the dollar had fallen from $4.50 to $4.30.
36 Robert E. Dowse (1966), *Left in the Centre: The Independent Labour Party 1893–1940*, London: Longmans, p. 106.
37 Norman and Jeanne MacKenzie, *The Diary of Beatrice Webb*, Volume Four, p. 25.
38 Dudley Sommer, *Haldane of Cloan*, p. 404.
39 Richard W. Lyman, *The First Labour Government*, p. 146.
40 Philip Snowden, *An Autobiography*, Volume Two, pp. 648–9.
41 HC Deb 1 May 1924 Vol 172 c1970.
42 P. J. Grigg, *Prejudice and Judgment*, pp. 135–6.
43 Winston Churchill, *Great Contemporaries*, p. 221.
44 Philip Snowden, *An Autobiography*, Volume Two, p. 642.
45 Philip Snowden, *An Autobiography*, Volume Two, p. 657.
46 Colin Cross, *Philip Snowden*, p. 206.
47 Diary entry dated 13 June 1924, APP.

7. CHARLES TREVELYAN: 'SECONDARY EDUCATION FOR ALL'

1 The coalition government's *Education Act 1918* had also paved the way for more free places in secondary schools, as well as more and better paid teachers.

2 Charles Trevelyan (1924), *The Broad High Road in Education*, London: Labour Party, p. 3.

3 Norman and Jeanne MacKenzie, *The Diary of Beatrice Webb*, Volume Four, p. 28.

4 A. J. A. Morris, 'Sir Charles Philips Trevelyan', *ODNB*.

5 A. J. A. Morris, *C. P. Trevelyan*, p. 156.

6 Keith Middlemas, *Thomas Jones: Whitehall Diary*, Volume I, p. 268.

7 *Evening News*, 16 February 1924, *The Times*, 4 March 1924 and *Time & Tide*, 29 February 1924.

8 *New Leader*, undated.

9 Charles Trevelyan, *The Broad High Road in Education*, pp. 3–8.

10 *The Times*, 23 April 1924.

11 A. J. A. Morris, *C. P. Trevelyan*, p. 160.

12 *The Times*, 22 April 1924.

13 Rodney Barker (1972), *Education and Politics 1900–1951: A Study of the Labour Party*, Oxford: Clarendon Press, pp. 53–5.

14 Norman and Jeanne MacKenzie, *The Diary of Beatrice Webb*, Volume Four, p. 27.

15 Memorandum by Sidney Webb on the first Labour government, Passfield 4/18, PBSW.

16 *Evening Standard*, 2 April 1924.

17 Rodney Barker, *Education and Politics*, p. 51.

18 HC Deb 22 July 1924 Vol 176 cc1149-269.

19 Sir George Otto Trevelyan to Charles Trevelyan, 24 July 1924, CPT/1/9/25, TA.

20 Randall Davidson to Charles Trevelyan, 5 August 1924, CPT/1/7/66, TA.

21 Philip Snowden to Charles Trevelyan, 22 August 1924, CPT/1/7/67, TA.

22 Charles Trevelyan to Molly Trevelyan, August 1924, CPT/3/70, TA.

23 He presumably meant David Lloyd George, who had actually been born in Manchester, and Ramsay MacDonald, who was from Lossiemouth.

24 Speech to National Eisteddfod, CPT/3/70, TA.

25 Charles Trevelyan (1927), *Education when Labour Rules Again*, London: Labour Party, p. 3.

8. 'RABBITS OUT OF A HAT'

1 Labour Party, *Labour's appeal to the nation*.

2 HC Deb 12 February 1924 Vol 169 cc757-67.

3 A third measure later extended this to 52 weeks in a year.

4 Keith Middlemas, *Thomas Jones: Whitehall Diary*, Volume I, p. 283.

5 J. S. Middleton, 'Thomas Shaw', *ODNB*.

6 Herbert Tracey, *The Book of the Labour Party*, Volume I, p. 188.

7 Rodney Lowe (1986), *Adjusting to Democracy: The Role of the Ministry of Labour in British Politics, 1916–1939*, Oxford: Clarendon Press, p. 32.

8 Philip Williamson, 'Margaret Grace Bondfield', *ODNB*.

9 Mary Agnes Hamilton, *Fit to Govern!*, pp. 71–2.

10 Margaret Bondfield, *A Life's Work*, pp. 255–6.

11 Keith Middlemas, *Thomas Jones: Whitehall Diary*, Volume I, pp. 273–4.

12 HC Deb 10 March 1924 Vol 170 c2003.

13 Herbert Tracey, *The Book of the Labour Party*, Volume I, p. 263.

14 MacDonald to the King, 19 February and 11 March 1924, PRO 30/69/228, RMP.

15 *Time* magazine, 4 February 1924.

16 Keith Middlemas, *Thomas Jones: Whitehall Diary*, Volume I, pp. 273–4.

17 HC Deb 12 February 1924 Vol 169 cc711-12.

18 Colin Cross, *Philip Snowden*, p. 200. Webb was said to resemble a goat.

19 Herbert Tracey, *The Book of the Labour Party*, Volume I, p. 202.

20 Andrew Thorpe (1996), 'The industrial meaning of "gradualism": the Labour party and industry, 1918–1931', *Journal of British Studies* 35:1, p. 93.

21 Norman and Jeanne MacKenzie, *The Diary of Beatrice Webb*, Volume Four, p. 28.

22 J. R. Clynes, *Memoirs*, pp. 56 and 60.

23 This advisory committee was abolished in 1965.

24 Harry Gosling, 1927, *Up and Down Stream*, London: Methuen, p. 326.

25 Harry Gosling, *Up and Down Stream*, p. 327.

26 J. R. Clynes, *Memoirs*, p. 60.

27 Manny Shinwell, 1955, *Conflict Without Malice*, London: Odhams Press, p. 91.

28 HC Deb 16 May 1924 Vol 173 c1751.

29 HC Deb 16 May 1924 Vol 173 c1770.

30 MacDonald to Manny Shinwell, 29 August 1924, LSE 3/1, Manny Shinwell Papers, London: London School of Economics Library.

31 Mary Agnes Hamilton, *Fit to Govern!*, p. 41.

32 Mosa Anderson (1952), *Noel Buxton: A Life*, London: George Allen & Unwin, pp. 117–18.

33 'The first Labour government', CA RBD MS 951-2-012, NBP.

34 Mosa Anderson, *Noel Buxton*, pp. 119–20.

35 Herbert Tracey, *The Book of the Labour Party*, Volume I, pp. 255–6.

36 *Spectator*, 31 May 1924.

37 J. R. Clynes, *Memoirs*, p. 42.

38 *The Times*, 14 May 1924.

39 Richard W. Lyman, *The First Labour Government*, p. 141.

40 HC Deb 20 May 1924 Vol 173 c2072.

41 HC Deb 22 May 1924 Vol 173 cc2505-06.

42 HC Deb 22 May 1924 Vol 173 c2510.

43 Norman and Jeanne MacKenzie, *The Diary of Beatrice Webb*, Volume Four, p. 28.

44 MacDonald to the King, 30 May 1924, PRO 30/69/228, RMP.

45 HC Deb 29 May 1924 Vol 174 c651.

46 Fenner Brockway, *Inside the Left*, p. 151.

47 Fenner Brockway (1977), *Towards Tomorrow: The Autobiography of Fenner Brockway*, London: Hart-Davis, MacGibbon, p. 67.

48 Fenner Brockway (1946), *Socialism Over Sixty Years: The Life of Jowett of Bradford (1864–1944)*, London: George Allen & Unwin, pp. 212–13.

49 HC Deb 30 July 1924 Vol 176 c2092.

50 Colin Cross, *Philip Snowden*, p. 208.

51 Philip Snowden, *An Autobiography*, Volume Two, p. 702.

52 Colin Cross, *Philip Snowden*, p. 208.

53 G. D. H. Cole (1948), *A History of the Labour Party from 1914*, London: Routledge & Kegan Paul.

54 Labour Party (1924), *Labour's Great Record*, London: Labour Publications Department, p. 5.

55 Labour Party, *Report of the Twenty-Fourth Annual Conference of the Labour Party*, p. 107.

9. WILLIAM ADAMSON: 'FAR FROM REVOLUTIONARY'

1 The position was upgraded to a full 'Secretary of State' by Stanley Baldwin in 1926.

2 Lord Macmillan, *A Man of Law's Tale*, p. 90.

3 David Howell, 'William Adamson', *ODNB*.

4 Norman and Jeanne MacKenzie, *The Diary of Beatrice Webb*, Volume Three, p. 330.

5 Mary Agnes Hamilton, *Fit to Govern!*, p. 41.

6 Anonymous, *The Scottish Socialists*, p. 105.

7 This Bill passed its second reading but did not become law. An Equal Franchise Act was not passed until 1928.

8 Ian S. Wood (1989), 'Hope Deferred: Labour in Scotland in the 1920s' in Ian Donnachie, Christopher Harvie and Ian S. Wood (eds), *Forward! Labour Politics in Scotland 1888–1988*, Edinburgh: Polygon, pp. 35–6.

9 Mary Agnes Hamilton, *J. Ramsay MacDonald*, pp. 44–5.

10 Richard W. Lyman, *The First Labour Government*, p. 232.

11 Gordon Brown, *Maxton*, p. 160.

12 *Glasgow Herald*, 15 September 1923.

13 Roland Muirhead to MacDonald, 3 January 1924, Acc 3721/6/108, Papers of the Scottish Secretariat and of Roland Eugene Muirhead, Edinburgh: National Library of Scotland.

14 Peter Dorey (2008), *The Labour Party and Constitutional Reform: A History of Constitutional Conservatism*, London: Palgrave Macmillan, pp. 206–7.

15 Michael Keating and David Bleiman (1979), *Labour and Scottish Nationalism*, London: Macmillan, p. 83.

16 Miles Taylor (2000), 'Labour and the constitution' in Duncan Tanner, Pat Thane and Nick Tiratsoo (eds), *Labour's First Century*, Cambridge: Cambridge University Press, p. 159.

17 Michael Keating and David Bleiman, *Labour and Scottish Nationalism*, p. 81.

18 *The Times*, 28 April 1924.

19 Gordon Brown, *Maxton*, p. 161.

20 Graham Walker (1988), *Thomas Johnston*, Manchester: Manchester University Press, p. 70.

21 HC Deb 9 May 1924 Faber & Faber 173 cc789-874.

22 HC Deb 9 May 1924 Vol 173 c871.

23 HC Deb 9 May 1924 Vol 173 cc872-74.

24 MacDonald to the King, 10 May 1924, PRO 30/69/228, RMP.

25 HC Deb 14 May 1924 Vol 173 cc1341-42.

26 MacDonald to the King, 15 May 1924, PRO 30/69/228, RMP.

27 HC Deb 15 July 1924 Vol 176 cc216-23.

28 Cabinet paper dated 29 May 1924, CAB/23/167/25, CPC.

29 Cabinet paper dated 4 June 1924, CAB/23/48/11, CPC.

30 'Material for Reply to Deputation on Scottish Home Rule', 21 July 1924, PRO 30/69/59, RMP.

31 HC Deb 18 June 1924 Vol 174 c2119.

32 Richard J. Finlay (1994), *Independent and Free: Scottish Politics and the Origins of the Scottish National Party 1918–1945*, Edinburgh: John Donald, p. 12.

33 Invitation card, Acc 13461/7, Papers of James Ramsay MacDonald, Edinburgh: National Library of Scotland.

34 'Material for Reply to Deputation on Scottish Home Rule', 21 July 1924, PRO 30/69/59, RMP.

35 Michael Keating and David Bleiman, *Labour and Scottish Nationalism*, p. 82.

36 *Scotsman*, 25 August 1924.

37 Roland Muirhead to MacDonald, 19 June 1925, Acc 3721/6/108, PSSREM.

10. JIMMY THOMAS: 'NO MUCKING ABOUT WITH THE BRITISH EMPIRE'

1 'What Holding Office has taught me', *Parsons Magazine*, March 1925, U1625/Z13, JHTP.

2 *Morning Post*, 8 March 1924.

3 Herbert Tracey, *The Book of the Labour Party*, Volume I, p. 185.

4 Philip Williamson, 'James Henry Thomas', *ODNB*.

5 Anonymous, *The Scottish Socialists*, p. 63.

6 Edward Marsh (1939), *A Number of People: A Book of Reminiscences*, London: Heinemann, p. 401.

7 Gregory Blaxland (1964), *J. H. Thomas: A Life for Unity*, London: Frederick Muller, p. 170.

8 Edward Marsh, *A Number of People*, pp. 400–1.

9 Hugh Dalton, *Call Back Yesterday*, p. 147.

10 Gregory Blaxland, *J. H. Thomas*, p. 169.

11 *Daily Herald*, 1 February 1924.

12 Gregory Blaxland, *J. H. Thomas*, p. 168.

13 The Metropolitan Police helpfully sent a copy to Thomas (U1625/8-13, JHTP).

14 *Daily Express*, 5 February 1924.

15 Keith Middlemas, *Thomas Jones: Whitehall Diary*, Volume I, p. 271.

16 *Sunday Times*, 8 March 1924.

17 *Parsons Magazine*, March 1925.

18 Gregory Blaxland, *J. H. Thomas*, p. 173.

19 Kenneth Rose, *King George V*, p. 331.

20 Norman and Jeanne MacKenzie, *The Diary of Beatrice Webb*, Volume Four, p. 11.

21 *Westminster Gazette*, 18 September 1924.

22 Edward Marsh, *A Number of People*, p. 402.

23 *Financial Times*, 29 January 1924, and Gregory Blaxland, *J. H. Thomas*, p. 170.

24 Memorandum by Kevin O'Shiel, 28 January 1924, NAI DT s1801D, Department of the Taoiseach Papers, Dublin: National Archives of Ireland.

25 Rough notes by Kevin O'Shiel, 30 January 1924, NAI DT s1801D, DTP.

26 Conversation with Denis Gwynn of the *Freeman*, February 1924, LA1/H/106/6, Eoin MacNeill Papers, Dublin: University College Dublin Archives.

27 D. G. Boyce (1988), *The Irish Question and British Politics 1868–1996*, Basingstoke: Palgrave Macmillan, p. 78.

28 Keith Middlemas, *Thomas Jones: Whitehall Diary*, Volume I, p. 269.

29 Keith Middlemas (ed.) (1971), *Thomas Jones: Whitehall Diary*, Volume III, *Ireland 1918–1925*, London: Oxford University Press, pp. 226–7.

30 Keith Middlemas, *Thomas Jones: Whitehall Diary*, Volume III, pp. 229–30.

31 MacDonald to Sir James Craig, 15 February 1924, CAB/9/B/4/1, Cabinet Secretariat Records, Belfast: Public Record Office of Northern Ireland.

32 Notes of conference at Chequers on 31 May 1924, PRO 30/69/1/71, RMP.

33 William T. Cosgrave to MacDonald, 4 June 1924, NAI DT s1801H, DTP.

34 MacDonald to William T. Cosgrave, 6 June 1924, TAOIS/s1801 H, DTP.

35 *Report of the Judicial Committee … on the Questions connected with the Irish Boundary Commission* (Cmnd 2214), 31 July 1924.

36 HC Deb 1 August 1924 Vol 176 c2401.

37 Proceedings of conference on the Boundary Commission, 2 August 1924, NAI DT s1801J, DTP.

38 Sir Ronald Waterhouse to Clive Wigram, 3 August 1924, PS/PSO/GV/ C/K/1949/11.

39 Diary entry dated 4 August 1924, PRO 30/69/1753/1, RMP.

40 MacDonald to Lady Londonderry, 5 August 1924, D3099/3/20/1/5, LP.

41 Lady Londonderry to MacDonald, 12 August 1924, D3099/3/20/1/6, LP.

42 Gregory Blaxland, *J. H. Thomas*, p. 171.

43 *The Times*, 16 May 1924.

44 *South Wales News*, 9 May 1924.

45 'Mr. J. H. Thomas's Empire', *The Weekly Despatch*, 3 February 1924, U1625/18-26, JHTP.

46 Richard W. Lyman, *The First Labour Government*, p. 213.

47 John Callaghan (2007), *The Labour Party and Foreign Policy: A History*, London: Routledge, p. 81.

48 Graham Walker, *Thomas Johnston*, pp. 66–7.

49 *The Times*, 9 August 1924.

50 J. H. Thomas, *My Story*, p. 81.

51 Mary Agnes Hamilton, *J. Ramsay MacDonald*, p. 179.

52 J. R. Clynes, *Memoirs*, p. 55.

53 John Callaghan, *The Labour Party and Foreign Policy*, p. 85.

54 Paul Mulvey, *The Political Life of Josiah C. Wedgwood*, pp. 142–5.

55 Partha Sarathi Gupta (1975), *Imperialism and the British Labour Movement, 1914–1964*, New York: Holmes & Meier, p. 108.

56 Keith Middlemas, *The Clydesiders*, p. 170.

57 *Socialist Review*, November 1924.

58 Hertzog had initially refused to take part.

59 *The Times*, 10 September 1924.

60 J. H. Thomas, *My Story*, p. 79.

61 Gregory Blaxland, *J. H. Thomas*, p176.

62 *Daily Sketch*, 18 September 1924.

11. Viscount Haldane: Tidying Up the Constitution

1 Presumably on foot. Haldane lived not far away at 28 Queen Anne's Gate.

2 Richard Burdon Haldane (1929), *An Autobiography*, London: Hodder & Stoughton, p. 326.

3 Richard W. Lyman, *The First Labour Government*, p. 100.

4 Norman and Jeanne MacKenzie (eds) (1984), *The Diary of Beatrice Webb*, Volume One, *1873–1892: Glitter Around and Darkness Within*, London: Virago, p. 345.

5 H. C. January G. Matthew, 'Richard Burdon Haldane', *ODNB*.

6 David Kirkwood, *My Life of Revolt*, pp. 221–2.

7 Lord Haldane to Asquith, 22 1924 and Asquith to Haldane, 23 January 1924, MS 5916/75-78, LHP.

8 Harold Begbie to Lord Haldane, 31 January 1924, MS 5916/78, LHP.

9 Stephen E. Koss (1969), *Lord Haldane: Scapegoat for Liberalism*, New York: Columbia University Press, p. 245.

10 Dudley Sommer, *Haldane of Cloan*, p. 404.

11 Stephen Roskill, *Hankey: Man of Secrets*, Volume II, p. 366.

12 Maurice Cowling, *The Impact of Labour*, p. 373.

13 See John Bew (2016), *Citizen Clem: A Biography of Attlee*, London: Riverrun, pp. 64–5, for an account of this stage in Attlee's career.

14 Jack Lawson, *A Man's Life*, p. 268.

15 Sir Frederick Maurice, *Haldane 1915–1928*, p. 177.

16 HC Deb 21 February 1924 Vol 169 c1971.

17 HC Deb 21 February 1924 Vol 169 cc1970-73. Thurtle was married to George Lansbury's daughter Dorothy.

18 HC Deb 21 February 1924 Vol 169 c2129.

19 W. S. Chalmers (1951), *The Life and Letters of David Beatty: Admiral of the Fleet*, London: Hodder & Stoughton, p. 373.

20 Stephen Roskill, *Hankey: Man of Secrets*, Volume II, p. 360.

21 W. S. Chalmers, *The Life and Letters of David Beatty*, p. 395.

22 Stephen Roskill, *Hankey: Man of Secrets*, Volume II, p. 361.

23 Sir Frederick Maurice, *Haldane 1915–1928*, p. 158.

24 Jake Vaughan, 2007, 'The first Labour Government and the civil service', PhD thesis, London: King's College, p. 149.

25 HC Deb 18 March 1924 Vol 171 c322.

26 Stephen Roskill, *Hankey: Man of Secrets*, Volume II, p. 361.

27 Partha Sarathi Gupta, 'Imperialism and the British Labour Movement, 1914-1964', pp. 71 and 97–8.

28 *The Times*, 3 October 1924.

29 Sir Frederick Maurice, *Haldane 1915–1928*, pp. 157–8.

30 Diary entry dated 1 July 1924, PRO 30/69/1753/1, RMP.

31 LCO6/861, Lord Chancellor's Department Papers, Kew: The National Archives.

32 Cabinet Conclusions dated 9 July 1924, CAB/23/48/15, CPC.

33 HL Deb 17 July 1924 Vol 58 cc696-711.

34 Cabinet Conclusions dated 27 March 1924, CAB/23/47/17, CPC.

35 Sir Frederick Maurice, *Haldane 1915–1928*, p. 176.

36 Labour Party (1924), *Report of the Twenty-Fourth Annual Conference of the Labour Party*, p. 48.

37 Since the *Sex Disqualification Act 1919*, women were no longer barred.

38 Memorandum on Justices' Advisory Committees, 7 November 1924, MS 5923, LHP.

39 John Shepherd and Keith Laybourn, *Britain's First Labour Government*, pp. 81–2.

40 HC Deb 30 June 1924 Vol 175 c937.

41 Cabinet Conclusions dated 15 July 1924, CAB/23/48/16, CPC.

42 Lord Parmoor to Sidney Webb, 18 August 1924, Passfield 2/4/H, PBSW.

43 Sir Patrick Hastings (1948), *The Autobiography of Sir Patrick Hastings*, London: Heinemann, p. 234.

44 Dudley Sommer, *Haldane of Cloan*, p. 404.

45 Sir Frederick Maurice, *Haldane 1915–1928*, p. 165.

46 Sir Henry Slesser (1941), *Judgment Reserved: The Reminiscences of the Right Honourable Sir Henry Slesser: Late Lord Justice of Appeal*, London: Hutchinson, p. 95.

47 The club was located at No. 11 Tufton Street.

48 Unsigned note, 18 May 1924, MS 5916/110, LHP.

49 Keith Middlemas, *Thomas Jones: Whitehall Diary*, Volume I, p. 284.

50 Richard Burdon Haldane, *An Autobiography*, p. 332. The CCR was established by Baldwin in 1925.

51 Keith Middlemas, *Thomas Jones: Whitehall Diary*, Volume I, p. 284.

52 Sir Maurice Hankey to Lord Haldane, 20 August 1924, MS 5916/145, LHP.

53 Unsigned note by Lord Haldane, 13 September 1924, MS 5916/150, LHP.

12. Ramsay MacDonald as Foreign Secretary:
Creating a New Atmosphere

1 Spey Bay Golf Club to MacDonald, 22 March 1924, PRO 30/69/1433, RMP.

2 John McConachie (1988), *The Moray Golf Club at Lossiemouth 1889–1989*, Elgin: Moravian Press, p. 46.

3 Malcolm MacDonald to Ishbel MacDonald, 5 August 1924, 123/4/51, MMP.

4 Alice G. Vines, *The MacDonald Women*, p. 163.

5 Lord Macmillan, *A Man of Law's Tale*, p. 95.

6 MacDonald to Lady Londonderry, 17 June 1924, D3099/3/20/1/4, LP.

7 Lord Thomson to MacDonald, 9 February 1924, PRO 30/69/208, RMP.

8 Keith Middlemas, *Thomas Jones: Whitehall Diary*, Volume I, p. 276.

9 Richard Burdon Haldane, *An Autobiography*, p. 332.

10 Sir Frederick Maurice, *Haldane 1915–1928*, p. 182.

11 David Marquand, *Ramsay MacDonald*, p. 330.

12 Norman and Jeanne MacKenzie, *The Diary of Beatrice Webb*, Volume Four, p. 18.

13 This treaty tied up loose ends left by the disintegration of the Ottoman Empire.

14 John Callaghan, *The Labour Party and Foreign Policy*, p. 32.

15 Lord Parmoor (1936), *A Retrospect: Looking Back Over a Life of More Than Eighty Years*, London: Heinemann, p. 197.

16 Kevin Morgan (2006), *Ramsay MacDonald*, London: Haus, p. 50.

17 *Time*, 4 February 1924.

18 *The Times*, 15 April 1924.

19 *The Times*, 2 November 1923.

20 Diary entry dated 3 February 1924, PRO 30/69/1753/1, RMP.

21 MacDonald to Lord Haldane, 3 March 1924, MS 5916/96, LHP.

22 Hubert H. Tiltman (1929), *James Ramsay MacDonald: Labour's Man of Destiny*, London: Jarrolds, p. 176.

23 A. J. P. Taylor, *Beaverbrook*, p. 220.

24 Sheldon Spear (1978), 'Pacifist Radicalism in the Post-War British Labour Party: The Case of E. D. Morel, 1919–24', *International Review of Social History* 23:2, p. 217.

25 Donald Mitchell, *The Politics of Dissent*, pp. 198–9.

26 Fenner Brockway, *Inside the Left*, p. 152.

27 Trevor Wilson, *The Political Diaries of C. P. Scott*, p. 459, and Philip Snowden, *An Autobiography*, Volume Two, p. 669.

28 David Bryn-Jones (1937), *Frank B. Kellogg: A Biography*, New York: G. P. Putnam's, p. 138.

29 Sibyl Crowe and Edward Corp (1996), *Our Ablest Public Servant: Sir Eyre Crowe 1864–1925*, Braunton: Merlin Books, pp. 454–5.

30 John F. Naylor, *A Man and an Institution*, p. 140.

31 MacDonald to Isabella Ramsay, 17 July 1924, PRO 30/69/799, RMP.

32 Diary entry dated 7 August 1924, PRO 30/69/1753/1, RMP.

33 Philip Snowden, *An Autobiography*, Volume Two, p. 675.

34 Diary entry dated 15 August 1924, PRO 30/69/1753/1, RMP.

35 MacDonald to Philip Snowden, 14 August 1924, PRO 30/69/1753, RMP.

36 Patrick Gower to Clive Wigram, 14 August 1924, RA PS/PSO/GV/C/K/1949/21.

37 Carolyn J. Kitching (2011), 'Prime minister and foreign secretary: the dual role of James Ramsay MacDonald in 1924', *Review of International Studies* 37:3, p. 1413.

38 David Bryn-Jones, *Frank B. Kellogg*, pp. 138–9.

39 Diary entry dated 18 August 1924, AAP.

40 Hubert H. Tiltman, *James Ramsay MacDonald*, p. 177.

41 David Marquand, *Ramsay MacDonald*, p. 351.

42 The King to MacDonald, 16 August 1924, RA PS/PSO/GV/C/K/1949/24.

43 Patrick Gower to Clive Wigram, 18 August 1924, RA PS/PSO/GV/C/K/1949/28.

44 Diary entry dated 16 August 1924, PRO 30/69/1753/1, RMP.

45 Sir Frederick Maurice, *Haldane 1915–1928*, pp. 166–7.

46 Sir Maurice Hankey to Clive Wigram, 20 August 1924, RA PS/PSO/GV/C/J/1935/6.

47 *Liberal Daily News*, 18 August 1924.

48 Labour Party (1924), *Can Labour Rule? No. 6, The Anglo-Soviet Treaties*, London: Labour Joint Publications Department, p. 10.

49 *Daily Herald*, 14 August 1924.

50 Mary Agnes Hamilton, *J. Ramsay MacDonald*, pp. 107–8.

51 Diary entry dated 25 August 1924, APP.

52 Colin Cross, *Philip Snowden*, p. 211.

53 Carolyn J. Kitching, 'Prime minister and foreign secretary', p. 1408.

54 Diary entry dated 25 August 1924, APP.

55 Raymond A. Jones, *Arthur Ponsonby*, p. 146.

56 Raymond A. Jones, *Arthur Ponsonby*, p. 148.

57 Stamfordham to Sir Ronald Waterhouse, 5 June 1924, PRO 30/69/197, RMP.

58 *The Times*, 21 July 1924.

59 MacDonald to Christian Rakovsky, 26 July 1924, PRO 30/69/197, RMP.

60 HC Deb 18 June 1924 Vol 174 c2095.

61 Raymond A. Jones, *Arthur Ponsonby*, p. 149.

62 Diary entry dated 13 August 1924, APP.

63 Arthur Ponsonby to E. D. Morel, 31 July 1924, Morel F8/123, EDMP.

64 Raymond A. Jones, *Arthur Ponsonby*, pp. 149–50.

65 Memorandum by Sidney Webb on the first Labour government, Passfield 4/18, PBSW.

66 John Campbell, *Lloyd George*, p. 103.

67 Stuart Ball (ed.) (1992), *Parliament and Politics in the Age of Baldwin and MacDonald: The Headlam Diaries, 1923–1935*, London: The Historians Press, p. 42.

68 Sir Henry Slesser, *Judgment Reserved*, p. 107.

69 Sibyl Crowe and Edward Corp, *Our Ablest Public Servant*, p. 458.

70 Raymond A. Jones, *Arthur Ponsonby*, p. 152.

71 Diary entry dated 14 August 1924, APP.

72 Memorandum by Stamfordham, 12 August 1924, RA PS/PSO/GV/ C/K/1956/1.

73 Richard Burdon Haldane, *An Autobiography*, pp. 328–9.

74 John Campbell, *Lloyd George*, p. 104.

75 Stanley Baldwin to John Strachey, STR/2/3/15, JSP.

76 MacDonald to Lord Parmoor, 11 August 1924, PRO 30/69/200, RMP.

77 Rhiannon Vickers (2004), *The Labour Party and the World*, Volume 1, *The Evolution of Labour's Foreign Policy, 1900–51*, Manchester: Manchester University Press, p. 87.

78 MacDonald to Isabella Ramsay, 20 August 1924, PRO 30/69/799, RMP.

79 MacDonald to Joseph King, 15 December 1924, PRO 30/69/1433, RMP.

80 Kevin Morgan, *MacDonald*, p. 54.

81 Hubert H. Tiltman, *James Ramsay MacDonald*, p. 181.

82 Sir Maurice Hankey to Lord Haldane, 9 September 1924, MS 5916/147, LHP.

83 Arthur Ponsonby to E. D. Morel, 6 September 1924, Morel F8/123, EDMP.

84 Sheldon Spear, 'Pacifist Radicalism in the Post-War British Labour Party', p. 218.

85 *The Times*, 9 September 1924.

86 Mary Agnes Hamilton, *J. Ramsay MacDonald*, p. 114.

87 *The Times*, 10 September 1924.

88 J. Ramsay MacDonald (1924), *Socialism: Critical and Constructive*, London: Cassell, pp. vi–vii.

89 *The Times*, 12 September 1924.

90 *The Times*, 13 September 1924.

91 James Margach (1978), *The Abuse of Power: The War between Downing Street and the Media from Lloyd George to Callaghan*, London: W. H. Allen, p. 40.

92 Norman and Jeanne MacKenzie, *The Diary of Beatrice Webb*, Volume Four, p. 39.

93 *The Times*, 15 September 1924.

94 Lauchlan MacNeill Weir, *The Tragedy of Ramsay MacDonald*, p. 165.

95 Sir Alexander Grant to MacDonald, 15 September 1924, PRO 30/69/194, RMP.

96 Unpublished memoir by Ishbel MacDonald, Add MS. 89304/3/8, IMA.

97 Philip Snowden, *An Autobiography*, Volume Two, p. 688.

98 MacDonald to Lady Londonderry, 13 September 1924, D3099/3/20/1/7, LP.

99 Philip Snowden, *An Autobiography*, Volume Two, p. 689.

100 Norman and Jeanne MacKenzie, *The Diary of Beatrice Webb*: Volume Four, pp. 39–40.

101 J. S. Middleton to MacDonald, 22 September 1924, PRO 30/69/175, RMP.

102 Lord Haldane to Beatrice Webb, 17 September 1924, Passfield 2/4/H, PBSW.

103 *The Times*, 22 September 1924.

104 Martin Gilbert (1976), *Winston S. Churchill*, Volume V, *1922–1939*, London: Heinemann, p. 54.

105 *The Times*, 28 September 1924.

106 Diary entries dated 26 and 27 September 1924, PRO 30/69/1753/1, RMP.

107 Unpublished autobiography by Lord Ammon, DMN/9/6, PLCGA.

108 Diary entry dated 24 September 1924, APP.

109 Diary entry dated 27 September 1924, APP.

110 Harold Nicolson, *King George the Fifth*, p. 388.

111 Philip Snowden, *An Autobiography*, Volume Two, p. 690.

13. Sir Patrick Hastings: 'By whose representation?'

1 Monty Johnstone, 'John Ross Campbell', *ODNB*, and Francis Beckett (1998), *Enemy Within: The Rise and Fall of the British Communist Party*, London: John Murray, p. 24.

2 J. J. Edwards (1964), *The Law Officers of the Crown*, London: Sweet & Maxwell, p. 199.

3 HC Deb 29 July 1924 Vol 176 c1897.

4 HC Deb 30 July 1924 Vol 176 cc2060-61.

5 Memorandum by Sidney Webb on the first Labour government, Passfield 4/18, PBSW.

6 J. J. Edwards, *The Law Officers of the Crown*, p. 200.

7 Sir Patrick Hastings, *Autobiography*, p. 236.

8 Sir Patrick Hastings, *Autobiography*, p. 5.

9 Sir Patrick Hastings, *Autobiography*, p. 147.

10 John Shepherd and Keith Laybourn, *Britain's First Labour Government*, p. 163.

11 Anthony Lejeune (revised by Mark Pottle), 'Sir Patrick Gardiner Hastings', *ODNB*.

12 For a full account, see F. H. Newark, 'The Campbell Case and the First Labour Government', *Northern Ireland Legal Quarterly* 20:1, March 1969, pp. 19–42.

13 HC Deb 6 August 1924 Vol 176 cc2928-30.

14 Francis Williams (1950), *Fifty Years March: The Rise of the Labour Party*, London: Odhams Press, p. 309.

15 John Scanlon, *The Decline and Fall of the Labour Party*, pp. 75–6.

16 It was sometimes claimed Campbell was missing both feet.

17 Sir Henry Slesser, *Judgment Reserved*, p. 106.

18 MacDonald to Stamfordham, 22 August 1924, RA PS/PSO/GV/C/K/1958/2.

19 Keith Middlemas, *Thomas Jones: Whitehall Diary*, Volume I, pp. 289–90.

20 HC Deb 8 October 1924 Vol 177 cc606-07.

21 F. H. Newark, 'The Campbell Case and the First Labour Government', p. 40.

22 J. J. Edwards, *The Law Officers of the Crown*, p. 205. Author's emphasis.

23 *The Times*, 15 August 1924.

24 J. J. Edwards, *The Law Officers of the Crown*, p. 206.

25 *The Times*, 15 August 1924.

26 Stamfordham to MacDonald, 25 August 1924, Add MS 89304/2/36, IMA.

27 John F. Naylor, *A Man and an Institution*, p. 147.

28 Keith Middlemas, *Thomas Jones: Whitehall Diary*, Volume I, pp. 290–91.

29 John F. Naylor, *A Man and an Institution*, pp. 144–7.

30 MacDonald to Hugh Macmillan, 24 September 1924, MS 25261, HMP.

31 F. H. Newark, 'The Campbell Case and the First Labour Government', pp. 38–9.

32 Unpublished memoir by Ishbel MacDonald, Add MS. 89304/3/8, IMA.

33 J. R. Clynes, *Memoirs*, p. 62.

34 J. J. Edwards, *The Law Officers of the Crown*, p. 178.

35 *The Times*, 26 September 1924.

36 HC Deb 30 September 1924 Vol 177 c35.

37 Diary entry dated 30 September 1924, PRO 30/69/1753/1, RMP.

38 HC Deb 30 September 1924 Vol 177 cc8-16.

39 Margaret Bondfield, *A Life's Work*, p. 261. Bondfield was leading a delegation to investigate Empire settlement.

40 HC Deb 30 September 1924 Vol 177 c16.

41 Keith Middlemas, *Thomas Jones: Whitehall Diary*, Volume I, p. 296.

42 MacDonald to the King, 1 October 1924, PRO 30/69/228, RMP.

43 MacDonald to Stamfordham, 2 October 1924, RA PS/PSO/GV/C/K/1958/4. Lloyd George had suggested MacDonald was about to embrace Protection as part of a Conservative–Labour coalition.

44 HC Deb 2 October 1924 Vol 177 cc316-17.

45 MacDonald to the King, 2 October 1924, PRO 30/69/228, RMP.

46 Mortimer Epstein, *The Annual Register 1923*, p. 106.

47 MacDonald to the King, 3 October 1924, PRO 30/69/228, RMP.

48 Sir Patrick Hastings, *Autobiography*, pp. 241–2. It appears MacDonald's intention was to immediately reappoint him.

49 Sir Frederick Maurice, *Haldane 1915–1928*, pp. 169–70.

50 *The Times*, 8 October 1924.

51 Charles Trevelyan to Molly Trevelyan, 7 October 1924, CPT/3/70/90, TA.

52 Stamfordham to Alex Hardinge, 7 October 1924, RA PS/PSO/GV/C/K/1958/12.

53 Stamfordham to MacDonald, 4 October 1924, PRO 30/69/197, RMP.

54 Jane Ridley, *George V: Never a Dull Moment*, p. 331.

55 Memorandum by Sidney Webb on the first Labour government, Passfield 4/18, PBSW.

56 Charles Trevelyan to Molly Trevelyan, 7 October 1924, CPT/3/70/90, TA.

57 Sir Patrick Hastings, *Autobiography*, p. 244.

58 HC Deb 8 October 1924 Vol 177 cc512-13.

59 Philip Snowden, *An Autobiography*, Volume Two, pp. 694–6.

60 Sir Patrick Hastings, *Autobiography*, p. 245.

61 Sir Patrick Hastings, *Autobiography*, p. 245.

62 HC Deb 8 October 1924 Vol 177 c638.

63 The Jameson Raid took its name from a botched attack against the Transvaal; the Marconi Affair of 1912 concerned insider trading in the Marconi Company.

64 HC Deb 8 October 1924 Vol 177 cc641-42.

65 David Marquand, *Ramsay MacDonald*, p. 374.

66 Vivian Phillipps, *My Days and Ways*, p. 123.

67 Sir Patrick Hastings, *Autobiography*, p. 246.

68 Cabinet Conclusions dated 8 October 1924, CAB/23/48/28, CPC.

69 HC Deb 8 October 1924 Vol 177 c679.

70 Philip Snowden, *An Autobiography*, Volume Two, p. 697.

71 MacDonald to the King, 9 October 1924, PRO 30/69/228, RMP.

72 Diary entry dated 8 October 1924, PRO 30/69/1753/1, RMP.

73 Philip Snowden, *An Autobiography*, Volume Two, p. 698.

74 Margaret Bondfield, *A Life's Work*, p. 260.

75 Kenneth Rose, *King George V*, p. 335.
76 Memorandum by Stamfordham, 9 October 1924, RA PS/PSO/GV/ C/K/1958/19.
77 Memorandum by Sir Francis Bryant, 9 October 1924, RA PS/PSO/GV/ C/K/1958/1.
78 Diary entry dated 9 October 1924, GV/PRIV/GVD/1924: 9 October. The King feared the election might return 'the three political parties in numbers similar to those of the present House of Commons.' (Memorandum by the King, 9 October 1924, RA PS/PSO/GV/C/K/1958/22).
79 Diary entry dated 9 October 1924, PRO 30/69/1753/1, RMP.
80 Keith Middlemas, *Thomas Jones: Whitehall Diary*, Volume I, p. 295.
81 HC Deb 9 October 1924 Vol 177 c731.
82 Diary entry dated 9 October 1924, PRO 30/69/1753/1, RMP.
83 HL Deb 9 October 1924 Vol 59 c667.
84 Ross McKibbin (1974), *The Evolution of the Labour Party 1910–1924*, Oxford: Clarendon Press, p. 130.
85 Labour Party, *Report of the Twenty-Fourth Annual Conference*, pp. 115–16, 182–5.
86 Sir Henry Slesser, *Judgment Reserved*, p. 95.
87 Diary entry dated 9 October 1924, PRO 30/69/1753/1, RMP.

14. The 'Red Letter' Election

1 Mary Agnes Hamilton, *J. Ramsay MacDonald*, p. 133.
2 Norman and Jeanne MacKenzie, *The Diary of Beatrice Webb*, Volume Four, pp. 41–2.
3 F. M. Leventhal, *Arthur Henderson*, p. 130.
4 Ralph Miliband, *Parliamentary Socialism*, p. 116.
5 Labour Party (1924), *Labour's Appeal to the People*, London: Labour Party.
6 *Daily Herald*, 13 October 1924.
7 Lauchlan MacNeill Weir, *The Tragedy of Ramsay MacDonald*, p. 185.
8 *The Times*, 14 October 1924.
9 *The Times*, 14 October 1924.
10 Lauchlan MacNeill Weir, *The Tragedy of Ramsay MacDonald*, p. 186.
11 Philip Snowden, *An Autobiography*, Volume Two, p. 608.
12 Robert C. Self, *The Austen Chamberlain Diary Letters*, p. 258.
13 Lauchlan MacNeill Weir, *The Tragedy of Ramsay MacDonald*, p. 188.
14 *The Times*, 14 October 1924.
15 *The Times*, 15 October 1924.
16 Philip Williamson (2007), *Stanley Baldwin: Conservative Leadership and National Values*, Cambridge: Cambridge University Press, pp. 83–4.
17 John Shepherd and Keith Laybourn, *Britain's First Labour Government*, p. 181.
18 Roy Jenkins, *Baldwin*, p. 83.

19 Philip Snowden, *An Autobiography*, Volume Two, p. 708.

20 Mary Agnes Hamilton, *J. Ramsay MacDonald*, p. 75.

21 A. J. A. Morris, *C. P. Trevelyan*, p. 162.

22 Molly Trevelyan to Lady Bell, 17 October 1924, CPT/6/1/29, TA.

23 North Camberwell Election News, October 1924, DMN/10/34, PLCGA.

24 Raymond A. Jones, *Arthur Ponsonby*, p. 152.

25 Diary entry dated 19 October 1924, APP.

26 *Daily Express*, 21 October 1924.

27 Hubert H. Tiltman, *James Ramsay MacDonald*, p. 188.

28 *The Labour Woman*, October 1924.

29 Lewis Chester, Stephen Fay and Hugo Young (1968), *The Zinoviev Letter: A Political Intrigue*, London: Lippincott, p. 123.

30 MacDonald to Hugh Macmillan, 10 September 1924, MS 25261, HMP.

31 Ian S. Wood, *John Wheatley*, p. 155.

32 J. R. Clynes, *Memoirs*, pp. 66–7.

33 See LP/JSM/MON/1-5, JSMP, for bad-tempered correspondence between J. S. Middleton and Sir Alfred Mond.

34 Philip Snowden, *An Autobiography*, Volume Two, p. 689.

35 Unpublished memoir by Ishbel MacDonald, Add MS. 89304/3/8, IMA.

36 Thomas N. Graham, *Willie Graham*, p. 153.

37 *South Wales Daily Post*, 18 October 1924.

38 Philip Snowden, *An Autobiography*, Volume Two, p. 709.

39 Rose Rosenberg to J. S. Middleton, 24 October 1924, MID/18/62, JSMP.

40 David Bryn-Jones, *Frank B. Kellogg: A Biography*, p. 138.

41 A. J. P. Taylor, *Beaverbrook*, p. 223.

42 Richard W. Lyman, *The First Labour Government*, p. 254.

43 John Ramsden, *An Appetite for Power*, p. 264.

44 John Ramsden, *An Appetite for Power*, p. 264.

45 Lewis Chester et al., *The Zinoviev Letter*, pp. 125–7.

46 *Daily Mail*, 25 October 1924.

47 J. H. Thomas, *My Story*, p. 78.

48 Lewis Chester et al., *The Zinoviev Letter*, p. 138.

49 Adrian Addison (2017), *Mail Men: The Unauthorized Story of the Daily Mail*, London: Atlantic Books, p. 86.

50 John Ramsden, *The Age of Balfour and Baldwin*, p. 205.

51 *Manchester Evening Chronicle*, 22 October 1924.

52 Gill Bennett, *The Zinoviev Letter*, p. 151.

53 Copy of Note of protest to Rakovsky, LP/JSM/ZI/1, JSMP.

54 Gill Bennett, *The Zinoviev Letter*, pp. 58–61.

55 Diary entry dated 31 October 1924, PRO/69/1753/1, RMP.

56 Sir Eyre Crowe to Stamfordham, 25 October 1924, RA PS/PSO/GV/C/K/1958/33.

57 The King to Stamfordham, 26 October 1924, RA PS/PSO/GV/C/K/1958/35.

58 John Ramsden, *The Age of Balfour and Baldwin*, p. 205.

59 Philip Snowden, *An Autobiography*, Volume Two, pp. 710–11.

60 Lewis Chester et al., *The Zinoviev Letter*, p. 116.

61 Diary entry dated 31 October 1924, PRO/69/1753/1, RMP.

62 Philip Snowden, *An Autobiography*, Volume Two, p. 711.

63 J. R. Clynes, *Memoirs*, pp. 64–5.

64 J. D. Gregory (1929), *On the Edge of Diplomacy: Rambles and Reflections 1902–1928*, London: Hutchinson, pp. 219–21.

65 Philip Snowden, *An Autobiography*, Volume Two, p. 712.

66 John Ramsden, *The Age of Balfour and Baldwin*, p. 204.

67 *The Times*, 28 October 1924.

68 Lewis Chester et al., *The Zinoviev Letter*, p. 134.

69 Anonymous to Arthur Ponsonby, 28 October 1924, MS. Eng. hist. c. 669, Ponsonby Archive, Oxford: Weston Library.

70 Memorandum by Neville Bland, 27 October 1924, RA PS/PSO/GV/C/K/1958/36.

71 Trevor Wilson, *The Political Diaries of C. P. Scott*, p. 472.

72 Roy Jenkins, *The Chancellors*, p. 283.

73 Norman and Jeanne MacKenzie, *The Diary of Beatrice Webb*, Volume Four, pp. 42–3.

74 Diary entry dated 31 October 1924, APP.

75 Margaret Bondfield, *A Life's Work*, p. 262.

76 Mary Agnes Hamilton, *Arthur Henderson*, p. 255.

77 Philip Snowden, *An Autobiography*, Volume Two, p. 716.

78 *The Times*, 5 March 1928.

79 Thomas Johnston (1952), *Memories*, London: Collins, p. 57.

80 *The Labour Woman*, December 1924.

81 John Ramsden, *The Age of Balfour and Baldwin*, p. 206.

82 Lucy Baldwin to Ishbel MacDonald, 29 October 1924, Add MS 89304/2/36, IMA.

83 Ralph Miliband, *Parliamentary Socialism*, p. 119.

84 Memorandum by Sidney Webb on the first Labour government, Passfield 4/18, PBSW.

85 Ralph Miliband, *Parliamentary Socialism*, p. 119.

86 Diary entry dated 31 October 1924, MIC665/18, LCP.

87 RA GV/PRIV/GVD/1924: 30 October.

88 Simon Heffer, *Henry 'Chips' Channon*, p. 133.

89 A. J. P. Taylor, *Beaverbrook*, p. 224.

90 Keith Middlemas, *Thomas Jones: Whitehall Diary*, Volume I, p. 305.

91 Roy Jenkins, *Asquith*, p. 502.

92 Malcom MacDonald to Ishbel MacDonald, 31 October 1924, 123/4/56, MMP.

93 Margaret Bondfield, *A Life's Work*, p. 261.

94 Molly Trevelyan to Lady Bell, 30 October 1924, CPT/6/1/29, TA.

95 Sir George Otto Trevelyan to Charles Trevelyan, 31 October 1924, CPT/1/9/25, TA.

96 *The Times*, 31 October 1924.

97 Diary entry dated 31 October 1924, PRO/69/1753/1, RMP.

98 Fenner Brockway, *Socialism Over Sixty Years*, p. 222.

99 Colin Cross, *Philip Snowden*, pp. 213–14.

100 Keith Middlemas, *Thomas Jones: Whitehall Diary*, Volume I, pp 298–301.

101 Kevin O'Higgins' address, 31 October 1924, LA1/F/305, EMP.

102 MacDonald to George Glasgow, 31 October 1924, PRO 30/69/2, RMP.

103 MacDonald to Hugh Macmillan, 1 November 1924, MS 25261, HMP.

104 Diary entry dated 2 November 1924, PRO/69/1753/1, RMP.

105 Memorandum by Stamfordham, 3 November 1924, RA PS/PSO/GV/C/K/1958/41.

106 Roy Jenkins, *Baldwin*, pp. 83–4.

107 Earl of Oxford and Asquith, *Memories and Reflections*, p. 209.

108 Diary entry dated 4 November 1924, APP.

109 Lord Macmillan, *A Man of Law's Tale*, p. 99.

110 Gill Bennett, *The Zinoviev Letter*, pp. 81–5.

111 Cabinet Conclusions dated 4 November 1924, CAB/23/48/33, CPC.

112 Diary entry dated 4 November 1924, PRO/69/1753/1, RMP.

113 RA GV/PRIV/GVD/1924: 4 November.

114 Memorandum by Stamfordham, 4 November 1924, RA PS/PSO/GV/C/K/1958/42. The *Annual Register* noted mischievously that Labour MPs with Royal Household positions had all been returned with increased majorities.

115 Diary entry dated 4 November 1924, PRO/69/1753/1, RMP.

116 RA GV/PRIV/GVD/1924: 4 November.

117 Jane Ridley, *Never a Dull Moment*, p. 332.

118 See, for example, 'NEW RESPECT FOR THE CROWN', *Sunday Express*, 9 November 1924.

119 Correspondence with John Wheatley's private secretary, November 1924, RA PS/PSO/GV/C/K/1958/65.

120 David Howell, *A Lost Left*, p. 259.

121 Lord Haldane to Mary Haldane, 6 November 1924, MS 6007, LHP.

122 Gregory Blaxland, *J. H. Thomas*, p. 179.

123 *Westminster Gazette*, 4 December 1924.

124 Charles Trevelyan to Molly Trevelyan, 5 November 1924, 4 November 1924, CPT/3/71/99, TA.

125 Diary entry dated 5 November 1924, APP.

126 Sir Eyre Crowe to Lord Haldane, 8 and 14 November 1924, MS 5916/166 & 172, LHP.

127 MacDonald to T. P. O'Connor, 6 November 1924, PRO 30/69/1433, RMP.

128 *The Times*, 8 November 1924.

129 Diary entry dated 6 November 1924, APP.

130 RA GV/PRIV/GVD/1924: 7 November.

131 Diary entry dated 7 December 1924, APP.
132 Ishbel MacDonald to Malcolm MacDonald, 11 November 1924, Add MS 89304/2/36, IMA.
133 'After the Battle', *Forward*, 6 December 1924.

15. WHITHER THE WILD MEN?

1   Diary entry dated 16 November 1924, DPP.
2   F. M. Leventhal, *Arthur Henderson*, p. 131.
3   Diary entry dated 3 December 1924, PRO 30/69/1753/1, RMP.
4   David Howell, *MacDonald's Party*, pp. 33–4. Maxton had proposed George Lansbury as MacDonald's successor.
5   MacDonald to Jupp, 9 December 1924, PRO 30/69/1433, RMP.
6   Correspondence between Lord Dawson and MacDonald, 2 & 3 December 1924, PRO 30/69/2, RMP.
7   Robert Boothby (1947), *I Fight to Live: Autobiography*, London: Victor Gollancz, p. 37.
8   Clifford Allen to Arthur Ponsonby, 2 February 1925, MS. Eng. hist. c. 669, PA.
9   PRO 30/69/2 & PRO 30/69/194, RMP.
10 *The Argus* (Melbourne), 4 December 1924.
11 Raymond A. Jones, *Arthur Ponsonby*, p. 154.
12 Austen Morgan, *Ramsay MacDonald*, p. 123.
13 Harold Spender (1926), *The Fire of Life: A Book of Memories*, London: Hodder & Stoughton, p. 276.
14 John Buchan to MacDonald, 4 December 1924, PRO 30/69/1433, RMP.
15 1931 Labour Party election poster, NMLH.1993.499, Manchester: Labour History Archive and Study Centre.
16 Philip Williamson, 'Margaret Grace Bondfield', *ODNB*.
17 Philip Snowden, *An Autobiography*, Volume Two, p. 656.
18 Anonymous, *The Scottish Socialists*, p. 107.
19 In 1935 Adamson lost to the communist Willie Gallacher.
20 J. J. Edwards, *The Law Officers of the Crown*, p. 213.
21 Lord Olivier to Charles Trevelyan, 12 December 1924 CPT/1/7/67/81, TA.
22 Trevor Wilson, *The Political Diaries of C. P. Scott*, pp. 477–8.
23 HC Deb 19 March 1928 Vol 215, c53.
24 Gill Bennett (1999), *The Zinoviev Letter of 1924: 'A most extraordinary and mysterious business'*, *History Notes* 14, London: Foreign & Commonwealth Office.
25 Robin Cook, 'The hidden hand', *Guardian*, 4 February 1999.
26 Newspaper cutting, November 1937, Iona Kielhorn Collection (IKC), Lossiemouth: The Hillocks.
27 David Marquand, 'Ramsay MacDonald', *ODNB*.
28 David Marquand, 'Ramsay MacDonald', *ODNB*.
29 Ishbel MacDonald to Malcolm MacDonald, 27 April 1957, 134/13/1-2, MMP.

16. Reassessing Britain's First Labour Government

1 *The Times*, 17 May 1924.

2 Paul Mulvey, *The Political Life of Josiah C. Wedgwood*, p. 139.

3 Martin Pugh (2010), *Speak for Britain!: A New History of the Labour Party*, London: Bodley Head, p. 184

4 Kevin Morgan (2005), 'The problem of the epoch? Labour and housing 1918–1951', *Twentieth Century British History* 16:3, pp. 227–55.

5 Gordon Brown, *Maxton*, p. 154.

6 Labour Party, *Labour's Appeal to the Nation*.

7 *New Leader*, 11 April 1924.

8 Ian S. Wood, *John Wheatley*, p. 143.

9 Clement Attlee (1937), *The Labour Party in Perspective*, London: Victor Gollancz, p. 52.

10 Labour Party, *Labour's Appeal to the Nation*.

11 Richard W. Lyman, *The First Labour Government*, p. 181.

12 Jake Vaughan, 'The first Labour Government and the civil service', p. 249.

13 Lewis Chester et al., *The Zinoviev Letter*, p. 153.

14 Earl of Birkenhead (1924), *Contemporary Personalities*, London: Cassell, p. 49.

15 Michael Meadowcroft (2018), 'The 1924 Labour Government and the Failure of the Whips', *Journal of Liberal History* 100, p. 33.

16 Sir Henry Slesser, *Judgment Reserved*, pp. 96–7.

17 These were set out in 1950 as the 'Lascelles Principles'.

18 Ivan Gibbons (2009), 'The First British Labour Government and The Irish Boundary Commission 1924', *Irish Studies: An Irish Quarterly Review* 98:391, pp. 321–33.

19 The Boundary Commission completed its work in late 1925, though its recommendations – minor transfers from Northern Ireland to the Irish Free State and vice versa – spooked London, Belfast and Dublin so much that the border was left unaltered.

20 Peter Dorey, *The Labour Party and Constitutional Reform*, p. 206.

21 British Pathé (1930), 'MacDonald In America With Roosevelt': https://www.youtube.com/watch?v=KtYgvKKCBm0&t=281s

22 Richard W. Lyman, *The First Labour Government*, p. 281.

23 Sir Patrick Hastings, *Autobiography*, p. 236.

24 Clement Attlee, *The Labour Party in Perspective*, pp. 51–2.

25 Fenner Brockway, *Socialism Over Sixty Years*, p. 218.

26 David Marquand (1997), *Ramsay MacDonald*, London: Richard Cohen, p. xv.

27 Mary Agnes Hamilton, *J. Ramsay MacDonald*, p. 191.

PICTURE CREDITS

1. Labour leader Ramsay MacDonald and the MPs Margaret Bondfield, Jimmy Thomas and Robert Smillie at a 'victory' rally at the Royal Albert Hall on 8 January 1924 © Topical Press Agency/Getty Images.

2. Ramsay MacDonald, Jimmy Thomas, Arthur Henderson and J. R. Clynes surrounded by well-wishers outside Buckingham Palace © Daily Mirror/Mirrorpix/Mirrorpix via Getty Images.

3. The 'biscuits' man Sir Alexander Grant playing golf with Ramsay MacDonald © KEYSTONE-FRANCE/Gamma-Rapho via Getty Images.

4. Ramsay MacDonald sporting Court dress at a Royal levee in early 1924. *Le Petit Journal*, 23 March 1924, © Mary Evans Picture Library.

5. A miniature of Ishbel MacDonald by Winifred Cécile Dongworth © National Portrait Gallery, London.

6. The first Labour Cabinet in the garden at 10 Downing Street © Universal History Archive/Universal Images Group via Getty Images.

7. John Wheatley and Charles Trevelyan, respectively Minister for Health and President of the Board of Education © Mary Evans Picture Library.

8. William Adamson circa 1920 © Hulton Archive/Getty Images.

9. The 1st Viscount Haldane, politician, lawyer and philosopher © Culture Club/Bridgeman via Getty Images.

10. Fresh from his foreign policy triumph regarding German war reparations, Ramsay MacDonald featured on the cover of *TIME* magazine © steeve-x-art/Alamy Stock Photo.

11. MacDonald invited W. T. Cosgrave, President of the Executive Council of the Free State, and Sir James Craig, Prime Minister of Northern Ireland, to Chequers in an attempt to resolve the 'boundary' issue © Firmin/Topical Press Agency/Getty Images.

12. King George V as featured on 'Wembley' stamps commemorating the Empire Exhibition, which he opened in April 1924 © Historic Illustrations/Alamy Stock Photo.

13. Sir Patrick Hastings, the Attorney General for England and Wales © Colin Waters/Alamy Stock Photo.

14. Ramsay MacDonald addressing the October 1924 Labour Party conference © Kirby/Topical Press Agency/Getty Images.

15. This poster by Harry Woolley set the tone for the bitter general election of October 1924 © Topical Press Agency/Getty Images.

16. The Zinoviev affair as depicted in the Illustrated London News © Illustrated London News Ltd/Mary Evans.

INDEX

and unemployment 115–17,
122–5, 127, 157–8
valedictory speech 212
and Viscount Haldane 153,
155–6, 165–6
workload 42–3
and Zinoviev Letter 222,
225–30, 237, 240, 248
MacDonald, Joan 37, 39
MacDonald, John 37
MacDonald, Malcolm xix, 3, 13,
37–9, 42, 44–5, 167–8, 219,
233, 249
MacDonald, Margaret 37, 40–1,
169, 249
MacDonald, Sheila 37, 248
Machinery of Government
Committee 165
McFadden, Pat viii
McKenna, Reginald 6, 101
MacKenzie, Muir 35
MacKinnon, Frank Douglas 162
Mackintosh, Sir Alexander 13, 36
McLean, Iain 87–8, 93
Maclean, Neil 134–5, 137
Macmillan, Hugh 51–2, 64, 128,
168, 201, 218, 235
Macnamara, Thomas 122–3
McNeill, Ronald 68
MacNeill Weir, Lachlan 64, 188,
215, 243, 249
Macpherson, Ian 134
magistrates 163–4
Maguire, Patrick xviii
*Manchester Evening
Chronicle* 223–4
Manchester Guardian 9, 14, 23,
174, 178, 185, 228–9

Mann, Tom 199
Marconi Affair 208
Markwald, Henry 244
Marquand, David xix, 3, 37, 46,
58, 169, 178, 249, 258
Marsh, Eddie 140, 142
Marx, Chancellor 177
Mary, Queen 19–20, 44–5, 66,
99, 164, 184, 203, 210
Massey, Vincent 232
Massingham, Henry 14, 24, 36
Masterman, Charles 93
Maurice, Sir Frederick 162
Maxton, James 16, 50, 52, 88–9,
243
and Campbell Case 195–6, 199
and Scottish Home Rule 130,
132, 134
Meechan, Mary 84
Middleton, J. S. 54, 56, 131, 163,
190, 212, 219
Miliband, Ralph 72, 215, 231
Miller, W. Reid 218
Miners' Federation of Great
Britain 128
mines 119–20, 252
Mitchell, Rosslyn 50–2, 232
Mond, Sir Alfred 85
Moore, Sir Thomas 221
Moray Golf Club 167
Morel, E. D. 23–4, 37, 50, 53–4,
170, 178, 185, 226, 243
and Soviet treaties 180–1
Morgan, Kevin 170, 185, 251
Morton, Desmond 223
Mosley, Oswald 231
Muir, John 16
Muirhead, Roland 131, 137